THE JEWS OF KURDISTAN

Mürre (Miriam), a Jewish girl from Amadiya.

THE JEWS OF KURDISTAN

BY

ERICH BRAUER

COMPLETED AND EDITED BY

RAPHAEL PATAI

WAYNE STATE UNIVERSITY PRESS DETROIT

Books in this series
The Myth of the Jewish Race, revised edition,
by Raphael Patai and Jennifer Patai, 1989
The Hebrew Goddess, third enlarged edition, by Raphael Patai, 1990
Robert Graves an the Hebrew Myths: A Collaboration, by Raphael Patai, 1992
Jewish Musical Traditions, by Amnon Shiloah, 1992
The Jews of Kurdistan, by Erich Brauer,
completed and edited by Raphael Patai, 1993

99 98 97 96 95 94 93 5 4 3 2 1

Library of Congress Cataloging-in-Publication Data

Brauer, Erich, 1895–1942.
The Jews of Kurdistan / by Erich Brauer; completed and edited by Raphael Patai.
p. cm. — (Jewish folklore and anthropology series)
Includes bibliographical references.
ISBN 0-8143-2392-8
1. Jews—Kurdistan—Social life and customs. 2. Kurdistan—Social life and customs.
3. Judaism—Kurdistan—Customs and practices. 4. Jews—Kurdistan—Folklore.
5. Folklore—Kurdistan. I. Patai, Raphael, 1910– . II. Title. III. Series.
DS135.K8B73 1993
956.6'77004924—dc20 92-46105

Book design by Joanne Elkin Kinney

Note on the Illustrations: All the objects photographed, as well as some of the photographs of persons, were in the Brauer Collection of the Hebrew University until the Arab-Jewish war of 1948, when the entire collection was lost.

CONTENTS

ILLUSTRATIONS

PREFACE

Taking Up Brauer's book after almost fifty years is for me like revisiting the haunts of my youth, like going back in time to a Jerusalem very different from what the city has become in recent years. In the intervening decades not only has Jerusalem become the capital of Israel and its physical appearance greatly changed, but it has developed into a center of manifold and intensive research activity in scholarly fields that were in their infancy in the 1940s. Among them was the study of the Jewish communities, whose number was to be soon thereafter so drastically reduced—tragically by the Nazi holocaust and messianically by their in-gathering in Israel.

In the 1930s Brauer was the only ethnologist (this is how he styled himself) to study any Jewish community; and the time granted him was enough only to complete one book, (on the Jews of Yemen) and to bring close to conclusion a second one (on the Kurdish Jews). It was while he was working on this book that I made his acquaintance; and it was partly, at least, under his influence that my interest shifted from the historical folklore of the biblical and talmudic periods to the anthropology of the modern Middle East in general and its Jewish communities in particular. After his untimely death in 1942, I felt truly alone in the huge terra incognita of contemporary Jewish anthropology; and it took me some two years before I reached the determination that it was up to me to initiate and organize research in this field. In 1944 I founded the Palestine Institute of Folklore and Ethnology and soon thereafter started to work on the completion and Hebrew translation of the English manuscript of *The Jews of Kurdistan* left behind by Brauer. Looking back on those years, I feel that one of the most important publications of the institute was this book, which appeared in 1947.[1]

In the course of the decades that have passed since, various aspects of the life of the Kurdish Jews have been studied by a dozen or so scholars. A. Ben-Ya'aqov wrote on their history,[2] J. J. Rivlin on their oral poetry,[3] Edith Gerson-Kiwi on their musical traditions,[4] Irene Garbell on their language,[5] Yona Sabar (himself a Kurdistani Jew) on their folk literature,[6] and so on. Yitzḥaq Ben-Zevi (patron of the institute and later the second president of Israel) and I both devoted parts of our general, survey-type books to the Kurdish Jews.[7] Yet with all these studies, Brauer's book has not only not been superseded by new research, but it has not even been augmented or duplicated—hence the importance of its publication in English, which makes what is still a unique ethnological monograph available to the wider scholarly community and, at the same time, serves as a monument to a scholar whose work has to this day remained largely unknown outside the narrow circle of Hebrew-reading anthropologists.

In my first preface, written in 1946, I said what I felt had to be said about the life and work of Erich Brauer and the circumstances in which he wrote his Kurdish book and in which I subsequently completed and published it. In this second preface I feel called to present a few data I consider important for supplementing Brauer's book and a few observations on how I see today—fifty years after be wrote it—its values and limitations. To begin with, some statistical data on the Kurdish Jews are in place.

Demographic studies, carried out by Abraham Ben-Ya'aqov, have shown that shortly prior to the establishment of Israel (1948) there existed 187 Kurdish–Jewish communities; of them, 146 were in Iraqi Kurdistan, 19 in the Iranian region, 11 in the Turkish region, and another 11 in the Syrian region and other places. As for population figures, for lack of statistical data, it could only be estimated that their total number was between 25,000 and 30,000. Some statistics of questionable accuracy were available only for Iraq, where, in 1947, 3,109 Jews were said to live in the Irbil (Arbil) province; 4,042 in the Kirkuk; 10,345 in the Mosul; 2,271 in the Sulaymania; and 2,851 in the Diyala provinces—a total of 22,618 for the whole of Iraqi Kurdistan. These figures were published in the *Encyclopaedia Judaica*,[8] (s.v. "Kurdistan") by Ben-Ya'aqov, who, however, with H. J. Cohen gives somewhat different figures in the same *Encyclopaedia* (s.v. "Iraqi"),[9] quoting the same official Iraqi statistic. Moreover, Cohen there writes that in 1948 "about 19,000 Kurdish Jews lived in Iraq." This vacillation as to their number in Iraq, where "official" statistics were available, illustrates the difficulty in estimating the number of Kurdish Jews outside Iraq in the same period.

Immigration of Kurdisb Jews to Palestine began in the sixteenth century and was directed to Safed in the Galilee, which at the time was the most important Kabbalistic center. For three centuries thereafter no information of any Jewish movement from Kurdistan to Palestine is available. Then, between 1900 and 1926, there was a Kurdish immigration to Palestine of about 1,900 Jews and in 1935 of another 2,500. The establishment of Israel was followed by the arrest of hundreds of Kurdish Jews in Iraq but subsequently, the Iraqi authorities relented and permitted Jewish emigration. As is well known, in 1950–51 practically the entire Iraqi Jewish community—some 125,000 strong—was airlifted to Israel, including almost all the Jews of Iraqi Kurdistan. Therewith the entire Iraqi (originally Assyrian and Babylonian) diaspora was liquidated, and the twenty-six centuries of Jewish history in Mesopotamia came to an end.

Once in Israel, the rapid assimilation of the Kurdish Jews to Israeli life and conditions began; and their specific type of Jewish culture, which had its origin in biblical and talmudic times started to disintegrate. Because of these developments (which could, of course, not be foreseen in the early 1940s), Brauer's book, which at the time of its writing was devoted to a vibrant and highly individual Jewish community became, within a few years, a monument—the only existing monument—to a community that has survived physically but only at the price of losing its remarkable cultural specificity.

What can we learn from Brauer's book on the Jews of Kurdistan? Above all, the student of Jewish life in the Middle East is struck by the intensity of the interrelationship between the Targum-speaking Jews and their Muslim neighbors in the villages and towns of Kurdistan. The accounts gathered by Brauer from the mouth of Kurdish Jews in Jerusalem about their life in Kurdistan prior to World War II show with great clarity that there was a lively participation by the Muslim Kurds in the folk life of the Kurdish Jews, including, in the first place, the popular Jewish religious observances. His book contains many examples showing that the Muslim Kurds attended Jewish folk rites—often even actively participating in them—and that there were numerous Jewish rituals in which such participation by the Muslim Kurds, including their headmen (the aga and the *pish-mire*) was either expected or required. The Muslim Kurds, for their part, considered such participation desirable because they were convinced of the beneficial effects of the religious folk rites performed by the Jews and believed that they, too, would derive benefits from them. Elsewhere I had occasion to point out that such religious cooperation between Muslims and Jews existed in Morocco.[10] From the present book it appears that a similar mutuality existed also between the Jews and the Muslims in Kurdistan.

This, of course, does not mean that in either Morocco or Kurdistan the Jews were not subordinated to the Muslims; nor does it mean that there were not (occasionally at least) indignities, exploitations, and even atrocities inflicted by the Muslims on the Jews. But my impression is that on the whole, the Jews and the Muslims got along reasonably well and that the former found ways in which they could hold their own vis-à-vis the latter.

Brauer's informants (as well as mine some five years later) convey the definite impression that the Kurdish Jews were, in the period preceding World War II, a rough, rude lot, given to violent behavior toward each other, whether in earnest or in jest. Beatings of weaker persons by stronger ones—-inferiors by superiors, weak men by strong men, children by teachers and parents, women (wives) by men, those guilty of crimes by those who had jurisdiction over them—were the order of the day. Thievery, often sanctioned by folk custom, and sabotage were nothing out of the ordinary. The humor of Kurdish Jews tended to be sexual and scatological. Some of these character traits were carried over by the immigrants to Israel, where many stories circulated about the violence and recklessness—but also the bravery and physical strength—of the Kurdish Jews.

What was not pointed out either by Brauer or by me in the supplementary notes I gathered for the book in the mid-1940s was that in all these character traits the Kurdish Jews closely resembled the Kurdish Muslims. Since the Jews were few and the Muslims many, we would have been led to the conclusion that the presence of these traits among the Kurdish Jews was the result of cultural-environmental influences absorbed by the Jewish minority from the Muslim majority. The fact that the Jews, despite having found a modus vivendi with the Muslims, were definitely dependent on them for their survival, also points to influences emanating from the mores of the Muslim majority and making themselves felt in the behavioral and attitudinal patterns of the Jewish minority. In other words, we have here a Jewish community that absorbed these traits (rather unusual among Jews) from the non-Jewish social environment in which they had lived for more than two millennia.

More remarkable is the fact that the Jews of Kurdistan succeeded in retaining so many typically Jewish traits that continued to distinguish them down to the days of their emigration to Israel. One of these was literacy. Although the literacy of the Kurdish Jews was not as high as that of the Yemenite or even of the Moroccan Jews, they *were* a literate population element in the midst of a largely illiterate majority population. To send a child to school, and to make him learn to read Hebrew and (to a lesser extent) also to write it was a matter of course for the Kurdish Jews, while nothing comparable existed among the Muslims. Likewise, it was a Jewish, but not a Muslim, trait to insist on the observance of many religious precepts. This was never easy; and in the case of the small and isolated Jewish groups in the Kurdish villages, it was quite difficult. The similarities and differences between the Kurdish Jews and the Kurdish Muslims is a broad subject with many ramifications, but we must leave it here.

I think I am justified in saying that this book is a historical document, on two counts. First, it presents a picture of Kurdish Jewish life and culture prior to World War II. Brauer's work on the book was cut short by his death in 1942. In the interviews I conducted with Kurdish Jews in Jerusalem in 1944–46 my informants were individuals who had left Kurdistan before the outbreak of the war, so that whatever data they supplied pertained to the same prewar period. In 1950–51, with the mass immigration of Kurdish Jews to Israel, their world as it had existed before the war suddenly ceased to exist. Hence, this book is a unique historical record of the life and culture of a Jewish community that has since disappeared from the country it had inhabited from antiquity, and has undergone a total transformation after its settlement in Israel.

Second, this book is a historical document because it presents the results of an ethnological method of investigation and interpretation that itself has been superseded by more modern anthropological approaches. As I point out in the Preface to the Hebrew Edition, written in 1946, Brauer was an adherent of the Kulturkreis school, which has since completely disappeared from the horizon of anthropological research. Although he referred in the body of the book only rarely to "culture circles," still, the scope (and the limitations) of his interest in the community he studied reflects the approach of his masters Luschan, Weule, Graebner, and others. Hence, the book as it stands is a monument to what a "Kulturkreisist" was able to do in studying a community from a distance, without ever having visited it.

Looking at the Brauer book fifty years after it was written, one cannot help noticing several omissions. One is the absence of a chapter on *language*. Although the book contains a profusion of linguistic materials (single terms, compound expressions, phrases, sayings, etc.) richly illustrative of the colloquial as spoken by the Jews of Kurdistan, there is no attempt in it at giving a general analysis and characterization of their language. This being the case, the reader gets no overview of the various language elements that had gone into shaping the Targum of the Kurdish Jews: the neo-Aramaic base, enriched by Kurdish (Kurmanji), Arabic, Turkish, Old Aramaic, and Hebrew expressions. It would have been interesting and valuable to investigate, in addition, the *types* of concepts covered by vocabularies derived from each of these languages.

In this connection, a comment must be made on the problems connected with the transliteration into Latin characters of words in the Targum language of the Kurdish Jews. Since Targum is a purely oral language, which was never written, the student had to rely on his ear in listening to the way it was pronounced and then try to render it phonetically as best he could. This was the method used by Brauer, by me when working on the completion of the book and interviewing Kurdish Jews, by Joseph J. Rivlin when he collected and put in writing the orally preserved poetry of the Kurdish Jews,[11] and by others. This is more difficult than it sounds for several reasons. First of all, there are variations in pronunciation between people from different areas, as well as inconsistencies in the speech of one and the same person, such as *ghulāma/khulām* (slave); *hitna/khitna* (bridegroom); *semka/smaka/samkisa* (pregnancy); *ṣuṣita/sisita* (braid); *chāla/shāla/shala/shalo* (trousers); *chehil/chilke/chilqe/cheli* (forty); and *ṣebā'ta/ṣubo'eta/ṣuwātha* (dyeing).

Next, there are divergences from old Aramaic that the student is inclined to mishear, such as Targum *khevrāye* from Old Aramaic *ḥevraye*, Targum *'eda* from Old Aramaic *'ēda* and Targum *z'aora* or *zora* from Old Aramaic *z'ēra*. The linguistically educated student knows that in these words there *should* be a *ḥet* or an *'ayin*, and may hear it even if, because in the course of centuries the phonemes in question have disappeared, the informant does not pronounce it.

Even with regard to place names, there are variations. For example, one and the same town is pronounced (and written by travelers and mapmakers) Arbil, Arbela, Erbil, and Irbil. Similar examples are Zakho/Zakhu, Nusaybin/Nesibin/Nisibin/Nisebin, Dehok/Dohuk/Duhok, Ravanduz/Rawandūz/Rowanduz/Rawandiz. Added to all this are the considerable variations between the Iraqi and the Iranian usage and between one locality and the other, as becomes evident on practically every page in the book.

Dr. Brauer had no time to prepare a glossary for this book; feeling that it would be useful, I have prepared the glossary that appears at the end of the book.

The musical traditions of the Kurdisb Jews are yet another area not touched upon in Brauer's book. True, be speaks of their musical instruments, of the occasions when the *muturbaye* performed, and the like; but nothing is said about the music itself, the melodies, the so-called "musical dialects," the melodic styles of the renditions of Targum texts. These, as Edith Gerson-Kiwi subsequently found, are distinct from the general Oriental–Sephardi style used in the presentation of Hebrew texts, so that the Kurdish *ḥazanim* (cantors) tended to be musically bilingual.[12] She has also established that in Iraqi Kurdistan (for example) there were no less than four musical styles current among the Jews, each associated with one language: (1) Hebrew for the liturgical synagogue music; (2) neo-Aramaic (Targum) for the religious and paraliturgical music of the school (midrash), the yeshiva, and some rituals connected with the studies, translation, and paraphrasing of the sacred texts; (3) Kurdish for the folk traditions, including epics, ballads, and dances; and (4) Arabic for secular songs, taken over from popular and urban art music serving purely social gatherings.[13]

Yet another subject not dealt with in the book is the belief system of the Kurdish Jews. Brauer has recorded much on religious rituals (both their official and popular varieties) that accompany the feasts of the religious year and the life cycle. But he said almost nothing, except for a few occasional remarks, about the beliefs that underlay the religious ceremonies, rites, and customs. What features were contained in the Kurdish Jewish God concept? What was the attitude to the Holy One Blessed Be He? What were the beliefs in angels, in demons, in spirits, in the evil Lilith?[14] We learn nothing of this important aspect of the Kurdish Jewish religious beliefs; and by now, I am afraid, it is probably too late to fill this lacuna.

Finally, no chapter in the book is devoted to the Kurdish Jews' self-image or their views of the Muslim Kurds and their Nestorian Christian neighbors. True, Brauer provides a very large number of details about the actual relationship between the Jews and the non-Jews;

but we miss a summary analytical presentation of how the Jews saw the non-Jews with whom they had such close contact and how they evaluated themselves in relation to them. It would, for instance, have been most interesting to know whether the traditional East European contempt for the *goy*, who was stereotypically considered ignorant, stupid, brutal, and a lush, had any kind of counterpart in the Kurdish Jews' image of the Kurdish Muslim and Nestorian.

Perhaps had Brauer lived to complete his book, he would have added chapters devoted to these subjects. I consider it equally regrettable that when I worked on the completion of the book, I made no attempt to supply such.

Finally, a few technical details. I left Brauer's text untouched, except for minor stylistic changes. All the additions I made to the original uncompleted manuscript are placed in square brackets. I substituted my English translation for all the foreign language quotations given by Brauer in their original Arabic, Hebrew, French, German, and so on. If I found that English translations of the works quoted by Brauer were available, I used them instead of making my own. All these translations are likewise put between square brackets. Where I had reason to retain quotations in the Hebrew original, I substituted English transliteration for the Hebrew characters. In many places, where Brauer gave Hebrew, Targum, or Arabic words and phrases in his own transliteration in Latin characters, I found it necessary to substitute a transliteration with which the English reader can be assumed to be more familiar.

Only in a very few exceptional cases did I find myself in disagreement with what Brauer wrote. If so, I expressed my view in a note, in square brackets.

Forest Hills
January 1993

RAPHAEL PATAI

PREFACE TO THE HEBREW EDITION

THE FIRST ETHNOLOGICAL monograph ever written on a Jewish community was the book of Erich Brauer on the Yemenite Jews published in German in 1934 by the Kulturgeschichtliche Bibliothek of Heidelberg University. The present volume of Brauer, published posthumously, is, after an interval of over a dozen years, still the only other study of this kind to be published and the first to appear in Hebrew. In these two books Brauer applied modern ethnological methods to the study of Oriental Jewish communities and thus paved the way for future researchers into the complex subject of Jewish ethnology.[1]

Erich Brauer was born on June 28th, 1895, in Berlin. After finishing high school in 1914, he studied ethnology at the universities of Berlin and Leipzig, where he had among his teachers F. von Luschan and Fr. Weule. In 1923 he was awarded the Ph.D. in Leipzig for his thesis *Züge aus der Religion der Herero: Ein Beitrag zur Hamitenfrage*, an amplified version of which was later (1925) published by the Institut für Völkerkunde, Leipzig. This book dealt with religious and magical ideas, ceremonies, and usages among pastoral peoples in Africa; and it received considerable attention from ethnologists and anthropologists. Even then, however, Brauer's interest was focused on Jewish ethnology; and in the very year in which his study was published he went to Palestine with a view to investigating Oriental Jewish communities. In 1930 he was awarded by the Hebrew University the Lord Plumer Prize, which enabled him to prolong his sojourn in Palestine for another year. Returning to Germany, he published the first results of his studies in two papers on the Yemenite Jews, both printed in 1931—the one a lengthy paper, "Die Frau bei den südarabischen Juden" (*Zeitschrift für Sexualwissenschaft und Sexualpolitik* 18), the other a short review on studies among Yemenite Jews (*Zeitschrift für Ethnologie* 63). These were followed in 1934 by his comprehensive monograph already mentioned, *Ethnologie der jemenitischen Juden*.

From 1934 and until his untimely death on May 9th, 1942—he was then in his 47th year—he again lived in Jerusalem, where he devoted himself entirely to his scientific work. From 1936 to 1940 he was research fellow of the Hebrew University and laid the foundations of an ethnological collection now in the possession of the Hebrew University. He was a passionate collector, endowed, over and above his scientific training and approach, with talents very valuable for an ethnologist: he was an accomplished painter and an expert photographer. The financial means at his disposal were pitifully inadequate; but he made the most of them and collected hundreds of dresses, articles of personal adornment, jewels, amulets, and other objects of folkloristic and ethnological interest; and made thousands of photographs, often uniting in them anthropological precision and artistic value. These he supplemented with his facile brush and pencil by sketches, portraits, and studies in oil. The greatest part of this pictorial material is still unpublished and has kindly been put at the disposal of the Palestine Institute of Folklore and Ethnology by Brauer's sister, Mrs. Gerta Heller of Petach Tikvah, together with part of the exhibits collected by him.

Though time was granted to Brauer for the systematic investigation of only two Jewish communities, those of the Yemenite and of the Kurdish Jews, he also studied other Oriental Jewish communities and published papers on the Jews of Afghanistan. His other papers include two on the Palestinian *Fellaḥin*; while in three papers published in his lifetime he presented some of the results of his studies in the ethnology and folklore of the Kurdish Jews.

Brauer based both his monographs on investigations conducted not in the homelands of these communities but in Palestine, more precisely, in Jerusalem. In his preface to *Ethnologie der jemenitischen Juden* he emphasized the advantages of such a study which, to him, outweighed its more obvious drawbacks. He wrote:

> During a sojourn in Palestine extending over a number of years, the author has studied Yemenites who have been immigrating in the course of several decades into that country. As against the disadvantages involved

> in such an investigation conducted outside their proper places of habitation, disadvantages of which the author is fully aware, there are in the present case considerable advantages. In Yemen the stranger is even today entirely in the hands of the Imam who enables him to see only what he wishes to show him. Since Halévy no foreigner has succeeded in visiting Northern Yemen, and most of the travelers are bound to follow the Ḥodaida-Ṣan'ā route. The Jews, too, are less accessible in Yemen, as the pressure under which they live obliges them to be cautious. In Palestine, it is possible to have a much freer intercourse with them. The young people are the first to develop this freedom, and the older people soon follow suit. One can even obtain information from women, a thing that would be most difficult in Yemen, where the sexes are kept strictly apart. In addition, one has the opportunity in Palestine to question Jews from all parts of Yemen, even from districts such as Ṣa'dah, which no European has yet been able to visit.[2]

Despite the above argument, it seems to me almost certain that were it not for his physical handicap—he was small, frail, and hunchbacked—Brauer's spirit of inquiry would surely have surmounted every obstacle, and he would have put the finishing touches to his studies of the Yemenite and Kurdish Jews during a sojourn of appropriate duration in these two Jewish communities.

It is noteworthy that in both cases Brauer chose as the subject of his investigations not the Jews of any single, narrowly circumscribed community, such as a township, but of a whole country, within which there existed a number of varied Jewish settlements often showing quite considerable differences in tradition and mode of life. When dealing with the Yemenite Jews, he considered, in addition to their main centers such as Ṣan'ā, also variations of custom and usage occurring in Northern Yemen on the one hand and in Aden on the other, separated by a distance of some three hundred miles.

In the present book, this tendency of taking into consideration the variations of usage in different settlements dispersed over a large area is even more pronounced. Kurdistan extends over an area that belongs politically to five countries: Syria, Iraq, Iran, Turkey, and Soviet Russia. Even before World War I, it was divided between three states: the Turkish Empire, Russia, and Persia. Political dependence obviously facilitates cultural influence to a certain extent, even if only by shutting off the community in question from influences emanating from the other side of the political boundary. Thus, there are considerable divergences of custom between the Jews of Amadiya, Barzan, Alqosh, Mosul, Arbil, Dehok, Kirkuk, and Sulaimaniya (belonging to Iraq) and of Sinne, Ushnu, Maragha, and Urmia (belonging to Iran)—to mention but some of the places that the reader will find figuring very often in the following pages.

The fact that the Jews inhabit three profoundly different types of countryside in Kurdistan—those of the mountain tracts, the volcanic lake region, and the plains—adds its share to their cultural diversity. The constant taking into account of several local variations of a cultural trait dealt with makes Brauer's treatment somewhat like a patchwork, so that the book demands concentrated attention from the reader who wishes to find its general pattern. I had occasion to discuss with Brauer the obviously disturbing effect such a method of treatment must have on the general picture of the life and culture of a community—to present which is, after all, the ultimate aim of this sort of ethnological monograph. He pointed to two circumstances that not only justified this method but even made it desirable: first, the underlying basic identity of the cultural traits varying in detail that are to be found among the Jews of a territory such as Yemen or Kurdistan; and second, the sadly neglected state of Jewish ethnology, which made a regional survey of entire Jewish tribes a task of primary urgency, compared with which the investigation of one single community was of only secondary importance.

While studying at German universities, Brauer came under the influence of the ethnological school known as that of the Kulturkreislehre (Culture-Circle Theory). The foundation of this school dates back to 1904, when Graebner and Ankermann gave their lectures on culture circles and culture strata in Oceania and Africa, respectively. The significance of the doctrine of culture circles was greatly augmented when Pater Wilhelm Schmidt incorporated it with minor variations into his book, *The Culture-historical Method of Ethnology*. The theory held that component parts or traits of cultures have an innate coherence and travel in closed "circles," that is, as complexes; when they clash with other complexes spreading from another center, either they blend or one gives way to the other. Outside Germany and Austria—Vienna was the seat of Schmidt's school—this theory met with but little approval. In America its most outstanding exponent is Clyde Cluckhohn.[3] Brauer remained faithful to the *Kulturkreise* to the end of his life and was, moreover, a militant exponent of this theory. How well I remember one day in the autumn of 1940 when, after having read a part of the first draft of my *Man and Earth*, he asked me point blank, "To what school do you adhere?" There followed a heated discussion on theoretical points, in which he expounded the convictions of his school with great force and clarity. It is all the more characteristic for his scientific integrity that from both of his books he excluded every theoretical discussion most conscientiously. In the present volume the term *Kulturkreis* itself occurs not more often than once or twice in an occasional note. It was Brauer's conviction that a descriptive study of this kind must present facts, all the facts, and nothing but the facts.

Brauer's choice of the Jews of Kurdistan as the subject of his second ethnological monograph was no less happy than that of his first study. While the Yemenite Jews were especially suitable to form the subject of an investigation on account of their relatively isolated development during many centuries, the Jews of Kurdistan are one of the very few Jewish communities in which agriculture in a traditional primitive form is still practiced and has a by-no-means-negligible importance as a source of livelihood. The way of life and the folk culture of Jewish agriculturists are of greater interest from the point of view of completing the general picture of indigenous Jewish life in all lands than those of a trading community could be. In addition to this, the Jews of Kurdistan inhabit a territory partly adjacent to, and partly overlapping, that country which can justly be regarded as the second homeland of Jewry after Palestine—namely, Babylonia where Jews have been living uninterruptedly for more than two-and-a-half millennia. From the talmudic and Gaonic periods rich literatures have preserved ample data pertaining to the way of life and culture of the Jewish people in that country. We know that in talmudic times they were to a large extent agriculturists, artisans, and shippers—all three occupations still pursued by the Jews of Kurdistan. Altogether, when reading Brauer's study, one gains the impression that a great many ancient Jewish usages and beliefs, both religious and secular, have been preserved and kept alive among the Jews of Kurdistan. To substantiate this impression a special comparative study should be made, based on the present book and talmudic literature. By way of example we may mention the beatings with branches on Sukkoth, the dances performed by old men (with swords among the Jews of Kurdistan), the belief that the wooden columns of the synagogues (as in the Temple of Jerusalem) are living trees with roots in the ground, and so on. Brauer himself pointed out such historical connections only very occasionally. In my additional notes, always in square brackets, I have called attention to several more of these historical parallels. Most of my notes will be found in the chapters dealing with religion. Shortly before his death, Brauer gave me this part of his study to read; and I drew his attention to several customs described by him that reminded me of customs known to me from my historical studies. He welcomed every such "tracing back" most heartily, but illness and death prevented him from utilizing them himself.

I also attempted to supplement the data gathered by the author with additional information elicited from Kurdish Jews in Jerusalem. My chief informant was Ḥakham Alwan Avidani, formerly of Amadiya, whose extensive knowledge and great familiarity with every aspect of his community's life proved an unfailing source to which I never applied in vain. The table of contents as drawn up by Brauer himself showed that it was his intention to write a number of additional chapters and sections. One of the section headings, for instance, in the chapter on marriage was The Bride's Costume; of this section, however, not a single line was written. I supplied a paragraph on this topic and also added another one, The Bridegroom's Costume. All my additions, whether short or long, have been put in square brackets.

The table of contents attached to Brauer's manuscript also showed that it was his intention to write one chapter on the somatology, and one on the statistics, of the Kurdish Jews. However, a search among the notes left behind by him, instituted upon my request by Mrs. Heller, brought to light only the scantiest of notes on some anthropometrical measurements. To supply a chapter on this subject would have demanded prolonged independent investigations among the Kurdish Jews, a task that I was unable to undertake:

Again, a comparison with the contents of Brauer's book on the Yemenite Jews shows that while there is throughout a general agreement between the structure of the two studies, the book on the Yemenites contains two sections and an entire chapter whose counterparts are lacking in the book on the Kurdish Jews. The two sections are Children's Games and Judicial Affairs, the chapter is on magic. Though some of this material is incorporated into other chapters of the book, it is more than probable that had Brauer lived to complete his study, he would have devoted special sections to these topics.

Apart from the additions referred to above, my editorial task comprised the verifying of some of the quotations, the correcting of some passages inaccurately translated from Hebrew authors, the substitution of the English version of the frequent quotations from Benjamin II in place of the German found in Brauer's manuscript, the completion of the bibliography, and the addition of occasional references to parallel traits to be found in other Oriental Jewish communities, mainly in order to counteract the impression that might otherwise be gained that a certain trait described is unique, found only among the Kurdish Jews. Nowhere did I interfere with the text itself, which is here presented to the reader in the very form given it by Brauer with the exception of minor stylistic changes.

Jerusalem
January 1946 RAPHAEL PATAI

PUBLICATIONS BY ERICH BRAUER

Züge aus der Religion der Herero: Ein Beitrag zur Hamitenfrage. Institut der Völkerkunde, 1st series (Ethnographie und Ethnologie). Leipzig: R. Voigtlanders Verlag, 1925.

"Die Frau bei den südarabichen Juden." *Zeitschrift fur Sexualwissenschaft und Sexualpolitik* 18 (1931): 152–71.

"Forschungen bei den jemenitischen Juden." *Zeitschrift fur Ethnologie* 63 (1931): 226–32.

"Yehude Teman: Bibliografiya" [The Jews of Yemen: A Bibliography]. *Qiryat Sefer* 10 (1933/34): 119–30, 236–48, 515–24.

Ethnologie der jemenitischen Juden. Kulturgeschichtliche Bibliothek, 1st series (Ethnologische Bibliothek), vol. 7. Heidelberg: Carl Winter, 1934.

"Fellachen in Palästina." *Almanach des Schocken Verlags* (Berlin) 1936/37:100–110.

"Der heilsame Granatapfelbaum: Nach Erzählung eines kurdischen Juden aufgezeichnet." *Almanach des Schocken Verlags* (Berlin) 1937/38:164–73. (Included in the present volume in chapter 18.)

"Minhage Yehude Kurdistan ba'Atzirat ha'-Geshamim" [Rites and Customs in Times of Drought Among the Jews of Kurdistan]. *Sefer Magnes* (Jerusalem) 1938:vii–ix, 50–61. (Incuded in the present volume as chapter 24.)

"Qivre Qedoshim we-Sifre Torah 'Ose Nifla'ot" [Holy Tombs and Miracle Working Torah Scrolls]. In Yisrael Yesha'yahu, ed., *Mi-Teman le-Ziyon.* Tel Aviv: Massada, 1938, pp. 165–73.

"Bräuche der kurdischen Juden: Kinder und Kindheit." *Almanach des Schocken Verlags* (Berlin), 1938/39:105–12.

"The Jews of Afghanistan," *Jewish Social Studies* (New York) 4 (1942). "On The Folk Museum in Palestine and the Style of Living of the Fellahin." In *Ba'ayot* (Jerusalem), May 1942.

"Yehude Afganistan" [The Jews of Afghanistan]. *Sinai* (Jerusalem) 7:12 (1944): 324–42.

"Minhage Leda Etzel Yehude Kurdistan" [Birth Customs of the Jews of Kurdistan]. *Edoth* (Jerusalem) 1 (1946): 65–72. (Translated from English into Hebrew by Raphael Patai.)

Milah we-Yaldut Etzel Yehude Kurdistan" [Circumcision and Childhood Among the Jews of Kurdistan]. *Edoth* (Jerusalem) 1 (1946): 129–38. (Translated from English into Hebrew by Raphael Patai.)

ABBREVIATIONS

A.	Amadiya
Arab.	Arabic language
BAIU	*Bulletin de l'Alliance Israélite Universelle*, Paris
D.	Dehok
EI	*Encyclopaedia of Islam*
EJ	*Encyclopaedia Judaica*, Berlin
EJJ	*Ethnologie der jemenitischen Juden*, by Brauer
ERE	*Encyclopaedia of Religion and Ethics*, ed. Hastings
Ḥ.	Ḥakham
Heb.	Hebrew language
HUBC	Hebrew University, Brauer Collection
HUCA	*Hebrew Union College Annual*
JAOS	*Journal of the American Oriental Society*
JI	*Jewish Intelligence*
JR	*Jüdische Rundschau*, Berlin
JRGS	*Journal of the Royal Geographic Society*
Kurd.	Kurdish language or people
OW	*Ost und West*, Berlin
Pers.	Persian language
REJ	*Revue des Etudes Juives*
RETP	*Revue d'Ethnographie et des Traditions Populaires*, Paris
S.	Sinne
Targ.	Targum language
Z.	Zakho
ZDPV	*Zeitschrift des Deutschen Palästina-Vereins*
ZVV	*Zeitschrift des Vereins für Volkskunde*

PART ONE

Introduction

1

Ethnological Research

The natural seclusion of the Kurdish highlands, which discourages traffic and communication, the political confusion prevailing there, and the rough character of the inhabitants have been a serious hindrance to all attempts at a scientific study of the country. Thus, the geographer Carl Ritter declared that prior to the journeys of C. R. Rich (ca. 1820) Kurdistan proper was literally terra incognita.[1] And strictly speaking, our knowledge of Kurdistan even today is confined to the environs of its trade routes and is very limited in extent.

All this applies to the inhabitants of the country even more than to its physical features. We do not yet possess any methodical ethnological study of the Kurds. The situation is somewhat better as regards the Christians. But the Kurdish Jews are among the least known of Jewish groups, the descriptions given in the meager accounts of travelers being of the vaguest. Travelers rarely came into contact with the Jews of this area; and most of them, in consequence, omit all mention of the Jews in their reports. Hence, many travel books, otherwise among the most important, find no place in a history of research in our field.[2] None of the travelers remained in the country long enough to gain a close acquaintance with the Kurdish Jews; and no work corresponding, for instance, to that of Saphir on the Jews of Yemen, exists on the Jews of Kurdistan.

Benjamin of Tudela and Petaḥya of Ratisbonne

The first authentic accounts of the Kurdish Jews are those of Benjamin of Tudela and Petaḥya of Ratisbonne in the twelfth century. Both were entirely under the influence of Arab geographers, and their aim was probably to find the [legendary] lost ten tribes [of Israel], a quest that lured many non-Jewish, as well as Jewish, travelers down to modern times.

Benjamin of Tudela left a description of his journey (1166–71) in a book that is deservedly famous.[3] But this book includes information Benjamin obtained from others, on Jewish communities that he himself did not visit; and this fact is not made clear in the book by either the author or his editors. Hence, the book lacks precision, and scholars have not yet succeeded in completely establishing Benjamin's actual itinerary.[4] Nevertheless, it can be regarded as virtually certain that Benjamin visited only the border districts of Kurdistan and did not penetrate the mountain region.

Starting from Palestine, Benjamin journeyed to Nisebin via Damascus, Aleppo, and Qal'at Jaber. Thence he went on to Mosul by way of Jezirat al-Omar "at the foot of mountains of Ararat. It is a distance of four miles to the place where Noah's Ark rested" (p. 52). Benjamin gives a detailed description of Mosul, which he calls Ashur (as is customary among the Jews even today); and he also mentions the ruins of Nineveh.

The text that follows at this point is defective. Something has evidently been lost before the mention of Arbil, and it is consequently impossible to determine whether Benjamin visited Arbil or not; it seems most likely that he turned westward from Mosul and reached the Euphrates, down which he traveled on a *kelek* [Arab. *kalak*, a raft of inflated skins] to Baghdad and Basra. It is improbable that Benjamin got beyond Basra. His reports of Persian localities (particularly Amadiya) were acquired from others, which does not, however, detract from their value. That Benjamin was never in Amadiya is clear from the exaggerated figure (25,000) he gives for its population. This may possibly be the error of a copyist;[5] but the entire account of Amadiya gives the impression of being hearsay rather than an eyewitness report. Benjamin evidently returned by way of Egypt after leaving Basra.

The book of travels by his contemporary, Rabbi Petaḥya of Ratisbonne[6] (fl. 1175–90)[7] has survived only in a version that has been tampered with by editors that Petaḥya's actual itinerary can no longer be ascertained. Petaḥya was a good observer, and his descriptions are more vivid than those of Benjamin.

Petaḥya did not enter Mesopotamia and Kurdistan from the west, like Benjamin, but from the north. He cut through Russia to the Crimea, crossed the Black Sea, and put ashore at a place unknown to us, whence he journeyed through the "Land of Ararat," that is, Armenia: "In the Land of Ararat he traveled as far as Nisebin and the city Hisn-Kepa (Hasan Kef) on the Tigris" (p. 18).[8]

He then proceeded to New Nineveh (Mosul), where he was detained for a considerable time by illness (p. 8). It took him fifteen days to reach Baghdad from New Nineveh. At this point, there follows a list of holy graves, including those of Ezekiel in Kefil, Nahum in al-Qosh (p. 34), and Ezra in al-Uzair. Whether he personally visited all these tombs is uncertain. From Baghdad he journeyed to Palestine by way of Mosul and Nisebin.

The descriptions we find in this book of a *kelek* and of "manna" are of special interest to us (pp. 10, 48).

Al-Ḥarizi

Only a few decades after Benjamin and Petaḥya, another famous Jew traveled through these regions—the Spanish Hebrew poet Jehuda al-Ḥarizi (ca. 1190–1235). Ḥarizi had translated into Hebrew the *Maqāma*s of the Arab poet Hariri, and this aroused in him the desire to emulate the Arab poet in an original Hebrew work. With the object of gathering experiences to this end, he set out from Toledo on a long journey that brought him to the lands of the Euphrates and the Tigris (ca. 1225). There he sustained himself for several years as an itinerant poet. His experiences on this journey are set down in his *Maqāma*s, entitled *Taḥkemoni* (2 Sam. 28:3), a work whose importance both as a poem and as a source for thirteenth-century Jewish life and customs has not been sufficiently recognized.[9] The *Maqāma*s, not being chronologically arranged, give no clear idea of Ḥarizi's itinerary; but in any case, he came to Mesopotamia from Aleppo. The Kurdish towns mentioned by him are Mosul (Ashur or Nineveh, *Maq*. 24, 29.1, 46.8.18, 47.7, 50.128) and Arbil (*Maq*. 18.4.144, 24.3); but apparently, he visited other Kurdish communities, as well, though he does not refer to them by name. From Baghdad he visited the graves of Ezekiel and Ezra (*Maq*. 35.2.49, 5.8; 35.2.26, 50.9.121). Ḥarizi's work gives little actual information about the Kurdish communities; but his portrayal of popular life and customs is a valuable contribution to the history of civilization.

Yiḥya al-Zāhiri

For centuries after al-Ḥarizi we hear nothing about the Kurdish Jews. The upheavals caused by the Mongol invasions and the destruction that accompanied them discouraged traveling in the area, and the dangers of the road were a deterrent. We must not imagine that the Jews of Kurdistan were entirely cut off from other Jewish communities during these centuries. It was not, however, until three hundred years after Ḥarizi that another Hebrew poet described a similar journey, likewise in *Maqāmas*. This was Yiḥya (Zekharya) al-Zāhiri (Avner ha-Temani), who lived in the second half of the sixteenth century and came from Ṣan'ā in Yemen.

His book bears the title *Sēfer ha-Musar* (Book of instructions).[10] The third chapter contains a description of his journey from Baghdad to Arbil, including his visit to the graves of Daniel and his companions in Kerkuk. In chapter 5 he describes his journey from Baghdad via Mosul, Kalne (Raqqa), and Nisebin.

The *Sh'liḥim* (Emissaries)

These two odysseys are sufficient evidence to show that the Kurdish Jews were not by any means entirely isolated. At all times there were connections between Palestine and the Kurdish diaspora; and if we possess only few written documents attesting to such connections, this is because those who sought out these distant Jewish communities were not men of letters. They were emissaries (*sh'liḥim*) of Palestinian institutions sent to the Jews of the Galuth to collect money for the maintenance of the institutions concerned. They also represented the ties between Palestinian Jews and their distant brethren.

From the beginning of the eighteenth century there is documentary evidence that *sh'liḥim* from Palestine visited Kurdistan regularly, both in order to empty the collection boxes of the various funds[11] and to preach and exhort the communities to observe the law. They also gave decisions in difficult legal cases (e.g., divorces).

Among the letters published by Mann are two that bear witness to such connection with Palestine. A letter from Sundur from the year 1702 (letter 17)[12] is addressed to Jacob Benjamin of Jerusalem. The writer requests Benjamin to send him certain books.

Letter 11, dated 1768 and evidently sent from Amadiya, has on its reverse[13] a letter of introduction for Mordekhai Sidon b. Eliezer of Safed. Mordekhai had visited the communities of Persia as a *shaliaḥ* (emissary), had been robbed on the way back, and arrived in Amadiya stripped of everything. The letter of introduction requests that contributions be given to him and help extended him for the return journey. It also mentions that Mordekhai's brother had been sent twice to these regions as a *shaliaḥ*.

Similar letters from Palestinian emissaries to the communities of Nirwa, Tchalla, and Sundur, asking for gifts for the Palestinian communities, have been published by S. Assaf,[14] who establishes their date as ca. 1788.

Among the emissaries from Palestine who visited Kurdistan was R. Yehuda b. Amram Diwan,[15] author of the collection of homilies and responses *Ḥut ha-M'shullash* (*The Triple Thread*), published in Constantinople in 1739. R. Yehuda undertook a number of journeys between 1710 and 1740 as *shaliaḥ* for the communities of Safed, Hebron and Jerusalem. These journeys took him also to Kurdistan and Persia.

From the headings of the sermons collected in his book we know that he visited Aleppo, Mosul, Diar Bekr, Sinne, Tabriz, and Hamadan. The *Ḥut ha-m'shullash* does not, however, make any substantial contribution to our knowledge of the Kurdish Jews.[16]

Because of the dangers of the road and the difficult nature of the country, the *sh'liḥim* often turned over the collection of money, on a percentage basis, to local representatives instead of visiting these out-of-the-way places themselves. This was a great disappointment to the inhabitants, for the arrival of an emissary from Palestine was always an eagerly awaited event. Thus, a *shaliaḥ* writes as follows from Amadiya: "It is my intention to go myself to the camp of your community; but the way is rendered very dangerous through difficult mountains and hills and through rivers and bridges, but my strength is small, I have not enough strength to go to you, especially as it is the rainy season and the cold is great."[17] The emissaries also made threats of heavy penalties if a suitable sum should not be delivered to their representative.[18] Still, the institution of *sh'liḥim* must be regarded as an exceptionally important one for remote and isolated communities.

R. David d'Bet Hillel

The first European traveler[19] after Benjamin of Tudela and Petaḥya to give a detailed account of the Kurdish Jews and to penetrate to the Kurdish highlands in person was R. David d'Bet Hillel, whose journey took place in the early nineteenth century. His report attracted little attention, owing to the peculiar circumstances of its publication. R. David was a native of Vilna. He settled in Safed in 1815;[20] but in 1824 he left his home, ostensibly "to see the world." Actually, his purpose must have been, like that of his predecessors, to find the lost ten tribes—a quest which he was probably prompted to undertake by the reports of *sh'liḥim* who had visited remote communities before him or had had information about them.[21] His route led him by way of Syria and Kurdistan to Baghdad (1827). There he sojourned for a year, after which he left for India from Basra. He traversed India in many directions. On his way back he was detained in Madras, where he supported himself by giving Hebrew lessons to the English clergy; and it was these circles that urged him to publish an account of his travels. Thus, it came about that the book appeared in Madras, where its chances of becoming known were small.[22]

Only his journey through Kurdistan need concern us here.[23] R. David went by way of Mardin to Diar Bakr and back to Nisebin (Tsintsebbin), then on by way of Salga[24] (Tsallaga) and Peshkhabur (Pasavoor) to Zakho (Zachoo), which he describes in detail. From Zakho he turned southward to Mosul. He paid a visit to al-Qosh and the grave of Navi Naḥum, then proceeded to the Kurdish mountains, visiting Dehok (Dehook), the Jewish village of Sundur, and Amadiya (Amadya). From Amadiya—whose importance for Kurdish Jewry he failed to recognize—his route led again to the mountains: to Shosh and Sukho (Sochoo), the latter of which he likewise declares to be a purely Jewish village.[25]

Returning to Mosul, he visited Arbil (Arvil)[26] and Kerkuk (Koorkook), then proceeded to Baghdad, whence he made his way to Southern and Eastern Kurdistan: Sulaimani (Sleemania), Bana (Bannah), Sakis (Sakees), Sabhlakh (Sabblagg = Saudi Bulaq),[27] and Tazqala (Tazcalla). He traversed the Urmia Lake region (Oormyan, Salamas) and even penetrated as far as Bashqala (Bascallan)[28] between the Urmia and Van Lakes—a bold undertaking that puts him on a level with such explorers of Kurdistan as C. J. Rich. Returning to Saudi Bulaq, R. David visited Mian-doab (Mean Davab), the Garus (Groosh) districts, Sinne (Sena), Kaslan, and finally Hamadan, which lies deep in Persian territory.

Undoubtedly, R. David's journey was a significant achievement. Only a few travelers, such as the daring Ker Porter, or Rich,[29] had visited such large sections of Kurdistan. Because of the danger of attack on travelers by the Kurdish tribes, the government authorities refused to issue travel permits. Indeed, several years later (1829) the orientalist Schultz of Giessen was murdered on the road between Julamerk and Bashqala.[30] The success of R. David's journey—the fact that he was able to pass through areas peopled by Kurdish tribes and almost untrod by the foot of an outsider—is due to his having come from Palestine as a ***hakham***, a method to which Saphir and Halévy likewise owed their success in Yemen.

R. David's book suffers from the fact that he spent only a short time in each place (he fails to specify the length of time) and was therefore not able to familiarize himself with the life of the people. Concerning the Jews of Amadiya, for instance, he writes as follows: "In the town are about two hundred families of Israelites who speak the same language as the Israelites in Zachoo, and have the same customs. Some of them are rich merchants, some workmen, and some owners of cattle" (p. 57). Such a description is not merely inadequate: from a scholarly point of view it is also misleading. R. David usually confines himself to establishing that the Jews of such-and-such a place are "using the same customs and language as the Israelites at Bahadina." When he then proceeds to say the same thing about the Jews of the Urmia district and of Sinne (pp. 73, 83), one is compelled to discount the scientific value of the report.

It was probably R. David's aim to write a sort of Baedeker for the English colonial officials in Madras who were the subscribers to his book. Therefore, the book is little more than an itinerary, confining itself to statistical information and the mention of a few objects of interest. Perhaps R. David's original manuscript may yet be discovered. According to a statement in his introduction, the description of his journey must have comprised six or seven hundred pages.

The Nestorian Mission

Almost simultaneously with R. David's visit to Kurdistan began the journeys of the Christian missionaries to the Nestorians (Assyrians) of the Urmia district and the mountain region of Julamerk. This was an important period in the exploration of our area; for these travelers furnished not only an excellent picture of the country and its inhabitants but likewise important comparative material concerning the *Surai*,[31] the Christian neighbors of the Jews. The mission reports have the greater value in that they supply us, for the first time, with the observations of men who had many years' experience on which to draw rather than with the impressions of casual visitors to the country.

Through the journeys of Eli Smith and H. G. O. Dwight,[32] who came to Kurdistan in 1830 on behalf of the Prudential Committee of the American Board of Commissioners for Foreign Missions, the Nestorians were, so to speak, rediscovered. Owing to the murder of Schultz, Smith and Dwight did not venture into the mountain districts but remained in the vicinity of Lake Urmia. Their journey provided the stimulus for the founding of the Urmia Mission by the Presbyterians and the dispatch of Justin Perkins and Asahel Grant.

Perkins[33] remained in Urmia from 1835 to 1841 and, in several journeys traversed the whole of the Urmia district. Though he did not penetrate into the mountain region, he came into contact with Nestorians from that region. His voluminous work gives no detailed account of the customs on the Nestorians. While therefore not of outstanding importance, it is nevertheless valuable as a source, especially for the Urmia Lake district.

The physician Asahel Grant[34] arrived in Urmia in 1835 and won friends in all parts of the country through his medical practice. Patients came to him from far and near. With the ground thus prepared, he succeeded in penetrating, in several journeys, into the actual mountain country of the Surai—the first European to do so.[35] In 1839 he went from Mosul to Amadiya by way of Akra (p. 59). He gives an interesting description of the ruined city and also mentions the Jews (p. 61). From Amadiya he pushed on into the Hakkiari Mountain region and visited the patriarch Mar Shimon in his mountain residence, Qudshanis. After spending five days with the patriarch, he returned to Urmia by way of Bashqala and Salamas. On a second visit in May 1840, Grant met the patriarch again, this time in the castle of the Hakkiari chief of Julamerk (p. 115).

In Grant's account of his travels there is little mention of the Jews, because he seldom came into contact with them. The value of the book lies in its authentic material on the Nestorians of the mountain district round Amadiya, the manners and customs of this community being of special interest to him in view of the fact that they were to serve as evidence for his thesis that the Nestorians were descendants of the lost tribes of Israel.

Following the Presbyterians, the Church of England began its activities among the Nestorians through the Society for Promoting Christian Knowledge. In 1842 it sent out W. F. Ainsworth,[36] and shortly afterward, George Percy Badger, who made a thorough study of the

Kurdish highlands. Badger also visited the principal Jewish centers and even penetrated as far as Ashita, where he saw the patriarch, Mar Shimon. His book on the Nestorians is a standard work and is indispensable in any investigation of the Kurdish Jews.[37]

Missionary Work among Jews

At this time the London Society for Promoting Christianity amongst the Jews, an organization of the Church of England, began to work among the Jews of Kurdistan and Mesopotamia. Most of the missionaries sent out by the Society were converted Jews.[38]

The first missionary to come in contact with Kurdish Jews was Joseph Wolff,[39] a German Jew who was in the service of the London Mission and later gained worldwide fame through his daring journey to Bukhara. He should, in fact, have been mentioned before R. David, because his early travel among the Jewish communities of Western Asia brought him to Salamas and Urmia in 1821–26.[40] On his great journey in 1831–34 he went by way of Mardin, Nisebin, Mosul, and Arbil to Baghdad and visited the Urmia district a second time.[41]

His reports contain no new information of importance on the Kurdish Jews and are, in the main, a record of quite fantastic missionary conversations that he held with these people.

His successor was Henry Aaron Stern,[42] another converted Jew. The London society had decided to open a mission in Baghdad; and in 1844 it sent Stern along with Murray Vicars and P. H. Sternschuss (likewise a convert) to that city, which had a Jewish population of sixteen thousand. Seeing that their missionary labors encountered the greatest difficulties, Stern and Sternschuss took the opportunity of seeking out the neighboring Jewish communities.

On his first journey (1848),[43] Stern set out from Baghdad and visited Tuz Khurmat, Kerkuk, Arbil, Mosul, el-Qosh, Dehok (his Tahook) and the Jewish village of Sundur, which he describes in detail. Guided always by local Jews, to whom he sold printed Bibles at very low prices, he proceeded to Zakho, Jezire, and Amadiya. From Amadiya he penetrated into the Nestorian district as far as Ashita, then turned eastward to Shosh, which had been visited also by R. David. From Shosh he returned to Mosul. His description of this journey, though very brief, contains many items of interest.

In 1848 Sternschuss, too, visited the Jewish communities of Kurdistan, among them those of Kerkuk, Arbil, and Mosul. Everywhere he sold Bibles: "Many of them have also been taken to Ravanday (Rowanduz)."[44]

Stern and Sternschuss were followed in 1855 by J. H. Bruhl and J. M. Eppstein, who were, like their predecessors, Jewish converts. But in Baghdad all Jews who came into contact with the missionaries were excommunicated, so that the work of the Baghdad mission became virtually impossible. Bruhl and Eppstein consequently undertook a number of journeys, visiting Kerkuk, Khoi-Sanjak, Sulaimani, and Tuz Khurmat.[45] The Baghdad mission was given up in 1866.[46] It would be highly worthwhile to investigate its activities from the Jewish point of view.

Joseph Israel Benjamin (Benjamin II)

Among the most celebrated sources for material on the Kurdish Jews is the journey of Joseph Israel Benjamin (b. 1818 in Falticeni in Rumania, d. 1864 in London).[47] Benjamin, who considered himself the successor of Benjamin of Tudela, called himself Benjamin II (*Acht Jahre in Asien und Afrika*, p.290) and has become known under that name. (Mendele Mokher Sepharim then brought this "dynasty" to a satirical close through the travels of his Benjamin III.) What could have induced Benjamin to give up his calling of timber merchant at the age of twenty-seven, part with wife and child, and set out on such a fantastic and, to all appearance, aimless journey is by no means clear. Evidently, he, too, was lured by the quest of the lost tribes.[48]

Benjamin set out on his travels in January 1845. In August 1847, after having visited Turkey and Egypt, he reached Jerusalem. He spent considerable time in Palestine, then journeyed through the Syrian cities and entered Kurdish territory at Urfa. Unfortunately, Benjamin fails to give exact dates, merely saying that his first two trips in Kurdistan occupied fifty-five days.

From Urfa he traversed the western Taurus (Suwerek, Tchermuk), passing through Diar Bekr, Mardin, and Nisebin to Salga (his Zelma). For ten days he journeyed over "the mountain chain of Djebel-Sandjack [Jebel Sanjak]," the villages of which "are inhabited mainly by Jews and learned in the course of these visits, in what abysmal ignorance they live." Benjamin gives only a short, general account of these ten days (p. 75).[49]

From Jezire he went to Zakho (Zachu), sojourned there awhile, then proceeded on his "first trip into the mountains of Kurdistan," visiting Sundur (Sandur), Dehok (Daik), Betanure (Tanura), and al-Qosh (Alkusch). At al-Qosh he took part in the feast of Shavu'ot (5th Sivan 1848).

He then went on to Mosul whence he set out on his second Kurdish journey. "After a journey of three days through a desert [*sic*]," he reached Akra, then traveled in a northwesterly direction to a remote and seldom visited mountain village Barzan (Birsani).[50] His stay in Barzan was too brief for any real insight into the life of the people, as the following statement attests: "The ignorance of our Jewish brethren here is so great that they are not even capable of reciting a prayer; and nowhere, I must confess with pain, did I find them in such a debased state, and sunk in such moral turpitude, as here." This is certainly an exaggeration, seeing that the famous Barzani family, which has produced many *ḥakhamim*, came from Barzan. Benjamin climbed the Piris Dagh (called Zibari by the Jews and Baris by the Kurds, according to Benjamin); and at the foot of the mountain he found four Jewish nomadic families who assured him "that never before had a Jewish European traveler been seen or heard of here" (ibid., pp. 106–7).[51]

Benjamin proceeded to Sündu, where he was detained for considerable time by illness, (probably an attack of malaria) and eventually returned to Barzan still suffering from the effects of the attack. Guided by a number of Jews and Kurds, he then set out for a destination "near to Urmia in the mountains, on the side of lower Persia" (first half of July 1848) (Germ. ed. pp. 80–81). On the fourth day, this journey came to an abrupt end through a variety of causes. Benjamin, unfortunately, does not give the names of the villages that he visited or that sent representatives to him.

Benjamin returned to Mosul and a month later (mid–August 1848) traveled with a caravan to Arbil (Erbil) from which he set out on his third Kurdish journey, visiting Rowanduz (Rowandis) and Khoi-Sanjak (p. 108). His travels in Kurdistan ended at Kerkuk.

Since his book was the only available source for material on the Kurdish Jews, it acquired the reputation of being a reliable report; and its author was reckoned among the very few outstanding Jewish travelers. The book should, however, have been approached critically, and the true value of its contents weighed, bit by bit.[52] Benjamin's account of his journey is without question an important document and bears witness to no inconsiderable daring on his part. It is to be regretted that a man who saw so much and lived in a period that had plenty of examples of excellent travel books should have left so vague and unscientific a description of his journeys. The book undoubtedly contains many important items; but only after all the material has been subjected to methodical and critical investigation will it be possible to use them in a scientific work.

Alliance Israelite Universelle

The Alliance Israelite Universelle began its work among the Kurdish Jews comparatively late. In 1903 it founded a school for boys and girls in Sinne and boys' schools in Kirmanshah (1904), Mosul (1907) and Hanekin (1911). Yet even before these schools were established, the monthly bulletins of the Alliance contained reports from various communities in central Kurdistan, some of which comprised valuable materials.[53] Furthermore, the Alliance teachers, particularly those of the Baghdad schools, undertook journeys of which they reported in the bulletins; and these reports often included information quoted directly from Kurdish Jews who came from the mountain region.[54]

Recent Journeys

The reports of the travelers who toured Kurdistan since 1870 contribute almost nothing to our knowledge of the Kurdish Jews. Even after the war of 1914–18, Kurdistan continued, as before, to offer great obstacles to systematic work requiring a prolonged stay in the country.[55] There are, however, several works that deserve special mention, chief among them being those of Henry Binder,[56] A. M. Hamilton,[57] and Lamec Saad.[58] The books of the two latter differ from those of their predecessors in being, not a record of the casual impressions acquired on a brief sightseeing tour but the observations of men who remained in the country long enough to gain real knowledge of the land and the people.

There are also several Jewish travelers who visited Kurdish Jewry in recent years. Ephraim Neumark[59] went only as far as Mosul, and his contribution is slight. The journey of W. Schur[60] merits some attention, however. Schur visited Urfa, Mardin, Nisebin, Jezire, Zakho and Mosul; and his short, general survey (*Maḥazot ha-Ḥayim*, p. 19–23) is among the best of the writings published up to that time on the Kurdish Jews.

In 1935, Hanekin, Kirmanshah, Sinne and their environs were visited by A. J. Brawer,[61] and the Jewish village of Sundur by Walter Schwarz (*Jüdische Rundschau* [Berlin], 1935).

Beginning of the Scientific Study of the Country

Up to this point we have considered only general works of exploration that included our area, consisting for the most part, of travelers' accounts of their journeys. Apart from a few minor studies on special topics, no scientific work of research specifically devoted to the Kurdish Jews has appeared.

A. Z. Idelsohn, who has made a study of many Oriental Jewish communities, rendered pioneer service in our field by carrying on researches among the Kurdish Jews living in Jerusalem. He published, with a general introduction, a collection of tales in the Aramaic dialect of Saudi Bulaq.[62] The material was still scanty at that time, for the total number of Kurdish Jewish families in Jerusalem did not amount to more than twenty-five. Several songs sung by the Kurdish Jews were also taken down by Idelsohn from the lips of a *ḥakham* who came from Saudi Bulaq.[63]

Idelsohn was preceded by Albert Löwy, who had collected information on the Kurdish Jews from a Jew of Urmia.[64] These notes contain much important material, and it is strange that research workers in this field have not made greater use of them.

Some manuscript material, consisting almost exclusively of letters, has also appeared in recent years. Jacob Mann has published a number of texts,[65] which are in possession of the Hebrew Union College Library in Cincinnati; and Simḥa Assaf has published various valuable documents,[66] some of which were collected by Walter Fischel on his two short trips to Kurdistan.[67]

A number of papers on the language of the Kurdish Jews—called Targum or Jebeli, a neo-Aramaic dialect similar to that of the Christians of Kurdistan—have appeared since R. Duval published his collection of tales in the dialect of Salamas.[68] In his standard work on Aramaic,[69] Franz Rosenthal has dealt in detail with the question of neo-Aramaic and has covered all the material of importance on this subject.

Joseph J. Rivlin is making a special study of the dialects of the Kurdish Jews and has published a number of minor texts.[70] In behalf of the Hebrew University in Jerusalem, he has also taken down the oral Bible translation of the Kurdish Jews. This work is still in progress.

2

The Land

It is not easy to give a hard-and-fast definition of the term Kurdish Jew. We may perhaps best define a Kurdish Jew as one who lives in the territory occupied by the Kurds and speaks Aramaic (Targum); but we must also include in our territory a few scattered districts where the Jews speak mainly Arabic (e.g. Nisebin).

The Kurdish Jews, like their Muslim neighbors, are actually a highland folk. But the Kurds have gradually pushed their way down from the hills into the plains and even into the Mesopotamian lowlands. Thus, they have drawn into the zone of their influence areas formerly dominated by Arabic culture; and in this way Jews, who in fact belonged to the Mesopotamian area, came into the orbit of Kurdish culture. It must nevertheless be clearly understood that the direction of migration of the Kurds is east–west, that of the Jews originally west–east; but the direction of Jewish migration varies, since, (as we must again emphasize) the Kurdish Jews are not a homogeneous people but came to Kurdistan in several waves. In any case, at present there is among them a strong east–west direction of migration, just as among the Kurds. We cannot as yet distinguish their separate migratory waves, and it is even possible that Jews have made their way into Kurdistan from the north.

The center of the settlement area of the Jews is the mountain region of the Zagros and the Taurus. In the latter, the number of the Kurds gradually diminishes in the territory of the Armenians, where there are today no Jewish settlements at all. Back of the mountains lie the Van and Urmia Lake regions, of which the latter in particular belongs to the Jewish settlement area. In the west, the Tigris may be considered the boundary of Jewish settlement. Thus, the Jews occupy three types of natural region in Kurdistan: the mountain tracts, the volcanic region of the lakes, and the plains as far as the Tigris.

The center is (as mentioned) the mountain region: in the north the Taurus, in the south the Zagros. The Taurus, stretching from east to west, is a ridge of old crystalline schist. The south–east section of the Taurus, which comes within the scope of our investigation only in connection with the Hakkiari Mountain range, the ancient seat of the Nestorians, is richer in water than the rest of the Taurus and therefore bears more resemblance to the Zagros.

In structure the Zagros is a folded mountain composed chiefly of limestone; and its chains run northwest to southeast, parallel to the Tigris. The water courses of this region, which abounds in springs, first follow the longitudinal valleys, then break through the chains toward the west in deep-cut gorges.[1] This excessive dissection makes the mountain tract very difficult of access and furnishes sites for settlement that, before the days of modern military technique, were virtually impregnable. Hence, this area is a classical example of a place of retreat in which remnants of different people and tribes have survived for centuries.

The northern and eastern division of the mountain ranges are characterized by volcanic formations. The Ararat is an extinct volcano; and the volcanic matter that spread itself in layers over the old stratified formation built the Van and Urmia Lakes, both of which are the result of the damming up of rivers by volcanic matter.

At the base of these mountain ranges is spread the calcareous plain of Mesopotamia, in which the Tigris and the Euphrates have cut their channels. The Kurds penetrated only as far as the Tigris, which is therefore to be regarded as the boundary of the Jewish area of settlement, as well. Eastern Mesopotamia likewise belongs geographically—and in part also geologically—to the Taurus and Zagros region, since it is not purely flat country but rises in a series of waves to the Zagros. The area is abundantly dissected by the rivers and streams that flow into the Tigris. Toward the south the landscape changes: here, the space between the Tigris and the Zagros becomes progressively wider; and this tract consequently takes on a character more akin, climatologically as well, to that of Mesopotamia proper.

Our territory belongs to the climatic region of the dry continental area, occupying a belt extending over both hemispheres at about the thirty-fifth parallel, for which winter rains and dry summers are typical. Kurdistan would be a dry area like Persia or the tableland of Arabia were it not for the Taurus and Zagros, which cause the wet winds blowing in from the Mediterranean Sea and the Persian Gulf to rise and precipitate their moisture.

The Zagros, in particular, with its severe winters and abundant snowfall, is a storehouse of water for this area. Rich in springs and streams (which flow throughout the year), it waters the whole tract as far as the Tigris and makes irrigation feasible where the rainfall does not suffice.[2]

The Zagros is covered to a height of 1,800 meters with a growth of dwarf oak that occurs in many varieties and produces oak apples, one of the principal export articles of the country. The dwarf oak is, in fact, Kurdistan's national tree. We can hardly speak here of a forest for there is only a sprinkling of trees on the slopes of the mountains. The picture presented is the characteristic one, often described, of a district of numerous deep-cut valleys, whose sides are covered with a sparse growth of dwarf oak. Beside the dwarf, there are certain forest trees—principally the walnut (whose fruit is highly prized), the poplar, and the wild mountain pear.

The absence of actual forests in this region is due, no doubt, to the complete lack of measures of conservation. The trees are ruthlessly cut down, both for fuel and for winter fodder. An occupation in which Jews are especially active is the lopping off of leafy twigs in the autumn to sell as feed for cattle. A further hindrance to afforestation is the presence of the numerous herds, which not only strip the young branches of their leaves but even attack the bark of the trunk.

The comparative mildness of the summers, due to the altitude and the abundant supply of water, have produced a rich flora.[3] Owing to the sparseness of the trees the mountain slopes enjoy a great deal of sunshine and are thickly covered with herbs and shrubs (Daphne, juniper, wild roses). Higher up, the dwarf oaks disappear, leaving only the alpine meadows. The mountain tract is therefore the district occupied by the Kurdish nomads and their herds. In the spring, after pasturing their herds in the plains, the Kurds move up to their mountain pasturelands, the *zozan*. They follow the snow line up the mountain sides until the onset of snow and rain in the autumn forces them back again, farther and farther down the valley. The winters are spent in the farming districts below, where the herds graze the fields after the harvest.

The descent of the nomads in the winter months is fraught with danger to the farmers.[4] The latter are settled mostly in the valleys, where their villages, often very small and primitive, nestle against a ledge at the foot of the mountains. Their chief protection lies in their remoteness from the highways. This isolation is also responsible for the survival of so many ethnic remnants. The villagers cultivate wheat, barley, and (in the warmer and better-watered districts) rice and cotton. They also engage largely in market gardening (for the most part on irrigated land) and grape growing. They grow an abundance of fruit and nut trees as well.

Though we are dealing with a rough, inaccessible mountain region, we find no teeming wildlife here. The beasts of prey have been virtually exterminated. The bear, which plays an important role in the tales of both Kurds and Jews (the Jews love to relate heroic tales of encounters with bears) is now found only on rare occasions. The land is rich in partridges and squirrels (see the tale "King of the Squirrels");[5] but the most formidable residents of the mountain area are, in fact, the demons.

The village settlements of the plain (i.e., of Mesopotamia and the lake region of the volcanic zone) do not differ substantially from those of the hill country. The plains, however, do not have the hard winter with its snowstorms that confines the villager to his house and forces him to make careful provision for his winter food supply. The village Jew even undertakes a change of profession in the winter, for he works as a weaver at home.

The location of a village settlement depends not only on the presence of arable land and a water supply but also on political factors: in so far as it is possible, districts remote from the highways are selected for settlement. The urban settlements, on the contrary, developed precisely on the highways and trade routes. Here, from time immemorial, great transverse valleys have marked the route from Persia into the Mesopotamian lowlands, and it was at these points that the urban settlements developed. Such valleys are those of the Khabur and of the Great and Little Zab.

One of the most important of these highways is the road that Hamilton transformed into an automobile road. It runs along the valley of the Great Zab, passing through Arbil and Rowanduz on to Teheran. Thus, by connecting with the railway in Turkey via Nisibin and Mosul, it makes possible direct communication between Western Europe and Persia in place of the previous roundabout routes.[6]

Another important road is that which runs from Mosul through Dehok, Amadiya, and the Taurus (Julamerk, Bashkala) to the Van Lake, utilizing the upper course of the Great Zab.

The old urban settlements in the mountain region acquire their distinctive character from their position at naturally protected spots. They are true natural fortresses, usually with their own water supply;

and it was only our modern military technique, with its air attacks, that rendered them valueless.[7]

Thus, Amadiya is situated on a plateau that rises to a height of 300–400 meters above the valley of the Great Zab (see illustration in Binder, *Au Kurdistan*, p. 200)* and can be reached only by difficult paths hewn in the rock.

Travelers were particularly impressed by the unique site of Rowanduz. Hamilton, for instance, writes:

> In this land of mountain, rivers, gorges and natural ramparts, the town could have been built in no more commanding position. It lies between two mighty chasms on a narrow tongue of rock that slopes down from the high range of the Kurrek Dagh. This tongue as it descends becomes a strip scarcely one hundred yards in width, which falls steeply until it reaches a flat platform of rock by the confined banks of the Rowanduz River, which here turns sharply into the canyon that bounds the promontory on the west. . . . High on the steep and narrow slope and perched thus between two great precipices is the town of Upper Rowanduz. (*Road Through Kurdistan*, p. 19; see also his plates 11, 28.)

A further safeguard to the settlements is the fact that the roads leading to them—or at least the settlements themselves—are protected by the castles of the Kurdish chieftains. These castles likewise served as points from which to launch attacks. One finds such castles scattered all over the country; but most of them, especially those on the main highways, are now in ruins.[8]

Of a different character are the urban settlements that lie at the mouths of the transverse valleys. These bear more resemblance to the settlements of the plains. Most of them are situated at points where the rivers become navigable for large *keleks* (rafts); they have consequently grown into trading centers. Thus, Zakho, which is virtually an island, with the Khabur flowing almost completely around it, has become a timber-exporting center. It is here that the large *keleks* are put together for transporting timber and other export articles to Mosul. Similarly, Khoi Sanjak owes its importance to its position at the point where the Little Zab (Zab al-Asfal) becomes navigable for *keleks*.

The cities in the plains are among the world's oldest known urban settlements. The antiquity of Arbil, for instance, is obvious in its distinctive external appearance. It lies on a *tell* (mount) 120 feet high.

*For this and all subsequent references, see Notes to chapter 1.

> Rising above the plain . . . like the truncated cone of some extinct volcano and topped with great brick walls, there stood the most ancient of all inhabited cities on the face of the earth. . . . Who built the great mound on which the modern city stands? . . . It merely grew. City upon city decayed into the mound which slowly rose through countless ages till today it stands about twice as high as any other such mound in the world. (Hamilton, *Road Through Kurdistan*, p. 63)

All the roads lead to the Tigris; and here, it is Mosul, the ancient Nineveh, "a city of border-zones and at the same time centrally situated," that is both industrial and spiritual center to the Kurdish Jews. Mosul is excellently situated for river, as well as land, traffic.

The question why Jews exist in one settlement and not in another can certainly receive no unequivocal answer. Though the Kurdish Jews are peasants and more closely identified with their country than most Oriental Jews, the geographical factor played no great role in the matter, even among them. Kurdistan as a place of retreat offered security to remnants of Jewish as well as other communities; consequently, the Jews survived there. Furthermore, there can be no doubt that the Jews were formerly attracted to certain settlements by their importance as trading centers. It is, however, probable that political reasons were the chief factor.

Following World War I and its political and economic aftermath, important changes took place in Kurdistan. The discovery of the oil fields, their modern exploitation, and the introduction of the automobile and the airplane caused certain settlements to prosper and others to decline.

The oil fields are situated in the neighborhood of Hanekin, Kerkuk, and Mosul. These cities have, in consequence, received a fresh impetus, the employees of the oil fields being drawn partly from their inhabitants. Similarly, the automobile and the airplane brought with them great changes. The country was opened up and made safer for travelers, for much traffic and swift communication spell ruin to the robbers who prey upon the caravans.

3

History of the Kurdish Jews

The present-day Kurdish Jews are not historically minded. In contrast with the Jews of Yemen, for instance, who have produced a number of historical works, the Kurdish Jews have, so far as we know, left no historical records of their own. Löwy's[1] experience with his Kurdish Jewish informants was the same as mine: none of them knew anything about the ancient history of their people. All historical events to which they referred were generally placed a century or a century-and-a-half too early.

The scanty material that we possess can give us no satisfactory conception of the history of this community. It can at best serve as a partial framework. Thorough archaeological investigation of the country might help fill out the structure to some degree. The Jewish settlements of Kurdistan are undoubtedly very old. And it is remarkable that we find Jews who speak an Aramaic dialect (Targum or Jebeli) in an area that represents the perimeter of settlement of the exiles from Israel and Judah (2 Kings 17:7, Isa. 11:11, 27:13) or at any rate lies adjacent to it.[2] Have we here before us the descendants of those exiles? Although in this general form, the assumption must be rejected, it may be said with some assurance that we have here Jews among whom are included remnants of the old Jewish population. We shall give some proofs of this hypothesis in our anthropological chapter.[3]

That our area was settled by Jews at a very early date is evident from the success of Christianity and the astonishing expansion of Nestorianism. Here, too, the Jews were undoubtedly the best material for proselytism, especially because the conversion of the rulers of Adiabene (first century C.E.) to Judaism resulted in the absorption of many non-Jews into the community and the settlement of Jews was supported by the converted princes.

It is surprising how rarely Kurdistan is mentioned in the Talmud, although Sura and Pumbadita were only a stone's throw away.[4] Mosul (Ashur) is not mentioned at all. Evidently, in talmudic times it was a very unimportant town. Mention is made of Arbil (Arbela), which is one of the world's oldest cities and which took the place of Nineveh after the fall of the latter; yet it is astonishing how insignificant is the place it occupies in the Talmud. Of central Kurdistan we hear nothing at all.

In regard to the position of the Jews in the period under Muslim rule, we are likewise merely groping in the dark. The Arab historians scarcely mention the Jews. Yet even the infrequent references to Jews in the cities show that this period, when the Arabs flourished, was a time of growth for the Jewish communities also.[5]

Twelfth Century: David Alroy

We are somewhat better acquainted with the position of the Jews in the twelfth century. Our knowledge rests on the meager information given by Benjamin of Tudela and R. Petaḥya, who, as we have seen, never visited central Kurdistan.

The time was the period following the Second Crusade. The cities were enjoying a new prosperity under the rule of the Seljuks. From the reports of Benjamin and Petaḥya, we gather that the Jews shared in this prosperity. Mosul, the "great Ashur," called "New Nineve" by Petaḥya, had a Jewish community of seven thousand souls according to Benjamin (*Sefer Massa'ot*, p. 52), six thousand according to Petaḥya (*Travels*, p. 8). The urban population had been augmented by Jewish immigrants from Palestine, fleeing before the approach of the crusaders. These immigrants gave a new impetus to the academy at Baghdad and also to Mosul, which had made itself independent of Baghdad and had its own exilarch.[6] Since Mosul was at the time unquestionably the spiritual and commercial center of our area, we may assume that among the many students whom the exilarch gathered in his court, there were also some Kurdish Jews.

The Jews of Mosul enjoyed autonomy. The exilarch even had a prison of his own. Half the head tax—which the Jews as unbelievers (*dhimmi*) had to pay—accrued to the state, and half to the exilarch.

The other cities of the plain also had important Jewish communities. In Nisebin there were one thousand Jews (Benjamin, *Sefer Massa'ot*,

p. 51) and three synagogues (Petaḥya, *Travels*, 2^b, 7^a). Petaḥya remarks that at Nisebin begins the land of Ashur (Mosul) [and that "Khazaria (Azerbaijan) has one language, and Togarma (Turkey) has another language"].

Jeziret al-Omar even had a community of four thousand Jews (Benjamin, *Sefer Masacot*, p. 51). As to Arbil we have no information, for (as previously noted) there is an evident gap in the text at this point.

Most important and illuminating of all, however, is the passage in Benjamin of Tudela that records the appearance of the false Messiah David Alroy of Amadiya (ibid., pp. 78–79). This passage gives us an insight into Jewish life in inner Kurdistan. And the negative inference to be drawn from the report is no less significant than the positive: this casual reference by Benjamin shows how much historical material on the Kurdish Jews has been lost to us.[7]

Benjamin describes Amadiya as a town having a Jewish community of twenty-five thousand—a palpable exaggeration:

> This is the first of those communities that dwell in the mountains of Hafton, where there are more than 100 Jewish communities. Here is the commencement of the land of Media. These Jews are descendants of those, who were first led into captivity by King Shalmanesser; they speak the Targum language and among them are learned men. They reach from the province of Amadiya[8] unto the province of Gilan, twenty-five days distant on the border of the kingdom of Persia." (ibid., pp. 76–77).

The Jews of Amadiya were also Persian subjects, and every male from the age of fifteen had to pay the head tax.

As we have said, the report on the false Messiah David Alroy is the most important single item we possess on the history of the Kurdish Jews. This David al-Ro'i, as Benjamin calls him, had studied at the Baghdad academy under the exilarch Hisdai and the Gaon Ali haLevi, and was a scholar of no mean attainments. This, again, shows us that the Jews of Kurdistan, far from being isolated during this period, had connections with the centers of learning in Mesopotamia. Benjamin's account of Alroy's activities is a mixture of fact and legend. He writes that "he conceived the idea of rebelling against the King of Persia and collecting the Jews who live in the mountains of Hafton to go forth and to fight against all nations and to march and capture Jerusalem" (ibid., p. 78).

The movement had a great following among the Jews, who called him Messiah; and the King of Persia, fearing clashes and disturbances, summoned Alroy and had him imprisoned in Tabaristan. Alroy, however, freed himself in a miraculous way and reached Amadiya in one single day, though it was a journey ordinarily requiring ten days.

The king then applied to the exilarch of Baghdad through the caliph of Baghdad and warned him that if Alroy did not stop his seditious activities, he would have all the Jews in his realm put to death. In great dismay, the exilarch turned to his colleague in Mosul[9]—which shows us clearly that Mosul was looked upon by the Jews of Kurdistan as their chief city. When all attempts to halt David on course had failed, treachery was resorted to. One of the king's vassals bribed Alroy's father-in-law, "so he went to Alroy's house, and slew him whilst he was asleep in his bed" (ibid., p. 81). Nevertheless, the king was not appeased until the Jews had paid a fine of one hundred gold talents.

An important source supplementing Benjamin's narrative has recently come to light. In the *Ifḥān al-Yahūd* (*Silencing of the Jews*) of Samaw'al b. Yaḥyā al-Maghribī, a Jewish convert to Islam, we find a more realistic version of Alroy's uprising, although due allowance should be made for the author's anti-Jewish attitude.

According to this source, David, here called M'naḥem b. Sh'lomo al-Rūḥī,[10] had won great renown among the Jews, wherefore the commandant of the fortress also wished to meet him. al-Rūḥī realized at once that this person was a mediocrity and conceived the plan of seizing the fortress with the help of the Jews:

> Therefore he wrote to the Jews who were roaming about in the cities of Azerbaijan and its surroundings, for he knew that the Jews of Persia were the most foolish of all the Jews, and let them know in his letter that he arose to be their savior from the hands of the Moslems. . . and also wrote to them that it was desirable that each one of them, when coming here, should have a sword or some other weapon hidden under his clothing'.[11]

When the Jews began to stream in, the commandant first thought that they were making a pilgrimage to al-Rūḥī, for he was familiar with such pilgrimages on the part of the Kurdish Jews. When, however, he realized the true situation, he had al-Rūḥī put to death. Great was the consternation of the Jews, and they stampeded in all directions:

> Yet the Jews of Amadiya extol him to this day in their assemblies, and many among them look upon him as the expected Messiah. I saw Jewish communities in Persia, e.g., in Khoi, Salamas, Tabriz and Maragha, which invoke his name in the holiest vows. The Jews of Amadiya are the most extreme opponents of the Christians in all things that relate

to Jews. In this city there is a sect that believes in a religious doctrine which, according to its members, comes from that impostor.[12]

Jacob Mann believes that Alroy's conspiracy was connected with events arising from the Second Crusade. The Seljuks in Mesopotamia and Syria were a source of great danger to the crusaders; and 'Imad al-Dīn Zangī, the Attabeg of Mosul (after whom Amadiya is said to have been named) had conquered Edessa. In this time of great political ferment, Mann believes, David Alroy was inspired with the prophetic spirit and conceived the plan of leading the Jews to Palestine.

In my opinion, Mann's explanation is not very convincing. I think it far more likely that Alroy considered this a propitious time for the Jews to make a bid for political independence, a status to which they had never, and to this day have never, yet attained. To understand the situation, it is well to recall similar occurrences among the Christians: "In 1310, in the reign of Uldjaitu, the Christians, after bravely defending themselves for over three months on the citadel of Arbil against the besiegers, Arab, Kurd, and Mongol, were overcome and exterminated."[13] Kurdistan has always been a land dominated by its chieftains, and the forays of these chieftains may well have spurred Alroy to make a similar attempt with the help of the Jews and in their behalf.

For an inquiry into the question of what elements had gone into the making of the Kurdish Jews, the fact that Jews from Azerbaijan had come to Kurdistan (which we learn from the Alroy episode) is of special importance. This was neither the first nor the last instance of the penetration of Jewish–Persian elements into Kurdistan. The boundary line between Kurdistan and Persia fluctuated for centuries; and there was no doubt an active exchange of population, in which the Jews also participated.

Thirteenth Century: Al-Ḥarizi

Not many decades after Benjamin of Tudela, the same area was visited by Ḥarizi (ca. 1230). His portrayal of the Jewish communities is a masterpiece, and it is hard to believe that Benjamin of Tudela and Ḥarizi were contemporaries. While we get scarcely a hint of Benjamin's personality in his work, Ḥarizi's *Maqāma*s are permeated with the personality of their author. This Jewish François Villon portrays the life of the Jewish communities with keen irony. He detects in them the signs of decay, although it was still before the time of the Mongol invasions that ruined the cities. Not only are Ḥarizi's *Maqāma*s modern as poetry, but they give a picture of the urban Jews which differs little from that of the Jews of today.

Ḥarizi gives scant attention to Arbil.[14] He recognizes the ignorance concealed beneath its glittering surface (*Maq.*24.3). The life of Mosul is rather more fully portrayed,[15] and from the picture of Baghdad we are able to glean much that is of interest for our subject.[16]

Ḥarizi views with wonder and admiration the size and beauty of Mosul and its palatial synagogues and gives an impressive lyrical description of the city in its winter garb (*Maq.* 29.1).[17]

As an itinerant minstrel dependent on the charity of men, he divides mankind into two groups, the hard-hearted and the kindly. The Jews of Mosul fare badly in this classification, with the exception of the two heads of the community, the exilarch R. Nissim, and the "Head of the Galut" David (*Maq.* 46.8.18–19; *Judae Ḥarizi Macamae*, ed. Pauli de Lagarde, p. 176). On the community itself he pours scorn and ridicule:

> When I came there, I saw their assemblies.
> Every one of them was nodding on the bosom of folly, there was no man, neither voice of man
> But the horses tied and the asses tied. [2 Kings 7:10]
> And it was for the Jews like a well, and ox and ass fell in.
> On the day on which the community of the Rock [the Jews] were exiled from Jerusalem, the pious were exiled to Damascus and Egypt and settled from Havila to Shur; but the rabble came to Ashur. (*Maq.* 46.8.28–32)

The description reaches its climax in the famous *Maqāma* 24 on the cantor of Mosul, wherein the ignorant congregation and their ignorant cantor, of whose performance they are so proud, are portrayed with a satirical outlook that is astonishing for the time.

After a brief description of the wealth and splendor of the city, and the avarice of its inhabitants, Ḥarizi tells how he comes to the synagogue in Mosul on Friday evening. He sits down among the crowd beside two old

> Longbeards, strong as oaks, of the sort that sell praise but do not earn it,
> Of the destroyers of charitable institutions, but not of their builders,
> Men of high stature, with bellies like heaps of corn, but with detestable souls and arrogant eyes. (*Maq.* 24.1.13–15)

They tell him proudly of the wisdom of their leader in prayer and his beautiful singing,
. . . And behold, the cantor appears,
On his brow the frontlet and on his head a shawl, white and beautiful, two-hundred-cubits long.
His beard reaches to his navel. And he covers it with a blanket.
Its fringes trail on the ground so that he nearly trips over the hem. (ibid., 22–26)

Contrasted with this external display is the utter ignorance of the cantor, who makes the most ridiculous mistakes; for he does not understand what he is reading. He accompanies his words with the most extraordinary gestures, thinking thus to show his devoutness. And as for the congregation,

Some of them sat there, others lay and slept like the dead.
Others again fled and did not return, left the house of prayer.
The oxen strayed from their herdsmen, herd and cattle fled,
There remained only four asses, who screamed and brayed with the cantor
And thought that they were singers (ibid., 53–57).

Ḥarizi might have been describing a Kurdish congregation of today, where the learning of the *ḥakham* exists only in the minds of the ignorant worshipers. And from this it is evident that the Mesopotamian and Kurdish Jewish communities must have received a continual stimulus from without in order to survive at all. With his sharp pen Ḥarizi also sketches scenes from the general life of the people. These might well be pictures of the present-day Oriental world, for it is already a world fallen into decay. The scene of the story of Ḥever ha-Qēnī and the poor peasant is laid at Raḥaba (Rehovot) on the Euphrates, south of Raqqa; but this gluttonous meal of the two proletarians at the cookshop in the bazaar might easily have taken place in Mosul or some other Kurdish city today, instead of at the beginning of the thirteenth century.

Ḥazan David and Ḥazan Yosef

As yet, there has been no scientific examination of the graves, holy sites, and synagogues of Kurdistan—a study that would undoubtedly yield many clues to the history of the Kurdish Jews. These Jews, who share with their Muslim neighbors the joy in the *ziyāra* (pilgrimage), possess a large number of holy graves and other shrines, some of which bear the names of historic personalities or of Kurdish Jewish *ḥakhamim*;[18] but no definite statement on their historical significance can as yet be made.

In the Bē Ḥazāne, which is one of the most famous of their places of pilgrimage, we have an exception. The Bē Ḥazāne is adjacent to the Navi Yeḥezqel synagogue in upper Amadiya, and it is here that we find the graves of Ḥazan David and Ḥazan Yosef.

We possess two documents bearing on the lives of these two men, but they show certain discrepancies. On the graves is a wooden shrine with an inscription [which reads, in English translation, "Ḥazan Yosef the son of Ḥazan David the son of Ephraim the son of Yosef the son of Yakob."][19] The second document, which was published by Assaf,[20] is in the *Sefer Pitron Ḥalomot* (Book of interpretation of dreams), written in 1738. There, in a passage of great importance for the history of Amadiya, we read: "The age of the settlement in Amadiya counts today, in the year 5548 (= 1788), 993 years. Some say: the year in which that wise Ḥazan David died was the 141st since the founding of Amadiya. For since the day on which that wise man died until today, there have passed 852 years."

According to this, Amadiya was founded in the year 795 C.E., and Ḥazan David died in the year 936 C.E. The origin of this tradition is not known. What is surprising is that only Ḥazan David is mentioned and not Ḥazan Yosef as well; for the old oral tradition always pairs these two names, as do the graves. This oral tradition, according to my informant, is known only to a few of the initiated. The tale runs as follows.

The brothers Josef and David came to Amadiya as dervishes and, seeing the beauty of the place, begged the pasha's permission to settle there. When the pasha asked them to what tribe they belonged, they answered, "We are of the tribe of B'ne Israel." But the pasha was an enemy of the Jews and he replied, "I have no place for you here." So the brothers went on toward Bebade. On the way, however, they used their magic powers to cast a spell upon the pasha, so that he fell ill. In his distress, the pasha sent horsemen after the brothers, bidding them to return and promising to grant their wish. They returned, healed the pasha, and asked for as much ground as the skin of a large ox could enclose. The pasha agreed. Thereupon, they took a large oxhide, soaked it in water for several days to make it pliant, and cut it spirally into a long narrow strip. With this they measured out a large flat surface of land, on which they built houses and a synagogue.[21]

Ḥazan David and Ḥazan Yosef evidently came from Persia. They probably settled in Amadiya at about the middle of the thirteenth century, since the synagogue referred to is without doubt the Sayyid Yeḥezqel synagogue. This is another instance illustrating the close relations existing between the Kurdish Jews and Persia. From the two succeeding centuries we have no reports on our area. This is due, no doubt, to the devastation spread in these regions by the Mongols under Jenghiz Khan and Timur, in which the cities suffered most. We must assume, however, that the urban population sought safety in the mountains, to which the Mongols had no access. The history of the Jews parallels that of the Nestorians, who withdrew to the mountains from their settlements in the plain and consolidated their holdings in central Kurdistan precisely at this time, when their power was rapidly declining elsewhere (their missions had previously reached as far as China).

Sixteenth Century: Yiḥya al-Ẓāhiri and Documents (Letters)

After a gap of two centuries, our records of the Jews are renewed. Kurdistan was never free from inner crises, owing to the struggles of its chieftains among themselves; and in the sixteenth century it was involved in the wars that broke out between the Ottomans and the Persians. After the capture of Tabriz by Sulaiman I in 1534 and the recovery of Baghdad from the Persians, who retreated behind the Zagros, the Turks became the rulers of Kurdistan and, except for a few unimportant intervals, have remained so up to our own day. In this connection it must be stressed that the real masters of the country were the local Kurdish chiefs, who took advantage of the struggle between Ottomans and Persians to consolidate their own positions.

Our records consist of the *Maqāma*s of the Yemenite Yiḥya al-Ẓāhiri and a series of letters in Mann's collection.

Ẓāhiri describes Arbil in the third canto of his *Maqāma*s.[22] Setting out from Baghdad, he visited Kerkuk, where he saw the graves of Daniel and his companions. The Jews of Kerkuk he labels "men of sin, wantonness, and guilt." From Kerkuk he went on to Arbil, "the lofty city": "I came to the city after ten days and took a fine attic room with bed, table, and lamp."[23] Several days later, he went into the streets to see the life of the city, "the fame of which reaches to the skies." He relates how he chanced upon a company of youths and old men whom he easily recognized as students and whom, after reciprocal greetings, he joined. They conversed about wisdom (*divre ḥokhma*) and finally came to the subject of Kabbala. Thereupon, one of the men arose and said he would give a great feast if one of those present would compose a song on a certain Kabbalistic theme. The men assembled in the house of their host:

And it happened in the Beginning of the night
When our minds were clear
That the men divided themselves
Into groups of two. . . .
And they cast lots
With drums and dances
For preparing the meal and what appertained thereto
In proper order
Some became slaughterers
And some judges and guards
And some went to look for spices
And gathered vegetables
And one became cook
Another baker
One strong, another weak
And one a seer and interpreter
For good fortune and happiness
And the lot fell on Yona
On me and on the host
To sing songs.

Nowhere else have I heard of this unique custom of assigning by lot the various tasks in the preparation of a meal. Yet we shall see that the Kurdish Jews, who love a feast above all things, choose a king and guards at their feasts, which are often quite formal. [In the first half of the sixteenth century, divination by casting lots was prevalent among the Jews of Kurdistan. In a letter written by Judah b. Simon of Amadiya to Yaḥya of Mosul, the writer repeatedly refers to his having cast lots in order to know future events (Mann, *Texts and Studies*, 1: pp. 485, 520–21). Judah informs his correspondent that he cast a lot as to who will become "king" (probably the tribal chief in the district of Amadiya), and the lot fell on a certain Aḥmed Beg; but since it was a cloudy day he could not be quite sure of the correctness of the lot. The same doubt was attached to a second lot indicating that the vizir of this Aḥmed Beg was in danger of his life. Again, the lots showed Judah that the wedding of his daughter should be celebrated on the fourteenth, fifteenth, or sixteenth of a month whose name is not mentioned. A passage in the letter seems to suggest that the divination was made by means of biblical verses, a method prevalent to this day in many an Oriental Jewish community.]

The second piece of documentary evidence is a series of five letters published by Mann, who was able to establish their date (beginning of the sixteenth century) through the mention of a well-known Ashkenazi Jew.[24] The main value of these letters probably lies in the fact that they portray a milieu that scarcely differs from that of the present. The contents alone give no clue whatever to their age. They were sent by the master of a school in Mosul (R. Yacob Mizraḥi) and his heirs to various communities in the Kurdish highlands, begging for continued and regular support of the school. The master had been a teacher in Amadiya and had later founded a school in Mosul evidently intended for the children of Jews who came to Mosul from central Kurdistan. At the time, Mosul was clearly the intellectual center to which Kurdish Jews of means sent their sons for an education (*Texts and Studies*, vol.1, p. 107). The school received contributions not only from central Kurdistan but also from Aleppo, Baghdad, Diar Bekr, and Maragha (on the eastern shore of Lake Urmia) (ibid., p. 69).[25]

In these letters, we find the earliest existing list of the Jewish communities of the Kurdish highlands. The communities mentioned are those of Amadiya, Betanura, Barwilnaya, Goharze, Kara, Mezuran, Nirwa, Sundur, Sharanish, Shukho (Sukho), and Tchalla. These localities, most of which Mann could not identify, all lie in the Amadiya district. Amadiya is the place most frequently mentioned, and one of the letters gives a long list of its notables (ibid., vol. 2, p. 16).

The letters give no hint as to the size of the communities. Today some of them are insignificant settlements, and others have been totally deserted by their Jewish populations (e.g., Goharze). Betanura is said to have had fifteen hundred Jewish families; today it has only twenty. Nirwa was a center of learning; it is today an unimportant place, with only a few Jewish families. In most of the places listed, the present Jewish community numbers less than ten families.

We can therefore assume with certainty that the Jewish population of Kurdistan has greatly declined since the sixteenth century. However, the same thing is, no doubt, to be said of the Christian and Muslim populations, which suffered perhaps even more under the disturbed conditions prevailing in Kurdistan.

On the whole, the letters portray situations that reproduce those of today. We see this, for instance, in the smallness of the matters they deal with. In letter 4, for instance, the widow of R. Mizraḥi tells how she was turned out of house and home because she could not pay one of her husband's debts, amounting to 100 *grush* (lines 55 ff.). It is certain that the Kurdish Jew did not belong either then or later to the class of large-scale merchants like those, let us say, of Baghdad. As the letters show, they lived a hard life and earned a meager livelihood. We shall have to return repeatedly to the contents of these letters in the course of our further investigations.

Nineteenth-Century Uprisings

Turkey's final conquest of Kurdistan was accomplished by Murad IV, who succeeded in recovering Tabriz—and in 1638 also Baghdad—from the Persians. Since that time, Kurdistan has remained firmly in Turkish possession. It was divided into three vilayets—Mosul, Baghdad, and Kerkuk—and was formally under the jurisdiction of the pasha of Baghdad, who was appointed by the sultan.

In actual fact, however, the power lay in the hands of the half-independent Kurdish chieftains, of whom, in particular, those of Amadiya, Khoi Sanjak and Rowanduz still exerted great influence and power. The main concern of the Turkish administration was the subduing and pacification of these chieftains, whose system of robbery, along with the disorders accompanying the seasonal wanderings of the nomads, kept the land in continual ferment.

Attacks and uprisings, some of them by no means localized, were the order of the day. The Turkish government was obliged again and again to send troops to Kurdistan. Notwithstanding these efforts, Kurdistan still remained one of the least secure of countries. By the middle of the nineteenth century, Turkey finally succeeded in crushing the last of the Kurdish chiefs without, however, affecting the status of the Kurdish tribes.

From the reports of travelers, we are particularly well informed of events of the years 1832–47, when the uprisings followed one another in quick succession and the Turkish government mustered all its strength in a final effort to overthrow the Kurdish lords and set up Turkish governors in their place.

One of the most serious uprisings was that of the aga of Rowanduz, Mehmed Bek Kura the Blind,[26] who had been created pasha by the Sultan Mejid.[27] In a swift victorious course he had taken Arbil, Kerkuk, Sulaimani, and Akra. Then, in 1832, he laid siege to Amadiya, which is a strong natural fortress, capable of offering prolonged resistance. An act of treason finally enabled him to take the town. The Jews tell the following tale of the siege and fall of the city.

In Amadiya there lived a family by the name of Manoaḥ, who were so rich that they even possessed a table and a jar of pure gold. Two centuries ago (*sic*) a hostile *shekh*, Mīre Kōra, "the blind king," advanced against Amadiya and laid siege to it. Thereupon, the head of the Manoaḥ family, Yosēf Manoaḥ, went to the *shekh* of Amadiya, Mer Sevdina, and said to him: "Do not be afraid of Mīre Kōra. Raise an army. I will provide for its food, pay and equipment."

Mīre Kōra invested Amadiya for seven years, yet could not take it. During this time he laid out vineyards and gardens around the city. But within the walls the hunger grew and grew. Yosēf Manoaḥ climbed the city wall each day and cursed Mīre Kōra: "Why do you assail Amadiya, Mīre Kōra? For seven years you have beleaguered our city without being able to take it. I shall use bullets of gold and silver against you."

In the city there was famine. Then Yosēf Manoaḥ's grandmother took her last handful of rice, milked a bitch, and cooked the rice in its milk. And she fetched a partridge (*qoqwanta* which the Jews keep as pets), cooked it like a chicken, laid it on the rice, and sent the food to the camp of Mīre Kōra with the message: "Why do you stay before Amadiya? You see we still have everything: meat, rice and milk." "Truly, it is so," said Mīre Kōra. And he contemplated withdrawing.

But in Amadiya there lived a Muslim witch who was so skilled in her art that she could even milk the moon. She went to Mīre Kōra and said: "It is all a lie. The city has no more food." And Mīre Kōra replied: "But I cannot force an entrance. The mountains and the walls prevent me!" The witch replied, "Dig an underground passage!"

So Mīre Kōra dug a tunnel under the wall, put explosives into it, and blew up the wall, so that he was able to break into the city. When he was inside, he demanded the name of the Jew who had cursed him from the wall. He made his soldiers loot the Jew's house, and he had the booty sold in the marketplace. But Yosēf Manoaḥ still had enough money left to buy it all back.

The city suffered greatly through the siege and the brutal treatment meted out by the conqueror after its fall.[28] Grant, who visited Amadiya in 1839 writes: "The town I found almost depopulated by wars consequent on the invasion of the Ravendoos Koords; and of one-thousand houses, only two-hundred and fifty are inhabited. Most of the remaining three fourths, and a part of the public markets, have been torn down or much dilapidated" (*The Nestorians, or the Lost Tribes*, p. 60). Badger also describes the plight of the city, which was "little better than a heap of ruins, and the rest is chiefly occupied by graves (no 'sacred groves' as Ainsworth writes)" (*The Nestorians and Their Rituals*, vol. 1, p. 199).

In 1836 Mīre Kōra was defeated and taken prisoner by Rashid Pasha's troops. But the population did not fare much better under Turkish rule. On the road between Mosul and Amadiya, Badger met a delegation of Amadiya Jews who were on the way to the pasha to enter a complaint "against the exactions of the Mutsellim of Amadiya" (ibid., p. 198). Jews and Nestorians alike groaned under his tyranny. Many wished to leave the city, but the pasha had issued a decree forbidding emigration: "Here, then, these poor creatures are obliged to remain ground down to the dust, with scarcely any means of obtaining a livelihood; their dwellings more fit to harbor wild animals than human beings, and without any other prospect of deliverance nearer than the grave" (p. 203).

Even in 1886 Binder found the city in a miserable state;[29] for if the Kurds had plundered the inhabitants in their fashion, the Turks did so in theirs. The Turks were not interested in building up the country. Hence, they permitted ill-paid officials to drain the people dry without doing anything for the development or well-being of the land.[30] Furthermore, the Turks incited one section of the population against the other. And as Kurds and Nestorians (Assyrians) were equally ruthless and cruel, the results of this policy were such as might have been foreseen.[31] Attacks of one section upon the other (such as that of the Kurdish Aga Badr Khan in 1847) were of frequent occurrence and led to heavy losses in life and property on both sides. The Jews stood between the two; and here, it was precisely their lack of political organization that probably redounded to their advantage.

The Young Turks also did little to reform the administration. Economically, the country had greatly deteriorated when the Turks entered the war of 1914; and Turkey, having need of the Hakkiari Mountains, which were an important military point, made great promises to the Assyrians. But since the massacres of the Armenian Christians began at about the same time, the Assyrians ranged themselves in May 1915 on the side of the Entente. The chequered fate of this alliance cannot be related here. It ended in the catastrophic retreat of the 70,000 Assyrians from Urmia to the south, during which they were massacred by Turks and Kurds alike. Only 50,000 Assyrians reached Hamadan.

Kurdistan in the Iraqi State (up to 1939)

In the redrawing of the map following the war, England assumed the mandate over Iraq for twenty-five years. In 1921 Iraq became an independent state, with Feisal as king. The mandate, however, still remained in force. Iraq was divided administratively into provinces (*līwa*s), which are governed by a *mutaserrif*. Every *līwa* is divided into districts (*qādas*) under a *qaimaqam* and subdistricts (*nahīyas*) under a *mudīr*. The Kurdish *līwa*s are Mosul, Arbil, Kerkuk, Sulaimani, and Diyala.

The seat of the government is Baghdad, where Parliament also meets. Hamilton states that this Parliament is chosen by "so-called" elections (*Road Through Kurdistan*, pp. 297–98). The government was in the hands of the Arab nationalists, who opposed Feisal and his pro-British policy and were both anti-Kurdish and anti-Christian. Their policy prevented the peaceful development of the country and involved it continually in new disorders. Instead of bending its energies to the task of economic upbuilding, the government was obliged to maintain a strong army to carry out its nationalistic policy.

This is not the place for a criticism of England's policy in Iraq. Suffice it to say that after Iraq's entrance into the League of Nations in 1932, England deemed the right moment to have come for relinquishing the mandate. The establishment of the Arab state under Feisal was a great disappointment to the Kurds, who had hoped for political independence. Nevertheless, we gather from recent accounts of Kurdistan (by William R. Hay, A. M. Hamilton, and R. S. Stafford) that the power of the Kurdish tribal chiefs had in no wise been broken. The various uprisings marking this period likewise bear witness to this.[32] The failure of the Kurds to attain a position of power is due to their lack of unity; for in view of their strategically favorable location and the poorness of the Iraqi army as a military power, the Kurds, united, would have been a force to be reckoned with. To be sure, air power has altered the situation here also—as the Kurds have already discovered.

Their internal dissension, with its continual clashes, weakens the Kurds as a nation; and the personal feuds of the chieftains demand sacrifices that strike the Kurds as a whole. An instance is the murder, by Nuri—as the result of a blood feud—of so able and progressive a man as Ismail Bek of Rowanduz (see Hamilton, *Road Through Kurdistan*, p. 270 ff.).

Along with the problem of the Kurds, that of the Nestorians, or Assyrians, has kept the country in a turmoil and checked its development. This problem of the Assyrians was fateful also for the Jews.

The dispute over the Iraqi–Turkish border seemed incapable of settlement. The Turks demanded an important part of northern Kurdistan, and in 1925 the League of Nations decided in their favor.

Through this award, the Hakkiari highlands fell to Turkey.[33] Thus, the Assyrians lost all hope of returning to the mountain territory, which they regarded as their ancestral home and in which their spiritual head, Mar Shimun, had had his seat.[34] The Assyrians, feeling themselves uprooted, did their bit in adding to the existing difficulties. It would be a mistake to assume that the Nestorians were morally superior to the Kurds or the Arabs merely because they were Christians. It has been repeatedly observed that their moral standard was not particularly high. "There is, indeed," writes Stafford, "no reason to think that the Assyrians had greater regard for the sanctity of human life and property than had the Kurds, nor that the Kurds had a lower standard of conduct, . . . in their raids and fights, than the Assyrians" (*Tragedy of the Assyrians*, p. 22).[35]

After the relinquishment of the mandate by England, the Iraqi government soon found a favorable opportunity of ridding itself of this undesirable element, especially as the army was thereby enabled to win some easy laurels. Hence, there followed the slaughter of the Assyrians that culminated in the massacre of Simmel and Dehok in 1933 (ibid., p. 177). Thus, it came about that the number of the Assyrians in Iraq, which before the war had totaled 100,000, was reduced to 20,000–25,000.

Between these two forces lived—and still live—the Jews. What appeared to be wholly a disadvantage—that is, the lack of minority status such as the Nestorians possessed—came at this juncture to be actually an advantage. Since the Jews were politically powerless, the Kurds and Arabs saw no danger in them.[36] Hence, the time-honored function of scapegoat was fulfilled by the Assyrians instead. The Jews remained comparatively unmolested, yet the general confusion and the growing spirit of nationalism had repercussions for them also.

The problem of the Assyrians was of importance to the Jews because the decision in the Turkish-Iraqi boundary dispute, which resulted in the loss of the Hakkiari highlands and the withdrawal of the Assyrians, deprived them of a valuable hinterland (Amadiya, Zakho), and pushed them to the very border at the north. Some ancient Jewish communities such as Tchalla and Nirwa, also fell to the Turks; and the Jews, not wishing to live under Turkish rule, emigrated.[37] In Tchalla, which had twenty-five families before the war, only five remained. Most of the others moved to Betanura or Mosul, and some to Palestine.

The situation of the Kurdish Jews was adversely affected by the disturbances in Palestine in 1929, 1936, and the years following. The Arab National movement made use of these events for propagandizing against the Jews. Since about 1812, individual Kurdish Jews, actuated by religious motives, had emigrated to Palestine.[38] But this emigration now took on a new and important form.[39] Lured by the letters received from the emigrants, in which the situation in Palestine was painted in rosy hues,[40] most of the Kurdish Jews were filled with the desire to join their brethren in their ancient homeland and have done with the Galuth.[41]

Little is known about the present situations of the Jews in Kurdistan, because the reports received by Kurdish immigrants in Palestine are scarcely reliable. The rebellion of the nationalists under Rashid Ali and the pogroms in Baghdad that followed his overthrow, speak a plain language. There was also a press report that several Jews were murdered in the Jewish village of Sundur. It may be assumed that the occupation of Iraq by the British has resulted in the restoration of order in the central areas at least[, now that the hopes of the fascists have been dashed].

How the fate of the Kurdish Jews will shape itself after the war depends on political developments. Still, every effort should be made to preserve Kurdish Jewry in Kurdistan; for this element is truly bound to the soil, and it would be a grave error to uproot it. Through improvement of the educational system and support of native handicraft, the Jewish settlement could become an integral part of the country's economy and one possessing potentialities.

PART TWO

The Material Culture

4

The Dwelling

Although the Kurdish Jews live a much freer life at present (1940)—and probably lived a much freer life in the past—than the Jews of Yemen or Persia, who are subject (as in earlier periods) to the Islamic laws governing the *dhimmīs*, their condition nevertheless resembles that of the Yemenites and Persian Jews in that they occupy segregated Jewish quarters. This segregation is voluntary—at least today. The Jew, by living among his own people and in the vicinity of his own house of worship, can observe the prescriptions of his religion with much greater freedom. We see the same phenomenon among the various racial groups in cities like London or New York.[1]

The Jewish quarter is not walled in, and it directly adjoins the Muslim Kurdish quarter. There are even Kurds who live inside the Jewish quarter (e.g., in Sinne).[2] The Jewish quarters in the various towns are named as follows:

Town	Kurdish	Targum
Arbil	Haret Ta'agil	—
Zakho (Z.)	Maḥala Juhiya	Makhalit Huzā'e
Amadiya (A.)	Maḥalit Jū'a	Makhalit Hudāi[3]
Ushnu	Garaki Julaka	Makhale Hudē
Sinne (S.)	Maḥala Musāikan	Mekhale Hudai

The streets of the Jewish quarter are usually named after the families who own most of the property in them. There are old families who possess whole rows of streets. Thus, in Zakho about fifteen streets are called by the names of the oldest families, for example, Makhalit Bē Zākin, Makhalit Bē Avo Bē Varde, and Makhalit Bē Hoja.[4] The same situation obtains in Amadiya. There, for instance, the synagogue Yehezqel [Said Yeḥezqel] is in the Kolāna Bē Shamo [Street of the House of Samuel], the synagogue Ezra haSofer, in the Kolāna Bē Dawrīke in the lower city.

Houses of the Jews

Almost every Jew in Kurdistan owns his own house, which passes by inheritance from one generation to the next. Very few live in rented houses, and part of these live in houses belonging to the synagogue and acquired by it through gift or bequest. Thus, the synagogue Navi Yehezqel in Amadiya owns fifteen houses, which it puts at the disposal of newcomers. The value of a house is remarkably small. The Kurdish Jews who leave the country can rarely obtain a reasonable price for their houses. As a rule, therefore, they leave them behind unsold.[5]

In many districts, building land has no market value whatsoever. Only fields and vineyards, especially irrigated fields, are salable. Anyone who wishes to build a house in Amadiya takes whatever piece of land he pleases.[6] At the worst, only his neighbor will protest if he happens to want the space for an extension to his own house. In Zakho, on the contrary, the land is valuable and must be purchased, because Zakho is on an island, and the land available for building is limited.

There are no building regulations in Kurdistan. The efforts of the British, who wished to introduce such regulations, came to naught. The rent paid for a house is extraordinarily low. In Zakho and Amadiya, one can get a house at a yearly rental of £ 1. In Sinne, the charge is from £ 2 to £ 3.

The houses of the Jews, like those of the Kurds, are primitive in the extreme. They do not differ from those of the Muslim Kurds, because the Jews are not subject to definite building regulations as are the *ahl al-dhimma* in Yemen.[7]

Most of the houses, especially in the smaller settlements, have only one story. In the hilly districts, each house adjoins the next above it, so that, as one mounts the slope, one may climb from roof to roof as on a series of steps. The village houses consist, for the most part, of one room only.

The usual building material in the plains and, to some extent, also in the hill districts (e.g., Rowanduz), is unbaked brick. In Arbil and

Sinne, baked brick is used (Arbil *karpīj*, S. *ajurē*), and in the hills, uncut stone[8] *kēpit kilsha*). The manufacture of mud bricks (Z. *lubne*, Rowanduz *liqbine*, S. *khishte*, [A. *lubni*]) lies largely in the hands of the Jews, who also travel from village to village to prepare bricks for local needs. The work is often done by women.[9] Finally, there are Jewish dwellings of the sort called *tanke* [only in the villages, around Amadiya]. They have walls made of wickerwork covered with clay (*tīna*) and are especially seen in country districts.[10]

Nowadays, the houses everywhere have flat roofs (*qāre*)[11] made of crisscrossed beams covered with a layer of brushwood (Z. and A. *tarpa*) and then a layer of earth.

Construction of the House

In Sinne all the builders are Kurds. In Amadiya and Zakho, on the other hand, there are also Jews engaged in the building trades. In Zakho the Jews are even considered the better workers in the building of *lubne* (mud brick) houses. Every building under construction is in charge of a master-builder (Z. and A. *ma'amirāna*). His workmen or assistants are called *pā'ale*. The *ma'amirāna* gives orders to the *pā'ale* during the work by singing

hālin lubnā	Bring a mud brick
ṭīna bāb	Clay for the father
hālin waṣla	Bring a piece (of a brick)
hālin ṭīna	Bring clay. (Z. A. being, similar)[12]

When the excavation work for the foundation (Z. and A. *isas*) is completed, the owner invites his relatives, friends, and the *ḥakham* to a festive meal at which nut cakes (*klēcha*) are served. [According to my informant, from Amadiya, this nut cake is called *kādē*, while a similar cake sweetened with sweets is called *klēcha*.] The *ḥakham* then takes a white cock and slaughters it, letting the blood run down into the pit. The cock's head is placed in the pit under a stone. Then the owner lays the cornerstone (Z. *kēpit benīza*, [A. *kēpit issas*]), first putting a gold or silver coin under it. The workmen begin the structure by laying down two parallel rows of stones, and each of the quests throws a stone into the space between the rows. The workmen are regaled with arrack and *maza* and the master of the house distributes coins among the poor (A.).

In Zakho a white cock is slaughtered in the *sūpa* [a central hall] at the west side (the direction of Jerusalem), the place intended for the beds. The *ḥakham* puts a little of the blood-soaked earth in the four corners of the *sūpa*, and throws in a gold or silver coin. The master or the mistress of the house then lays a cornerstone (*kēpit isas*) in each corner and recites the benediction. In Sinne, also, a chicken is slaughtered and its blood poured into the excavation. The flesh is distributed among the poor.

The building of the roof is often a community affair, which is quite usual in the Orient. The night on which this is accomplished is called the *lēl zebara* [A.]. For this occasion, the owner asks about fifty young men over. They bring up sand, mix it with chopped straw (*tibn*, [A. Targ. *tuna*], hoist it up to the roof, and roll it with the *mandurta* [A.]. The work is accompanied with dancing and singing. At midnight it is finished, and everyone sits down to the meal that the owner has prepared for them. (Z. and A.).

The one-story house in Zakho has a courtyard (*hosh*, Kurd. *haush*). At one side of the courtyard is a covered veranda (*birbanke*, Kurd. *bar sifke*), the roof of which is supported by a row of wooden pillars. From the *birbanke* one enters a long, broad room (*sūpa*, Kurd. *sik*), the main room of the house. An oven (*kanun*) stands at either side. There are no windows in the *sūpa*; the light enters from the door and through apertures in the ceiling (*kāwa*, Kurd. *kulak*). Small doors lead from the *sūpa* to the storerooms (*manzāle*).[13]

Amadiya boasts some two-storied houses (*bekhtāya*, *be'elaȳe* [ground and second floors, respectively]).[14] The lower floor contains storerooms and the stable, the upper floor a summer room (*manzar qēta* [or *manzal qēta*]) and a winter room (*bēthit süswa*). Both rooms have a separate washroom, which is used chiefly for purification after sexual intercourse. [In some of the houses there is a room whose floor is below street level. In this room, called *sardawe*, the people living in the house spend the hot hours in summer.]

A separate kitchen is unknown. In summer the wife cooks and bakes in the courtyard or in the *birbanke*, in winter in the *sūpa* or wherever the oven happens to be.

Until the coming of the British, the Kurdish Jews had no latrines; and even today they suffer such a thing only in the courtyard—not in the house, as among the Kurds. Until 1914, it was the universal custom for old and young to repair to the river in the morning to attend to the calls of nature. Benjamin II describes this proceeding in great detail and tells how business deals are arranged and quarrels settled during this rite (*Acht Jahre in Asien und Afrika*, pp. 64–65). For washing—especially washing hands—they use a can (A. and Z. Kurd *mesīna*, [A. Targ. *kuraza*,] S. *aftabha* and a bowl (A. and Z. Kurd. *dashō*, [more accurately *dastasho*; Targ. *kāpā*;] S. *lagan*); see illustration no. 16; specimen in HUBC 37:46).

Furnishing the House

The furnishings of the house are as primitive as its construction. In this respect, the Jew is exactly on a level with his half-nomadic neighbor, who can easily carry about all his worldly goods on a mule. The nomad or semi-nomad displays aesthetic interest and feeling only in connection with such things as carpets, drinking vessels, and weapons. It is much the same with the Jews, but the last remnants of their artistic sense has been destroyed by the ruin that has overtaken the country in recent times.

The rooms are entirely unfurnished. Better articles of clothing are kept in chests (A. *sünduq*, [Kurd. *sabatqa*,] S. *yigdan*) or in niches in the walls (Z. *kāwa*, S. *tāq*). The occupants of the house sit on mats (Z., D., A., S. *hasīra* [or *ḥaṣira*]) or carpets (Z., A., S. *gāla*; Z. and A. *makhfūra*). [*Gala* is a woven carpet (Kurd. *bereq*, Pers. *qelim*), while *makhfūra* (A. *maḥfura* or *sh'vita*) is a knotted carpet of the kind known in the West as "Persian carpet".] They eat at a low table (Kurd. and Targ. *kursī*) from a round bowl (Z. *faraksēni*, A. *sinīya*, S. *langerī* or *sīnī*). [In Amadiya the following names are used: *farkhasēni* is a round, flat tray with very low brim, made of copper and plated with tin, some 80 centimeters in diameter; *ṭashta* is a tray similar to *farkhasēni*, with the exception of the brim, which is some 15 centimeters high and perpendicular; *lagan* is a smaller plate; and *siniyē* is a plate with a brim sloping outward.]

Lately, European tables and chairs have found their way into Kurdistan; and chairs are the first thing the Kurdish Jews who have become somewhat acclimatized to conditions in Palestine provide for themselves on, move frequently, receive as gifts.[15]

On the other hand, the Kurdish Jews in Palestine do not readily give up the habit of sleeping on the floor, to which they were accustomed in Kurdistan.[16] They spread out carpets and mattresses—in winter in the main room, as near the oven as possible, and in summer on the roof. The roof, which is reached from the outside by a ladder (Z. *jarāde*, A. *simalta*) is the regular living place in summer. In order to protect themselves from scorpions, they elevate their beds a little by making a platform *qaprāna* [A.] of beams and boughs, resting on four stones.

In the country districts, (e.g., Betanura), the beds are made on a high platform (*barzēle*), which is supported by four poles and must be reached by a ladder. [According to my informant from Amadiya, this bed is called *qiprāna*. It comes in two kinds: one is low and rests on four stones, the other is high and supported by wooden posts. *Harzēle* is a wooden platform built on the branches of a tree, and upon it the fruit is stored from the summer until midwinter. Also, the baskets in which fruit is stored, which are placed among the branches, are called *harzēle*.] Anyone not accustomed to this kind of bed gets a fright when he sleeps in it, because the platform sways violently in the wind. The *harzēle* gives excellent protection against mosquitoes, however.[17]

Initiation Ceremony

After the completion of the house, the initiation ceremony ([Heb.] *ḥinnukh habayit*) must take place before the owner may move in. The *ḥakham* and a number of friends are invited to this function and must accompany the owner when he enters the new house. His wife throws out a handful of wheat and breaks a vessel. The women formerly poured out some water, waved a cloth in each hand, and called out, *Kisha, kisha āzi beshiyāsa āthe hawiyātha hawakh benōne benātha khitne kalawatha*, "Kish, kish,[18] go, demons, come in living creatures [i.e., good angels], you shall have sons and daughters, sons-in-law and daughters-in-law."

The men then sit down and read Mishna for some hours, after which the master of the house puts on his new clothes, especially made for the occasion and recites the benediction. Then the *mezuzot* [parchment scrolls containing Deut. 6:4–9 and 11:13–21, fixed to the doorpost in a wooden or metal case] are brought, and the *ḥakham* fastens them in proper places. The reading is renewed, lasting about five hours, and is followed by a meal. The guests depart at about two in the morning.

Next morning, the master of the house invites the whole community to an initiation feast ([Heb.] *s'udat ḥinnukh habayit*); and only then may the household articles from the old house be moved into the new one.

Amulets for the House

The Jewish religious apotropaion, the *mezuza*, is usually of a very primitive type in Kurdistan. Most frequently, a hole is left in the wall and the piece of parchment is put inside and protected simply with a piece of glass (Arbil). The use of a reed tube with a glass-covered aperture for the word *Shaddai* is also very widespread. The reed tube is sometimes inserted into the wall (A., Z. and S.).[19]

In Rekan, also, a reed tube is used for this purpose; but the aperture for *Shaddai* is protected not with glass but with a piece of cloth that hangs over the *mezuza* and is lifted up when the *mezuza* is kissed. There are some *mezuzot* in leather[20] or tin cases[21] or in wooden tubes[22] and these also are inserted into the wall. It is noteworthy that in Rekan the *mezuza* is fixed horizontally. The *mezuza* case consequently has a different shape here, the opening being oblong and the word *Shaddai* written to fit this opening.[23]

In Zakho, at times, the antlers of a stag (Kurd. *qanānith paṣquvi*) are fastened to the door or a cast horseshoe (*na'ala*), sometimes with green beads (*quṭnaskath yerūke*) attached to it, is nailed to the middle of the lintel. [In the two-storied houses in Amadiya, the antlers of a mountain deer are inserted into the outer walls of the upper floor by way of decoration.]

In each of the four corners of the *sūpa* they bury an amulet, designed, as a rule, to counteract the influence of Lilith (Z.). House amulets are resorted to when a succession of illnesses or deaths in the family causes the house to be regarded as being in the power of the demons. In such a case, an amulet written in the blood of a white or a black dove is put under the threshold. A wolf's tail will serve the same purpose (A.).[24] In cases of death, an old hoof, the tail of a wolf, and a piece of skin from a donkey are laid on the roof under a stone (A.).

The Kurdish household is run on the patriarchal system. When the sons marry, they continue to live in the father's house, either in a room cleared out for them or in a new one built on. For this reason, Kurdish houses often show a ground plan that could not have been originally so designed.

It often happens that thirty persons or more will occupy a single house, the space in which is at best very limited. The household of the entire family group is conducted as a unit. The oldest man is the head of the house. A. Kurd. *malukhve bētha*, ["leader of the house"; A. Targ. *urwit bētha*]. The *reshith bētha* (A.)[25] is in charge of the domestic work, and the other women must carry out her orders. [According to my informant from Amadiya, *reshith bētha* is the name of the male head of the house. The woman is called *kabānit bētha*, "leader of the house," or *rapthit bētha*, "great one of the house"].

5

Clothing

The costumes of its inhabitants makes it again apparent that Kurdistan is definitely a place of retreat. The most varied influences came together here; and with our present meager knowledge of the subject, it is not yet possible to give an altogether accurate picture of the details of the costumes worn by the different ethnic elements occupying this area.

This applies also to the costume of the Kurdish Jews; for here, too, there is no uniformity—in fact, their dress conforms almost entirely to that of their neighbors. Apart from ritual garments, there is no conspicuous difference between the dress of the Kurds, the Christians (Surai), or the Jews. This is most noticeable in the case of the simple man, for the primitiveness of his costume permits of no great variation. The reason for this uniformity of costume among Muslim Kurds and Jews is obvious: there are no definite regulations concerning dress in Kurdistan (as there are in some Muslim countries where Islamic laws regarding unbelievers are in force).[1]

In order to obviate complications, we shall confine our study to two districts: Amadiya in the central or mountain region and Sinne in the Persian-Kurdish area. We have no old illustrations of Kurdish Jews that might give us an idea of the possible development of their costume. We are compelled, therefore, to rely on early descriptions, which unfortunately show many lacunae in the matter of costume.

Costume of the Kurds

The situation is better as regards the Kurds and the Surai. Binder gives the following description of the dress of the Kurds living in the vicinity of Amadiya in the year 1860:

> They wear the mustache and cover their heads with white, conical, felt hats, around which they wind enormous turbans. Their trousers of exceeding width are of a material made of the hair of red goats and often splashed with color. They wear a small jacket reaching barely to the waist; above it, they often wear a coat longer than the goat-hair jacket, decorated at the front with coarse trimmings. For footwear they have boots of red leather with strong shoeings on the heel. (*Au Kurdistan*, p. 109, [trans. from French by R.P.])

In Binder's illustration the Kurds[2] are wearing white shirts (*krās*) with long sleeves, long baggy trousers (*darpe*), and a sash (*shālik*) wound around the waist (ibid., p. 106). The trousers shown in the illustration are of a special sort of which we shall have more to say later. Over the shirt is an open vest or jacket (*yeshlak*), with sleeves that are slit from shoulder to wrist and can be buttoned up or left open. Over the *yeshlak* comes another vest (Kurd. *chokhik*, [Targ. *chukhta*]), which is no longer worn today. It is made of wool and its back is covered with long black goat hair of very find texture.[3] Nowadays the Kurds often wear two jackets: on top the sleeved *yeshlak*, and under it the sleeveless *yēlak*. Both of these garments are obviously of Turkish origin.[4]

The Kurd in the illustration is wearing the conical felt cap (Kurd. *kolāw*), which is little used by Kurds today. This conical cap is evidently an ancient type of headgear and should probably be attributed to the tribes to which the Nestorians belong, rather than to the Kurds. A long, brightly colored linen cloth (*ashḥadaqāye*) is wound thickly around the cap. Today the *ashḥadaqāye* is replaced by the *jamadāni*, a black woolen cloth with a white design woven in. The *jamadāni* is imported from Europe.

The shoes worn by the Kurds are high red or yellow leather boots, *chakme*,[5] with long curled-up, pointed toes and heels tipped with iron.

Costume of the Nestorians

Binder gives another picture showing the costumes worn about a hundred years ago by the Nestorians in Julamerk in the vicinity of Amadiya (*Au Kurdistan*, p. 168).[6] Here we see the conical cap (*kushisa*) with a cloth wound around it.

The upper part of the body is clad in a long-sleeved white shirt (*sudra*) and a sleeved jacket. But apparently, in earlier times, the Nestorians did not wear the Turkish vest affected by the Kurds. The trousers are drawn over the *sudra*. These trousers, which we have already described in connection with the Kurdish costume and a jacket of the same material (*chāla chapuksa*,[7] Kurd. *shālō chapek*) form the characteristic dress of the Surai (Christians).

The cloth in good specimens is like silk, being woven of the finest goat wool (*kulye subya*). The Surai, in particular, are skilled in the manufacture of cloth of beautiful color and varied designs, embellished with embroideries and patterns woven over the original web. The Kurd in the picture just described is wearing trousers of this kind.[8] The Kurds of today are also partial to such trousers.[9]

In the trousers-and-jacket we evidently have a garment of great antiquity, the origin of which I have not yet succeeded in tracing. It is found not only among the Surai but also among certain sections of the Armenians[10] and among the Aissors of the Caucasus.[11]

Several of the Nestorians depicted in Binder's illustration wear a long, heavy, sleeveless cloak (*badan* or *abayika*) of goat's wool. This is nowadays replaced by the thick woolen jacket *(chukta)*, the *chokhik* of the Kurds.

On their heads they wear the conical felt cap (*kushīsa*) described above. In former times the *asḥadaqāye* was wound about it, but this has now given way to the *jamadāni* also among the Nestorians.

Costume of the Kurdish Women

Before proceeding to consider the dress of the Jews, we must observe that of the Kurdish and Nestorian women. Binder gives a picture of Kurdish women; but it is not at all clear, and there is no description (*Au Kurdistan*, p. 161).

The dress of the ordinary Kurdish woman is simple in the extreme. It consists of trousers (*darpe*)—the lower part of which *(sār daringe)* is of colored material—and a long blue or blue-and-white-striped gown (*tras*) with wide, wing-shaped sleeves *(lewandīya)* not unlike those of a kimono. The gown is worn over the trousers, and is sometimes confined at the waist by a simple cloth (*shāle*). Around the head is wound the *jemadāni*. The feet are usually bare; but heelless red slippers (*palawe* or *kalāsha*), a kind of footgear made of patches, are sometimes worn. The jewelry with which the women are often lavishly adorned is described in another connection.

The Nestorians

Of the Surai women we have some old illustrations in Justin Perkins (*Residence of Eight Years in Persia*, facing pp. 319, 335, 336) and the descriptions in George Percy Badger (*The Nestorians and Their Rituals*, vol. 1, p. 55). The latter pertain, indeed, to the Christians of Tur; but the dress of these women resembles that of the Surai women of the mountain region.

The female attire comprises a pair of *shalwar*, and a red robe somewhat resembling a surplice, the long sleeves of which are generally tied together and thrown behind the shoulders. This is secured to the waist by a narrow girdle with two large ornamental silver clasps. The headdress is peculiar to these parts, and in form is not unlike an archer's helmet made of a pointed cap, and covered with large pieces of silver money.

In the opinion of my informants, Perkins's plates are inaccurate. The women there wear green trousers and a gown reaching the knees. This gown lacks the wide-hanging sleeves and is obviously too short. A Nestorian girl wears a *mekatana* over the gown (*The Nestorians and Their Rituals*, facing p. 335). The capelike wrap worn by a Nestorian mother is, at all events, no longer used; and it is doubtful if it was ever worn in this fashion (ibid., facing p. 336).

Nowadays, the dress of the Surai women in the vicinity of Amadiya consists of long, colored trousers (*shirwāle*) and, over these, a long red gown (*sudra jangōso*) with wide sleeves. The women wear no jacket.

Costume of the Jews of Amadiya

In the costume of the Jews of Amadiya (which town we shall consider first), we note a mixture of Kurdish and Nestorian elements. The description given by Benjamin II is inaccurate and not at all illuminating:

> On week days the men only wear a shirt with a girdle round their waist, short pants, which only reach to the knee[?], and a little cap, round which is rolled a thin piece of black stuff; they likewise go barefoot. I inquired why they wore such garments, to which I received the answer, that it was more convenient for work. . . . On the Sabbath they lay aside this dress, and wear a long dark robe of woolen cloth. This robe is buttoned from the neck down to the girdle, from which it falls in two large flaps down to the knees; the sleeves extend to the waist and are quite tight. Only the richest wear shoes, the others generally leather sandals. (*Eight Years in Asia and Africa*, p. 129)

This account, in which there is a confusion of various items, shows the weakness of Benjamin II's description. The attire of the men in Amadiya includes the *sudra*, a shirt of white linen (*grawe*). At the neck, in the middle, is an opening, closed with one button. Short trousers are not worn in Amadiya. What Benjamin II took to be short trousers may have been ordinary trousers with the legs rolled up.

The characteristic feature of the shirt is the long, winglike sleeves,[12] which we find also among the Kurds (especially in Persian Kurdistan). During work, the sleeves are turned up, drawn over the shoulders, and tied together at the back of the neck. Here again we see that utility is quite an irrelevant factor in clothing styles. The wide, hanging sleeves resemble those worn by the dancing girls in Chinese statues of the Tang period. In Kurdistan, also, these sleeves actually belong to the dancing costume. In earlier times they did not form part of the dress of the common people but were affected only by the upper classes. H. Naumann has brought out the same point in connection with German national costumes: "The so-called 'folk costumes' did not originate in the folk, and they certainly do not represent the creative spirit of the people. . . . Hence they are not primitive community property, but are cultural assets of the higher layers that have come down" [trans. from German by R.P.].[13]

The men of Amadiya wear broad white trousers (*shirwāla*), with legs tapering off to the ankle. Over the shirt comes the "small *ṭallith*" ([Heb.] *ṭallith qatan*) then the two vests or jackets of Turkish origin that we found among the Kurds. The sleeveless one (*ēlāka* or *hēlāka*), with its characteristic horseshoe-shaped armhole, is donned first. On either side, the *ēlāka* has a crocheted color border to which is attached a closely set row of loops on the left and buttons on the right—the ancient type of fastening found in old Persian garments. The loops and buttons are also crocheted and multi-colored. They actually serve, for the most part, merely as ornaments, the vest being buttoned at the top and bottom with a special button. In Amadiya we also find embroidered vests called *ēlāka sundūri*—after Sundur, where their use is commonest.

Over the sleeveless *ēlāka* comes the sleeved jacket (*yeshlāka* or *eshlāka*). This is also provided with loops and buttons, but is worn open. Specimens of these two garments are made of black and yellow striped material and were intended for Sabbath and holiday wear (HUBC 38:68). The sleeves of the *yeshlāka* are 48 centimeters long and 15.5 centimeters wide and have a three-cornered armhole. Both garments have a breast pocket on each side; but the one at the right is a blind pocket, intended only for ornament. The tail of the shirt is worn inside the trousers (contrary to the habit of e.g., the Afgans), and the sleeves are often drawn over those of the jackets.

This is the basic style of dress of the Kurdish Jews, especially in the rural districts around Amadiya. But the basic style has acquired many variations, partly due to the dictates of fashion and partly to the fact that every garment is patched over and over again and is worn until it literally falls to pieces.

The basic garb, we observe, shows the influence of the Kurds more than of the Surai. Still, we find the *chāla chapuksa* [A. *shāla shapuksa*, trousers-and-jacket] of the Surai used as holiday attire and especially as the bridegroom's wedding costume. Though in some districts (Betanura, Kara, Tchalla, and Rekan) the Jews are the only weavers of *chāla chapuksa*, they know how to make only the simple kinds; whereas the splendidly colored and richly ornamented models are obtained from the Surai. The Jews are known as weavers of the simple type of trousers (*chāla*), which are worn at times without a matching jacket.

Some Jews wear a long sash (*shāl*) wound around the waist [or a *kharkhasa*, belt]. On feast days and Sabbaths, aged men and wealthy folk wear the *kurtāke* [or *kurtak*], a cloak cut like a caftan, without buttons. It is made of striped material and is imported from Mosul.

The old-time garb is fast disappearing today. Everyone imitates the European styles; and it is considered genteel, so to speak, to possess a *sāko*, that is, a European jacket. The *sāko* is bought in Mosul, where it is manufactured both by Jews and non-Jews. Hamilton also notes how, among his workmen, especially those coming from Persian-Kurdistan, there is a strong desire to own European clothing, sometimes with most extraordinary sartorial results.[14]

Every Friday the Jews have their heads shaved clean. Their headgear consists of a skullcap (*kusīsa*) made of felt or cloth and is not cone-shaped like that of the Surai. Around the cap is wound a cotton cloth of the greatest possible proportions, the *jemedāni*. Young men and youths attach to this cloth a number of long tassels (*jifke*, *jemedani mere jifke*), which hang down back of the right ear. The *jifke* are quite commonly found as trimming on clothing. They recall the tassels that appeared on the garments of the Hittites.[15] In place of the cotton cloth, old men and notables wear a [black] silken cloth (*poshīye*).

In the country districts it is customary to go barefoot, as Benjamin reports. In winter, heavy stockings (*gurwe*) made of white sheep's wool and knitted in artistic patterns by the women serve as protection against the cold. There are also stockings with colored designs, of the sort worn in Persia and Afghanistan.[16] Red slippers (*pelāwa smōke*) are used in the house. The commonest footgear is the ***kundare***, an ordinary low shoe. [The leather shoes worn in Amadiya are called ***kalkē***.] In the mountain districts the extremely practical ***reshke*** are worn.[17] These are made of skins (Rekan) or cloth (Tchalla [and Amadiya]) and are indispensable in the Kurdish mountains because of their elasticity.[18] Sandals, which Benjamin II mentions, are quite unknown in Kurdistan.[19]

Costume of Jewish Women

Benjamin II gives the following brief description of the dress of the women: "The women wear a colored vest; round the head they fold a cloth or a piece of stuff, from beneath which their black hair falls down to the shoulders. They go barefooted, but decorate their hands, arms and feet with gold and silver rings; sometimes they wear through the nose a ring, which hangs down to the mouth" (*Eight Years in Asia and Africa*, p. 129).

This description applies to the Jewish women of the country districts, whose costume in the main resembles that of the Surai women. But there are numerous minor variations.

The gown (*sudra*) is similar to the shirt worn by the men, but is brightly colored and is longer, reaching to the knee. The gown of the Jewish bride is red; that of a Kurdish bride, green. The women's *sudra*, like the men's, has wide, hanging sleeves; and when it is made of material figured on one side only, the pattern comes on the inside, because the sleeves are generally turned back and tied behind the neck like those of the men. The gown is often embellished with rows of ornamental needlework ending in a tassel.

The broad trousers (*shirwāla*), which are of the "diagonal trousers" type (Max Tilke *Kostüm*), are either wholly of colored material or are in two sections—the lower section, called *sar dalinga*, "end of the feet," being colored, and the upper section, white.

Characteristic of the women's costume (as of the men's) is the vest (*ēlāka*) with armholes shaped like a horseshoe. The women's *ēlāka* clearly reveals its erotic purpose; it is very short and acts as a corset, throwing the breast into prominence. The *ēlāka* is often made of fine silk. It is buttoned only at the top and bottom, with the remaining loops and buttons serving merely as ornaments (HUBC 37:3–4).

The erotic character of the *ēlāka* is especially evident in a certain type of this vest called *ēlāka korunfele*, "clove *ēlāka*" (HUBC 39:19). This is decked out at the breast with chains of cloves. Cloves, like nutmeg, are considered aphrodisiac and therefore play an important role in love songs.[20]

The *ēlāka* is often richly embroidered. A specimen has a design that evidently harks back to ancient tradition and includes the figure of a tree (HUBC 37:60).

Over gown and vest comes the long outer garment (*fistāna*) which gives the Kurdish Jewish women their typical appearance. Though the *fistāna* is probably of Turkish origin[21] and a recent importation, it has nevertheless become firmly entrenched.

This long, flowing garment is a combination of open bodice and skirt. To the short open bodice with its long sleeves and three-cornered armhole is attached a wide, pleated skirt. The material used is figured cotton cloth of European origin. The colorfulness of this gown is sometimes enhanced by combining cloth of different colors. Instead of the *fistāna*, old women wear a *kurtāka* with a shawl wound around the waist. It resembles the *kurtāka* of the men.

The *kebā'a*, a long garment without buttons, similar to the *kurtāka* is worn wide open if worn by the women of Zakho and Arbil in place of the *fistāna*. The *kebā'a* is girded with a shawl that in Zakho, for instance, is generally of white material.

Girls and young women are partial to the *kutkit chokh kalabdūn*, "woolen *kutka*, with silver threads." This is a black open jacket with very short, almost square sleeves, and is lavishly embroidered in front and in back with brightly colored silk threads.

In Amadiya and neighboring districts (Betanura, Tchalla, Rekan, and Barzana) the girls receive, at the time of their marriage, the *abāye ketāwa*, "shoulder *abāye*," which they don for the first time eight days after the wedding as a symbol of their married state. This is the so-called diagonal upthrow (*schräge Emporwurf*) of Tilke,[22] which was evidently a Semitic garment in very early times and appears frequently on monuments.[23] This rectangular cloth (Kurd. *charoke*), as worn by the Jewish women, is generally made of black goat wool (*ma'az*).[24] It is placed around the body and fastened over the left shoulder with a blue glass button. The Surai women also wear a wrap of this kind.[25]

The women dress their hair in numerous [usually seven or eight] small braids (*süsyāta, sosiyāsa*), often as many as ten to twenty, and wind about their heads a cloth of gaily striped black cotton trimmed with tassels (*poshīye mere jifke*). In place of this cloth, old women wear the *kasrawan*, a black headcloth with threads of white silk woven through it.

It is customary for the women to go barefoot in summer. Formerly, they sometimes wore the *chakme*, boots with curled-up toes; but nowadays, they use ordinary slippers (*kundare*).

Costumes in Sinne: Men

Let us briefly consider the costumes of Sinne, which clearly reveal Persian influence. The men's attire here also includes a white shirt (*sura*); but the opening at the neck is on the side,[26] and there are no wide hanging sleeves. The trousers (*shirwale*) are white, but narrower than those worn in the mountain district.

Over the shirt comes the small *tallit*. The vest (Arab. *sukhma*, [more accurately *zakhma*]) was introduced in Sinne only about thirty years ago. The outer garment is the *alkhalkha*, a long collarless cotton-lined cloak quilted in parallel stitchings (*miol miol*). The sleeves are slit from elbow to wrist, and are buttoned up by means of loops and buttons of the sort already described (*dugmi halke*). Later, the *alkhalkha* was replaced by the *kebā'a*. The *kebā'a* is not lined and is made of material of various colors but in cut resembles the *alkhalkha*. Young men often have their *kebā'a* lavishly embroidered.

For outdoor wear, the *'aba*, a coat imported from Persia and Damascus, was formerly in vogue; but about the beginning of the century it was supplanted by the collarless coat (*lewada*). Young men aspiring to fashion wear the Persian *sardari* or *kulatchā*. This is a close-fitting garment reaching to the knee, and is often richly embroidered with colored thread.

The headgear consists of a skullcap (*arakchin*) over which is often worn a felt cap (*kesīla*; Kurd. *kolā*) covering the entire head. Old men wind a shawl (*dasmal*) around the *kesīla*. Another type of head covering is the *chakā*, a tall cap made of real or artificial fur.

As Sinne is Persian, it was subject to Riza Shah's secularizing decrees; and the Jews, also, were compelled to adopt European dress.

Sinne: Costume of the Women

Like that of the men, the attire of the women in Sinne shows strong Persian influence. Feminine undergarments include a shirt (*sura*), which has not the wide, hanging sleeves prevalent in Amadiya, and long, colored trousers (*pāntolē*).

Over the trousers come several skirts: first a narrow strip of cloth (*kamar band*) fastened around the waist with a string and kept on at night, then a short skirt (*shalte*), and finally a longer one (*shirwale le'ēfāne*), which is lined with cotton to make it stand stiffly out. Some women were accustomed to wear, in addition, the Persian ballet skirt (*shirwāla tanaka*).

Over the shirt came a blouse (*alkhalkha*). This was open in front and had sleeves made in the Persian fashion, that is, slashed and with cuffs trimmed on the inside. The *alkhalkha* was later replaced by the *yelak*, a jacket resembling the *yelaka* but with ordinary sleeves. It was worn closed. The sleeves were slit from armpit to wrist and laced up with a string and buttons. The cuffs were sometimes turned back. Over the blouse or jacket women often wore the *kūla jah*, a knee-length garment open in front and commonly used in the winter because it covered the entire trunk.

Older women were accustomed in former times to wear a cap (*ksīla*) with a silken cloth (*pūshīn*) wound around it and on top a large cloth (*lajaga*, which was sometimes tied under the chin. Among the wealthier women this headdress gave way around the year 1900 to a new fashion. A long strip of cloth (*kalagābī*) was wrapped around the *ksīla* to form a thick turban, which was set on the head a little to one side. It was adorned with pins and pendants of all sorts and often weighed as much as four kilograms.

When walking in the streets the woman are enveloped in a large black cloth (*charchau*).

White stockings are the customary footgear, older women drawing over them the *siame gurji*, shoes made entirely of cloth, that is, without leather soles. Ordinary shoes, made in the Russian fashion and called *erūsi*, are also worn.

Europeanization is quite as strong in the women's costume as in the men's.

6

Food

In comparing the diet of the Kurdish Jews with that of the Yemenite Jews, the great differences between these two Jewish communities that live under not-too-dissimilar conditions are once more thrown into strong relief.

Both the Kurdish and the Yemenite Jews inhabit a hill country. But Yemen is a land of irrigation and highly developed vegetable gardening. It is not a grazing country. Kurdistan, on the contrary, is preeminently pastoral. It possesses, however, the additional advantage of an amount of rainfall sufficient for the cultivation of unirrigated crops and also of conditions favorable for crops requiring irrigation, such as fruit growing and vegetable gardening.

The Yemenite Jew, like his Arab neighbor, is almost completely vegetarian. Even in the cities he eats meat only on the Sabbath and feast days. Fat—butterfat—is likewise a delicacy.[1] Bread, porridge and vegetables are the staple food of the Yemenites; therefore (as we have often previously remarked) "picnic types" are rarely to be found among them.

Quite different is the case of the Kurdish Jew. Standing, as he does, between the nomadic Kurd and the agricultural Kurd or Christian, he enjoys the advantage offered by both forms of economic subsistence. The Kurdish Jew is a meateater; his type of diet exploits to the full the benefits to be derived from stock farming. At the same time, he is quite partial to cereals, vegetables and fruits. He consumes all these different kinds of food; and since, in addition, food is cheap in Kurdistan, he eats a great deal. He loves to eat, and the quantity that a healthy man can devour is often astonishing. Therefore, we find among the Kurdish Jews strong, powerful physiques. However, the tendency to grow fat (they are exceedingly fond of fat food) is checked by their living conditions. Kurdistan is a rugged, inclement land; and its people cannot lead the quiet, sedentary life that inhabitants of warmer climes enjoy.

Bread

To the nomadic Kurds bread is a delicacy, and travelers often remark with surprise that they are able to obtain it in Kurdish camps. Among the Kurdish Jews bread is one of the staple foods. The grain for the bread is bought at harvest time, usually for the entire year. in general, part of it is acquired by the merchants through barter.

The grain is kept in large earthen jars[2] that often hold as much as 60 rotl (154 kilograms), the lids of which are sealed with clay. It is sometimes stored, also, in sheepskin sacks (A. and Z. *mezīde*). In Ushnu it is stored in the age-old fashion, that is, in pits dug for the purpose. Such *chāle* (Kurd.) are used in Zakho and Amadiya only when there has been a bumper crop and other receptacles do not suffice.

Before being ground, the grain is cleaned by the women and sifted through sieves (*arbala*) of different degrees of fineness. The grinding is done in water mills (A. and Z. *irkhe*, S. *urkhel*), some of which are owned by the Jews.

In Zakho a piece of iron is laid on the sack when the grain, (or flour, as the case may be) is brought to or from the mill. In Amadiya the custom is practiced only in the latter case.[3] The first loaf of bread baked from the new flour must be eaten by the head of the family.

Grinding with a handmill (Z. and A. *gerüsta*)—a task that in the eyes of the Yemenite Jewess symbolizes, as it were, the hard lot of woman (see *EJJ*, p. 208)—is no longer customary in Kurdistan except in country districts (e.g., Rekan). In the cities. the handmill is used nowadays only for grinding wheat groats (*girsa*), burgul (*gürgur*), and oats (Z. *kashkiri*), Sulaimani *dastar*), for grinding the Passover grain. The flour is stored in the house in large, four-legged clay receptacles (Z. *sekhōpa*, [A. or *kwara*]). For example, if asked on a fast day, *Āhit sīma wētin*? "Are you fasting?," a person who is not fasting will often reply, *He wēn sīma som sekhōpa* "Yes, I am fasting the *sekhōpa*-fast," (Z. and A.)

In the towns bread is made almost exclusively from wheat (*khite*). Only in times of want is durra (*khurūvi*) or millet (*prāge*, Kurd. *gāres*) substituted. In the country, on the other hand, durra bread is the rule, rather than the exception. The poor of the cities make bread also of barley (*se'āre*) or millet (*tahla*).

There are two types of bread: that baked on the baking sheet, and that baked in an oven. The dough (*lēsha*) for bread baked on the baking sheet contains no yeast (*khamīra*). When the woman takes the flour out of the sack, she says *Brākhit Eliyahu nāvi hōya gāwe*! "The blessing of the Prophet Eliyahu be in it!" While she is pouring the water into the dough, she whispers several times, *Shem Shaddai*! [Heb. "(In) the name of God!"]; and as she kneads the dough in the kneading bowl[4] she says, *Idāsit sāra imēnū hāwe gāwe rizqit faqīre jāre mampelit gāwe* "The hands of Sarah our mother be in it, support for the unhappy poor send in it" (A.).

A lump of dough (*gūsa*)[5] is laid on the low baking board (*khuwāna*). In Amadiya and Zakho this is made of *gāsa* [lime]. The dough is rolled out first with a thick bread roller (*dorāna*), then with a thin one (Z., A., S. *gēra*), to a flat, round loaf (*ṭlumṣa* [*ṭlumtha* or *ṭluma*]). The *ṭlumṣa* is placed on the baking sheet (*dōga*; A., Z., D., Ushnu, and S. Kurd. *saj*) with a stick. The baking sheet is a shallow bowl of sheet iron, resembling a section of a hollow sphere, and is set, curved side up, either on the *kanūna* or on the oven (*tanūr* or [*tanūra*]). The bread is baked lightly on both sides, removed, and put into baskets.

This bread (*lakhmit dōqa* or *lakhmit raqēqa*, flat bread) is the sort ordinarily eaten, especially in winter when it is difficult to bake on the *tanūr*. In Amadiya, a sufficient quantity of *lakhmit dōqa* to last a week is baked at one time. Many families make a two-weeks' supply at each baking. The stale bread, if too dry, is softened a bit with water. In other places, the baking is done once or twice a week.

Leavened bread, thicker than *lakhmit dōqa*, is baked in an oven. After the yeast (*khamīre*) is put in, the dough is left standing over night to rise. The *tanūra* looks like an earthenware cask and is set on the ground or else sunk into the ground. A wood fire is kindled within it, so that its sides get heated up.

As in the case of *lakhmit dōqa*, the dough is rolled out on a baking table into more or less flat loaves. Then it is laid on the baking cushion[6] and clamped on the inside wall of the *tanūra*. When ready, the bread is removed with the aid of two sticks.

Whereas the urban Jews bake only wheat bread, (as mentioned), the village Jews eat bread made of durra. The unleavened, moderately thick *prāge* bread, baked on the *dōqa*, is called *taptapinke* in the Betanura and Rekan district (also Kurd.).[7] In this area, the thick, leavened durra bread baked in the oven *kanūna* is called *qulēra* or *qolora* (A., from Greek κολλύρα).[8]

Besides bread, the Kurdish Jews bake a great many kinds of cakes and fancy breads, such as those prepared for the different feast days, and the like.

Meat Dishes

We have already mentioned that the Kurdish Jew, in contrast to the Yemenite, is a meateater. Meat is cheap and plentiful in Kurdistan. The economic foundation of Kurdistan rests on the great number of its herds. The livestock of the Kurdish nomads consists chiefly of sheep and goats. Cattle, being obviously less suited to this mountainous pasture country, is a rarity.

In the towns, slaughtered animals are procurable daily. Not so in the country, where, although to be sure, animals are always at hand, the *shoḥeṭ* to do the ritual slaughtering is not. Hence, the village Jews usually eat fresh meat only twice a year, and content themselves at other times with preserved meat, of which they lay in great quantities.

Mutton (*pisrit irbe*) is the meat most commonly eaten, the flesh of the ewe (Z. and A. *iwanta*, pl. *iwāne*) being preferred. Goat's flesh (*ize*), on the other hand, is despised. It is called *pisrit kōme*, "flesh of the black," in contrast with *pisrit huwāre*, "the flesh of the white," that is, of the sheep (A. and Z.).

The Jews of Sinne eat beef (*pisrit tōra*) for the most part. In other places, however, beef is eaten only in winter, because in summer the cattle are put to pasture for fattening.

The most highly prized of all the meats is chicken.[9] No Sabbath dinner or other festive meal must be without it, and during marriage festivities one of the evenings is called *lēl kethētha*, "night of the chicken," from the great number of chickens consumed on that occasion. Cold chicken cut into small pieces is served as *maza*, the Kurdish hors d'oeuvre, with which all feasts begin.

Another fowl that is considered very palatable is *qoqwāna* or *qoqwanta*,[10] a kind of partridge (*Perdix cinerea*). These birds are caught alive by the Kurds and sold to the Jews, who keep them in cages (*sute*, [A. *lisa*]) and rear them like domestic fowl, for these birds please them on account of their singing. Indeed, some of the Kurdish Jews are so fond of their *qoqwanta* that when they came to Palestine, they brought their *qoqwanta* along.

Sparrows[11] are also eaten. They must, of course, be ritually slaughtered. They are caught in traps.[12] When the children catch a sparrow, they seize it by the head and sing *Chūche chūche qūna bāda gaza nada dēta bardem*, "Sparrow, sparrow, with your tail shake, do not scream, your prison I am opening" (Z. Kurd.). The sparrows are spitted on long iron needles and roasted. The children eat them or else they are used for *maza*.

Preserved Meat

Preserved meat occupies an important place in the diet of the Kurdish Jews. There are several kinds of preserved meat, those consumed in the largest quantities being *qalya*, which is made by the Kurds, also, and *qawürma*, salted beef, which keeps more than a year and is used for Sabbath dishes. *Qawürma* is unknown to the Kurds.

The widespread use of preserved meat has two causes. First, the Jews of many of the smaller places. which cannot afford a resident *shoḥeṭ* and are visited by the itinerant *shoḥeṭ* only at long intervals, would have to go meatless most of the year if they had no preserved meat. Second, preserving the meat enables them to make use of the fat autumn stock and thus ensure for themselves a supply of good, fat meat for the pastureless winters.

A comparatively large family will slaughter about eight fat sheep for preservation by *qalya*, the most widely used of the preserved meats. The work is done in the upper floor of the house. First the tail fat (A. *ēlītha*) is cut into small pieces and boiled until it melts. Care must be taken not to mix the fat of the male and the female animals: the sexes fight, it is said; and the fat boils over. The flesh is then cut into large pieces and boiled for a short time. The pieces of fat that fail to melt are called *sisqe* and are used for making *zātit sisqe*, bread baked on the *dōqa* and containing some of this unmelted fat (Amadiya). Finally, the liquid fat is poured over the thoroughly cooked pieces of meat; and when cool, the meat put into large earthen casks (*sidanka*), of which a fairly large family will possess about ten or twelve, that is, approximately one for each month. *Qalya* is eaten from Sukkot to Sukkot.

The *qalya* intended for Passover is prepared with exceptional care. Not only are the *ḥames* regulations punctiliously observed, but no menstruating woman and no child may be present during its preparation (A.).

The second type of preserved meat is corned beef (A., Z., S. *pisra qawürma* or A. *pisra maksūd*, [Targ. *pisra dwīqa* or *pisra kefita*]; Z. *pisra kezīda*), which, as mentioned, is unknown to the Kurds.

Qawürma is made only of very fat oxen or cattle, such as the *Surai* (Christians) are experienced in breeding. Every Jewish family prepares one such animal at Hanukka. The meat is cut into slices and pickled in tall earthen vessels (*elīna*), which are then covered with hides and in which the meat remains until Shavu'ot. While making *qawürma* the Jews of Sinne sing

qawürma pazan mana	Pickled meat from our sheep
jashen khomana	Is a feast for ourselves
qawürma pazāna	Pickled meat from our sheep
gusht harzāna	Is cheap meat.

In the country the Jews make a third type of preserved meat, that is, dried meat, *pisra vīsa* (Arbil, Rekan, Hora, Nirwa, Tchalla, and Cakhon).[13] The meat from animals slaughtered during Sukkot, especially cattle, is salted and hung up to dry. It keeps until Passover.

The Nestorians prepare their *tilye* in much the same way. They hang up a whole sheep to dry, and keep on cutting pieces off it from time to time. Some of this meat is eaten uncooked.

Dairy Products

Milk production is even of greater importance for the people of Kurdistan than meat production. The numerous herds of sheep and goats furnish a far greater quantity of milk than the inhabitants can consume.

The milk of their sheep and goats, and the great variety of products made from it, form the staple food of the Kurdish nomads. In some districts grain fills a very insignificant place in their diet. Bread is a delicacy in which they can indulge only on rare occasions, and milk and cheese are the only fare at hand. The abundance of the milk supply also results in an exceptionally low price of all dairy products.

Though the Jews bear less resemblance to the Kurdish nomads than to the settled population, which subsists largely on cereals and vegetables, dairy products nevertheless play an important role in their diet, especially in the country districts, where they seldom eat meat except on the Sabbath. The Jews obtain most of their milk and dairy products from the Kurds. Some of the Jews, however, have sheep and either goats or cows of their own. As the flocks of sheep far outnumber those of goats or cattle, dairy produce is made chiefly from the milk of sheep.

Fresh milk (Z. and S. *ḥalva,* [A. *khalva,*] Kurd. *shīr*) is little used, being reserved only for children and patients. It is the curdled milk that is of importance in Kurdistan, as in most stock-farming countries.[14]

To form curdled milk (*masta,* Pers. and Kurd. *māst*),[15] the fresh milk is strained and warmed, a bit of sour milk (Z. and A. *heven*) is added, and it is left to stand till next morning. The cream (A. *sertun,* Z. *sertīka*)[16] floats on top. *Masta* is used either for making butter or as an ingredient in other dishes. For butter making, the *masta* is put into a churn (A. and Barashe; Kurd. *mashqa,* Targ. *gūda*)[17] that is simply a bag made of sheep's hide. It hangs on a tree and the women keep shaking it, singing, as they do so, "churning songs."

The sweet butter (A. and Z. *nivishk* or *kara*) and the buttermilk (*dō'e*) are then removed from the churn. Sweet butter must be used while it is fresh. It is eaten, for instance, with tea (*nivishk chai*). Salt is added to the butter that is to be kept for any length of time. Salted butter is called *mishka* (A. and Ushnu).[18]

Curdled milk is much used in cooking, especially in spring and summer when the milk supply is great. *Masta* is eaten also with *burgul.* Combined with the roots of *karange* [A. *kangerē*; a root with thorns and thick leaves] cut into small pieces, *masta* forms *karange mast* (Z) or *kangire gō masta* (A.), which is brought to the bride in the ceremony known as *tabaqe.*

Cheese (Z., A., S., Ushnu, *gubta*; Kurd. *panir* or *panīr*) is another product made of *masta. Gubta* is sometimes dried and kept for the winter.

The buttermilk (*dō'e*)[19] remaining from the churning is a very popular article of food, the more so as there are such quantities of it in summer that it costs next to nothing.

A large part of the skim milk is used for making white cheese (A. and S. *kashke*). A supply of dried *kashke* is likewise laid in for the winter, when it is grated (in a *mego,* grater) and dissolved in water like powdered milk. Grated *kashke* is also cooked with wheat grits to form *kashkiye* (A). [The cheese is made in a bag and is called *dō'et kista,* bag cheese. This is lean cheese. When this cheese is dried in the sun it hardens and is then called *kashke.* The *kashke,* softened in water, is cooked together with rice and either honey or butter. In Amadiya, *kashke* cooked with burgul, or such like, is called *kashkiye.*]

Jājīk is made by adding *siābō*, a kind of celery, to *dō'e* that is kept in *mezīda*, sacks made of [sheep] skins (Maclean, *Grammar*, p. 43). This is eaten in winter in Amadiya with the morning tea.

Vegetables (*Yirke*)

The Kurdish Jew, as we have already remarked, bears more resemblance to the settled Kurds of the towns and the village farming population than to the nomadic Kurds. He has a mixed diet that includes vegetables and legumes, as well as meat and dairy products.

The commonest vegetables in Amadiya are: *ba'injāne smōke* (tomato), *ba'injāne kōme* (egg plant), *badūnis* (parsley), *bāmiya* (Ochrea bamia), *bisle* (onion), *kalāme* (white cabbage), *tūma* (garlic), *qar'a* (pumpkin), varieties of beets [*silqa*] and turnips (e.g., *shargumta*), peas [*ḥumus*], and beans [A. *fasuli* or *lubia*].

Burgul and Rice

One can almost say that there is no meat or milk dish eaten by the Kurdish Jews in which burgul or rice does not figure. Burgul (A. *gürgur*, Z. *girgur*) is made as follows. Wheat is boiled in the large *marigla* [tub] until the grains burst. This boiled wheat is spread out on the roof to dry and is then pounded by two hefty young men, who sit opposite each other beating the *gürgur* rhythmically with a wooden mallet (A. *danguchke*, Z. *mekutke*, S. *mikūt*). Water is poured on the *gürgur* during the pounding; and when the pounding is finished, the *gürgur* is again put on the roof to dry. Next morning, the housewife invites several girls to the house to grind it in the handmill, after which it is stored in sheepskin sacks (*mezide*). Every family provides about ten sacks of *gürgur*.

It is interesting to note that the Jews or Amadiya and Rekan and their surrounding districts prepare the *gürgur* during the Omer nights [i.e., between Passover and Shavu'ot]. In Zahko only a small amount is made at that time, the main supply being prepared during the *seliḥot* nights of [the month of] Elul.

Rice (*riza*, Kurd. *birinj*), although cultivated in Kurdistan, is considered something of a luxury, and serves, therefore, as the basis of all festive meals and all ceremonial dishes. *Riza kethētha*, "chicken with rice," or *riza qoqwāna*, "partridge with rice," must not be absent on any festive occasion. At weddings, the families of the bride and groom send each other a *sīnīye* [tray] of rice "with a chicken enthroned on top."

Rice is prepared in various ways. The Kurds term rice with meat *pilaw*. The Jews of Sinne also eat *pilaw* in combination with all sorts of other foods. In Amadiya there is a particularly delicious dish of rice and meat [boiled with water and oil] called *riza kabūli*. Rice with buttermilk (*dō'e*) forms *gulul* (A.), which is eaten with melted butter and honey. (In Tchalla, Nirwa, and Rekan it is called *madīra*.)

Another rice dish that may, so to speak, be considered the national dish of the Kurdish Jews, is the *yiprakh* or *yaprakh* (Z., A., S.).[20]

The real *yiprakh* is rice wrapped in vine leaves. It is made by forming balls of rice mixed with raisin and sometimes meat, wrapping them in the vine leaves, and placing them carefully in a pot in circular rows, very close to each other. A little water and some grease are added; and the pot is left to stew for several hours or even, over a small fire, the whole night. For winter use, the vine leaves are dried in the spring, strung on a cord, and hung up till needed. If cabbage leaves are substituted for vine leaves, the dish is called *yiprakh kalamīye*. For *yiprakh pishpishe*, young vine leaves are chopped up and mixed with the rice (A. and Z. Jews only). *Yiprakh* is also cooked in butter. This is called *yiprakh mishka* and is eaten with buttermilk (*dō'e*).

Dumplings

Rice or wheat grits (*girse*) form the basis of another national dish of the Kurdish Jews, that is, dumplings (Z. and A. *kutele*, S. and Arbil *kufte*). The Jews are inordinately fond of these, and are capable of consuming an astonishing number of them—ten or more—at a time.

For *kutēle pisra* meat is pounded in a mortar (*makīna*), formed into dumplings with ground rice, and cooked in *dehena*, tail-fat. The stomach of a sheep, filled with rice (A. *kāsa*), is often added. There are also a great many other kinds of dumplings, such as *kutēle riza*, rice dumplings, and *kutēle girsa*, groat dumplings. *Kutēle* are the favorite form of *mebōsa*—the *ḥammim*, that is, the warm Sabbath food, of the Kurdish Jews.[21] In Sinne the Muslims call the dumplings *kufte musā'i khan*, that is, "Jewish dumplings," or *kufte sham'a*, "Sabbath dumplings." In Amadiya the dumplings are called *kutilkit shambiye*, "Shabbat dumplings," or *kutilkit Jehā*, "Jewish dumplings." The Kurds come to the Jews and ask them for *kutēle*, to give to their sick, for this food is believed to be a remedy against fever (A.).

Dumplings are often cooked with vegetable soups, especially the sour vegetable soups, *khamuṣta*,[22] for which a great many different kinds of vegetables are used, according to the season. They are made sour with *smōke* and cooked with meat. The usual Purim soup, for instance, is *khamuṣta kūwi*,[23] "sour soup of wild vegetables," a soup made of onions, garlic leaves, and *smōke*. [*Smōke* or *smoqe* is a vegetable with a vinegary taste.] *Kutēle khamuṣta*—sour soup containing large dumplings made of groats and *qalya*—is a very popular Sabbath evening dish (Z.).

Another soup often cooked in the spring is *maslōqa* (Z. and A.). This is a fat, meat soup to which *kutēle girsa* made with tail fat have been added. [Another kind of soup is *maraqit lilātha*, a soup of beet leaves, which is made of the leaves of young beets before the root develops. In Amadiya this soup is also called *abhka barsilqe*.]

Fish

Fish (*nunītha*, pl. *nunyātha*; Kurd. *māsi*), though abundant in the waters of Kurdistan, are hardly ever eaten by the Kurds and only moderately—and without any special enthusiasm—by the Jews.

The Jews are in the habit of eating fish at Purim, during Passover, on the eve of Rosh Hashana and during Hanukka. They generally catch the fish by means of a poison (*dermān* [A. *dermān nunyātha*, fish poison]), whose chief ingredient is the excrement of certain birds. The poison is twisted into flat pills and inserted into angleworms. The worms are thrown into the water and when the fish swallow them, they soon rise to the surface drugged (Z., D., and A.).

Fish are also caught with baskets (*suta*), with nets, *shabāqa* [or *mirokha*; a long pole with a round wooden frame and a net attached at one end about 1 meter in diameter], or with hook and line. It is one of the pleasures of the rich to sit on the river bank in the evening and fish with hook and line (Z. and D. *shiṣa*, [A. *shaṣa*]). Fish are also brought by the Muslim Kurds from distant rivers and placed on the market for the Jews.

The fish are either fried in butter or steamed. To steam them, a little water is put into the pot, some sticks are laid over it like a grate, then a layer of fish is laid over the sticks. Then come another grate and another layer of fish, and so on. The pot is tightly closed and set over a small fire (A.).

Maza

A festive meal among the Kurdish Jews never begins with the meal itself. It is always preceded by a social hour in which there is dancing and singing and the guests are regaled with arrack and *maza*.[24] *Maza* consists of cold fish, cold chicken or *qoqwāne*, partridge, roasted or boiled meat, mushrooms [A. *kwarke* or else *kame*, a sort of fungi not known in Amadiya], fruits, and nuts. The men often bring along their own *maza* (e.g., on Sabbath afternoon); and each invites his neighbor to partake of it. The meal itself, however, unless furnished by the host, is brought later by the women.

Sweets

The Kurdish Jews are not fond of sweets. Candy is eaten mainly by children. But, as in Persia,[25] sugarloaf (A. *rēsh shākar*) is held in great esteem, especially by way of a gift. In addition to its value as a sweet, it has a certain ceremonial significance. Witness, for instance, the *shirinē khorān*, "eating of sweets" in connection with the betrothal ceremony in Sinne (see p. 113). Besides the sugarloaf, the principal sweets used by the Kurds are [boiled] grape syrup (*mē pukhta*), honey, and *mana*. Grape syrup (*mē pukhta*) is made chiefly from grapes of inferior quality. *Mana* is plentiful in Kurdistan. [According to my informant, in Amadiya, the *mana* is called, in Targum, *ar'ūra*. It is found among the leaves of trees, especially among acorns. A cloth is spread beneath the branches, which are then shaken so that the *mana* falls off them onto the cloth.] The Jews regard it as the manna provided for the Israelites in the Wilderness. Hence, mention of it is often made in travel literature and is, indeed, rarely omitted from any description of a journey through this area. Benjamin II describes it thus: "Another extraordinary appearance which reminds us of the journey of the Jews through the wilderness, is the manna which here, in the form of grain, descends with the dew. The grain is of a whitish color and hard to the touch. It is collected in vases at break of day, and placed in the sun; in the warmth of which it melts, and becomes a cheesy kind of substance in which state it is eaten with bread at breakfast" (*Eight Years in Asia and Africa*, p. 136).

[Rabbi David d'Bet Hillel writes, of the *mana* that falls in the vicinity of Suleimani

> In summer manna is found here which falls every morning with the dew. When it falls on the rocks it is as white as snow, but it is difficult to obtain it as it is gathered for the governor and the notables. The mana which falls upon the trees and the grass, looks white and green as its color intermingles with that of the leaves and the blades. It is plentiful and is sold in the form of balls. Whatever is left in the field after sunrise melts like water. I have eaten some of it myself, and it is

sweet and of a pleasant taste. The people use it as a medicine. In the language of the natives, and in Arabic, it is known as *man shama*, that is, manna from heaven.][26]

The attitude of the Kurdish Jew toward sweets is obviously the result of outside influence. He looks upon indulgence in sweets as a sign of effeminacy—suitable, consequently, for women and children but unbecoming to men.

Candy, *shakarat* [A. Targ. *shakroke*], is imported from Mosul. It is distributed among the children on such occasions as the *ḥilyūta*, after the birth of a boy. *Baqlawa*,[27] a Turkish confection, consisting of about seven layers of dough alternating with a filling composed of nuts, honey, and butter, is eaten extensively throughout Kurdistan. It is baked in the *sīnīye* on the oven. *Luqma* is made by mixing flour with honey and almonds.

Beverages

The milk drinks *dō'e* and *masta* have already been discussed.

Tea, *chai*, though a comparatively recent importation, has nevertheless become firmly established in the daily life of the Kurdish Jew. How recent its introduction was is attested by a story which the Jews of Sinne tell about a certain Jewish physician. On drinking the new hot beverage for the first time, the physician was convinced that his insides were being burnt out and in his fright he jumped into the water.

The use of coffee (*qahwa*) is older than that of tea. It is drunk chiefly on festive occasions and is served in small cups, without sugar.

Among nonalcoholic drinks, there are in Sinne. as a result of Persian influence, a great variety of sherbets. In central Kurdistan sherbet is most commonly made of *mē pukhta*.

Khoshāve [good water] is a drink that is popular in the spring. It is made by soaking raisins, figs, and *khilu rashke*, dried pears, in warm water for several days. The Kurdish Jews like to drink *khoshāve* after their fat Sabbath food (A. and Z.).

In the summer, if they have no masta, they quench their thirst with *shamīza*, which consists of *ṭākhin* [sesame ground on millstones], *smōke* and onions, mixed with water (A.).

Alcoholic drinks fill an important place in the life of the Kurds,[28] as well as of the Kurdish Jew. He loves to drink and indulges his taste at every opportunity. Without arrack (*araqīn*) no picture of him would be complete. Arrack is a drink that accompanies him at every step in his journey through life, and gives flavor to all his feasts. In Amadiya, the *Ḥevra Qaddisha* has developed into a men's club that meets three times a week for a drinking bout (see p. 192). The Kurdish Jews regard their ability to consume a great quantity of strong drink as a sign of their physical strength, and are very proud of it.

Thus, it came about that when the English government, after the occupation of Iraq, forbade the manufacture of arrack in the home, the Jews felt it as an unwarranted attack on their private lives. The government encountered the greatest difficulties, and in some places there were actually riots.

The manufacture of arrack in the home is, indeed, still universal, since the distilling apparatus (*parch araqin*) is very primitive. The *sa'dani* (D) and *bejāra* (A. [choice]) are considered the best kinds of grapes for making arrack. Most of the distilling is done from dried grapes. There are three grades of arrack, depending on the number of times it has been distilled *araqīn khāmi*, once; *araqīn dubāra*, twice; *makrūr*, the best grade, distilled three times, in making which a chicken is laid in the receiver to absorb the impurities. Various spices are added to the arrack.

Compared with arrack. wine (*khamre*) is of minor importance. Each family makes its own wine at home, from black grapes (*inve takhlik*). The Jews of Herki and Tchalla have the reputation of making the best wine.

In Amadiya there was formerly a common wine press (*avisla*) at the synagogue,[29] but nowadays the grapes are put into huge vats and trod out with bare feet. The juice is then strained through a cloth, *ṣapiō* [more accurately *ṣapia*, A.] and poured into earthen casks (*ēlīne*). The *ēlīne* are up to two meters in height, and most of them are generations old. Their covers are sealed with clay. The *ēlīne* are opened at Hanukka or Passover, when much wine is drunk.

Wine is used also for the benedictions on the Sabbath and at feasts. In the winter, when the father and his grown sons return from the synagogue, they are accustomed to have a drink of wine and a bit of meat roasted on the spit (A.).

The wine for the benedictions is sometimes made of raisins. Such raisin wine, *qolkhīsa* [A. *qolḥītha*], is also provided for women and children at Passover in order to enable them to drink the four glasses as prescribed.

Narcotics

The Kurdish Jews indulge freely in tobacco (*tutun*), which is cultivated in many parts of Kurdistan, sometimes by Jews (Urmia and

Amadiya districts, see p. 208). Tobacco is smoked in a pipe consisting of a long tube (*baska*) and a clay bowl (*kalunka*). For a bridegroom, the tube is wound with cloth. Arrack is often poured over the tobacco. Tobacco is also pounded and mixed with various herbs for use as snuff (*barnūt*).

Meals

After this general survey of food and its preparation. let us consider the different meals served during a single day, taking Amadiya as an example. The cooking is done only twice a day, in the morning and in the evening.

For early breakfast (*fetara* [or *fetarta*]), which takes place after the return of the men from the synagogue, only bread and tea are taken.

At nine o'clock comes the first warm meal (*ghedāya* [or *gadāya*, *'edāya*]). In the winter, this consists of lentils, rice, or similar dishes; in the summer of vegetables, rice, or borgul with *masta*.

The midday meal (Z., D., A. *sharūsa*,; S. *khala kōra*—of which the children, returning from school, also partake—generally comprises only cold foods such as bread with *ṭākhin* or *pukhta* or, in the summer, sour milk. Cooked vegetables are occasionally served. A frequent dish for the midday meal is *ardoshavke* [Kurd., flour and grapewater]. This is made by mixing *mē pukhta* with uncooked flour. Another favorite midday dish is *arkhabke* [Kurd. uncooked flour] a kind of omelet.

The main meal is eaten in the evening, after the *Ma'ariv* prayer. It is called *'ashāya* (Z., D., A.) or *shām* (S.). The entire family assembles for the *'ashāya*. There is always a meat course; and it is customary to cook a specific dish on the same day of each week. Thus, every household in Amadiya cooks *kutēle* for Tuesday evening and *yiprakh* for Wednesday evening and for the eve of the new moon. On the other hand, for Thursday's dinner there is some inferior dish, this being the eve of Friday, the feast day of the Muslims.

PART THREE

The Family

7

Marriage

As among all Jewish tribes, the marriage ceremonies of the Kurdish Jews contain a strong admixture of non-Jewish elements—are, in fact, dominated by them.[1] In Kurdistan the customs as a whole are much alike, but local differences are so marked that their analytical description would require a separate book. In order, therefore, that our picture may be as compact and complete as possible, the customs of the two towns, Amadiya and Zakho, are taken as a basis; and brief descriptions are given of parallels and divergences found in other centers of Kurdish Jewish settlement.

Marriageable Age

The age at which marriage is contracted among the Kurdish Jews depends upon the financial situation of the family. If the father is rich, the son marries early. (Since the father furnishes the bride-price, there is no hindrance to an early marriage.) In less well-to-do families, where the youth must earn this money himself, the age for marriage is higher. It may even happen that the bridegroom, after all arrangements have been made, loses part of the money in business, and must therefore apply to his future father-in-law for a reduction of the amount or a postponement of the wedding.

It was customary to marry off the girls directly after their first menstruation. The usual explanation given for this haste is the desire to guard the girls against indiscretions. It is, however, clear that the custom among the Kurdish Jews[2] has a magic background.

Of a girl who sees the *dam nidda* (Heb. menstrual blood) for the first time, it is said, *Lakhmit bēthit bābakh ḥarimle* [A. *ḥaramle*] *illakh*, "The bread of [the house of] your father is taboo to you." If no betrothal is arranged for her, misfortune may overwhelm her and her children. If, for instance, the father has died and his daughter sees the *dam nidda* for the first time during the year of mourning, several old people come to the widow and say: "Marry your daughter, for the bread of your father is taboo to you. Otherwise misfortune will come." The betrothal ceremony (Heb. *ērūsīn*) is then performed very quietly because of the year of mourning.

If a girl who has lost both father and mother menstruates for the first time, several old people go to the *gevir* to give notice of the fact. The *gevir* takes counsel with other local notables; and the girl's dowry is at once got together from the *quppat arīkha*, welfare fund [lit., "meal fund"] and from donations (see p. 192).

Among the rich, the choice a bride for his son is altogether in the hands of the father, who carefully considers the social and financial standing of the family from which he is to select his son's wife. There is rarely any opposition on the part of the son. Still, in recent years—particularly among humbler families—we sometimes find the son making his own choice. In former times, the boys and girls were segregated after their tenth year; and the girls could appear in the street only with veiled faces. Today the situation has changed. The youths see the girls at weddings and other festivities, where they associate freely; and it is clear that such contacts break the ground for future love affairs.

My informant, who comes of an important family, was only thirteen years old when his father arranged a marriage for him. He was still a schoolboy. One day, his uncle came to the school, took him on his shoulder and carried him home, where his father and several *ḥakhamim* were discussing his marriage. He himself had no idea at all what marrying meant (A.).

A boy is usually not married before the age of eighteen or a girl before the age of thirteen (or fifteen).[3] When the father has made his choice, he sends an old woman to the father of the chosen girl; and since no one likes to do anything in a hurry in the Orient, the girl's father, if he consents, sends word to come again in a month.

The *Niqda* (Bride-Price)

A month later, the interested parties meet at the bride's home for the *tlaba*, the marriage agreement. The bridegroom's mother has food sent to the bride's house for the evening on which the negotiations over the marriage agreement are to take place. The bridegroom's father appears with several old men.[4] The *ḥazan* begins with a *drush* [sermon] in which he says that it is not good for a man to be alone; and finally he asks, *Niqda kema shaqlit minan*?, "How great a bride-price are you taking from us?"

About 1890, it was decided in Amadiya that the bride-price, excluding jewelry, should not exceed 130 *qeran* (ca. £6 10s.). [Similar decisions were passed also by other Oriental Jewish communities. In Meshhed, Khorasan, for instance, it was ruled about 1850 that the bride-price should not exceed 150 *qeran*.[5] The reason for such decisions was the tendency to outdo one another in paying higher and higher amounts in bride-price, which often led to the financial ruin of the family. The decision was carried out by the heads of the community.]

In recent years, money having become cheaper owing to the British occupation, the *niqda* increased to £20 (200 rupees). In Arbil the *niqdiya* amounts to £20 on the average. Out of this sum, the bride's father buys her jewelry. The bride-price may, however, be as high as £100.

In Zakho the *bartil* amounted to 50 *mejidi* (about £10) in Turkish times. In addition to this, the bridegroom had to give 2 *mejidi* as *ḥalvit jimma*, "mother's milk," to the mother of the bride.

In Sinne[6] there is no bride-price. The bridegroom must supply the trousseau and furnish the home. Only among the poor is a bride-price (*shervahi*; from *sher*, "milk," and *bahi*, "price") demanded.[7] Brawer writes that the bride furnishes her own trousseau ("A Chapter From My Journey in Iran," p. 17). This undoubtedly refers to the *jahāzie*, which is taken to the house of the bridal couple the day after the wedding.

In some places, one evening does not suffice for the negotiations; several meetings are necessary before an agreement is reached.

The situation so far described in regard to the youth and girl's consent and the bride-price is that which normally obtains among the Kurdish Jews. We are, however, in possession of material—mostly from documents that have come to us—acquainting us with quite deplorable circumstances under which marriages were sometimes contracted. We must, of course, take into consideration that we are dealing here with exceptional cases, which, as such, came before the Rabbis for decision and have thus been preserved in documents. Still, my informants declare that such things occur even today.

Under normal circumstances, marriage is not, either for the father of the bride, or for the father of the bridegroom, a "business deal," entered into merely for the sake of profit. On the contrary, both parties incur considerable expense. Among the poor, however, it is true that the fathers sometimes seek to gain a profit through their daughters. This leads to a situation in which the human side of marriage is entirely disregarded, and the fathers treat their daughters purely as merchandise.

As a result of a rabbinical inquiry we learn of such a case from Zakho.[8] A Jew of Zakho had fallen on evil days and was in such reduced circumstances that he sold his seven-year-old daughter for 8 *grush* to another Jew as maid—by no means an unusual transaction. The purchaser still owed the father a small part of the purchase money. When the father demanded this money, the buyer of the daughter gave it to him, saying, in the presence of witnesses, that this was for the *qiddūshim* (betrothal) of the daughter with his son. The girl's father consented. However, in the event, after the buyer's death, his son gave the girl back to the father (for she failed to find favor in his eyes); and the father married her to another man. The lawsuit concerned the validity of this second *qiddushim*, since the deceased buyer had actually already arranged the *qiddushim* for his son.

Another case that throws some light on the moral position of the Kurdish Jews in matters relating to marriage, is contained in one of the letters published by Mann.[9] A Jew of Sukho[10] had married off his daughter; and since he required some female help as a substitute for her services, he conceived the following solution, whereby he expected to "kill two birds with one stone." He took into his house a girl who was, for the time being, to do the necessary housework, but who was later to become the wife of his still unmarriageable son. While the son did not in the least know "what a woman is" (line 15), the girl obviously considered herself married; for when she fled from the house, she gave as the reason for her flight "that she doesn't want this (man) because he is not like other men" (line 27). A complicated legal case arose when the son died, because this brought up the question of *ḥalīṣa* (see p. 188).

When a father refused to give his daughter voluntarily, the youth sometimes had recourse to violence and abducted the girl. Thus, so it happened, as one of the letters published by Mann reports,[11] that a man by the name of Ḥanukō, of Nirwa, took a fancy to the eight-year-old daughter of another Jew and wanted to marry her. As Ḥanukō had a bad reputation, the father of the girl rejected his suit. Ḥanukō thereupon abducted the girl and took her to Baduk, a distant village near Amadiya, intending to have a secret betrothal ceremony performed there. [According to my informant, there is no village of this name near Amadiya; there is, however, a village called Bade there.] In the letter referred to, the *ḥakham* of Nirwa calls upon the *ḥakham* of Amadiya to do everything he could to prevent the marriage of this minor.

In Rekan and its vicinity, abduction of girls is even now not an uncommon occurrence. Such cases, however, are mostly those in which the girl agrees but the father refuses—whereupon the would-be bridegroom, through an intermediary, makes a rendezvous with the girl, appears at the appointed place with several armed Kurds, and takes the girl away by force. There is no *ḥakham* who will perform the betrothal ceremony against the father's will; nevertheless, such an act usually forces the father to give his consent.

Lēl Kethētha, "Night of the Chickens"

After an agreement on the bride-price has been reached, it is decided to meet at the close of the following Sabbath. This evening is called *lēl kethētha* (or *kesēsa*), "night of the chickens," because a great number of chickens are bought for the guests (A.).

The fathers of the bride and groom send the invitations through the *shammash* (sexton) saying, *Sāwun kethētha bē khitna (kālo)*, "Come to chickens at the house of the bridegroom (the bride)." The young men take a great number of chickens and several bottles of wine and accompany the bridegroom's parents to the bride's house. There, each is given a glass of arrack, after which they return to the bridegroom's house by a different road (*chape būke*)[12] from the one by which they came.

At the homes of *khitna* and *kālo*, the guests sit down together to the "feast of the chickens." That evening, at about ten o'clock, the father of the bridegroom sends an invitation to the guests who are with the bride to come to his house. They appear, accompanied by their wives, who assemble in a separate room. The usual merrymaking follows, including the dancing of the *ḥigga* in the courtyard (A.).

In Sinne, this feast at the close of Sabbath is called *shirinē khorān*, "eating of sweets."[13] The guests assemble at the bride's house. The bride sends the bridegroom sugarloaves (from ten to thirty, according to her means); and the bridegroom responds with a golden ornament.

Next morning, the preparations for the ceremony called *sīnīye* [plate] are begun. The cooking of the food is, according to custom, part of the ceremonial. The girls of the families of both bride and groom come to the house of the bridegroom's father to clean the rice for the feast. As they work, they sing (Kurdish) songs.

The meat is cooked in rice and peas and put on a large *sīnīye*. The plate is covered with a silken cloth and the mother of the bridegroom adds several articles of clothing as a gift. One young man takes the *sīnīye* on his head, another, the clothing. As the procession passes through the streets, it is pelted with nuts and sweets thrown from the houses along the way. An old woman is stationed on the roof of the bride's house, and, as the guests enter she showers wheat upon them, saying, *Ēnit ḥazda paq'a*, "The evil eye [lit., "the eye of him who covets"] shall burst."[14] When the guests present the gifts to the mother of the bride, the parents of the bridegroom dance before the two young men. The bride's mother puts on her daughter's finger the gold ring that is among the gifts. The silken scarf (*kasrawan*) is tied about the bride's head by one of the girls, and the shoes and stockings that have been given her are put on her by another girl.

In the bride's room the guests dance the *ḥigga*. The bride must take part in this dance. A donkey saddle (*qurṭāna*) is laid upon the shoulders of the mothers of the bridal couple, and a cooking spoon (*itrana*) is put into their hands in place of the sword; and in this costume they must dance.

The rice from the *sīnīye*, *rizzit bē kālo* [the rice of the bride's house] is distributed among those present and sent in small bowls to the homes of acquaintances. The bridegroom's people thereupon return to the *bē khitna*, where the dances are continued. Then the groom's father gives the people an invitation for the following Sabbath, called the Shabbat Ma'arafe, Sabbath of Preparation (A.).

The custom of the *sīnīye* is similar in Zakho. There it is called the *ashāyit kālo*, "bride's supper." When the empty rice dishes are returned to the bridegroom's house, the people sing

hai mintā, mintā, mintā
mintā min bābā hīwāle
kozinta rapsa tāle
malātā āwā
hai lenüsso zāwa

O thanks, thanks, thanks
Thanks for the father [who] gave [her]
a large mule for him
Your house is [steady]
O for Nissim, the bridegroom. (Z. and A. Kurd.)

Shabbat Ma'arafe

On the night preceding Thursday, the girls are again sitting together at the bridegroom's house; and all night long they grind wheat for *girse*. At midnight refreshments are served to them. On Friday, the cattle are slaughtered for the feast. On Sabbath morning the bridegroom is brought to the synagogue by a singing crowd. All the posts of honor are in the hands of the bridegroom's father, who bestows them for the most part on relatives.

After the service, the bridegroom is escorted home. Then all go together to the house of the bride. There they dance the "dance of the kerchiefs, *ḥiggit kaffiye* [A. *ḥiggit pathpāthā*]; and the mothers must once more perform the dance with the donkey saddle in order to amuse the company. Food is brought from the bridegroom's house and served to the guests, while two girls in rhythmic step, accompanied by singing women, bring in two vessels of food for the bride. At midday the company proceeds to the bridegroom's house, there to dance and sing again (A.).

In Amadiya, two weeks elapse between the *ma'arafe* and *qiddūsh ērūsīn*—the solemnization of the betrothal, *qadōshe*.[15] The *qadōshe* always takes place on Wednesday, the day of which the sun and moon were created.

In Zakho the *qadashta* often follows directly after—at the latest, one week after—the completion of the marriage agreement.[16] In Arbil the *arīsā* is delayed from one to two weeks, and in Sinne it often takes place four weeks after *shirinē khoran*.

The Betrothal (*Qadōshe*)

The women of the bridegroom's household again set about the preparation of the feast several days in advance. Rice is cleaned, and poultry and the remaining necessaries are provided. On Tuesday the food, entirely prepared, is taken to the bride's house.

The bridegroom is led in procession to the bride's house on Wednesday. There he takes a seat of honor beside the *ḥazan* and the notables, and the bride is brought in. She is veiled but has not yet undergone any of the ceremonies, such as the dyeing with henna, that are supposed to guard her against witchcraft and the "evil eye."

The *ḥazan* takes the silver betrothal ring (*esiksit qadōshe*), which may or may not have a stone, dips it in wine, and shows it to the witnesses, in order that they may confirm the fact that it is *shawe pruṭa*[17] [or A.

kṭoya kha para, worth a penny]. Then the bridegroom puts it on the bride's finger, while reciting the benediction. The bride is not veiled during this part of the ceremony, because cases have occurred in which another girl was substituted for the chosen bride. The groom, shy and awkward, is called [by the man who performs the betrothal ceremony and amid much laughter] to *dinshoq īdah*, "kiss her hand"; and the woman raise their *klīlīlī*. Then follows the breaking of the wineglass by the bridegroom.

The bride is led back to her room, and the men and women sit down to the *se'odit qadōshe* [betrothal meal].

After the meal, the bridegroom is escorted to his home, where his friends celebrate the *lēlit qadashta* [wedding night] by playing games and dancing till morning.

The girls and young women gather at the bride's house for the *lēl qadashta*. The women of the bridegroom's household also attend, bringing plates of sweets.

They dye the bride's hands, feet, and hair—or at least one of her fingers—with *ḥunna*, henna, and spend the whole night with her but must not sleep.

In the morning they take her to the bathhouse and then back home again, where a meal awaits them.

After the bath, they sing the song *Tirnīnī tirnīnī khā yōma ana mepiqlī lamsayōre*, "One day I went out to take a walk" (A. Z. being similar) In Sinne there is no *qiddūsh ērūsīn*.[18]

The Interim

There is an interval of half a year or more between the *qiddūsh ērūsin* and the *sheva' berakhot* [Heb. "seven benedictions," i. e., the wedding ceremony]. In Zakho the seven benedictions come at least six months after the *qadashta*. This applies to the well-to-do. If there is difficulty in getting together the money, there may be an interval of two years. In Sinne, on the other hand, it is precisely the rich who like to prolong the interval, to show how hard they find it to part with their daughter. They also want to show in this way the superiority of their daughter and their own reluctance to let her leave their home for one in which she will probably find conditions far less comfortable than those she is now enjoying.

This interim has its special customs. Throughout the whole period the bride must not show herself to the bridegroom or to any other male from his household. She must hide herself if one of them enters the house (Z., A., and Arbil, and Muslim Kurds).

After the *qadashta*, the bridegroom may not enter the bride's house until he has undergone the ceremony *petākhit urkhit khitna*, "opening of the way for the bridegroom." The bride's father invites the bridegroom and his people to a dinner. There are no practices peculiar to this dinner. Thereafter, however, the bridegroom is permitted to enter the bride's house; but he must always knock at the door beforehand, so that the bride may have time to hide herself (A.).

In Zakho, this dinner, which takes place about a month after the *qadashta*, is called *krēthit khitna*, "invitation of the bridegroom." The bridegroom must be the last guest to leave, and he may from that time on visit the house of the bride. There are similar dinners in Ushnu (*pesarkhīl khātan*) and in Sinne (*mehmāni*, feast).

The chief use to which this interim period is put is the preparation of the bride's trousseau. The bride has a number of things to make—gifts for the bridegroom and the guests[19] and the requisites for the cradle for her future children. The bridegroom's gift is an embroidered collar *basar qedāla*, "behind-the-neck." For the guests she prepares the bright-colored knitted gloves (*daz gorka*) and stockings (*kistit pāre*), wallets for the money or watches, and crocheted covers for bottles (*pemōdit zivirta*). She must provide the cradle with the wrappings (*benūde*) and a coverlet (*keramta*), which is made of "a thousand patches" (A. Z. is similar).

Preparations for the Wedding

Most marriages are solemnized at Passover, other favored seasons being Sukkot and Shavu'ot (A. and Z.). The time for the wedding was formerly—and is sometimes even today—determined magically, by "casting lots." This is shown by a passage in the letter sent by Juda b. Shim'on of Amadiya to Yiḥya in Ashur (Mosul).[20] The letter apparently dates from the sixteenth century. It tells us that the writer had cast lots in regard to some political affair but was not entirely satisfied with the result: "But I am not entirely convinced because it was cloudy when I did the casting." Then he continues: "In the matter of the wedding of your son—God preserve and protect him—it shall take place on the 14th, 15th or 16th of the month, for this I have long since sought for and investigated, and it is correct."[21]

One month before the wedding the bridegroom's father invites the women to buy the clothes for the bride. The mother of the groom, the mother of the bride, and several other women thereupon go to the market place and get the necessary dress material, the shoes, and so on.

The dresses are sewed at the bride's house. The dressmakers work without pay, but their food is furnished by both households (A., Z., and S.).

In Zakho, as soon as the dressmaker has cut the first piece, the women who have gathered there raise their *klīlīlī* and cry, *Brīkhe, brīkhe, hāwe brīkhe, beliba besīma*, "Blessed, blessed, may [the clothes] be blessed with happy hearts." [In Amadiya they also say, *Brīkhe, brīkhe, naqsha khāre ilu bnōne ubenātha bith khitne wkhalātha*, "Blessed, blessed be (the clothes), may they be dirtied by sons and daughters, grooms and brides" (A.)]. In Sinne the bridegroom invites the dressmakers to a meal at his home.

During the month before the seven benedictions the youths and maidens gather every evening at the house either of the *khitna* or of the *kālo* and dance and sing. In Amadiya this is called *kam ḥelūla*, "before-the-wedding" (Kurd. *bar da'wat*).

The actual wedding festivities begin a week before the *sheva' berakhot*. The Sabbath preceding the *sheva' berakhot* is called Shabtha did Mashmō'e, "Sabbath of the Announcement" (Z.; formerly also A.).

On Saturday morning, while the men are in the synagogue, the women and girls take sweets, fruit, and arrack to the house of the bride. The musicians (*muṭurbāye*) also arrive, and there is dancing and singing of "Dalēlēle, Dalēlēle." The bride joins the dance. The young men come from the synagogue and dance *berīsa* in the courtyard, singing the song "*Lo Shewano*" (O Shepherd). Then the young men go to the bridegroom's house and continue their dancing there.

After the *Minḥa* prayer several women are invited to the house of the bridegroom. Two of them, whom it is especially desired to honor, take two dishes of food, *fēkit kālo*, "fruit for the bride," and bring it in procession, surrounded by the rest of the women, to the bride's house.[22] If the bride happens to be dancing in the courtyard with the girls when the women arrive with the *fēkit kālo*, she must quickly flee to her mother's room; for it is not considered proper for the bride to receive the dishes out of doors.

The close of this Sabbath is termed *shekālīsit ḥelūla* or *shekalisit da'wa*, "beginning of the wedding" [A. *shekalteth khlūla*]. The relatives of the bride are invited to the home of the groom, while the bride sends there a female relative to invite the girls to her house. They sit in two rows facing each other and sing to each other alternately. (Z. and A.)

In Sinne the bride is taken on Friday evening to the house of her uncle or another relative. There the women and girls gather on Friday evening and Sabbath to dance and sing. The same thing takes place at the bridegroom's house. The bride is taken back to her father's house on Sabbath afternoon. The close of Sabbath ushers in *īlat dewaqāne*, "night of the dancers" [A. *lēlet dwākat khigga*, night of festive dancers] at the house of the bridegroom. In this, both the youths and the men take part.

The provision of food for the wedding festivities holds an important place in the preparations during the week preceding the seven benedictions. The women are occupied in cleaning the rice for the various feasts, baking bread, and so on. The cattle must be slaughtered and the poultry, fruit and other essentials provided.

In Amadiya all assemble on the evening before the seven benedictions (Tuesday evening) at the house of the bridegroom for *nānūpaz* (Kurd.), "bread and mutton." A messenger is sent to the bride's father to inquire who will be his representative (*qāṣūt*) at the *nānūpaz*. A member of the bride's family appears. He takes his seat beside the bridegroom's father; and the latter has the supply of provisions brought in, which, by the marriage contract, the bridegroom must send to the house of the bride for the wedding feast. The supplies to be furnished are determined by tradition and consist of rice, flour, meat, *dehina* (tail fat), *smōke*, onions, cucumbers, *shergumme*, *silqe* (turnips), pepper, petroleum for the lamps, and a load of wood for the stoves. All these provisions are brought to the bride's home with songs and merriment.

The Dyeing with Henna

First among the magic practices to which a bridal couple in Kurdistan must submit is the dyeing with henna. In Zakho the dyeing takes place on two evenings—on Thursday evening and at the close of Sabbath. The first henna night is called *lēl ḥinne bedugle*, "false henna night."[23] Ostensibly, this designation refers to the fact that the dyeing with henna is not immediately followed by the wedding; but it is clear that the idea is to outwit the demons.

On Thursday morning, the people are apprised through loud playing by the musicians that they are invited to come to the bridegroom's house. The henna is brought in a bowl and is received by the women with the *klīlīlī*. Several women knead the henna in the *tashta*, dissolving it in lukewarm water and adding *ḥamīrit ḥinna*, which is made of *smōke*. The *ḥinna* must ferment like dough until evening.

The Invitation to the Aga

When the henna is ready, the next step is sending the first invitation to the aga [local Kurdish chieftain] and obtaining his permission to proceed with the wedding. It is with this object in view that the ceremony of sending henna to the aga is carried out. Three vessels, each containing powdered henna and a piece of soap, are placed on a brass platter and covered with a silken cloth. A youth takes the platter on his head (as is customary) and, escorted by the musicians and several men and women, goes to the house of the aga. The group stops before the closed door of the aga's house. The latter sends out a servant to ask for whom the henna is intended. "It is henna for the marriage of so-and-so," is the reply. As a rule, the aga accepts the henna, but in cases where for some reason the relations between him and this particular Jewish family are strained—if they would not lend him money or did not ask his permission for the marriage beforehand—he refuses to accept the henna. Then the delegation goes back home without any music, and the aga sends his servant to the bridegroom's house to tear the parchment of the musician's drum. Through bribes and the intercession of some of the notables, the Jew must then try to make his peace with the aga before he can even think about the wedding.

If, however, the aga has accepted the henna, the musicians play, and the group enters the courtyard of the aga's house to dance. The servant (*julāma*, Kurd. *khulām*) takes the platter of henna to the aga's wife. The aga throws *shabāshe* to the musicians, which is announced thus: *Shabāshe agāi sarsare jewātera*, "The aga's *shabāshe* [or A. *dauate* or *khlulāye*, guests] for the assembled company". When the aga signifies that it is time to stop, he has a garment brought in as a present to the musicians, and the people return in procession to the bridegroom's house (only in Zakho; Kurds also send henna to the aga).

Then they take five or six bowls of henna and go to their Kurdish acquaintances. These first ask if the aga has accepted the henna; for if he has rejected it, he would punish them for admitting the Jews. On receiving and affirmative answer, the Kurds, too, make *shabāshe* and give a present to the musicians. The presentation of the henna serves at the same time as an invitation to the wedding (Z., A., and among the Kurds).

The Jews then return to the bridegroom's house, take several bowls of prepared henna and, escorted by the musicians, go to the homes of the relations of the bridal couple, where they proceed to dye the hair of all the girls between the ages of five and ten. The relations also make *shabāshe*. The dyeing is continued on Friday and on Sunday, because any family whose little daughter failed to get her hair dyed for the wedding would be greatly offended (Z.).

In the evening, the men gather at the bridegroom's house and the women at the bride's. The girls sit around the bride and sing. Then one of the girls from the bridegroom's family appears and invites the girls to go to the bridegroom's house and fetch the henna for the bride. There two bowls are filled with henna and carried to the bride's house on the heads of two young men. Especially powerful youths are chosen for this task because the boys try to steal henna from the bowls on the way. The procession is accompanied by the musicians. When they approach the bride's house, they cry, "The henna is coming!" so that the bride may veil herself. The women undo the bride's plaits and dye her hair with henna. Then they dye her hands and their own.

After the dyeing at the bride's house is finished, the henna is taken to the bridegroom, and his hands, forelock, and sidelocks, *gulage* [A. *gulangi*], are dyed. Then the young men present dye their own hands.

In Zakho, the Sabbath, with its special customs, comes between the *lēl ḥinna bedugle* and the true henna night. On Sabbath morning the musicians are awakened with jests: *Hüllo, hüllo, müturbo, ser subaḥīye lēbeda*,[24] "Up, up, musicians, it is dawn, beat (the drum)!"

The music brings all the Jews to their feet; and the bridegroom, simply clad, is taken to the synagogue, where, however, neither he nor his father is called to the reading of the Tora, because they are in the middle of the wedding.

While the men are in the synagogue, the women and girls of the bridegroom's family dance in the courtyard of his house to the music of the musicians. The groom's mother then takes some *mebōse* and a sieve *'arbala*), which she fills with raisins and fruit. Accompanied by the musicians, the women take this to the bride for the *subaḥīyit kālo* [A. *fetartet kālo*], "the bride's breakfast." Here, again, there is dancing; and the good things that have been brought are passed round.

Meanwhile, a girl is sent every now and then to the synagogue to see if the service is over, for at the end of the service the women go to the synagogue with the musicians to fetch the bridegroom. As we have mentioned above, several weddings are often solemnized at the same time, and the different musicians frequently meet on the way. The resulting din is such that the *shammash* comes out of the synagogue to restore a degree of quiet. The musicians then escort home their respective bridegrooms, each with his people.

After the close of Sabbath comes *lēlīye*[25] the night in which both bride and bridegroom are dyed with henna [Zakho].

The youths and maidens who are at the homes of the bridegroom and the bride, respectively, must not sleep during this night; for they must keep watch over the bridal couple (also among the Kurds).

The bridegroom sits on a low stool, and an old man washes his feet and arms and cuts his nails. During this process the men sing the song "Hai Chalaiyabi." Then they dye the bridegroom's sidelocks, both sides of his hands as far as the knuckles, and his feet to the ankles. Meanwhile they sing and make *shabāshe*; and finally they dye themselves.

After the dyeing, the men take several bowls of henna and, again with the musicians proceed to the bride's house. The bride, too, has just been dyed in the same way as the bridegroom. If her hair was not sufficiently well dyed on Thursday night, it is now dyed again. During the dyeing the company sings the song *Nariqe*.

In Arbil, where the seven benedictions likewise take place on Sunday, the henna night, *bēt ḥinne*, is also the night preceding Sunday. The bridegroom's little finger and index finger of the right hand are dyed.

The Henna Night in Amadiya

In Amadiya, too, the henna night (*lēl ṣevā'ata* [or *lēl ṣuwa'ta*]) comes a day before the seven benedictions, that is, on Tuesday evening. The fathers of the bridal couple send a *shammash* round to deliver the invitations: *Atētun ṣevā'ata bētit kālo* (*khitna*), "Come to the dyeing in the house of the bride (bridegroom)." [The formula of invitation sent differs in the case of a rich man from that sent to a poor man. If the man is rich, the invitation formula is *Adlel ṣuwatela beth kālo mbashlētun*, "Tonight there is painting at the bride's house, cook" (i.e., bring along food). If the man is poor, they say *la mbashlētun*, "do not cook," this is, do not bring along food].

The people gather at the bridegroom's house, where they dance, sing, and partake of *maza*. Then the meal is served. After the meal the *shushbīn yamīn* (*qarivāna raste* [groomsman]) leads the *khitna* as unobtrusively as possible to his own house. When the guests have finished the benediction, they ask each other, "Where is the bridegroom?" "He went away in anger (*mokhshimle*)," is the answer, "Come, we want to bring him back." On the way to the *shushbīn*'s house, they sing the song *Ya sar qantarke shā raban shā raban*, "She who is in the upper chamber is very fair, very fair" (Kurd.).

When they reach the house, they ask the bridegroom, "Why have you left us?" The *shushbīn* serves refreshments to the guests, and the *khitna* is led back home by another road, *chape būke.*

The henna had already been brought from the bride's house in the morning. It is now kneaded for the bridegroom by an immature girl. When the henna is ready, a boy is seated on the bridegroom's knees, and the whole process of dyeing is carried out on this boy before it is the turn of the bridegroom. First the right hand and the left foot, then the left hand an the right foot, are dyed and bandaged. The purpose of the dyeing of the boy is to ensure the blessing of many children in the future for the bridal couple. After the dyeing of the bridegroom, the young men present also dye themselves.

When the dyeing of the *khitna* is over, the girls go to the bride's house in order to dye her, *ṣō'akh kālo.* Here, too, the henna is kneaded by an immature girl, and the dyeing is first carried out on a girl who sits on the bride's lap. The bride's hair is dyed; otherwise, the process is the same as in the case of the bridegroom. During the dyeing the women sing *Khajuka semar kandi akh yaman* [Khajuka (a woman's name) shines like the moon, how beautiful! (Kurd.)]

In Sinne the henna night (*lēl ḥanna*) is on the night preceding Thursday, while the seven benedictions come on the night preceding Friday. The women dye both sides of the bridegroom's hands and his hair. The bride's hair, hands, and feet are dyed; and several lines are drawn across her forehead.

In Zakho, after the dyeing, a feast, *pashīvit khitna*, is served at the bridegroom's house to about one hundred guests. The women and girls, an the other hand, get only the food that was brought to the bride's house in the ceremony called *tabāqe*, "baskets," before the *lēlīye*. The bridegroom's people take about two hundred loaves of bread (*laḥmit dōqā*), which they divide among five or seven baskets—likewise some curdled milk (*karange mast*)—and carry it in procession, accompanied by the musicians, to the bride's house.

The bridal couple eat a great deal, since they must fast the next day. They are fed by the *shushbīnīm*, for their hands are bandaged and they cannot feed themselves (also A.).[26] When the *shushbīn* hands the bridegroom the first bite—a large piece of bread—everyone tries to snatch it away from him, and each one breaks off a bit of it as *segūla* [Heb. charm]. The same is done with the bride's first piece (Z. and A.)

The bride and the groom may lie down and sleep; but those who are spending the night at their respective homes must stay awake, since it is their duty to protect the bridal couple against the demons. They dance and sing and play all sorts of jokes in order to keep awake. Some take a needle and thread and if anyone falls asleep, they sew him (or her) to the mat or to his (or her) neighbor. A similar custom is observed on Tish'a b'Av.[27]

In Sinne, the watchers choose one of their number as *kad khoda* "chief of police," and two as policemen, *farash bāshī*. These play all sorts of tricks on the company. For instance, they refuse to let the youths dye themselves with henna until they have contributed some money. With the money thus collected they give a fine dinner after the wedding.

The Bride's Bath

The dyeing with henna is followed by the bathing of the bride and bridegroom as a further preparation for the seven benedictions. In Zakho the bride is given a warm bath in the house after the dyeing—while it is still dark, though close to dawn. A girl whose parents are both living is first bathed in water, next comes the bride, and finally several of the bride's friends.

After the bath in the house, two women take the bride to the river before daybreak; a star must still be visible in the sky. There she is undressed—she must not keep on so much as a ring—and she immerses herself in the river three times. This dip in the river has to be carried out even in winter.

In Amadiya the women and girls take the bride to the riverbank (*rubār*),[28] wash her there in warm water with the (knitted) *life* [lit., "sponge"; actually, a sort of bag in which the soap is kept], sprinkle her with rosewater, and so on.

In Arbil, the *shamash* brings the bride the following toilet articles from the bridegroom's house: soap (*sabon*), a washcloth (*lifke*), a comb (*mesreqe*), handkerchiefs (*pishta māle*), rosewater (*mā'at warde*), and depilatory ointment for the hair of the body (*darmāne gurē*). When the women of Amadiya comb the bride's hair at the river, they pick seven hairs out of the combings. These they take to the *ḥakham*, who combines them with silk threads and forms a braid, which is supposed to symbolize the intertwinement of bride and groom and against which no countercharm has an efficacy. At the *yiḥud* (see pp. 139–40), the bridegroom detaches one hair, the bride the next, and so on until all the hairs are detached.

After the washing, the bride is immersed three times in the river. Then she is dressed, but not yet in her wedding clothes. During the dressing the women sing *Dim khamlūlā, dim khamlūlā*, "Quickly adorn her" (Kurd.). [According to my Amadiya informant, the words of the song are: *Dim khaimula, dim khaimūla / Tolē randē, dim khaimūla*, "Adorn her, adorn her / she is beautiful and pleasant, adorn her.] *Kā'ke* and *yipraḥ* are served to the women at the river.

Singing songs, they bring the bride home completely veiled. The musicians go to meet them; and the people stand in front of their houses, pelting the bride with nuts, sweets, and wheat.[29]

As soon as the bride has entered the house and seated herself, a small boy is set on her knee with the words *Ishalla brōna qamāya hawēlakh hāwe urza* ["God grant that the first child you will have should be a male," or *Ishalla ilāha takhīrakh bkha urza*, "God grant that God remember you with a male," A.].

In the interval between the bath of the bride and that of the bridegroom, the *ketubba* [Heb., marriage contract] is written (Z., A.).

The bride's trousseau is piled in one corner of the room; for on Sunday morning, the *ḥakham*, several notables, and two men brought by the *ḥatan* [bridegroom] come to estimate the value of the trousseau and enter it in the *ketubba*, which has been prepared beforehand. Every piece is separately appraised and entered. It often happens that such violent quarrels arise between the two fathers at the valuation that the bridegroom asks the *ḥakham* to write the *ketubba* in accordance with his own valuation (Z. and A.).

The Bridegroom's Bath (*Khiyāpit Khitna*)

In Zakho, after the valuation, the *shammash* invites the young men to the bridegroom's house, where they dance and sing and make *shabāshe*. It was formerly the custom for about ten of the youths to go through the town toward midday with the musicians to collect food for the *pashīvit khitna* [lit., "after the groom's supper," A.]. Lately, this has been discontinued. Instead, about one hundred families living in the neighborhood send in the food. The dinner is a jolly affair (Z.).

After the dinner, an old man is sent with a cauldron and some wood to heat the water at the river for the bridegroom's bath. In a great procession, joined by everyone who can spare the time and escorted by the musicians, the bridegroom is led to the river. The father, if he is wealthy, buys the young men high, white felt caps (*kusīsa*, pl. *kusyāsa*; Kurd. *kūmik* [i.e., hat][30] like those worn by the Nestorians.

Even the non-Jews come to see the bridegroom's bath at the river. Several boys with bundles on their heads, *buqchit did khitna* [the bundle of clothing of the bridegroom], containing the bridegroom's clothes, bring up the rear of the procession.

When the boys with the bundles reach the river bank, first the women and then the young men dance *berīsa* [Z.; A. *khiga* or *khlula*, "a dance"] about them. The bridegroom's bath, like the henna-dyeing ceremony, is preceded by that of an unmarried prepuberty boy who still has both his parents. The bridegroom's bath lasts about an hour and is accompanied by the singing of special songs. After the bath, the bridegroom immerses himself three times in the river. Some youths, who want to show their prowess, immerse themselves six or seven times, till the people call to them *Gemāle, Gemāle*, "Stop!"

After the immersion, the bridegroom is dressed at the river's edge in his wedding clothes.[31] Into his belt he sticks a dagger (*khanjar*), which he borrows from the Kurds. The dagger serves not only to protect him from the evil eye but also to frighten the bride if she should, perchance, conduct herself with too much reserve. To his turban cloth (*kasrawan* [a silken kerchief, with colored embroideries, which is wound around the hat] are fastened protective charms against sorcery and the evil eye—for example, a band (*tīta*), to which little chains with silver scorpions, frogs, green stones, and buttons made of "fish bone" are attached. Besides all this, the bridegroom carries a very long pipe (*basika*),[32] which he must smoke at the river (also a Kurdistan custom).

The bridegroom is led home by two of the most important men of the town. Before and behind him, the people, both men and women, dance the *deranga*.

The Bridegroom's Bath in Amadiya

In Amadiya, the bridegroom rides to the river, escorted by *dola wezirne* [drum and flute]. The Muslims who join the procession fire their guns. The bridegroom is bathed on the river bank, and his old clothes are bestowed upon the man who bathes him. Then he is immersed in the river three times, sprinkled with rosewater, and dressed in his wedding garments. The song *Zawāye bena rubāri* (Bring the bridegroom to the riverbank is sung while he is being dressed [or else *Zawāye bena sershoyi—Ḥame mem dawo*, "Lead the bridegroom to the place of bathing, my Ḥame (a name), your mother (is calling you)]. He is then taken to the *bē ḥazāne*, [where he is dressed. The scribe is called in and he draws a large ט on [the groom's] forehead in black ink]. Roses are stuck into his headdress and his belt, and he is repeatedly doused with rosewater. [The groom leaves his shirt open at the neck, and it remains open until the marriage is consummated. If he has been able to consummate the marriage, he closes the neck of his shirt; if not, he leaves it open.

When the groom has finished dressing, he remains seated in his place, and many young men surround him. Every one of them has brought with him something to eat or drink—a bottle of wine or spirits, *maza*, or the like. The two *shushbīnīm* sit one on each side of the groom, and the whole company sings songs in his honor. So they spend the time between 3:00 p.m. and about 6:00 when they all set out to accompany the groom to the house of the bride's father, where the *sheva' berakhot* will take place (A.)].

Dressing the Bride

While the bridegroom is in his bath, the bride is being dressed in her wedding clothes. Only a few of her friends are with her, since the women and girls are all at the river watching the ceremonies attendant on the dressing of the bridegroom.

The girls sing *narīke* as they dress the bride. [The words are *Nārinē hai narē*, "The bride is adorned, the bride is adorned," Kurd.]. There are, however, no special ceremonies at the dressing and little joy; for the sadness of parting hangs over the women of the bride's family. The bride and her mother weep loudly, and it is considered fitting for the other women and girls who are present to weep also.

The Bride's Costume*

[The most important part of the bride's costume is not her clothing but the jewelry and adornment. Into her hair are plaited silver chains with little silver bells attached to them, which tinkle whenever she moves her head. In every braid she wears one such chain with silver bells. These chains are called *gadlē*. On her head the bride wears a *kuchma*, a head-kerchief, of wool embroidered with different patterns. The *kuchma* is shaped like a bull's leg (i.e., it is pointed on top);

*[Brauer intended to write this section, as well as the following one, on the bridegroom's costume, but he died before he could write them. The information as given here was supplied by Ḥakham 'Alwān Avidani from Amadiya and is presented in his own words. R.P.]

and from it down the sides of the bride's face, hang golden or silver ornaments, which fall upon her breast. These ornaments are called *shushlatha*.

Over the *kuchma* the bride wears a thin red veil (*khipo*), which covers also her face. In her ears she wears earrings (*marwade*)—of gold if she is rich or, if she is poor, of silver.

In the bride's nose a nose ring (*khezemta*) of gold is hung through a hole in one of her nostrils. Around her neck is a necklace (*qardana*)—of gold if she is rich, else of silver. In addition to this, she wears around her neck a broad necklace of red corals with a round golden plate hanging from it. This necklace is called *toqed kisnē*, "coral necklace," while the golden plate is called *dehwa urwa*, "big gold." From her right should across to the left hip hangs a silver chain with a silver plate attached to it. This plate is a talisman, upon which are inscribed Hebrew words and signs of apotropaic import, like the names Shaddai and Ṣevaot; the prayer beginning with the words *Ana bekhoaḥ*; the first letters of each word of the Psalm beginning *Shir hama'aloth essa 'enay*; the word *argaman*, whose letters are obtained from the initial letters of the names of the angels Uriel, Raphael, Gabriel, Michael, and Nuriel. This plate, called Shem Shaddai, is a present given to the bride by the groom. The bride's hands are adorned with gold and silver bracelets, *shubrasa*. On her fingers are numerous rings of gold, *isiqyasa* (sg. *isiqsa*); the wedding ring, however, must be made of silver. Round her ankles the bride wears anklets (*khalkhāle*).

On the upper part of her body the bride wears a thin white blouse, *sudret kitan*, "cotton blouse." Over this she wears a *yelaqa*, "bodice," of colored silk, and over this a long coat, *kurtak* or *fistana*. The rich make this coat out of silk or out of *kalabdun*, that is, a cloth made of a thread of silver and wool (or flax) spun together. Over this long coat she wears a short mantle, *qutked kalabdun*, a *kalabdun* mantle. Over the *kurtak* or *fistāna* she wears a linen girdle, *kināra*, which closes in front with a *kamar*—two silver plates. The bride wears ordinary linen drawers, *sharwala*, with embroidered stockings, *gurwe chakme*, and shoes. In Amadiya, the shoes are either *kundere* (leather), *pelāwe* (of red leather, a kind of slippers), or *chakme* (high shoes of red leather).]

The Bridegroom's Costume

[As against the bride, who is decorated all over with jewelry, the groom wears no adornment of any kind. Nor do his clothes differ from the usual everyday or feast day clothing of the young men. On his head he wears the *khusisa*, a hat, or *jamadāni*, a headgear of blue cloth, or *poshia*, a headgear of silk. On his body he wears a shirt of *kitan* (cotton) and trousers, *mkhizna*, of white cloth. Over his shirt he wears the *ṭallith z'ora* (the small *ṭallith*, the traditional square cloth with fringes at its four corners), and over that the *yelaqa* (bodice). Over this, again, he wears trousers and a coat *shalla shapuksa*. Round his waist he wears the *shāla turma* ("shawl from Turma"—a town in Persia where these shawls are made and exported to Kurdistan, A.)]

The Procession to the Bride's House

In the villages where the bridegroom is bathed in the bathhouse (S., Arbil, and Ushnu), the procession returns to the bridegroom's home, so that he may be led from there to the bride's house. This differs from the practice in the localities where the bath takes place at the river; for the river is actually a "place of worship," and the bridegroom is led directly from the river to the bride's house.

In Zakho, when the bridegroom passes through the town on his way to the bride's house, the roofs are filled with people and the women raise their *klīlīlī*. A man goes before the procession calling out, *Bahtātha chukha lā'āzil chukha lā khāyit*, "Women, none is to spin, none is to sew!" The women must then cease spinning—an occupation which Kurdish women pursue whether standing, sitting, or walking—nor may they engage in any kind of needlework or similar task (also A.); for this, it is believed, may cast a spell upon the bridegroom.

If the procession passes the house of a relative or friend, the woman of the house steps out of the door carrying a bowl of wheat, which she strews over the bridegroom's head, then breaks a pitcher of it in front of him. At this the people cry (in Hebrew), "The pitcher broke, but we are saved" (*Hakad nishbar w'anaḥnu nimlaṭnu*). Also, when the bridegroom crosses the threshold of the bride's house, a woman throws wheat over him and breaks a pitcher.

In Amadiya, as we have seen, the bridegroom is led directly from the river to the *bē ḥazāne*. There, the men and youths are sitting at *sherāthit qam khitna*, regaling themselves with arrack and *maza*. A number of youths and maidens proceed meanwhile to the bridegroom's house to fetch the *sham'it khitna* [the bridegroom's candle], which the *shammash* provides for the wedding. This is a large, thick wax candle, mounted on a cake of wax. Round the large candle are seven smaller candles, representing the seven benedictions. Every girl gets a small colored candle to carry in the bridal procession.

Everyone who can walk joins the procession. The aged, the disabled, and others who cannot go along fill the roofs of the houses that the procession must pass. In the van of the procession are dancers, who dance with sword and shield. Several old men dance wildly with *gōpāle* (sticks). A girl from his household walks before the bridegroom, carrying a censer. [The incense is a kind of glue, *bukharē*, made from the fruit of certain trees. It smokes considerably when it burns, emitting a pleasant odor. This smoke is said to frighten away evil spirits; that is, it protects the groom.] The *qerivāna raste* also walks before him with large *sham'e*. The *qerivāna chape* follows the bridegroom. He grasps the bridegroom's garment to prevent anyone's passing between them; for if this should happen, a spell might be cast upon the bridegroom.

The bridegroom is surrounded by girls carrying lighted candles and singing. One of the songs runs thus:

pēkēlē [pleṭlē] seherā yā bahūra
[lē bilhāya el sipsit ṭura]

There rose the moon, the shining
[It shines on the (top) of the mountain.]

In Sinne, the bridegroom is led in festive procession from his house to the house of the bride. The people carry wooden torches and candles and lead the horse that is to bear the bride to the bridegroom's house (see p. 134). The horse—borrowed from another Jew—is splendidly decked out: gaily colored cloths form his caparison, and gaily colored paper is braided into his mane and tail. On either side of the bridegroom walk the two *shushbīnīm*, with lanterns in their hands.

Arrival of the Procession; *Berakhta*

In Zakho the *berakhta*, "blessing" (i.e., the seven benedictions) takes place in the bride's house, the bridegroom being led thither. After sundown, following the seven benedictions, the bride is brought to the bridegroom's house. The usage in Amadiya and in Arbil is the same, but there is no uniformity in this respect throughout Kurdistan. In Ushnu the seven benedictions are said in the bride's house or in that of the bridegroom after the bride has been brought there. If it is feared that a spell may be cast upon the bride, the seven benedictions are recited at her house,[33] in secret, immediately after her bath. Otherwise, the ceremony may be performed either in the bride's house or in that of the bridegroom. In Sinne, on the other hand, the ceremony is always performed after the bride has been brought to the bridegroom's home. The reasons for this change in the custom are not clear.

There is just as little uniformity in regard to the day of the week on which the wedding is solemnized. In Zakho the *berakhta* comes on Sunday evening. The case is the same in Arbil. In Amadiya, the *barokhe* [blessing] always comes on Wednesday evening; in Sinne[34] and Ushnu (i.e., the districts under Persian influence), on Thursday evening; and in Dehok, on Friday evening.

As soon as the bridegroom enters the house, a woman breaks a pitcher and throws wheat over him (Z.) or he is pelted with nuts (A.).

In Zakho the ceremony takes place in the *sūpa*, in summer in the *birbanke* (see p. 78). Here it is not customary to spread out a cloth in front of, or over, the bride as *ḥuppa*, "bridal canopy." Candles are distributed among those present and are lighted at the time of the *berakhta*. The father gets a particularly large candle.

Before the seven benedictions, the *ḥakham* reads the *ketubba*. When he reads out the final amount, those present exclaim, *Illāha mā'amire bēt bābakh*, "God build up your (i.e., the bride's) father's house."

The ceremony of the seven benedictions is performed in one corner of the room. The bridegroom stands before the veiled bride and places his right foot on her left foot. This symbolizes the subjections of the wife.[35] After the benedictions the bridegroom crushes a pitcher with his foot.

In Amadiya, a cloth (*perdit kālo*) is spread out in front of the bride. During the reading of the *ketubba*, the *ḥakham* holds one end of the document and the bridal couple hold the two corners of the other end, the bride stretching her hand through the curtain. When the *ḥakham* reaches the passage *m'qara'e umṭalṭ'le*, those present stamp their feet and repeat the words.

In the Kurdish *ketubba* there are several dots indicating the moment for the *qinyan* [acquisition]. At this point the *ḥakham* and the bridegroom take hold of a silken cloth and make the *qinyan*.

If the bridegroom has already given the ring to the bride at the *birkat ērūsīn* [blessing of betrothal], the coemptio through the *p'rūṭa* (coin) now follows. The *p'rūṭa* is first dipped in wine, which the bridegroom and the bride then drink. Here, too, the bride is shown unveiled to the bridegroom and the two witnesses, so that they may be convinced that she is the genuine bride.

After the seven benedictions everyone kisses the bridegroom on the head and the *ḥakham* sings

hai bū m'bārak hai bū m'bārak
zawāwo beglē m'bārak

O, may he be blessed [repeat]
The bridegroom blessed for the bride. (Kurd.)

Dangers of the Seven Benedictions

The bridal couple are in special danger during the seven benedictions. The dyeing, the amulets, the bath—all these are intended not only to strengthen the bridal couple and prepare them for the new state upon which they are entering but also to protect them against the evil influences to which they are particularly exposed during this transition period.

Before the seven benedictions, the *ḥakham* warns the assembled guests not to cast a spell upon the bridal couple: *Yā rabotay līt reshūt lawet awid ziyāna ibbid irkhē katē ilēsa katē khetēsa gad gāna āhū qāṭil chūkha lā awid kha chūla zidāna min gāna wele ketība gō tōra dēni: lo yaḥavol reḥayim varakhev ki nefesh hu ḥovel,* "Gentlemen, there is no permission for him who works mischief to the millstones (of which) one (is) above and the other below. It is as if he were killing a living soul. Let no one do anything else than for himself. It is written in the Torah, "No man shall take the upper or the lower millstone to pledge: for he taketh a man's life to pledge" (Deut. 24:61).*

[Another version of this warning (from Amadiya) is *Rabotay, ktīva lē batōra dēni m'qodeshta lā awid ziyāna ib irkhē katē ilēsa ukatē ktēsa gad dyana awā qatel,* "Gentlemen, it is written in our Holy Bible, he shall do no damage to the millstones (of which) one (is) above and the other below, because it is as if he were killing a living soul." The man who arranges the wedding ceremony then says, *Līt reshuth min midrash ilēl min midrash iltekh awed kha shula zodāna min ganē,* "There is no permission from the upper council and from the lower council, that he do an act surpassing his strength"—a euphemism for sorcery.]

---

*[This passage was interpreted already by the Jerusalem Targum, etc., as referring to those who "bind" the bridegroom (by magical means), thus making it impossible for him to approach his bride. See also Ibn Ezra's comments ad Deut. 24:10, and my *Man and Earth*, vol. 1, pp. 196–97].

A spell may be cast upon the bridal pair during the seven benedictions by tying knots in a string while repeating certain magic formulas. The bridegroom protects himself against such spells by having his father or a relative tie a countercharm at the same time. This countercharm is untied when the bridegroom goes into the bridal chamber (Zakho, Ushnu). We have already met with such a knotted amulet in connection with the bride's bath at Amadiya. [In Amadiya, before the seven benedictions, the man who conducts the wedding is approached and is told, "We want to tie the bride and groom now." A silver or gold ring is brought, three or five silk threads of various colors, and two long hairs from the bride's head. The man who conducts the wedding then ties the threads and hair to the ring with seven knots, pronouncing over each knot the name of an angel. He also recites Psalm 20. The ring with the knots is then given to the groom. After the meal, the groom unties one knot, the bride unties the next, and so on until all the knots are untied. Then the groom takes off his shoes and the consummation of the marriage takes place.

In Amadiya, too, the groom may also be warned to take off one of his shoes before the seven benedictions and then, while these are being recited, to insert his foot slowly into the shoe, so that by the time the benedictions are over his foot should already be inside his shoe. In order that the groom should have control over his wife, he puts his right foot on the left foot of the bride as she stands next to him; and so he stands during the seven benedictions. This the groom can do only if the bride is ritually pure (i.e., not disabled by menstruation), for otherwise he must not touch her.]

It is also possible to bewitch the bridal couple by slowly closing a pocket knife (A. and Ushnu). In order to protect the bridegroom, four powerful young men are appointed as guards, whose duty it is to see that no sorcery is going on. They must also, for instance, take care that no one is smoking; for this may cause the bride to become barren (A.). The bridegroom may further protect himself by closing one finger during each of the seven benedictions (A.).

The hour of the seven benedictions is, however, a beneficient, as well as a dangerous, hour. For this reason, barren women, especially the ***kepista*** or ***kebista*** (see p. 159), are often placed beside the bride (A.).

In Amadiya the bride is taken to the bridegroom's home directly after the seven benedictions. In Zakho, on the other hand, the bridal pair at once sit down together to a meal, which serves to break their fast. Chicken is set before them, but they eat of it sparingly.

Taking the Bride to the Bridegroom's Home: *Shenōyit Kālo*

After the seven benedictions the men get up to escort the bridegroom back to his house. The young men and the women stay behind to take part in the festive procession, accompanied with music, in which the bride is to be conducted to her future home. No very great ceremonial attends the return of the bridegroom to his house. He is brought back *chape būke* [a roundabout way]. Guns are fired by those taking part in the procession, the children throw "caps," and the men sing the *yigdal* hymn (Israel Davidson, *Thesaurus of Medieval Hebrew Poetry*, p. 195). In the house the men recite the *minḥa* and *ma'ariv* prayers (Z.). The usage differs in Arbil. Here, the evening prayer takes place in the synagogue, to which the men repair with the bridegroom after leaving the house of the bride.

The bridegroom goes on foot, but the bride is usually conducted to the bridegroom's house mounted on a horse (Z., D., A., S., and Ushnu). In Arbil the bride, too, goes on foot, her father and mother leading her by the hand.

The horse for the bride is generally provided by the aga as a token of esteem for the Jews. The aga also provides a servant to hold the horse (Z., D., A., and Ushnu). The horse is splendidly caparisoned. Care is taken to procure a mare (Z. and A. *meḥine*); and the color is also important, brown being preferred (A.), black rejected (Ushnu).

The bride's people kiss her with tears. Their hearts are heavy at the parting, the more so as her close relatives are not allowed to accompany her to the bridegroom's house, a proceeding that would be regarded as improper. When the people come to take the bride out to the horse, the bride's uncle gets up and locks the door. On being asked what he wants, he demands *pishta dare* (Kurd.)[36] "behind-the-door." After considerable bickering, which sometimes degenerates into serious quarrels, he lets himself be induced (on payment of several *mejidi* by the bridegroom's relations) to open the door (Z.).

This custom of *pishta dare* obtains in Amadiya also, only here it is usually the water carrier (*saqāye*) who locks the door. In Sinne it is the *shammash* of the synagogue who opens the door—but only after payment of a proper sum.[37] The veiled bride is then taken out and mounted on the horse, which is led by relatives of the bridegroom. They keep hold of the bride because the music of the *muṭurbāye* or the noise of the crowd may easily cause the horse to shy. Candles or torches are carried in the procession.

The custom of *pishta dare* is practiced by the Kurds also. For example, at the marriage of an aga's daughter, his shepherd or his stableman locks the door and says, *Pishta dere min dewēt*, "Behind-the-door I demand."

In Amadiya the bride-price (*naqda*) is carried in the procession in the form of the trousseau. Powerful youths bear the *buqchit kālo* on their heads. This contains the bride's dresses and the like, wrapped in "cloths of a thousand patches." Others carry the pillows, the chest, the mirror, and so on. Bowls of food and fruit are also taken along; and one young man holds the bride's drinking cup (*zivirtit kālo*), over which is a special crocheted cover (*pedōmit zivirtit kālo*).[38]

[According to my informant, the bride is led to the groom's house on horseback only in winter, when walking through the streets is difficult. If no horse is available, one of the men of the bride's family carries her on his back. In summer the bride goes on foot. During the procession the women sing

har sēlan w'har musyālan
b'sēpē shlikhē m'pulṭālan
ul'flān khitna m'burkhālan

We have come already, we have brought already,
With drawn swords we have taken her out
And to this groom we have blessed her.

They also sing a Hebrew song:

Emet atta ḥatanēnu
K'mo sahar b'tokhēnu
Ukh'melekh atta l'fanēnu
B'khallatkha m'od tismaḥ
B'rov mamon uv'rov qemaḥ
V'tizke laḥazot ṣemaḥ
B'yamekha uv'yamēnu

Truly you are our groom,
Like a moon amongst us,
Like a king are you before us,
May our God bless you.
In your bride may you be most happy.
With plentiful money and plentiful flour,
And may you live to see Ṣemaḥ (the Messiah)
In your days and in our days.

This song is also sung on the Sabbath during the wedding festivities, when the groom is called up to the Torah in the synagogue.]

The bride's procession does not take the direct road but moves in a round about way toward the bridegroom's house. All along its way the women stand on the roofs and raise their *klīlīlī*, as in the case of the bridegroom's procession. Women relatives of the bridal couple step out of their houses, pelt the bride and her attendants with wheat and nuts, and break a drinking cup in front of the mare on which she is riding. Her mother-in-law does the same when she reaches the bridegroom's house; and as she enters, her father-in-law pelts her with small nuts, which the children scramble to pick up (Z., likewise A.).

In Sinne, also, the bride's parents and relatives remain behind, weeping. The bride, covered with a red cloth (*diwākh*) and wearing a red *shāl* about her hips as *siman ṭov* [good luck charm], is set on the horse and held on either side by an old man from the families of the bride and groom. Here, however, the bridegroom is led in front of the bride. When they reach the houses of relatives, the latter bring out a mirror, a basin of water, sherbet (lemonade), and arrack. The bridegroom (but not the veiled bride) looks into the mirror and the basin of water, while the bystanders say *Barūkh haṭov wehamēṭiv*, "Blessed be the Good and the Doer of good." Then sherbet and arrack are drunk, and the bridal couple is sprinkled with rosewater (*gūlab*). Rich families also bring golden ornaments and hang them (not as a gift but as a loan) on the horse.

The moment when the bride crosses the threshold of the bridegroom's house, which is thenceforth to be her home, is richly endowed with special customs; for it is a *moment de passage*. Some of these usages may not belong to Arnold van Gennep's *rites de passage*.

The practice of showering the bride with wheat is very general throughout Kurdistan. In Ushnu the bride is also doused with water. As the bride enters the house, the bridegroom, too, greets her by pelting her with things that are clearly symbols of fecundity. In Arbil, the bridegroom and several of his friends climb to the roof of the house, from which the bridegroom throws wheat and barleycorn upon the bride and the other young men shower her with raisins, almonds, and sweets. In Ushnu, the bridegroom likewise climbs to the roof; but he throws down apples, trying, if possible, to hit his bride on the head.

In Amadiya, as the bridegroom's mother showers her daughter-in-law with wheat, she says

shenōyakh berīkha
ibbid brōne ūbenāta
ḥazyat kalatakh
duchminakh duchmin gōrakh
napli khe eqlāthakh

Your coming here be blessed
In the midst of sons and daughters
May you see your daughter-in-law.
Your foes and your husband's foes
Shall fall beneath your feet.

The mother-in-law then takes a loaf of bread, sprinkles salt and wheat on it, and describes three circles with it around the horse's head, after which she feeds the bread to the horse. When the bride has been lifted off the horse, a boy mounts it and rises three times up and down the street at a quick trot.

In Sinne, the mother-in-law dances before the bride as the latter crosses the threshold. While she dances, she holds over the bride's head a bowl (*qāwa sīnī*), in the midst of which stands a candle with seven wicks, surrounded by little bowls of wheat, candy, honey, and the like, and also small, lighted wax candles. The large central candle burns seven days and seven nights in the bridal chamber. The honey is spread over the bride's feet so that she may be blessed and "sweet."

The Bridal Chamber

In the bridegroom's house, the bridal chamber (Arbil and Ushnu *ḥuppa*, S. *parda*, A. and Z. *gnūne*)[39] is prepared for the bride and groom. In Sinne, the *parda* consists of one piece of cloth that partitions off a section of the room. In Amadiya, the *gnūne* is made by the *shammash* of the synagogue out of four pieces of cloth (*sitre*) belonging to the synagogue. The four curtains are fastened to the ceiling with ropes, so that they form a sort of room. The *gnūne* is decked out with carpets and cushions. The bride is led into the chamber, and the female relatives of the bridegroom come to congratulate her. After them, the men enter the *gnūne* and congratulate her with the words, *Berikhta alpa khēre khazētun bigdāde*, "Blessed one, a thousand benefactors may you see together."

A small child is brought in and seated on the bride's lap. She presents him with some of the money that her father gave her at parting. Instead of one child, often, several children are brought in and placed on her lap, one after the other. This is done so that she may be blessed with children.

The same custom obtains in Amadiya. A boy of three or four is put in the bride's lap. She hugs and kisses him, then dismisses him with a gift of money.[40]

Food brought from her father's house is set before the bride. This *sapoyit kālo* must not fail to include some rice and a chicken. The relatives and the young men stand around the bride; and whenever she puts a bit into her mouth, they try to snatch it away—or if it falls to the floor, everyone grabs at it, for eating this bit of food is looked upon as *segūla*.[41] This function gives occasion for much jesting.

The Wedding Feast

During the *sapōyit kālo*, the bridegroom and all those who are invited to the *se'odat khitna* sit in the *sūpa*. Each of the relatives has the *sīnīya rēsh khitna* (chicken with rice) brought from home for this meal. In former times, it was customary for the young men to go out with the musicians and collect the *sīnīya* from the houses of the relatives. The cooking is, however, done in the bridegroom's house for the notables and *ḥakhamin* who have been invited and for the poor.

After the washing of hands and the benediction, the dish with the best chicken is set before the bridegroom. Then the bowls and spoons are distributed among the guests, and the *ḥakham* lifts his spoon, saying, *Ya jemā'a bekhabhod*, "O gentlemen, with deference." When the bridegroom begins to eat, the *sapōyit khitna* follows; and everyone snatches the bits of food from his mouth.

During the meal, some food is sent to the house of the bride, where the family are sitting like mourners, weeping and wailing. The bridegroom's father and uncle repair thither for a while in order to eat with the disconsolate family and cheer them up by telling stories. Then they return to the bridegroom's house to finish their meal.

The *ḥakham* again recites the seven benedictions, and a beaker of wine is sent in to the bride. Then everyone rises with the bridegroom; and, at a sign from the *ḥakhamin*, the singing and dancing in his honor begin. This continues about half an hour, after which, still dancing, and singing the *pizmon* called *Simḥū nā, simḥū nā*,[42] the men bring the bridegroom to the bride in the *gnūne*.

The *Yiḥud*

The bride, on hearing the singing, lowers her *izar*, the large veil covering both head and face, and rises to receive the bridegroom. The bridegroom enters and asks her for a cup of water. When she gives it to him, he lets it drop. This signifies that he will rule over her. Clever parents tell their daughter about this custom; and in that case, she does not hand the glass of water to the bridegroom but sets it down in front of him [so that he should not be able to drop it].

Thereupon, everyone leaves the room except the bridal couple. Outside the door, which the bridegroom locks, an old man waits and often, also, an old woman from the bride's family, who in given cases—when, for example, the bridegroom slanders the bride—is there to protect her.

The bridal pair always lies on the floor, never on a bedstead. When the marriage is consummated, the bridegroom opens the door, in order to let the people see the blood-stained cloth. Women from the bride's family also appear; for they must be able to act as witnesses should the bridegroom later, perchance, in moment of anger, cast suspicion on the bride.

The women raise their *klīlīlī*, and the musicians arrive. The music in the night apprises the town of the fact that the marriage has been consummated and the bride found to be a virgin. The people get up from their beds and go to the house of the bridal pair, saying, "He has become a bridegroom." One of the bride's relatives brings the blood-stained cloth to her father's house (Z.).

The usages are similar in Amadiya. The bride is led into the *gnūne*, and the bridegroom enters at the same time. On either side of the bridegroom sit the *qerivāne*, while at the side of the bride sits the *yimmat buke*, who is now called *sar sepīye*, "white head." Beside these, there are only a few old and respected people in the *gnūne*. They are served with food from the bride's house. The bride, being veiled, is often fed by the *sar sepīye*.

A boy of three or four is brought in and placed on the bride's lap. She hugs and kisses him. Then the guests leave the *gnūne*. [If anyone is slow to leave he is told, *plot*! "Get out!"] The *shushbīn* requests the bridegroom to unveil the bride: *Glī pātit kālo*, "Uncover the face of the bride." When the bridegroom lifts the *ḥuppit kālo*, he must present the bride with a piece of jewelry. Thereupon, the *qerivāne* and the *sar sepīye* also leave the *gnūne*.

To signify that the marriage has been consummated, the bridegroom says to the bride in a loud voice: "Bring me some water!" whereupon the *qerivāne* and the *sar sepīye* reenter the *gnūne*. The *sar sepīye* exhibits the cloth with the signs of virginity, and the bride is congratulated with the words *Pāsit bābakh jummakh khuwarta*, "The face of your father and your mother became white (lighted up)."[43]

The custom of *pishle khitna* obtains in Amadiya also. After the consummation, the bridal pair may fasten the button of their garments, which had previously been left undone for magic reasons.

[The following morning, the groom is asked by his friends, "*Find* or *found*," being a reference to "I *find* woman bitterer than death" (Eccles. 7:26) and "He who has *found* a woman has *found* goodness" (Prov. 18:22), according to the ancient talmudic tradition. Among the Jews of Amadiya, however, this question is a way of inquiring whether the groom has found the bride a virgin or not.]

In Sinne, the bride and groom are left along in the *parda*, and they eat their first meal together before their marriage has been consummated. An old woman, *pa khasu*, "in place of the mother-in-law,"[44] waits outside. After the consummation, the bridegroom summons the old woman and shows her the cloth. She takes it and, accompanied by the *shushbīnīm* and several young men, brings it to the bride's parents. The old woman and her companions then demand a present from the parents and refuse to leave until they have received a few chickens. In Sinne, no meal follows the seven benedictions.

In Arbil, a cock and a hen are brought from the home of the bride's parents. These are for the meal which the bridal couple eat together in the *ḥuppa*. The bride and the groom first eat the heads of the hen and of the cock respectively, then the rest of the body. This serves as *kappara*, "expiation," for the bridal pair. The bridegroom must leave the *ḥuppa* directly after the consummation. The people who are awaiting him in the courtyard receive him with benediction and the *klīlīlī*. An old woman from the bride's family, called *barbūk* (Kurd),[45] takes the cloth with the signs of virginity and shows it first to the bridegroom's family, then to the family of the bride.

The Seven Feast Days

The seven benedictions are followed by the seven feast days (*sho'a yomāthit khitna*). During this week of celebration, the bridal pair remains in the *gnūne*'; but the bride and the groom must sit apart because the bride is unclean. The bridegroom must take nothing from the hand of his bride and must not cohabit with her. It is therefore customary to put a small girl between the bride and groom at night to guard them from transgressions (Z.). The bride must not step outside the house during these eight days except in the company of a girl. When the bridegroom enters or leaves the room, the bride must rise. If the bridegroom has been away, a boy is usually sent ahead to announce his return.

The bridal couple are never left alone in the *gnūne*. One of the *qerivāne*, neither of whom goes to his work during this week, always keeps them company. Moreover, they have a steady stream of visitors. Throughout the week, the women and girls come in the morning, the men in the evening. No one may smoke in the *gnūne* or cut anything. In the whole house, the woman may not spin. Evidently the fear of the bridal couple's falling under a spell has not subsided.

Every morning, food for about twenty persons is sent in from the bride's house. This intended for the *qerivāne* and for the close relatives (Z., S., and Arbil). In the evening, on the other hand, part of the food—that served to the notables—is furnished by the bridegroom. However, most of the guests bring their *sīnīya* along.

Even a youth who does not ordinarily go to the synagogue on weekdays will not, as a bridegroom, miss a service during this week. Morning and evening, the *shushbīnīm* bring the bridegroom in procession, with song—and often with *dūla* [or *dola*] and *zirne*—to the synagogue. Part of the community assembles beforehand at the bridegroom's house in order to join the procession. In front of the house, they dance the *ḥigga*. Children bearing candles also take part in the procession in Arbil.[46]

Custom prescribes a very definite order in the rounds of visits paid during this week.[47]

On Thursday morning after the seven benedictions and the *pishle khitna* night, the bridegroom is led in an especially festive procession to the synagogue. Young men precede him, dancing the sword dance. Muslim Kurds also join the procession. After the service, the bridegroom is brought to the house of the *qeribhāna raste* for the *helūla*, "wedding feast," which the *qeribhāna raste* has already had prepared for the bridegroom in the night following his confirmation of the successful consummation of the marriage. The *helūla* now takes place if the marriage was consummated on the first night. When the dinner is over, the bridegroom is escorted home.

On Thursday evening, *sapōyit khitna*,[48] the first evening after the seven benedictions, the whole community assembles at the house of the bridegroom, if he is of a rich family, to dance and sing. Everyone brings his *sīnīya* of food along and offers some of it to the bridegroom, saying, *Besiman ṭov naqsha brōne ubbanāta*, "With good omen, may you dye [i.e., with henna] sons and daughters." And when the women give *sapoya* to the bridegroom's mother, they say, *Ēnakh behūre khazyat newaqīnakh*, "May your shining eye see your grandchildren."

On Friday morning, the left *shushbīn*, *qerivāna chape*, invites the bridegroom to his house as did the right *shushbīn* on the previous day. The women, in the meantime, have their hands full preparing the food for the Sabbath, when the whole community comes as the bridegroom's guests.

On this Sabbath, the posts of honor are given to the bridegroom. He recites the morning prayer, takes out the Torah, and puts it on the *teva*, while the congregation sings a *pizmon*. The bridegroom, along with the other wedding guests, is called to the reading of the Torah as "third." When he steps up to the Torah, the congregation intones another *pizmon*. The bridegroom returns the scroll to the Hēkhal [Ark]. He also recites the *musaf* prayer. Since *musaf* may be said only by a married man, the congregation wishes to bestow this honor at once upon the newly wedded youth. [In Amadiya they also sing the *pizmon* called *Atta hu y'didi, hadari hodi*.][49]

After the service the bridegroom is escorted with music to the *bē ḥazāne*, where the *ḥavērim*, the members of the *Ḥevra Qaddisha* [lit. "holy society," charity organization taking care of burials, etc.] of the Amadiya Jews (see p. 191) are assembled for their regular Sabbath morning meeting. The bridegroom presents them with a bottle of arrack, and a second bottle is provided out of the synagogue supplies in honor of the bridegroom. The two bottles are called *dake*.

After the bridegroom has returned from his visit to the *ḥavērim*, men and women, bringing their food, gather at the home of the bridal couple. There they celebrate in their characteristic manner. The men sit at arrack and *maza* and sing their songs, most of them Kurdish. The women dance *ḥigga* with the bride and the men with the bridegroom. These activities continue until the *drūsh* and are resumed after the *drūsh*.

Ṣubaḥīya Dekhitna (Breakfast of the Bridegroom)

Scarcely is Shabbat over before the bridegroom's mother must begin planning the preparation of the food for the next morning. The other women are again invited to help, and some of them who have no small children to care for stay and work until morning.

For the *ṣubaḥīya dekhitna*[50] "the bridegroom's morning meal," the whole community assembles at the bridegroom's house. The bride's parents are also invited. This is the first time that they and their people appear at the bridegroom's house, for they must not take part in the meals that are given after the seven benedictions.

The function begins with *feṭarta*, the early breakfast, which opens with three glasses of arrack. After *feṭarta*, the guests leave, only the relatives of the bride remaining at the bridegroom's house. The guests soon return, however, each with a bottle of arrack and some fruit. Everyone kisses the bridegroom on the head and sets the fruit and arrack before the *qerivāna raste*. The company then proceeds to drink arrack and sing and dance till the bridegroom's breakfast is brought in.

The meal is followed by the game *yesirit khitna*, "the bridegroom's prisoner." The *shushbīnīm* direct the *shavīshe*, "servants," to tie up the guests, one after the other (with the exception of the bride's family), and to hang them up by the heels. No one is released until he has promised to pay a ransom in the form of money, arrack, or chickens. Large contributions are thus extorted from guests who are exceptionally wealthy. The guests then proceed, with the bridegroom, the bride, and the ransom, to the river, where it is customary to go for such excursions; and they eat, drink, dance, and sing in the usual manner until sunset. The custom in Zakho is similar.

In Ushnu, one of the most respective relatives of the bridegroom is appointed *diwambagī*, "bey of the diwan." Beside him stand two "policemen" (*eshkase*). The *diwambagī* gives the order, "Bring So-and-so"—whereupon the "policemen" lay the victim on the ground and beat him until he agrees to give what is demanded of him either in money or chickens. With the loot, the company goes with the bridegroom and the bride to a vineyard, there to dance and sing and afterward to consume the "loot."

In Sinne, the custom is called *sēr khelūla*, "wedding excursion." On the morning following the consummation, the bridegroom sits enthroned like a king (as they say) with his *shushbinim* beside him. The "policemen" whom we mentioned in connection with the dyeing ceremony (p. 124) are also in attendance. These "policemen" go to the marketplace, and so on; and thence they bring before the bridegroom a number of people, including women, on whom the bridegroom imposes a fine (*jor*). With the money thus collected, the merrymakers buy food and drink and at the end of the wedding week make an excursion with the bridal pair.

The custom is known to the Muslim Kurds, as well, and was perhaps even taken over from them. Among the Kurds, the bridegroom is looked upon as a king; and three of his comrades act as his officers (*chavishen*). At the *girtenū bardānā zawāi*, "capture and release by the bridegroom," the bridegroom orders the officers to seize So-and-so. He is seized and brought before the king, who imposes a certain tax upon him, such as a sheep, chickens, a thousand nuts, or something similar. Should So-and-so refuse, he is bound and beaten until he submits. Sometimes people are even dragged out of their beds and brought before the bridegroom.

The Kurdish bridegroom has also his "thieves" (*dizēn zawāi*), who set out on this night and steal chickens and even sheep and slaughter them on the spot. They break into shops and steal rice, sugar, and other products. If any of their victims is indignant, the bridegroom refunds the value of the stolen articles. This is how the Muslim Kurds make merry at the bridegroom's home the night before he enters the bridal chamber.

Let us now return to our description of the marriage customs of the Jews of Amadiya. From the river the people go back to the bridegroom's home. All the guests, with the exception of the bride's relatives, bring their *sīnīya* with them. They dance and sing. First the men eat, as usual; then they have the food sent in to the women, who have their feast out of what is left over from the men.

After the meal comes the observance with the *tavsine*. These are a special kind of large bowl, of which Amadiya possessed but three. They are used only at weddings, for the *ṣubaḥīya*, and at funeral feasts.

The *shawīshe* are told to "go and pass round the *tavsine* of the bridegroom and of the *qerivāne*." The bowls contain rice with chicken on top, that is, the customary festive food of the Kurds. On this occasion, however, the food has purely ritual significance. Each guest receives three spoonfuls of rice and a bit of chicken out of each *tavsin*. After the lavish entertainment of the day, these nine spoonfuls have only a symbolic meaning. They are eaten as *segūla*. When all the men have been served, the women likewise receive their nine spoonfuls each from the *tavsine*.

On Sunday evening comes the ceremony known as *ṣubaḥīya*. A *sīnīya*, in which a collection is to be made for the bride, is set before the bridegroom. He puts in a piece of jewelry as the first gift, and everyone follows suit with a piece of jewelry or a coin. After the men have made their contributions, the *sīnīya* is brought to the women.[51]

This custom of giving presents is based altogether on the principle of reciprocity. The idea is that what I give today, I get back tomorrow. Or, as their proverb goes, *Nāne mēra qāra*, "The bread of man is borrowed" (Kurd.).

In return for the gifts, the bride distributes the small articles she had prepared before the wedding.

This custom is found also among the Muslim Kurds and is called *sar ṣobaḥīya būke*, "the bride's first morning." On the morning after the consummation, the guests gather at the bridegroom's house. A *sīnīya* stands in the middle of the room, and about it sit the people. The guests rise, one after the other, in accordance with their standing in the community, and lay their coin in the *sīnīya*. In return, each donor receives one of the small presents that the bride has made. The large donors, however, also receive large articles of clothing.

There is no special closing feast. The *khitna* and the *kālo*, who are so termed throughout the whole first year, go to the *miqve* [ritual bath] and at once begin their regular daily life. The garments of the "king" and "queen" are laid away in trunks.

Nevertheless, this first year also has its special ceremonies. One of these is the first visit of the newly wedded couple to the bride's parents. In Amadiya, the *sar sepīye* comes on Friday evening after the seven feast days and takes the bride to her father's house. This visit is called *bē shōde* (Z. *bē shōze*).[52] The bride remains there until Sunday evening, while the bridegroom stays home. On Sunday evening, the *qerivāne* bring the bridegroom to his father-in-law's house, where they proceed to celebrate in the usual manner. When the young couple leaves, the father gives his daughter a piece of jewelry. Should she be dissatisfied with her present, she says, "I am not going"; and the father is obliged to add something else (similarly Z.).

The Muslim Kurds, likewise, have this custom. Eight days after the wedding, the bride goes to her father's house—hence the expression *Būke cho hashtia mal bābē*, "The bride went for the eighth to the house of her father" (Kurd.). The bridegroom visits her in the evening. He does not sleep there, however, but returns home. The bride stays with her parents three days and nights and receives a present on leaving. [This custom can be found also among the Jews of Amadiya, where the bride goes to her parents' house on the eighth day after her wedding. The saying is *Kālo zila il bē shodē*, "The bride is gone to the house of joy."]

On the fortieth night (*arbi*) after the seven benedictions, the newly wedded pair must go again to the *miqve*. In the evening the *qerivāne* come to them for the last time; and once again, as in the wedding week, they all sit down together and dance and sing and make merry. The same custom, *chilke*, "forty," is found among the Muslim Kurds. In Sinne the *ḥuppa* is taken down on the fortieth night, and a hen and a cock are slaughtered as *kappara* for the bridal pair.

Throughout the first year, food is sent to the young wife from her father's house on every Sabbath and on all the feast days (Z., A., and S.). In Amadiya it was even customary for supper to be sent every evening by the bride's mother.

In Sinne, in former times, a newly married woman never went anywhere during the first year but always remained at home. In Ushnu the wife must be veiled both inside and outside the house until the birth of her first child. Only her husband may see her face.

Marriage among the Village Jews

As an example of the marriage customs of Jews living in the country, let us describe a village wedding from the vicinity of Sinne (Persian Kurdistan).

Only two or three Jewish families live in any one village; therefore, a young man is generally obliged to get his bride from another village. For this purpose, he sends an intermediary to the girl's father; and all the conditions are discussed with him. In contrast to the usage in the towns, the village father gets a sum of money from the bridegroom. The amount demanded varies from 150 to 250 *toman*.[53]

When the negotiations are concluded, the bridegroom's father proceeds to pay a visit to the father of the bride. He is accompanied by some of the Jews of his village, and the party is joined on the way by Jews from other villages; but the bridegroom himself remains at home.

The bridegroom's father and the guests are entertained at the home of the bride's father for two or three days. The festivities are called *shirinī khorān*, "eating of sweets" (see p. 113). The jewelry sent by the bridegroom as a gift to the bride is delivered to her, and she reciprocates with several sugarloaves.

Though the people in the villages, as already stated (p. 95), rarely eat meat under ordinary circumstances, for these occasions they send for a *shoḥeṭ* [ritual slaughterer], in order that the guests, who usually have a hard journey behind them, may be well cared for. At the time of the feasts of pilgrimage, the bridegroom remembers to send gifts to the bride (jewelry, an article of clothing, sometimes even a sheep), and the bride sends a gift in return.

After the wedding date is set, the bridegroom sends invitations to the people of the surrounding villages through a messenger. Non-Jews are also invited.

On the approach of the great day, several Jews, accompanied by Muslim neighbors, ride to the bride's village, where a number of festive meals await them—Jews and Muslims alike—at the home of the bride's father. Muslims also assist in the preparations for these feasts and Muslim women come to help the Jewish women in the cooking and baking.

Since the village Jews are even more completely in the power of the aga than the urban Jews, it follows as a matter of course that the aga's permission must be obtained before a father may send his daughter to another village or a bridegroom acquire a wife from another village. Therefore, the bride's father, accompanied by several notables, betakes himself to the aga, bringing sugarloaves and other presents, to get the aga's leave to proceed with the marriage.[54]

The bride is set on the horse. For her parents to accompany her would be regarded as improper, so they merely send an old woman along. The riders who take the bride to the bridegroom's village make merry on the way, singing and playing jokes. Each rider has a wooden spoon; and when the party passes through a village, the riders stick their spoons into their headdress to show that they are a wedding party. Nevertheless the villagers often demand a gift from them before allowing them to pass.

From the bridegroom's village the people come to meet them, on horseback, with the band playing. When the bride dismounts from her horse at the bridegroom's house, she is pelted with coins or nuts, and sprinkled with rosewater. Often, however, she refuses to dismount until a sheep has been slaughtered for her and a sign made on the door with hands dipped in the blood of the sheep.[55]

The seven benedictions take place in the country on Friday evening. The ceremony is the same as in the towns. If the seven benedictions do not take place on Friday evening, the bridegroom climbs to the roof of the house after the consummation and fires a shot as a sign that the bride was found to be a virgin. In the night preceding the Sabbath and on Sabbath there are feasts—which are attended by Muslims, as well as Jews. Since at weddings a minyan ([a quorum of ten adult men,] otherwise a rare occurrence) is present, there is also reading from the Torah. On Sabbath the gifts are presented. They consist of sugarloaves, sheep, or articles of clothing. The bride then distributes among the guests the presents she has prepared, part of which she herself made while she was still in her father's house (e.g., colored stockings).[56]

In Rekan, near Amadiya, the wedding celebrations occupy only two days. A messenger (*kasut*) is sent beforehand to the surrounding settlements to invite the Jews. After the henna night, the bridegroom is brought on horseback to the river, which is two hours distant from Rekan. There, before the bath, equestrian games (*jiridāne*)[57] take place.

The bride is brought to the river at the same time as the bridegroom. She rides a mule and is accompanied by the aga's wife, who sings *narīke*. After the bridal pair have bathed, sheep are slaughtered, and a great feast is held at the river's edge. Muslim Kurds likewise take part. This is the only meal given by the bridegroom, all the others being provided by the local Jews jointly. The Muslims who attend are entertained partly by the aga and partly by the local Muslims.

In the neighborhood of Sinne, the wedding festivities do not occupy a whole week. Those who attend return to their villages on Sunday, for their work calls them.

In the villages around Amadiya, a man stands on the roof of the house in which the marriage has taken place and calls down as a sign of the end of the celebration, *Khola qetā'ele qaisa birbizle* ["The rope broke, the wood scattered"]. This is done on the third day.

8

Birth and Childhood

Since women occupy a very inferior position among Kurdish Jews, women who are pregnant are treated with no more consideration than the rest of their sex. They are expected to continue their work right up to the time of giving birth. Some people assert that this is better for them than sitting still.

Any care bestowed upon them has in view the welfare of the child rather than that of the mother. On the other hand, the women of the community show great concern for the expectant mother and instruct her how to look after herself.

Popular expressions concerning pregnancy reflect this attitude: in keeping with the crude ways of the Kurds, they are far from delicate.

In Amadiya the so-called rejoicing over pregnancy (*farḥīya semāka*) was formerly celebrated on the occasion of a young woman's first pregnancy.[1] As soon as the bride realizes her condition, she is taken to her father's house. Here her mother and other women relatives bring cloth and sew clothes for the expected new arrival. The special task of sewing the *benuda*, the wrappings for the cradle, is assigned to some old woman who has brought many sons and daughters into the world. Musicians with *dōla* (drun) and *zirne* (trumpet) are invited to the house, and the women dance and sing. The expectant mother is given good advice as to what she should do and what she should avoid doing. In the evening there is a meal at the husband's house.

In Zakho the attitude is different. Here the bride is ashamed of her first pregnancy and tries to conceal her condition. In general, pregnant women continue to dress as usual; but there is also a special garment for women in their first pregnancy, the *sudra semāka kameta* (Amadiya, Betanura, Rakan, Tchalla, Herki). This *sudra* is like an ordinary dress but has a piece of cloth sewn on in front at the waist, giving the appearance of an apron.[2] It is also common for pregnant women to wear an apron called *birwana*,[3] ostensibly "to conceal the growing size of the body." But this custom undoubtedly has its origin in magic practices. Thus, in Anhalt (Germany), pregnant women tie an apron around their waists "so that the child later on may not refuse his mother's breast."[4]

The rules governing the conduct of pregnant women are varied.[5] For example, she must not eat anything sour but should, on the other hand, drink some wine each day, so that the child will become beautifully white and red, and she should eat honey because this increases the quantity of milk (A.). The child will be beautiful if the mother eats a great deal of fish (Z.).[6] Eating the flesh of cattle is forbidden (Z.).

She must be very careful with the parings of her nails. If anyone should step over them, she would have a miscarriage; and the same thing would happen if she should step over the parings of another person's nails. The fear of demons gave rise to the prescriptions that forbid a pregnant woman to pour water on the ground in the dark or to bring black utensils into the house (A and Z.).

Dangers to Pregnant Women and Protection against Them

Amulets to protect pregnant women are very numerous. Special stress is laid upon amulets in the case of women who have already had miscarriages (A. and Z. *trākhā*) or some of whose children have died.

The custom for a pregnant woman to wear a special kind of padlock on her body is very widespread (A., Z., D., and S.).

The skin shed by a snake is put into a little bag and carried by the woman in her girdle (D.).[7]

Five silken threads of different colors (red, green, yellow, white, and black) are twisted into a cord. While this is being done, the names of certain demons are pronounced. This cord is then worn diagonally across the body like a bandoleer. It is noteworthy that it is not worn around the waist, as we so often find to be the case.[8]

Sometimes amulets are also written by the *ḥakham*. These are buried under the threshold, burned while the woman stands over them, or used like other written amulets.

Amulets made of copper (*brünjuk* (copper) are regarded as a particularly efficacious. In Zakho the pregnant woman collects silver from seven immature girls who have had no sexual impulses (*'eshq*) and also from seven women in childbed who at the time have no *'eshq*; and out of this silver she has the Jewish silversmith make a plate on which the *ḥakham* engraves the names of certain demons. Both the silversmith and the *ḥakham* must observe the prescribed rules of purity while making this plate.

Still more efficacious, however, is an old copper amulet whose magic power has already been put to the proof. Such old amulets are in the possession of certain families, who lend them out in case of need. There are famous amulets in Betanura and Bashqala, for instance. A certain amulet from Sündu, made by H. Gedalya b. Ḥ. R. Raḥamim, is round and has a diameter of 47 millimeters (HUBC 38:114). The inscription engraved on it reads:

שדי	יהוה
בשם עזריאל	בשם אל אלהים
שמריאל יצדהיאל	שדי צבאות יהוה
יהדריאל יהואל יה	אל מיכאל גבריאל
לבשם פחדיאל ב נפ	רפאל נוריאל לימה
ורת יוס פבנפורת על	חזי ימחה יוהק ברפטיאל
יעינבנ ותץ עדה על	לבשם פנואל פנואל
שור סנוי סנסנוי	פנואל חי חי חי יד
סמנגלף לשמירת	פוניאל מריאל
דדה ומו עי	סיג וגד דוני
דיד	לווהי

[It is almost impossible to translate the text of an amulet such as this. However, it contains several divine names (YHWH, El, Elohim, Shaddai, *Ṣeba'ot*) the names of traditional angels (Michael, Gabriel, Raphael, Nuriel), as well as made-up angel names (such as Barfatiel, Mariel, Shamriel, Yehadriel, Yehoel, Paḥdiel). Lines 5–8 on the left side contain the verse "Joseph is a fruitful vine, a fruitful vine by a fountain, its branches run over the wall" (Gen. 49:22), which is used very frequently in Jewish amulets and is here given in a distorted form, with the words broken up and grouped into unintelligible forms. This is followed by the likewise very frequently used reference to the three angels Senoi, Sansenoi, and Semangelof, who also are supposed to drive off the arch she-demon Lilith.]

If there is fear of a miscarriage, the amulet is borrowed from the family that possesses it and hung around the pregnant woman's neck, to the sounds of the shofar (A.). A shoe nailed above the door will also prevent miscarriage (A.). The woman is taken to her parents' house or to some other place, on the principle that a change of residence can outwit the spirits (S.). In addition, the pregnant woman makes a pilgrimage to certain holy graves. Thus, the women of Sinne go to the grave of Esther at Hamadan.

If the woman is subject to fears, a basin of water is put on the roof at night to catch the starlight. In the morning, seven red-hot spits for roasting meat (*sabuza*), are plunged into the water; and this water is given to the woman to drink (Z.).

The following complicated procedure is also regarded as a very efficient remedy. A leaden bullet (*bariqsa*) is melted down, a basin of water set on the pregnant woman's head, and a broom held over the basin. The liquid lead is poured through the broom into the water, producing a hissing sound. The water is then spilled out at a crossroad and a loaf of bread and an onion are laid in each of the four roads (A., similarly Z.).

If a pregnant woman has feelings of anxiety, she may burn a snakeskin (*shelukhtit khūwe*) under herself or have a wolf's tail fastened over the door (A. and Z.). [These charms are efficacious against evil spirits, as is the right eye of a wolf, which brings luck in every case. If a woman has miscarried in previous pregnancies and she fears she will miscarry in the present case, she takes a snakeskin that has been shed by the snake and ties it over her stomach beneath her clothing. The snakeskin remains there until the time of pregnancy is ended. Then it must be taken off, or she will be unable to give birth, since the snakeskin "ties." The snake sheds his skin once in three years. (A.)]

The appearance of the child may be influenced by two factors: (1) prenatal cravings and "shocks," and (2) the moon.

The belief in the influence of prenatal shocks and cravings on the unborn child is, we may say, common to all mankind.[9] Therefore, even in Kurdistan, the pregnant woman is granted everything she craves. Otherwise, the child may come into the world with blemishes of some kind, (A. *shāme*, Z. *nishanqa*. [The *shāme* is a black soot that appears on the child's body at a place corresponding to that part of his mother's body which she touched when in fear during her pregnancy, A.]. If a pregnant woman should pass by people who are eating something, she is forced to stop and partake of the food. Similarly, if she is paying a visit, she is immediately served with any food that happens to be in the house lest she feel a sudden craving (A. and Z.).

Furthermore, since the moon is believed to have an influence on the appearance of the child, a pregnant woman is not permitted to leave the house during a lunar eclipse (A. and Z. *devhāqit sehara*). The child, it is thought, moves within the mother's womb during a lunar eclipse; and the part of its body that is turned toward the moon will be marred by red spots (A., Z., and S.). In Sinne these spots are called ***kal sera.***

The Delivery

During the delivery, the mother is attended by midwives (Arbil ***daipirka***, "grandmother"; A. and Rekan ***dapilka*** [***dāpirke***, "old mother"] or ***qablanta***; Z. ***jidika***; Ushnu ***mamata***; Sulaimani ***mamanji***).

The Jewish midwives are old, experienced women, who accept no pay for their services but receive a gift (some article of clothing) and their board during the eight days they spend at the house.

Jewish midwives are held in high repute, also among the Kurds, who often apply to them for help. Even the demons, it is believed, feel the need of their service and call them in to aid in delivering their wives. This happens chiefly in the case of half-demons, that is, changeling women. A story about a Jewish midwife who is called out by night to deliver a she-demon is widely current. [What follows is one version of it:

There was a man named Shakoko, who lived in Amadiya. He was poor and had an old mother who was a well-known midwife and did everything for the love of heaven. Once, at midnight, somebody came to her house and said, "Aunt No'omi!" "What do you want?" she asked. "My wife is about to deliver, come with me!" She replied, "By my eyes, I am coming right away!" She washed her hands and followed the man who was waiting outside. When they walked away from the town, she asked him where he was taking her. He said, "Auntie, close your eyes!" He led her into a cave; and when she opened her eye, she found herself in a big palace. In it sat a woman, ready to give birth, on two stones. Around her stood women who sang, "If it is a son, happiness for you—if it is a girl, sighs for you." She noticed that they were not human and was sore afraid.

The she-demon was delivered of a boy.[10] The midwife was very happy and did everything necessary. When the woman in childbed noticed that the old woman whom her husband had brought to her was no she-demon but human, she said to her, "Be careful, and don't eat anything. Only after my husband has sworn that he would do nothing to you, take what he gives you." When the man came, he said, "Auntie, I shall give you whatever you wish." She answered, "Please, only take me home, I take no fee for my services." The demon said to her, "I swear by this boy that I shall take you home unharmed!" Then he went and brought a rope and a few cloves of garlic. She was afraid and accepted it. She had to close her eyes again, and on the way she lost a few cloves of the garlic. Those that remained she put aside negligently in the house, and the rope she threw on a stack of wood.

When she got up in the morning, instead of the garlic there was gold in front of her; and where she threw the old rope, instead of one load of wood, there were ten. Everything on which they put the rope was multiplied tenfold. The family became rich through the rope, and therefore from that time on people called the family Rope.][11]

Some midwives are themselves suspected of practicing witchcraft. Thus, in Rekan there was a midwife who cast a spell on the children. Consequently, all the women had difficult deliveries. H. R. Menachem exposed the sorcery and decreed that a woman in labor should put one of her husband's garments under the pillow as a countercharm.[12]

The husband must not be in the room during the delivery (D. and Sulaimani).

Position during Delivery

The position assumed by the Jewish mother during delivery varies in Kurdistan. In Sinne she squats with her feet on two stones (*kista*) and is supported by three women. In Zakho she kneels, with pillows (*dazga*) under her knees. The midwife sits in front of her, and another behind her. The latter massages her abdomen. The woman sitting in front takes her by the hands and lifts her up a little when the child appears.

The custom that formerly obtained in Amadiya in the matter of position during delivery, appears to be very old. The woman squatted, leaning forward, and supported herself on a pair of T-shaped wooden bars. These bars were kept in the synagogue; indeed, a pair was kept in each of the two synagogues. The woman had no other support, the *dapilka* merely sitting in front of her.[13] This custom was done away with by Ḥakham Ya'aqov about 1840. Today, the woman supports herself on another woman. Ḥakham Ya'aqov likewise introduced a new custom, that is, that a barren woman should seek to cure her barrenness by rendering this service to a woman in labor. This is based on Genesis 30:3, which tells that Rachel sought to cure her barrenness by having her handmaid Bilhah bear upon her knees. (This was communicated to me by a ninety-year-old woman from Amadiya.)

It is customary to scatter earth on the place where the woman is giving birth, so that the child may come into the world on earth (S.). This earth, rubbed fine, is also used as powder. After a successful delivery, a little of this earth is out into a small bag and hung around the mother's neck in such a way as not to be visible. It is considered a means of ensuring future successful pregnancies. The rest is taken to some isolated place, lest someone be polluted by it.

Difficult Labor

In general, the birth proceeds normally. Still, difficult labor is obviously not unusual, since the expedients employed in such cases are very numerous. Apparently there is a connection between difficult labor and the spread of rickets among the Kurdish Jews as a result of insufficient nourishment and improper care of infants.

The means employed in cases of difficult labor fall into two categories: those based on magic with an admixture of religion and those based purely on magic. Among the former is the wide-spread custom of inviting several *ḥakhamim* to the house to recite Psalms for the suffering woman (S., Z., and Sulaimani). If this does not help, one of the *ḥakhamim* is required to blow the shofar. Thereby the names of certain angels are blown into the woman's ear (A. and Z.). From the tone of the shofar it is also possible to know whether the birth will pass off successfully (Sinne, Sulaimani, and Ushnu).

As *kappara* (expiatory sacrifice) a hen is slaughtered (or, among the rich, even a sheep), and the blood sprinkled on the place where the birth is proceeding or on the woman herself (A.). In Zakho a hen and a cock are taken—the former for the woman, the latter for the desired boy baby—and these are swung over the mother's head. The flesh of the slaughtered animals is distributed among the poor.

The husband of the woman in labor fetches from the synagogue the upper part of the "crowns" (Heb. *rimmonim*) decorating the Torah scrolls. In Kurdistan this cup-shaped upper part can be unscrewed. The husband takes it to a *ḥakham*, who, while reciting Psalms, fills it with *mayim ḥayyim* [Heb. "living water"], after which the husband, without uttering a word, must hasten home with the water and give it to his wife to drink, handing it to her from behind (S.).

The *ḥakham* writes amulets containing the names of certain angels, and these amulets are put on the woman's tongue (S.) or on her navel (Z.). Sometimes the writing is washed off the paper, and the water given to the woman to drink (a common custom).

The "seven-year-old *maṣṣa*" [unleavened Passover bread, matzoth] is regarded as a very effective expedient in cases of difficult labor. A small *maṣṣa* the size of a dollar is baked together with the *maṣṣa sh'mura* (see

p. 279); and then, for seven consecutive years, it is laid on the Seder dish in order that the benedictions may be recited over it. After that, the *maṣṣa* is sewed into a bag decorated with buttons and beads that likewise serve magic purposes.[14] The *maṣṣa* is hung round the woman's neck as an amulet (A.), or is laid on her heart (Z.). Water in which the *maṣṣa* has been soaked is also given to the woman to drink (Z).

Along with these customs, which have some connection with religion, there are the purely magic practices, part of which have been taken over from Kurds or Christians.

A piece of cloth large enough to make her shroud is bought and placed near the woman with the words "This is your shroud, this is for your shroud, we are giving it to the poor as *kappara*." Then the cloth is distributed among the poor (Z.).

For a medicine the woman is given a drink made of manna (*ar'ura*) dissolved in water (Z. [and A.]) or a broth prepared from fig leaves (D.).

The husband's foot and shoe play an important role in the customs performed in cases of difficult labor. These customs are also prevalent in southeastern Europe.

Among the Kurdish Jews, the husband strikes the wife on the back with his shoe (A. and S.). We find the same practice among the modern Greeks. There the husband strikes the wife three times on the back with his shoe and cries, "It is I who have put this burden upon you, now I take it away."[15]

Water is poured into the husband's shoe, and the wife must drink it (Z. and S.). The Serbs[16] and the Bosnians[17] also practice this custom.

Another remedy that obviously has the same basis in magic, consists in having the wife drink of the water in which the husband's foot has been washed (A. and Z.).

Care and Treatment of the Mother after Delivery

The afterbirth (Z., D., and A. *kawursa* "fellow"; S. *kurta*; Kurd. *hawala butzuk*, "companion of the little one") is buried or simply thrown out. The midwife cuts the umbilical cord with a pair of scissors. In Zakho the *jidika* cuts the cord over the two great toes of a barren woman in order to let the blood flow over them. When the remainder of the cord drops off, the midwife receives a gift (S.). The dry remnant of the cord is then put into a little bag and hung on the cradle. A year later it is buried (A.). In Zakho the bit of cord is put into the water in which the mother bathes forty days after delivery. The water is poured over the heads of mother and child, and this is said to promote the child's development.

The very widespread custom of laying the mother (Z. and A. *ḥeta.* or *ḥayata*, woman in childbed) on the bare ground is not found among the Kurdish Jews. The mother lies on some valueless cloth that can later be thrown away. She is given no water to drink during the first few days. In Sinne the women drink a great deal of oil. Sweet beverages, in particular, are recommended—for instance, sweet tea, which is believed to increase the quantity of milk (A.), or wine and *sherbet* from *me pukta*, grape syrup (Z. and D.). The first meals given to the mother must be sweet; therefore, grape syrup is added to them.

Care and Treatment of the Child after Delivery

Among the Kurdish Jews it is customary to rub the newborn baby with salt instead of bathing him (A.). It is clear that the use of salt for this purpose has its basis in magic.[18] The child is supposed to become healthy and strong through being rubbed with salt. For this reason, the Kurdish Jews say to a lazy fellow, *Pakhewit lēwit mümlēkha mā milkha lütwa bē bābokh*, "You are dull [lit., "bland"], you are not salty, there was no salt in your father's house" (A.)[19] or *Mā pakhalē öha amri yōmit hiwēle lā drēlū milkha gō māyit khiyāpa dīde*, "How dull this man is, they will say that no salt was put into his bath water on the day of his birth" (Z.).

The custom of sprinkling the child with salt immediately after birth is mentioned as far back as Ezekiel 16:4. One might therefore suppose that this old practice of cleaning the child with salt is an ancient Semitic custom that had survived among the Kurdish Jews. Such a conclusion, however, is scarcely possible. We have here an instance that shows clearly how difficult it is, where Jewish tribes are concerned, to prove that an existing custom is a genuine case of survival. In the form here described, (i. e., rubbing the child with salt, instead of washing him in salt water, as is done among the Jews of Sinne, and to some extent among those of Zakho),[20] the custom is practiced also by the neighboring peoples, such as the Nestorians,[21] Kurds, Georgians, Armenians, and Persians and is to be found in Greece[22] as well, so that our districts might be regarded as the center of the territory in which this custom prevails. We can perhaps assume that the Jews have taken over the practice from the Nestorians, and that in any case there is no question here of survival of an ancient custom.

After the cleansing, the midwife adjusts the body of the child, straightening the arms and legs, molding the head and forehead, and, in case of a girl, even forming dimples in the cheeks (A.). She also puts *kohl* [powdered antimony sulfide] into the eyes (Z.).

Typical of this *Kulturkreis* [culture circle, see p. 26] is the tight binding of the child in swaddling clothes. The Kurdish Jews further bind the child to the cradle [A. *dodiya*, Kurd. *landik*] with tight wrappings. A newborn baby is bound in special bands (*pechulka*) and laid in a grain sieve (*ribala*), with a bit of iron on him. The iron and the sieve are believed to guard him against the "evil eye" (A. and D.). [The child lies in the sieve (*arbala*) for seven days, with a candle burning beside him. (A.)] The Muslim Kurds, too, lay the newborn child in a sieve for six days.[23] Up to the time of the circumcision ceremony, the Jews of Zakho place the child in the round baking pan (*doka*), which is also made of iron. A girl is laid at the left side of the mother, and a boy at her right.

The Taboo on Women after Delivery

According to Jewish ritual, a woman is unclean after childbirth just as during the menstrual period. The idea of the uncleanness of women following childbirth is clearly among the earliest of human conceptions, and it is spread far and wide over the earth. Judaism has not been able entirely to eliminate the magical roots of the belief.

According to Jewish law, the mother is taboo forty days after the birth of a boy, and eighty days after the birth of a girl. The ultrapious among Kurdish women observe forty-one days in the case of boys, and ninety-one in the case of girls. In Amadiya, women nowadays usually observe forty and eighty days, respectively. The general unclean period is, however, forty days at present, owing, no doubt, to the influence of non-Jewish neighbors—hence the expressions *arbi* (Z. and S.) and *aribi* (A.), "forty," and, in speaking of women, *go aribi*, "in the forties" (A.) and *Arbī pillā'i rēshaw*, "Forty fell on her" (S.). The Kurds, similarly, call the period *chilke* (A.) or *chelle* (S.), "forty."[24]

We may say that the woman is taboo during this period and is subject to the appropriate taboo laws. She must not leave her room during this time. If possible, she must lie in bed during the first eight days (Z.). At night, she must not go into the courtyard. If she leaves her room, she must always be accompanied by another woman.

In Amadiya and Nirwa it was customary for the mother to remain in bed for eight days. Then, accompanied by the midwife, she repaired to the "segregation house," which is erected outside the town for the menstruating women. In this house there was always a large number of women to whom food had to be brought from the town. The mother remained there until the day of her purification. The custom is said to have been abolished about 1860.

There is a taboo on a woman who has just given birth because a dangerous, enervating force emanates from her and this affects her environment. It is clear that complex notions are here involved: on the one hand those around her must be protected against the enervating force; and on the other, the endangered woman must herself be protected. The protection of the woman extends to the room in which she is lying as well as to herself. During the first three (or eight) days it is forbidden to borrow fire or a utensil, particularly a copper vessel, from her house (Z. and A.). Here we have a very widespread custom.[25] Everything that comes in contact with the mother is taboo and is withdrawn from use. There is an obvious connection between this and the custom of bringing food to the mother. She must neither cook nor bake, not because she must not work but because the utensils are taboo. Hence, in some places it is forbidden to bake or to roast meat in the mother's house. It is said that the odor of roasted meat is injurious to the newborn child (B.). It is also forbidden to draw water in the dark from the cistern of her house (S.).

In order to protect the mother against the power of the demons and other harmful influences, the midwife draws a circle round the room with an iron rod or hangs a black rope round the mother's bed (S.).

The belief in the power of onions to drive away demons[26] is very widespread, and we find it also among the Kurdish Jews. In Zakho three onions are put upon a spit (*shebūza*) and set beside the mother. In Sinne, also, onions are put upon the spit, *shebūza*; but here there are seven onions to begin with, and one is removed each day.

Among the persons imperiled by approaching a woman who has just given birth are other women in the same condition and betrothed couples. The person from whom the demoniac influence emanates, in this case the mother, is called *kepāsa* (A.) or *kābsē* (Z.), the victim of the evil influence, *kebista* (A.).

In order to escape the dangerous force, women who have lately delivered are forbidden to pass the houses of other women in childbed (Z., A., and S.). If a woman has nevertheless accidentally committed this error, she must spit in the mouth of the other woman's baby (S.)[27] or touch the baby's foot with a finger moistened with spittle (S.)[28] The prohibition sometimes extends to the family of the woman concerned, that is, to her husband and her other children. The danger is greatest if the newborn baby is a girl (S.). Through disregard of the prohibition women may become barren or members of their family may fall ill and die.

Similarly, betrothed persons are forbidden to pass the house of a woman in childbed. In case of failure to observe this prohibition, various countercharms are employed. A bride, for example, must step back and forth across the feet of the mother three times. Or she must step three times over a vessel in which the mother has urinated (Z.). In Sinne, the measure prescribed for mothers who have failed to observe the prohibition applies also to betrothed persons. In Amadiya, the bridegroom or the bride gives the mother a piece of bread and receives a piece of her bread in return; or else they exchange needles with each other.

These ceremonies serves as preventives also. When betrothed persons live in a street where a woman is confined, they carry out these prescriptions and thus acquire the power of passing the house of the *kepāsa* thereafter with impunity (A.).

When the forty days of seclusion are over, it is said of the woman, *Nepiqla min arbī*, "She has come out of the forties." In Kurdistan there is no special ceremony marking the close of this period. The midwife cuts the mother's nails and takes her to the *miqve* (A.). In Sinne, on the day when the mother is to go to the *miqve*, she sends a bowl of porridge (*kesāne*) to her friends and relatives, as at Purim; and these return the bowl filled with almonds.

The Week before the Circumcision

The birth of a son is hailed with joy. The women at once raise their *klīlīlī*. News of the birth of a daughter, on the contrary, is received in silence.[29] If the birth takes place at night, the husband, who in any case is not greatly interested in the progress of the delivery unless it happens to be a difficult birth, and awaits events calmly, will not even be awakened if the child is a girl.

If the child is a boy, everyone hastens to notify the father should he, for instance, happen to be in his shop at the time. He rushes home, but must not immediately enter his wife's room; he must wait outside a little while, lest he "tire" the child (Z.).

A father to whom a daughter has been born is sometimes afraid to venture into the street. The children run after him and call, *Tūvā, tūvā khāra b'lakhīt abūhā*, "Daughter, daughter, dirt on her father's beard" (A.). [My friend S. Ben-Shabbath of Haifa, after having read the above passage in Brauer's "Mīlah weyaldut ētzel Yehudē Kurdistan," p. 129

(see Publications), informed me that the same doggerel was recited also among the Sephardi Jewish children in many a Middle Eastern country. The word, however, should read *tūhā*. The children surround, in the street, the father of a newborn girl and sing, *Tūhā tūhā khiryeh biliḥyet abūhā*! "Tūhā, tūhā, dirt in the beard of her father!" The word *tūhā* is derived, according to Ben-Shabbath, from the rhyme of a sonq that is sung on the Sabbath following a girl's birth, when her father is called up to the Torah in the synagogue. This song begins,

Bat n'imah mah qrātūhā
Uvizhavim 'atartūhā
w'al kisē shēn samtūhā.

Beautiful daughter, what did you call her,
With gold you encircled her,
And on an ivory seat you placed her.

Also, when congratulating the father of a girl upon her birth, it is customary to say mockingly, *Mazal ṭobh, tūhā, tūhā.*

I also heard another version of the saying, from H. Neḥama of Jerusalem: *Tūhā tūhā khāra fuwasṭ liḥt abūhā* "Tūhā, tūhā, dirt into the middle of the face of her father!"—whereupon the father answers *Khāra fuwasṭ limā shāfūhā*! "Dirt in the middle of him who has not seen her!" See also Ben-Shabbath, "Tuha, tuha," *Edoth* 2:1–2, p. 127.]

A poor man, in particular, is pitilessly baited in such a case. The children jump on his back and shoulders and pelt him with mud. Sometimes they torment him so that he does not venture to leave his house for a fortnight. In Sinne a woman who has borne a daughter must sit in the dark, the lamp being so placed that no light can reach her.

When a son is born, a meal (*shetāya*)[30] is served daily at the father's house, beginning with the day after the birth. About fifteen men come every evening, bringing with them *maza* and arrack, some of which they give to the mother, as well. They eat and drink and sing circumcision hymns (Z., D., and A.).

In Sinne, where, after the birth of a boy, a sheep (among the less well-to-do a hen) is slaughtered and the flesh given to the poor, guests are entertained every day the week before the *milah* [Heb. circumcision"].[31] The women come in the daytime, the men in the evening. Musicians are engaged, and sweets and fruit are set before the guests. For the men there is arrack, as well.

From the third day on, relatives and neighbors bring meat into the mother's house. But the meat must not enter her room until she has walked three times round it. It is therefore set down in the courtyard, where the mother, with the child and the midwife, goes through the necessary formality. This is done so that the mother may not become *kebista* (A.).[32]

The third day after the birth of a son is called *khilyūsa*. "sweets.[33] The father of the child has candy distributed among the children. If he is rich, he sends great bowls of sweetmeats to the aga and the other notables, who reply with congratulations. Their wives come to congratulate the mother (A.)

Shabbat Avī Haben

The Sabbath before the circumcision is the Shabbat Avī Haben [Sabbath of the Son's Father] or Shabbat Se'ūdat Mīla [Sabbath of the Circumcision Meal] in Amadiya and Sinna, respectively.

While the father of a son is honored on this Sabbath by having an *'aliya* [calling up to the Torah reading] bestowed upon him—by the synagogue, so to speak—the father of a daughter serves as the butt of the jests of the community. The father of a son is presented with a dish of *maza* by the *gabbai* and a jug of arrack by the synagogue. Instead of these gifts, the father of a daughter is given a water jug and a washbowl and told, *Shti khōshēba makimakhlokh sēfer tōra*. "Drink, on Sunday you will be called up to the Torah" (A.). The only exception occurs in Rekāna Dēm, Upper Rekan, where the father of a daughter is honored in the same way as the father of a son.

Otherwise, it is only the father of a son who is called to the reading of the Torah, usually as *shlīshī* (A. [third]).[34] The father sends out invitations beforehand, and the guests from the neighboring villages appear on the Shabbat Avī Haben. They remain until the circumcision.

In the places where all the *'aliyot* for the whole year are sold at Simḥat Torah, (see p. 320),[35] there is a convention that (as in the case of a bridegroom) all the *'aliyot* should be reserved for the *avī haben* on this Sabbath.[36] The father takes the *lū'aḥ* (see p. 321) and gives it to the Kohen and Levi. Then all the relatives and acquaintances are called up to the Torah as Israel. They recite the *mī shebērakh* blessing and present gifts to the synagogue, the *ḥazan*. and so on. Last of all, the father is called up.

The relatives and friends who habitually worship in another synagogue, come on this Sabbath to the synagogue of the *avī haben*.

In Amadiya, after the prayer, the *ḥaverīm* invite the father to drink with them (see p. 192). In other places where this custom does not exist, the "second meal" takes place in the father's house.

The women gather in the mother's room after the prayer. In Amadiya this function is called *feṭarta*, "breakfast."[37] In Zakho the morning is called *khilyūsit yāla*, "the child's sweets." The women take meat and dumpling (*kufte*) and go to the mother's house. They give some of the food to the mother and the midwife and also to each other. They dance and sing; and if the boy has been born to a rich woman, the feast is very sumptuous (A. and Z.).

In Sinne it is customary for the children to come to the door of the mother's house on Sabbath and sing, *Tenu lanu hozaban, yiḥye kesiman tov*, "Give us *hozaban*, may it be a good omen." They give the children *hozaban*, that is, nuts and candy. Sometimes the children stand on the roof, and the *hozaban* is thrown up to them. In acknowledgment, the children sing, *Pāv qidāmev berīkha hevē*, "His feet, his steps, be blessed."

On this Sabbath the *sandaq* [godfaṭher] is also chosen and apprised of the honor. He sends the child the clothes it is to wear for the circumcision.

Lēl Sheshe (Sixth Night)

One of the most dangerous nights for the mother is the *lēl sheshe*. In Sinne this is still (as it was originally) the sixth night, *lēl shishī* [Heḅrew], whereas in the rest of Kurdistan it coincides with the night before the circumcision, the *Wachnacht* of the European Jews.[38]

It appears that the word *sheshe*[39] has no direct connection with the Kurdish *shesh* or Hebrew *shisha* but was originally the name of a female demon (perhaps the demon of the sixth day), who lays traps for the children; for we find the same custom also among the Jews of Baghdad. On the sixth night after the birth the latter likewise celebrate a feast at which saffron water is distributed among the boys, who roam through the streets crying, *Shisha*! and are treated to sweets.[40]

The Muslim Kurds hold this celebration on the seventh night after the birth instead of the sixth. In this connection, B. Nikitine writes: "On the first six days . . . neither the *dapirk* nor the other women who were present at the delivery are allowed to leave the house. . . . The rule is above all strict for the night. If need be, the women can absent themselves during the day, but they must come back for the night, otherwise the evil spirit *sheshe* (the origin of this name is in the number six, *shesh* in Kurdish) could kill the mother or the newborn."[41]

In Sinne the women appear at the mother's house at about 4:00 P.M. They are entertained in the customary way, and food is distributed among the poor. This should, if possible, be a sour dish and the usual choice is therefore *shella tirshī lelē sheshe* (a sort of thin porridge made of rice cooked sour). Besides this, raisins and other sweets are given to the children. The ceremonies carried out are clearly aimed at providing the mother with means of protection similar to those of the *lēl ḥinne* in the case of betrothed couples (see p. 122). The midwife strikes the mother three times on the temples, and claps her hands three times, saying, *Se Līlīt*, "Depart, Lilith."[42] The women fetch blue dye (*nīla*) or yellow dye (*zaira*) from the dyers and paint the mother with it. On her face they paint a definite pattern, then they paint her hands, feet, and pudendum. The child is also painted. During the painting marriageable girls must leave the room. Finally, the women paint the wall opposite the bed in which the mother is lying.

This custom is called *rang kolekhīla*, "dye-they-are-making"; thus, the mother is also asked, *Rang wilalakh*, "Have they painted you?" After painting the mother, the women present paint their own foreheads, hands, and feet. It is looked upon as a good omen if the mother does some sewing during this night. For this night, the midwife puts a necklace of amber beads round the mother's neck; and two midwives lie beside her till morning. The men likewise come to the house to feast. Musicians arrive and the guests sing and dance.

The *lēl sheshe* takes place on the sixth night also in Ushnu. Men and women gather at the mother's house. The women say, *Sheshe berakhta*, "A blessed *sheshe*." Girl babies are named on this night. In Sinne and Ushnu, however, there still exists the custom of celebrating also the night before the circumcision.

The Night before the Circumcision: *Wachnacht*

In Dehok, Zakho, and Amadiya it is the night before the circumcision, that is, the eighth night, that is called *lēl sheshe*. Hence, the customs of the *lēl sheshe* and of the night before the circumcision are combined on this night.

In the evening the Chair of Elijah (Kursi Eliyahu) is brought from the synagogue to the father's house. The chair is adorned with *rimonim* and is placed, slightly elevated at the entrance. The men and women who arrive kiss the chair as they enter. Sweets are distributed among the groups of children who appear.

The men read the Zohar. Then the father has arrack, fruit and *maza* brought in; often the musicians appear (not in A.); and there is dancing and singing.

The women gather in the mother's room. In Zakho it is on this night that they paint the mother's palms and forehead with black dye (not in Z.). They likewise paint the child. If an outsider is present on this night, he, too, is painted.

A large *qandela* [candelabrum], called *qandelit Eliyahu hanavi*, with a great wax candle adorned with flowers, is brought from the synagogue and taken in to the mother. She lights the candle and throws a coin into a dish of water that stands on the *qandela*, which is then brought to the men. Each of them throws a coin into the dish and lights a small candle, which the *shammash* is holding ready. Thus, about fifty candles are placed upon the *qandela*. When the men have all discharged this duty, the *shammash* extinguishes the lights and goes to the women's room, where the same ceremony is carried out. The money thus collected is added to the *kuppa* of the synagogue, and the *quppat arīkhā*, the social welfare fund (A.).

The custom in Ushnu is similar. Here, also, the *shammash* takes a flower-bedecked *qandil* to the mother's house; but oil lights are used instead of candles.

The women do not sleep during this night but keep watch over mother and child. On the *lēl sheshe* the newborn baby must not sleep on the ground or in the cradle. Therefore, the women who spend the night with the mother hold him on their laps in turn (Z. and D.). But only women past the climacteric, *qeṭa'eta*, are allowed to hold him.

Special importance is attached to the celebration of the *lēl sheshe* in homes where the newborn child is also the firstborn or where other children have died.

On the morning of the eighth day the circumcision of the boy takes place. In Kurdistan this ceremony is commonly performed in the synagogue (A., Z., D., S., Ushnu, and Sulaimaniya). Bigar is an exception; there, the circumcision is carried out at home before *minḥa* prayer instead of after the morning prayer as in other places.

A general exception is made during the cold winter months or in the case of fathers who have already lost several sons. In such cases, the infant is circumcised at home lest the evil eye (*'ayin hara'*) blight him on the way to the synagogue (Z.).

Before the morning prayer, several men carry the chair of Elijah from the father's house, where it had stood during the *lēl sheshe*, back to the synagogue. The honor of carrying the Chair of Elijah is put up to auction, and the successful bidder has the privilege of placing the chair on the *teva* [reader's platform]. The men who escort him dance and sing all along the way (A.). This Chair of Elijah has short posts on which, by way of ornament, *rimmonim* are set in honor of the occasion. The chair is hung with silken scarfs, mostly green in color, to which amulets (bearing the name *Shaddai* [Almighty] and similar inscriptions) have been sewed. It is likewise the custom for mothers of sick children to fasten wolf's teeth[43] to the chair (Z.).

The Circumcision

After the prayer, the *ḥazan* announces that there is to be a circumcision that day and invites the men to remain in the synagogue. Meanwhile, the *shammash* goes to the father's house and asks the women to bring the child.

The women have already bathed the child and dressed him in the circumcision garment presented to him on the Shabbath Mila by the *sandaq*. In a merry procession, accompanied by the musicians, the women proceed to carry the child, swathed in scarfs, to the synagogue. At the sound of the *klīlīlī*, which they raise, other women come running out of the houses to join the procession. The infant is first carried by his two grandmothers, then by the other women in turn, it being considered a good omen and an honor to carry the child part of the way—for which reason, in Ushnu, he is carried also by a young woman who had not yet given birth to a child.

A delay in the arrival of the child occasions much banter in the synagogue. A stock joke is that he is late because Elijah is busy: *Hai hū ōha Eliyahulē izlē bid sho'i shūqē gimzabīnē*, "See, this Elijah is selling his wool yarn in seventy markets" (Z. and A.)

When the women appear with the child, everybody rises, for Elijah is believed to have entered together with the child. The grandmother or the midwife hands the child to the *sandaq*. The *sandaq* is generally the child's maternal grandfather. It is by no means uncommon for the father not to be present at the circumcision at all, since the men are often away from home for months at a time (e.g. in Z.).[44]

The *sandaq* passes the child three times over the Chair of Elijah and then sits down either on one of the steps of the *teva* or else on the circumcision chair, which they keep beside the Chair of Elijah for the purpose (Z., A., and S.). This chair, also, is adorned with silken scarfs.

The function of circumciser (*gazāra*)[45] is fulfilled by the *shoḥeṭ*,[ritual slaughterer]. The Jewish circumcisers are in such high repute that they are employed by Muslim Kurds also.[46] Among the Jews they receive no fee for their services as circumcisers, this task being regarded as a *miṣva* [religious good deed]. In Zakho a piece of homemade soap was formerly presented to the circumciser by way of a gift.

Since there is no *shoḥeṭ*—circumciser in the villages, it is not possible to have the circumcision performed exactly on the prescribed day. Therefore, the Jews in the villages around Rekan and Nirwa "collect" the children and have them all circumcised together during Sukkoth, when the *shoḥeṭ* arrives to slaughter the *qalya* meat. The villages, however, do not possess a Chair of Elijah.

For drawing forward and holding fast the foreskin, the circumciser uses a clamp (*mashqas*),[47] which may be either plain or ornamented and varies in size.

The blade of the circumcision knife *garē'eta*) has only one cutting edge. The circumciser uses a special knife or, at times, the one used for slaughtering poultry. To check the bleeding, he sprinkles the wound with ashes from the blue paper in which sugarloaves are wrapped (S.), or powdered caraway seed,[48] or pulverized wood scraped from the girders of the house (Begar). In Amadiya, the wound was first smeared with a paste made of *smōke* (see p. 101) and salt and then sprinkled with ashes from black cloth. During the *meṣiṣa* [ritual sucking out], the circumciser keeps some brandy—or else a mixture of water and *smōke*—in his mouth.

Magic

After the operation, the circumciser shows his blood-stained hands to the congregation; and the man who is holding the child say, *Minkhum bedima*, "Behold the blood!" It is believed that God forgives the sins of those who look upon the blood and that barren women are cured of their barrenness through gazing at the blood-stained hands (A.).[49] Likewise, the water in which the circumciser washes the blood from his hands is regarded as a remedy for barrenness. Women wash themselves with it (A. and Ushnu) and even drink of it (Ushnu). The flax with which the wound is covered is also regarded as a remedy for barrenness, and women fumigate themselves with it (A.).

The circumciser places the foreskin (A. *duluksa*, Z. *ṣarmuksa*)[50] in a bowl of ashes and says, *Nāḥash 'afar laḥmo*, "The serpent, dust is its food." The bridal cloth, with its magic erotic symbols, is spread over the bowl; and a boy takes it to the father's house. The mother hangs the foreskin on the cradle until it is dry, then takes it off and keeps it as an amulet (A.). Pieces of the dried foreskin, being regarded as a tried remedy for barrenness, are swallowed by barren women (Ushnu, Z., and S.) and sometimes also put into the vagina (Z.). However, the foreskin must be acquired and used surreptitiously, because the child's relatives will not allow it to be used for the practice of magic. [Such use of the foreskin is common in most Middle Eastern Jewish communities.]

When the benediction is recited over the wine, a few drops are put into the child's mouth. If he does not cry he is accepted as one of the community, and the men say to one another, *Zeh khebrāya*, "This is one of the community" (A.).

In Amadiya, when the father pronounces his son's name, the *mohel* dips his finger in wine and sticks it into the infant's mouth, "so that the child should not forget the name" (A.).

The Circumcision Feast

As the congregation leaves the synagogue, each member is presented with a small cake by one of the family who is stationed at the door. An especially powerful man, able to cope with the onrush of the guests, is chosen for this task.

The child is then taken home, accompanied once more by the musicians and the *klīlīlī* of the women. In Sinne, only the women enter the father's house. They present gifts and are served with refreshments. The men proceed to their work. The only circumcision feast they receive is that served during the *lēl sheshe*.

In most of the larger Kurdish Jewish communities, however, the circumcision feast takes place immediately after the circumcision ceremony. At all events, it must take place in daytime. Poor families often settle the matter right in the courtyard of the synagogue by distributing sweetmeats and pastry among the assembled guests (A.). The rich, on the other hand, serve a sumptuous feast at the father's house.

In Zakho, if the circumcision happens to fall on the Sabbath, the feast is dispensed with. Instead, the girls distribute rice and meat among about one hundred families. In Amadiya, however, the feast takes place also on the Sabbath. There is much merrymaking after the feast in this town, just as at weddings. The game *yesīra hakōma*, "the king's prisoner," is a special favorite on this occasion. There about ten servants (*sabusa*) on duty at the circumcision feast, and they do not permit any of the guests to leave before the end of the celebration. Their attentions are bestowed particularly upon the rich. These are not allowed to depart until they have contributed a gift of brandy, poultry, or money. If any of them refuses, he is punished by *talto'e*, that is, he is hung up by the feet until he submits (see p. 245).

With the money thus extorted the *sabusa* buy meat and brandy and with their friends—and several women to do the cooking for them—repair to the meeting place outside the town to celebrate.

Care of the Child; the Cradle

After the lapse of the time (mentioned earlier) during which the infant lies in a sieve or in the *doka* (baking sheet), he is put into the cradle [A. *dodiya*, Kurd. *landik*]. The Kurdish Jews use two kinds of cradles: the hanging cradle and the rocking cradle.

The hanging cradle is a sort of hammock. It is made of stout cloth attached to a rod on either side like a stretcher and is fastened with ropes to a beam in the ceiling. When the child is taken outside the house, the cradle is removed and carried along. This type of cradle is not intended for very young babies.

The ordinary cradle is that mounted on rockers.[51] The child, already wrapped in swaddling clothes that prevent the movement of arms as well as of legs, is so firmly bound to the cradle that he cannot change his position. This immobility is necessary for the functioning of the urine pipe [A. *sibak*]. A reed pipe is attached to the child's organ by means of a wax top which is made to fit the male or female organ. This drain pipe for the urine passes through the pillow on which the child is lying and through the bottom of the cradle into an earthen pot (A. *sinja*).[52]

The child is taken out of the cradle only twice daily to be swaddled afresh. It is not taken out for nursing. Moreover, as the cradle usually stands indoors, one may easily imagine how little air and sun the babies get and how readily they fall a prey to illness.

All sorts of amulets are fastened to the cradle, as (for example) a chain of almonds, nuts, blue beads, and a piece of wood from the *khilapta* tree (A.).

Feeding of the Infant

The infant is given its mother's breast on the day of its birth. In Zakho it is first fed melted butter (*mishkha*), and only after ten hours does the mother begin to nurse it. At any rate, there is no scruple about giving it colostrum. The mother nurses the baby from the beginning because (probably for fear of magic influence) she dares not give it to another woman to nurse, especially if the baby is a boy. A wet nurse (A. *dādōka*) is engaged when the mother is suffering from stoppage of the flow of milk or similar disabilities. Some rich women take a wet nurse in order the more quickly to become pregnant again—for there is a widespread popular belief that a nursing woman cannot conceive.[53]

Woman have a great variety of remedies that they employ when the flow of milk diminishes or ceases. The *ḥakham* writes a certain amulet, which is worn on the breast in a silver case. The women fetch earth from certain holy graves (e.g., Bē ḥazāne in Amadiya), which they stir into water and drink.

As mentioned, the child is not removed from the cradle for nursing. The mother kneels beside the cradle, leaning over the child, and supporting herself by resting one arm on the pole at the top of the cradle. (In this connection see the cradle song.)[54]

To facilitate nursing, there is a special shirt (A., Nirwa, and Rekan *sudra mamsanta* [wet nurse's shirt]) with a slit for each breast. This slit is covered with a flap.[55] The women sing cradle songs while nursing the child.

The child is nursed for two years. During the first year, milk is the only food and drink it gets. No water or tea is given. Not until the second year is the mother's milk supplemented by soup or porridge and also by drinking water. Then, however, great care is taken always to give the child plenty of water to drink, lest it fall ill. If the mother should forget to give it water and, in consequence, it then drinks too much at a time and falls ill, it is said, "Thirst fell upon him" (*Sokhwāna pillu*).

To cure the child, water is put into the bowl of a new pipe (*galunka*) and given to the child to drink. Then it is necessary to walk four cubits up and down the room, after which the pipe bowl is thrown into the river with the words *Sokhwāne, sokhwāne akhtum gō māye yala ṭarīs*, "Thirsts, thirsts, you in the water, the child is cured" (A.).

As far as we know, there is no special ceremony at the weaning (*khesala*) of the child. If the child wishes to continue nursing, the mother colors her breast black to frighten him or else sprinkles her breast with pepper.

Childhood; the First Tooth

[When the first tooth appears, they say *Yā ilāha yawit 'arzāni w'imnahi*! "Oh, Lord, give plentifulness and peace!" The meaning is that since teeth are created for eating, let there be enough to eat. (A.)]

Among the Kurdish Jews, as elsewhere, the appearance of the baby's first tooth is a happy event for which a feast is arranged.[56] They say, *Aggar dakī fakrā takhtē dargushtī maklālū tekhēla patīla kesāne bashla baki*, "The child demands this feast, even if the cradle must be burned to cook the food."

Porridge *kesāne* (see above p. 160) is generously distributed among the poor and sent to friends. Some of it is poured on the roof, so that the birds may also rejoice at the cutting of the tooth (S.).

This feast, however, often takes place only in celebration of the first tooth of the first son. In Amadiya, musicians are also invited; and sweets are sent to neighbors and friends.

An amulet made of a wolf's tooth (*kāka dēbha*) is hung round the child's neck bearing the words *Mānit bāne kākokh bāne kākit gāne*, "Who counts your tooth, let him count this tooth" or *Kud mēnekh kākokh mēnakh bāya kāka*, "Who looks upon your tooth, let him look upon this tooth" (A.).

In Nirwa, Rekan, and other towns, for the *plātit kāke* the parents send a bowl of *khashīsha*, a porridge made of wheat and peas, to relatives and friends, and receive in return a gift of cloth, a *megilla* [copy of the Book of Esther], and so on.

In Barashe, one bowl of sweets and another of salt are sent to acquaintances. As they present the bowls, they say, for instance, *Plitlo kāke la avramīnko*, "Abraham has cut teeth"; and the others answer, *Brīkhe hāwe ille*, "Blessing be upon him."

It is regarded as a bad omen if the first tooth appears on the upper jaw. In such an event, a "powerful" remedy is employed. The child is thrown from the roof into a cloth which several people are holding below (S.).

Growth of the Child

During the first year of his life, the baby's hands—but not his face—are washed with water in the morning. The mother squirts some milk out of her breast and washes the child's face with it, saying *Bröni pāse willu khulyela malākhe*, "My son, his face the angels shall wash" [or *malākhet shena*, good angels]; or she says, *Āna khālanna khalwa*, "I wash it with milk" (A.).

Learning to Walk

Babies are assisted in learning to walk by being put into a wheeled stand made for the purpose (A. and S.). Certain ceremonies are carried out if the child is slow in learning to walk. Some entrails (*talya*, i.e., heart, liver, etc.) are provided, and the child is undressed and held over the entrails while water is poured over him. He should then begin to walk very soon (A.).

If this remedy does not succeed, recourse is had to the stronger one of "binding" (*yisāra*). The child's hands and legs are bound and he is taken to the main street at a time when it is known that the aga will be riding by. The aga, knowing the custom, dismounts from his horse and cuts the child's bonds with a knife (D. and A.).

There is furthermore the method of fumigation with the horn of a stag based on Pirqe Avot 5:23: *Raṣ kaṣevī*, "Be as swift as a deer" (A.)

In Amadiya, the mother, with the child, goes in the evening to the place of the demons called Berē Awja, Round Stone. She puts some bread, salt and onions beside the stone and lays, also, the child there, with the words: "Please, my friend, let my child go free." After an hour she picks the child up again, and next morning he is certain to walk.

In Sinne, the child is laid in a winnowing sieve (*arbala*) and carried around to seven families, each of which must contribute some food. From these seven kinds of foodstuffs a meal is prepared and the child must consume it.

The first words that the child utters are *bābi* [daddy], *yimmi* (A. [mummy], *tata* or *baba* (father), *dai* (mother), and *Allah* (God) (S.). [If a child's first word is *bāba*, "daddy," it is a sign that the next child born to his parents will be a boy. If he says *yimmi*, "mummy," first, they will have a daughter. Another method of divination is that if a child, when he first starts walking, takes some ashes and puts them on his head, it is a sign that his mother will conceive and bear a male child. (A.)]

For a child who is slow in learning to talk, "binding" is employed, just as for the child who is slow in learning to walk (D. and A.). Another remedy is to place three grains of toasted rice under the tongue (A.).

Children Who Are Thought to Be in Danger

Parents who have already lost several children practice a special custom in order to protect their newborn child. Soon after his birth—thirty days at the latest—the child is "sold." He is sold to a female relative, who pays about a pound for him. She turns him over to the mother to nurse and makes a small symbolic payment each month for this service. In addition to this, she buys the child's clothing until approximately his tenth year.[57] Under no circumstances may the parents buy the child's clothing (Z., D., and S.). If possible, the mother of a large family of children is chosen as "purchaser"; and the child bears the name of her family (S.).

There is also another practice, namely, that of treating the baby as a pauper's child, instead of selling him. Money is collected for the purchase of his clothing;[58] or, immediately after his birth, scraps of cloth are gathered from different families and made into a "dress of a thousand patches" like that worn by the dervishes (*sudra qiche*).[59] This dress has a red bead sewn to it and is worn by the child on the morning of the Shabbat Mīla (A.; see also p. 162)

For such children, the *sudra* and the *kirtaka* are made out of grave clothes (*kitān mithe*). If an old man or a *ḥakham* dies, the cloth remaining from his shroud is sold by auction and acquired by the family of such a child. The *sudra* is further distinguished by the red bead[60] (A.).

In addition to the practice of selling the baby to another family, there is also that of selling him to the gypsies (*qarachāya*).[61] The latter buy the baby and another member of the family buys him back from them. This custom was quite common in Amadiya.

Finally, there is the practice of exchanging the baby for a young dog. The mother takes the baby to a female dog that has just born some young. She lays the baby beside the mother dog and takes one of the puppies to her breast. Then she walks back and forth with it three times saying, *Yā kalibta, hā sheqol brōni tālakh, ana sheqelli ōha brōnakh tagyāni*, "O mother dog, take my son for yourself. (In return) this your son I take for myself." Thereupon, she takes her son back, goes to the river and dips him in it three times (Z.). The custom of throwing the puppy into the water is probably older (D.). This custom is popular also among pregnant women who have previously lost several children. As they perform this rite they say, "O river, I give you the dead son, give me the living one in return" (D.).

As an amulet for these children who are thought to be in special danger, it is customary to have a *sēpa* (sword) made. Silver is purchased from three silversmiths—a Jew, a Muslim, and a Christian. Out of this, a small silver sword is made by a Jewish silversmith. The *ḥakham* then engraves upon it the names of certain angels. While doing so, he must observe the rules of purity as prescribed in the making of amulets. The child wears the sword on his shoulder or on his cap until he reaches the age for putting on the tefillin (A. phylacteries).[62]

A *sēpa* from Amadiya, which must be about two hundred years old (HUBC 39:56), bears the inscription

בשם יהו חרביאל
בשם אבלא בלא לאא ובשם
אריאל רפאל גבריאל מיכאל נוריאל
חיי גזגדר ומשמרת ל(נושא) ל(ה) ק(מע) וידו.

[A hand made of silver or gold also serves as an amulet for the same purpose. (A.)

If several children died at a tender age and the mother has given birth again, the child will be called by a name that will serve to protect him. My informant, Ḥakham Avidani of Amadiya, told me that before he was born, his parents lost three sons, each of whom died right after the circumcision. When he himself was born, his father called him 'Alwan, Sacrifice; this name protected him and so he remained alive.]

9

THE KURDISH JEWESS

To draw a picture of the Kurdish Jewess is a difficult task from the viewpoint of modern man. One has a tendency to be lured into a one-sided portrayal and thereby to deny to the Kurdish Jewess the place in the cultural structure that she actually occupies.

An anthropological examination shows the Kurdish Jewess to possess a robust, tough, and big-boned frame. One does, indeed, occasionally find an oriental beauty among the young girls; but an attractive figure among the women is a rarity. The hard work, the ungentle treatment, the frequent pregnancies, and the primitive conditions under which they live, rob the women very early of all grace and charm. There remain the heavy lineaments of the typical peasant woman.

The curses that roll easily from her tongue reveal the Kurdish Jewess as a product of this rough land. She is no tender being, and in her feelings and sentiments she shows little of what we are accustomed to call feminine. It is difficult to get a glimpse into her love life, but one has the impression that anything bordering on sentiment is quickly suppressed by the hard atmosphere in which she lives.

In cursing each other, the women use the names of Vashti and Zeresh, the two evil women from the Book of Esther.

A preliminary explanation is essential to the understanding of one of their curses, implicit in which is a revelation of the treatment of the woman at the hands of her husband. The *ketubba*, "marriage contract," is placed in a small bag immediately after it is read out at the seven benedictions, and the wife always sleeps with it under her pillow. To take the *ketubba* out of the bag is forbidden, for this would result in the husband's death. In this curse, one woman accuses the other of having taken out the *ketubba* in order to bring about this very result: *Vashti pitkhat ketubat ṭar gurakh māyis ishallah dāyim qāyim hāwe ṭar nekhīrakh tāwira*, "Vashti, you have taken out your marriage contract, so that your husband may die; but God grant (that) he remain alive, so that he may break your nose!" (A.; also Z.) [Vashti's name appears also in another curse, *Vashti merē duma*, "Vashti with the tail!" This is in accordance with a tradition which says that Vashti refused to appear before the guests of Ahasuerus because she did not want them to see she had a tail. (A.)]

Many of the curses are connected with the death customs. If a child dies, the mother sometimes cuts off her braids (see p. 89)—hence the curse *Hāī min ṣoṣiyākh qetī' īlakh*, "O, may they yet cut off your braids!" (Z.).

Again, since the dead are washed on a plank (*darga*), certain imprecations wish death upon the hated woman in the words *Rabī ṣoṣiyākh rēsh darga* [or *dāpa*] *khepīlū*, "God grant that they wash your braids on the death plank!" (Z. and A.) [or *Tnāshe mardashē*, "One hair washing!" i.e., "May you die and have your hair washed only once and no more!" (A.)]

The Yemenite Jew has something of the *Berufungstypus* [vocation-type]—to use Clauss's expression in the otherwise not very happy characterizations of his classification of types.[1] The same is true of the Yemenite Jewess, who is altogether a more refined and more sensitive type. This is a consequence of the religious attitude. The Kurdish Jewess, on the other hand, bears on her face the stamp of subjection.

One is impressed by the primitiveness and the peasant soul of the Kurdish Jewess. Her horizon is restricted to her family and the life of her own community. Girls get no schooling whatsoever. Only a few, under special circumstances, learn to read and write. Most of these are the daughters of *ḥakhamim*, who for the most part, teach them only when there is no son in the family on whom the effort can be spent; and there is usually a practical purpose involved. These *ḥakhamim* are schoolmasters; and if they have no sons or only very young sons, they teach the oldest daughter to read and write in order that she may help her father in his teaching. This is because a Kurdish Jewish village schoolmaster is at the same time *shoḥeṭ* and *mohel* and is often called away from his pedagogic duties.

A very interesting case of this kind, from the sixteenth century, has come to our notice through one of the letters of Kurdish Jews published by Mann.[2] This letter is one of several dealing with the same affair. Jakob b. Judah Mizraḥi,[3] who was obviously a Kurdish Jew, conducted a school in Amadiya and later in Mosul. This school, as we gather from his letters, was chiefly supported by grants from Jewish communities in Kurdistan (see p. 66). After Mizraḥi's death, his widow endeavored to carry on the school herself. The letter in question could hardly have been composed by her,[4] since it is full of *melitzot* [poetic expressions] and reveals no small knowledge of Hebrew and rabbinical literature. We gather from this letter that she was taught by her father, Samuel Halevi: ["He did not teach me any thing or work except the work of heaven to fulfill what is written, 'And thou shalt study it day and night'. Because of the many sins, he had no sons but only daughters"] (lines 65–66). Further, she states that her father, at the time of her marriage, insisted on her continuing the work with the Torah: ["And he also made my husband swear that he would not make me perform work, and he did as he had commanded him"] (lines 67–68).

Evidently, the entire burden of the school work rested on her shoulders: ["From the beginning, the Rabbi, of blessed memory, was busy with his studies and had no time to teach the pupils; but I taught them in his stead, I was a helpmeet for him. Now, because of many sins, he departed to (eternal) rest"] (lines 68–69). She begs the community to support her and reinforces her plea by appealing to ["the sake of Father, of blessed memory, and the Rabbi, of blessed memory, so that their Torah and names should not be brought to naught in these communities; for I remain the teacher of Torah and she who reproaches and demands that (they observe) the immersion, and the Sabbath, and the menstrual impurity, and the prayer, and the likes"] (lines 58–59). Thus, she also lays stress on her activity in spreading the Torah among the women, whom she exhorted to observe the regulations concerning *nidda* and the Sabbath laws.

A vivid memory of these learned women has survived among the Kurdish Jews. This fact also speaks for the rareness of the phenomenon. Thus, it is said that the wife of R. Simon, in the seventeenth century, was a teacher of children in Amadiya. In the late eighteenth century, the wife of a certain R. Asher pursued the same vocation, likewise in Amadiya. And about 1840, the sister of a R. Eliyahu was her brother's assistant in his teaching (according to the statement of Shabtai Joseph Barashe). Among the few Kurdish Jewesses in Jerusalem who know how to read and write is the daughter of a *ḥakham* of Nirwa. She is therefore also the adviser of all the women in the neighborhood. At the time my informant lived in Amadiya, there were only two women there who could read and write; and in Zakho and Sinne it is doubtful if there was even one.[5]

The women speak almost exclusively Targum. In certain districts (e.g., Amadiya) they also speak Kurdish fluently. In Zakho, on the other hand, where they have little opportunity to come in contact with Kurds, their knowledge of Kurdish is slight. True, the songs that the women sing at weddings and similar functions are for the most part Kurdish; but they little understand them. I found no evidence of a secret language among the women [as one finds among them in some places in the Near East].

In Hebrew the majority of the women know only a few benedictions and the *Shema'* prayer.[6] Still, they are very punctilious in the external observance of the religious precepts.

Polygamy

Polygamy is permitted among the Kurdish Jews but is rarely practiced. In Amadiya in about 1930 ten men had second wives, in Ushnu seven. In Sinne 1 percent of the men are polygamists. Men with three wives are very exceptional.[7] In Sinne, for example, at the time of my investigation [late 1930s], my informants knew of no single case of this kind.[8]

One of the principal reasons for marrying a second wife is the lack of a male heir. In the countryside, more than in the towns, economic factors also come into play. A thirty-year-old Jew living in the country town of Ushnu took a girl of twenty as his second wife. The only reason he gave me for this marriage was that the work in his house had increased to such an extent that one wife was not enough. He had four cows, and the care of these was mainly the duty of the second wife. Another case in which the economic motive is paramount is the marriage of a man who took a wealthy widow as his second wife. Such marriages, entered into for purely financial reasons, are not infrequent among the Kurdish Jews.

The first wife generally struggles with all her might and main against her husband's taking a second wife. Still, she knows that her weeping and wailing are in vain.[9] When her husband brings his second wife home, the first wife—probably making magic use of the custom described above in connection with the reception of the bride in the bridegroom's house—climbs to the roof, throws pebbles at her rival as she enters, and stamps her foot. In this way she ensures her supremacy over the second wife (A.).

The wedding customs of a plural marriage are substantially different from those of a first marriage. If the second wife is still a virgin, the preparatory ceremonies occupy three days. This applies only to the wife. The husband is exempt from the henna dyeing and the special ceremony at the bath. He must, however, sit in the *gnūne* for eight days with his new wife. [There may be in this custom a memory of the biblical usage; cf. Gen. 29:27.] If the second wife is a widow or a divorced woman *tolaqta*, then the customs peculiar to her state are carried out (see p. 187).

Treatment of Women

The Kurdish Jewess is treated as we are accustomed to find women treated among orientals, specifically among oriental peasants. The woman is in a state of complete subjection to the man. In view of this fact, one can scarcely speak either of loving, or of brutal, treatment. Most of the women look upon their husbands from the beginning as their lord and master. Even in districts where one speaks of the woman as well treated (e.g., Amadiya), the entire burden of the household work is thrown upon her. Not only that but she must wait upon her husband hand and foot. The more important the family, the more extreme is this treatment. The husband hardly takes a step in the house and never lifts a finger. He says to his wife, "Bring me the book. Bring me my pipe, the tea," and so on. It is actually a disgrace for a man to do anything for himself. Of a husband who is continually ordering his wife about, it is said, *Mane īla bakhte khabre khāye yerīkhelū*, "He whose wife stands under his orders, his life will be long."

On the other hand, it is said of a husband who is not given to ordering his wife about, *Mane lēwa bakhte khabre amre*[10] *krī le ajale*[11] *zīlēlū*, "He whose wife does not stand under his orders, his life is short, his days went."

The women have their meals apart from the men, generally after them.[12] At feasts, the *sīnīye* that is brought to them contains the men's leavings. If the husband and wife go to the same place, they never walk side by side, but the wife follows a few steps behind.

Although the husband treats the wife as a ruler treats his subject, she need not, for all that, be treated brutally. The Kurdish Jews, however, have a tendency to be brutal to their wives and to beat them—often so cruelly that the women must take to their beds. At weddings and feasts, when the men have gone ahead with arrack and *maza* and the women must bring them the *sīnīye* with the food, the women who happen to come late are beaten by their husbands in the presence of the other men. The husband wishes thereby to display his might before the other men.

Daily Work

It is, we may say, a matter of course that the whole burden of the housework should fall upon the wife. The wife gets up in the morning before her husband. While she washes herself, she recites the prescribed benedictions, which every woman knows, then goes to the mezuza on the door and says the *shema'*, which the women of Amadiya know as far as *Uv'khol m'odekha.*[13] After that, she brings her husband water to wash in. When the husband says the benedictions the women add *amen*. While the husband is at the morning service in the synagogue, the wife lights the stove and prepares breakfast (*gadāya*; see p. 105). Then the children get up and eat their breakfast.

After the boys have left for school, the mother puts her *talma* on her back and goes to fetch water from the river or the spring. In Amadiya, the wives of rich men do not fetch the water themselves but keep a water carrier (*saqāye*). The less fortunate women go to the river or spring in groups twice a day, morning and evening. In Sinne they go only in the evening.

The wife then sets the house in order and prepares the dinner (*sharūsa*, see p. 105). When she hears the voice of the muezzin (*mala*) calling from the minaret of the mosque, she knows that it is midday (*palgit yom*) and that the boys are coming home from school.

The laundry is done on a definite day in Kurdistan, usually on Thursday, so that there may be clean clothes and clean linen for the Sabbath. The women gather at the river with their washing and clean the clothes by dipping them in the river and beating them with a board (*khatōra*).[14] When the laundry is finished, the women proceed to take their Sabbath bath (*kiapa*). For this purpose, they bring a cauldron to the river to heat the water. In Amadiya they may also go in winter to a warm spring (*en khātūn*; Kurd. *kānī khatūne*), namely, the Spring of the Lad. This washday at the river is a holiday for the women. They dance and sing till late in the evening, then return home all together (A. and Z.).

In the afternoon the women sit and work in the courtyard in a shady spot, on the *birbanke*, or (in winter) in the house. The Kurdish Jewess, like Oriental Jewesses in general, is tied to the house. She does not go to the market and she rarely leaves the precincts of the Jewish quarter. Her human contacts are limited to relatives and neighbors. These afternoons, along with the feasts, form her social life. In summer, the women of Ushnu sit in the court of the synagogue—the closest thing to a garden that the Jewish quarter can boast.

Handicraft and Needlework

The Kurdish Jewess also differs from her Yemenite sister in that her needlework and other handwork does not show much skill—or perhaps it would be more correct to say that it no longer shows much skill. We find in it none of that fine technique and hereditary artistic taste that the Yemenite women have developed in their embroideries and basketwork.

One of the principal occupations of the Kurdish woman is the preparation of wool. She cards,[15] washes, and spins it. Whenever she has a free moment, she can be seen standing at her door with her spindle (*tashīya*).[16]

The women are also busy with weaving the wool. Thus, in Amadiya simple rugs (*gāle* and *shēwise*) are the work of the women. Their chief pursuits, however, are dressmaking and knitting (Z., D., A., and S.).

Their dressmaking comprises articles of linen and clothing, the latter often embroidered (Z., D., A., and S.). The greater part of their customers are Muslim Kurds.[17] Among the skilled manual crafts in which the Kurdish women even today show a high degree of artistic excellence is knitting. We have already spoken of the stockings, leggings and gloves, some of them exceptionally beautiful, which they knit of white or many colored wool in artistic designs (see pp. 87–88).

Instruction in these crafts is the only education the girls receive; and it is frequently given not by their mothers but by some woman who is reputed to be exceptionally skilled and who, though she often has many such pupils sitting in her house, takes no pay for her efforts. Apart from this type of instruction, the girls grow up entirely ignorant and illiterate.

Laws of Purity

The women resemble the men in their rigid orthodoxy. They, too, have the faith of the peasant, which is completely satisfied by the performance of external ceremonies. They observe punctiliously the rites that women are supposed to observe. Chief among these are the laws of purity.[18] We have seen that in Amadiya and Nirwa there were special houses to which the women retired in the period following childbirth or during menstruation and the seven days of impurity (p. 158). This custom was abolished about 1860.

The wife does not tell the husband when she is impure, but he realizes her condition from the special garments which she puts on at this time.[19]

When she is impure, the woman must not sit on the same carpet as the other members of the family. She must also eat apart from them. She has a special spoon and other dishes, which are separately washed (Z. and S.). She must not prepare the food, and she must not pass her husband the water.[20] There are, moreover, among the Kurdish Jews the ultrapious who will not at any time take anything directly from the hands of their wives. Thus, it is told of the *shammash* Yiṣḥaq of Amadiya, who lived about 1870, that in order to perform his duties at the synagogue always in a state of purity, he never at any time took any object directly from the hand of his wife or daughter.

The same regulations apply to unmarried girls as to women. There are no special ceremonies at the first menstruation. Among *ḥakhamim*, in particular, girls and women are treated alike; and the father takes nothing from his daughter's hand during her time of impurity (A. but not S.).

In Amadiya all women refrain from wearing white for seven days, In Sinne for five, six, or seven days. After a further seven days they go to the *miqve*, the ritual bath.

The *Miqve*

The *miqve* of the Kurdish Jews, termed *gara*, is generally a bath in the river (Z. and A.). The *miqve* in Amadiya (*garit alūchā*, "bath of the plum" [so-called because plum trees grow near the building]), is said to be very old. It is surrounded by ancient walls built up still higher with branches of trees, so as to be effectually screened from the road. Before taking their bath, the women cut their nails and clip the ends of their braids. The women of Zakho formerly went to the *miqve* either in the daytime or at night. In Amadiya, however, it has been customary from olden times to go at night. The reason given is that the woman must not meet a non-Jew on the way back. The immersion in winter, at a time of extreme cold, is a great physical strain; and women of exceptional piety perform prodigies of heroism, so to speak, in carrying out their religious duties in spite of snow and ice. Since it is a pious duty to the Kurdish Jew to sleep with his wife on the night before Sabbath, women who become pure on Friday go to the *miqve* on Friday night. This, it is said, is what the wife of the *ḥakham* Rabbi Shim'on of Amadiya once did. She went to the river in the night; and it was winter, a time of cold and storm. On the way home she met a man. She turned back with the woman who accompanied her, and immersed herself again; but again, she met a man on the way home. This happened fourteen times, and fourteen times she returned to her bath in the river. Then her skin began to peel off from the cold, so she put her shawl over her head and let her companion lead her home (told by S.Y.).

It is also regarded as a religious duty for a husband to cohabit with his wife directly after her purification.[21] Therefore the men, who are mostly away from home, make great haste to be back on the night after the immersion; but if their return is nevertheless delayed in some way, the wife is seized with a fear that a demon may become aware of her purity and sleep with her. As a protection against the demons, therefore, she keeps her husband's trousers under her pillow during the night (Z. and S.).[22]

Adultery and Divorce

Although the Kurdish Jews always talk about the seclusion of their women, who sit by themselves in the courtyards of their houses, it is remarkable how many cases of misconduct were reported to me. It would appear that the chief reason these transgressions remain so firmly fixed in the memory of the Jews is that they generally ended in the conversion of the woman to Islam.

The following story, which centers around a woman from Betanura, gives us a good insight into a case of this kind. It was told to me by the *urvat jemā'a* [head of the community] of Amadiya himself, Shabtay Yosef.

There was a girl in Betanura, who excelled in beauty above all the other girls of Barwilnaya. Her father gave her in marriage to a man; but there was, in Betanura, another man who was after her. And she did not resist but slept with him. The matter became known and reached the ears of the people of Amadiya. In his capacity of head of the community, Shabtay Yosef had the man brought before him, and remonstrated with him. But the man denied everything. They made him render an oath, and he did. Thereupon, they made a *danin agav sudar* with him: he had to get hold of one end [of a *sudar*], the *ḥazan* of the other; and he had to swear that under such and such penalty, he would not again go near the woman and would not enter her street.

The man returned to Betanura. But, a few months later, news again reached Amadiya that he had relations with the woman. They ordered him again to come to Amadiya, and Shabtay Yosef sentenced him to fifteen beatings; that is, he got beaten on his back and legs fifteen consecutive days, so that after the first few days he was unable to walk and they had to put him on a mule to take him home.

Thereafter, and after the imposition of a heavy fine and additional warnings, they took him back to Betanura, where he remained bedridden for several weeks, until finally he recovered from the wounds inflicted on him by the beatings.

About this time, a young man, a weaver from Tchalla, came to Betanura. This young man was extremely strong, he could break iron with his bare hands. He had left Tchalla because of some quarrel. He went to the mir [lord] of Barwilnaya, and asked permission to settle in Betanura. It was granted to him. This young man fell in love with the same woman. He made up to her and slept with her.

In the meantime, her first lover recovered. At first, he avoided the house of the woman; but soon desire grew so strong in him that he went to her and had relations with her.

The doings of the young man were reported to the mir of Barwilnaya. The mir warned him and threatened to have him killed. When the young man did not desist, the mir ordered his servants to fetch him. He warned him once more and said that although he had been willing to accept him in Betanura, he would under no conditions tolerate such things in his territory. Then he had him beaten cruelly (as it was customary with the mir) and finally had him immersed in icy water. But the young man, with his strong nature, soon overcame the effects of this torture and before long, again started to go to the woman.

One evening, when both lovers were with the woman, her husband, who had been keeping watch over his rice fields, returned. The young man threw himself upon him and twisted his limbs so that they thought he was dead. The young man fled.

But the husband did not die of his injuries. He recovered; and one day, without giving a *get* [letter of divorce] to his wife, he left Betanura in secret. He went to Mosul, then to Baghdad, and via Egypt reached Jerusalem, where he still lives today.

When the woman saw that her husband had left her without a *get*, she went to Amadiya to ask that they obtain a *get* for her so that she could marry again. They agreed to track down her husband but warned her to cease her misconduct or else she would be punished most severely.

But she did not stop and continued her relations with her first lover. Thereupon, the mir of Barwilnaya had the man apprehended and brought before him. He had two poles five meters in length stuck through the legs of his trousers and one pole through the arms of his jacket, put him thus against the wall, and had him beaten until blood streamed from all parts of his body. Then they took the man, who was half dead, to the place where the animals were kept, put him down there, and ignited the dung under him.

The young man, who had fled, heard that the husband remained alive; and he came again, in secret, to the woman. The mir of Barwilnaya, however, had enough of the affair. He summoned the relatives of the woman and told them that he was giving them a free hand to do what they thought was right.

Over night, her brothers, when they heard that the lover was with their sister, got up, broke into the room, and killed the man they found there. He turned out not to be that young man but another lover of their sister.

The brothers had to flee. The sister, however, married a Kurd and converted to Islam. That man died soon thereafter. She married another Muslim, and moved with him to Dehok. A few years later, when this man, too, died, a Jew wanted to marry her, but the woman did not want to become Jewish again.

Several years later, the brothers wanted to return to Betanura. But avengers of blood can only return if the locality calls them back. So the brothers, following their custom, set fire to a corner of a field. When, despite this, the people of Betanura did not call them back, they set fire to the fodder. Thereupon the people of Betanura wanted to make peace. The mir of Barwilnaya summoned one the five brothers and the father of the murdered man. Blood money in the amount of £25 was set, and in addition £5 for the mir. The money was taken from the cash of the prayer house, and the brothers undertook to repay it in the course of a few years.

[It is difficult to determine to what extent this is a true account of what happened, and to what extent it is colored by the storyteller's imagination. If it is a true account, one can learn from it important details concerning the relations between men and women and the power relations in the community.

The most remarkable feature is that the woman, guilty of multiple and repeated adultery, receives no punishment. In each case, it is her lovers who suffer. The punishments escalate from admonition to beating, to torture, to fines, and ultimately to death.

Interesting is also the power relationship between the *urvat jemā'a*, the head of the Jewish community, and the mir, the Muslim headman of the district. The former can sentence the culprit to beatings and fines, but only the latter can subject him to torture that can result in his death. It appears, moreover, that the relatives of the woman (her brothers) are allowed to take action against her lovers only if the mir grants them permission to do so. Even the husband seems intent only on attacking the lover, even though this results in his own bloody defeat. Nobody touches the woman. She can even go to the rabbis of Amadiya to ask their help in obtaining a divorce, and they agree to help her.

There can be little doubt that the heroine of the story must have been a quite exceptionally attractive woman. Her lovers risk torture, mutilation, and even death but are unable to keep away from her. After her conversion to Islam, two Muslim men are ready to marry her. And after all this—all the adultery and apostasy—there is still yet another Jewish man who wants to marry her. It is not clear from the story how this Jewish man could expect her to return to Judaism, seeing that to leave Islam is a capital offense in Muslim lands.

Interesting, also, are the details we learn from the last paragraph of the story about the rules governing blood revenge and blood money.

In any case, this story depicts a situation not at all consonant with the domination of the man over the woman repeatedly emphasized by Brauer.]

The punishment meted out to an adulteress is hard. In Zakho the wife of a rich Jew carried on a liaison with the son of the aga. The rav at once decreed a divorce. The hair of the erring woman is cut off,[23] and she is set backward on a donkey and given his tail as a rein. The children escort her, beating on tin pans, and douse her with sour milk (Z.).

The Muslim Kurds also punish adulteresses and prostitutes in this way. A Jewess of Sinne, who was considered to be exceptionally beautiful, became a prostitute and converted to Islam. When the government could no longer ignore her traffic, she was seized and her hair cut off; then she was dressed in men's clothing and driven out of the town.

Procurers (*kauwāde*) meet with a similar fate. In Amadiya there lived an old Jewess who engaged in pandering. The Jews could not induce her to cease her activities and lodged a complaint against her with the government. She was set backward on a donkey and brought to the town wall, from which she was hurled and stoned. She lived through all this, however, and is said to have turned over a new leaf.

Sometimes the husbands take the law into their own hands. A Jew of Rekan went out with his guilty wife to milk the sheep. On the way he stabbed her with his dagger (*ḥanjar*) and some time later killed her lover also.

The domination of the man over the woman, in every relationship and every phase of life is characteristic for the Kurdish Jews. It is very difficult for the wife to obtain a divorce from her husband. He, on the other hand, can easily get the *ḥakham* to draw up a *get*, a bill of divorce, for him.

Juridically, the wife is powerless to free herself from the bonds of marriage, a situation that is doubly hard in view of the fact that the girls are married by their fathers without regard to their own wishes. A case in point is that of a woman of Amadiya, reputed to be very beautiful, who had left her husband because she could no longer endure living with him. She had taken the child she had born to her husband and had returned to her father's house. All attempts to obtain the husband's consent to a divorce met with failure. These attempts continued for five years, and even the rabbinate in Ashur (Mosul) was approached—but without result. The case was finally settled through the mediation of a rabbinical emissary from Palestine. The father, however, had to pay the husband £40 to secure the *get* for his daughter.[24]

The situation of the husband is very different. If he can fulfill the obligations laid upon him in the *ketubba*, he can easily get rid of his wife. The *get*, which is drawn up by the *ḥakham*, is delivered to the wife, and then torn crosswise in the customary manner. After this ceremony, each of the parties goes to the *miqve*. Those taking part do not return home by the direct road but *chape* (roundabout): in this case they make a detour through the market place (A.). The husband who gives the *get* (*tulqa*) and the divorced woman (*tolaqta*) then distribute bread among the entire community.

The children remain with the father. The women, it is said, part easily with their children (A.). If the divorcee has an infant, she nurses him until his second year—a service for which she is paid—then this child also is sent to his father. There are no further relations, I am told, between the children and their divorced mother.

The *tolaqta* usually marries again,[25] although men are not very eager to marry a *tolaqta*. At her remarriage there are no ceremonies. She is not dyed with henna. She is bathed in the ordinary way and brought to her husband's house without any solemnity. The bridal meal consists of a very simple dish, *shorba* (a thin porridge made of rice). If the bridegroom is still a bachelor (*janka*) all the customary preparations are made for his wedding, and he must remain in the *gnūne* eight days, whereas the *tolaqta* may leave it after three days.[26]

Levirate Marriage

Levirate marriage (Heb. *yibbum*) is still practiced by the Kurdish Jews, although it is much less frequent than release through the *ḥalīṣa*.[27]

In the letter from Sukho that we have previously mentioned (Mann, *Texts and Studies* letter 19; see above, p. 112) the writer seeks to have the marriage declared invalid on the grounds that the woman's deceased husband was a minor and in order that the woman should not have to wait until the husband's only surviving brother, a child of six,[28] would reach majority (thirteen years) and either the levirate marriage or the *ḥalīṣa* could take place.

In Sinne the ceremony *ḥalīṣa*, the drawing off of the shoe [a ceremony performed for the purpose of releasing the widow and her deceased husband's brother from the duty of marrying each other], is performed outside the town in a place called *va'ad*. In Amadiya the *ḥalīṣa* was at one time performed in a certain cave outside the town, but about a hundred years ago a special house was built near the synagogue for this purpose. The age-old *ḥalīṣa* shoe (*pelaftit khalīṣa*) is kept there.

In Sinne, the dayyanim, the shammash and the witnesses, together forming a minyan, go with the *yavam* [levir] and the *yevama* [widow] to the appointed place on the day before the ceremony. There they seat themselves in exactly the same order as they are to sit the next day. The *ḥakham* says, "We have come here today to arrange the place for the *ḥalīṣa* between A and B." The latter are then enjoined to fast next day. On the morrow the *ḥalīṣa* party arrives early at the *va'ad*. Food and carpets are brought along. After another attempt to bring about the *yibbum* [considered a necessary formality], the ceremony of the drawing off of the shoe follows in the traditional manner. The woman lays her headdress about her shoulders and puts a small cloth on her head as soon as she reaches the place. She must not spit at this time. She has been well drilled beforehand by the *ḥakham* in the drawing off of the shoe, the spitting, and the sentence that she must recite. The witnesses receive a large sum of money for their services (A.), since the *ḥalīṣa* ceremony is believed to be dangerous for all the participants; consequently, no one wishes to have a hand in it. Likewise the *ḥakham* and the scribe who draws up and writes the *ḥalīṣa* document are highly paid. In Sinne the remuneration is ten times as great as for drawing up a *get*.

In Sinne a cock and a hen are slaughtered after the *ḥalīṣa* as *kappara*. In Amadiya the participants do not return home by the direct road but *chape*, in a roundabout way, as in the case of a *get*.

The man and the woman must both go to the *miqve*. Then they proceed to the market place, buy bread, and distribute it among the poor and the schoolboys. In former times, the distribution of the bread took place before the *ḥalīṣa* ceremony (A.).

10

Death and Burial

Whereas in the customs associated with the other crises of human life (such as birth and marriage) we clearly recognize among the Jews the influence of their non-Jewish environment, this is not the case in the customs associated with death. The Oriental Jews—and among them those of Kurdistan—have taken over scarcely anything from the death customs of the people around them, so that their death customs remain fundamentally Jewish.

If a man is in the throes of death, everyone without exception leaves the room. It is said that the soul would not take its departure if anyone should weep (S.).

A prolonged death struggle, it is thought, shows that the soul cannot get out of the body. Therefore various measures are adopted to facilitate its escape and thus relieve the dying man. The first and most effective measure is the ceremony of *ḥaṭṭara*, "releasing." Ten men, among them several *ḥakhamin*, assemble in the room, lift the patient to his feet and pronounce the *ḥaṭṭara*. Unless he is destined to recover, he will not survive the day (A.).

Again, the synagogue is locked, and the key put under the dying man's head. The soul will then make a great effort to depart, because the congregation is waiting for the key (S. and U.); or the dying man is given "water of *qri'at Shema'*" to drink (a glass of water over which a *ḥakham* has said the *Shema'* S.).

When the man has breathed his last, he is laid face down on the bare ground at the spot where he died, so that he may draw into himself the odor of the earth; otherwise, his skin will turn black. A bit of iron is laid on him; and candles are set about him at the head, foot, and sides (A.). The dead man lies in the middle of the room (Z.), with his feet to the west ([i.e. to Jerusalem,] Z. and A.)

Everyone who is in the room rends his garment. Formerly, a tear was made in the undergarment also. The people in the neighboring houses, especially those in which the weeping of the mourners can be heard, pour out all their drinking water. The explanation of this custom is the usual one, namely, that the angel of death washes his blood-stained knife in this water. The neighbors usually transfer their supply of drinking water beforehand to houses some distance away (D., A., and S.).

The community is at once apprised of the death. In Amadiya a man formerly went through the town wearing a black armlet on which was embroidered the word *aveluth*, "mourning," and carrying in his left hand a black flag, *sinjaq evel*, which bore the inscription, "Flag of mourning; for this is (the fate of) every man" (see Ecclesiastes 7:2).[1] If the dead man is a *ḥakham* or some other prominent person, a general stoppage of work is decreed; but for an ordinary individual, work is suspended only for a short time before the funeral.

The *Ḥavrāye*

The head of the *Ḥevra Qaddīsha* is immediately notified. Amadiya possesses an especially well qualified and apparently very old organization of *ḥavrāye*. It comprises from twenty-two to twenty-four members,[2] among whom are always included the *ḥakham*, the *gabbai*, and two *gevirim*.

The members choose their chief, the *shekh ḥavrāye*, and the chief appoints his deputy *bar shekh*, and a *shammash*. These hold office for a number of years, but the *shekh* can be deposed if he fails to give satisfaction.

At the time of his election, the *shekh* is presented by the *ḥaverim* with some article of clothing (e.g., an *abāyika* [or a *shāla turma*, a shawl from Turma]); and he reciprocates by inviting them to a banquet at his house.

It is the specific duty of the *ḥabrāye* to care for the sick, to take charge of the body after death, and to make all funeral arrangements; but in Amadiya the association has, in fact, developed into a men's club with the ordinary activities of a club, and it likewise exercises a degree of control over the community.

The *ḥaberim* have what amounts to a "men's house." This consists of a room in the Bē Ḥazāne, the house built near the graves of Ḥazan David and Ḥazan Yosef in the precincts of the Sayyid Yeḥezqel synagogue (see p. 250).

In this room the *ḥaverim* meet three times a week for their drinking parties: on Sunday evening, on Wednesday evenings, and on the Sabbath immediately after the morning service. At these parties arrack is served, three glasses to each *ḥaver*. The *ḥaverim* bring along their own *maza*. After the refreshments, the *ḥakham*, at the *shekh*'s invitation, delivers the *drāsha* [sermon]. The arrack consumed by the *ḥaverim* is paid for out of the various contributions that flow regularly into the fund of the *ḥavraye*.

These contributions come from the men who are called to the reading of the Torah—the *ḥaverim* and the *gevirim* when thus honored must pay special fees—from the *ḥatan Torah*, the bridegroom, the *shushbinim*, the *avi haben*, and so on. All the men from the outlying districts who come to Amadiya for the services or who make the pilgrimage (*ziyāra*) to the graves of Ḥazan David and Ḥazan Yosef—by no means a negligible number (see p. 62)—contribute to the fund of the *ḥaverim*.

The fund is further augmented through fines, especially fines for offenses committed by the *ḥaverim* themselves. The strictness of the code regulating the behavior of the members to each other, especially at their meetings, is conducive to many fines of this kind. All disagreements among the members are settled by the *shekh*, and a fine in the shape of several bottles (*kanīna*) of arrack is laid on both the contending parties. Similarly, all the other resources of the *ḥavrāye* are used for supplying the *ḥaverim* with arrack. In short, we have here, in effect, a kind of *Freibier*.

The *ḥaverim* have a meeting place not only in the Bē Hazāne but also at the riverbank. There, at the *duke ḥavrāye* [place of *ḥaverim*], are a number of walnut trees. At the drinking parties in winter the produce from these trees is very formally distributed, the *shekh* calling out the names of each member and giving him ten nuts. The *serāne* ["excursions"] take place at the festivals and on the occasion of the departure of members of the community for Ashur (Mosul) on business (see p. 212).

The twenty-four *ḥaverim* comprise sixteen actual members (with the *shekh* at their head), four men who wash the dead bodies, and four notables (*ḥazan*, *gabbai*, and two *gevirim*). Their service to the sick consists in arranging for two men, appointed by the *shekh*, to keep constant watch beside them; but their chief duty is the care of the dead.

When death has taken place, the *shekh* is first of all notified. The *shekh* then notifies the *bar shekh*, and the latter notifies the *shammash*, who summons all the *ḥaverim* to the house of the *bar shekh*. Thence they go to the house of the *shekh*, where each *ḥaver* is handed two glasses of arrack. Apparently, this drink has a ritual significance. After the *shammash* has brought the necessary implements, the fourteen gravediggers, with the *shekh*, proceed to the cemetery to dig the grave and the four washers to the house of the dead man to wash the body.

The transformation of the *ḥebra qaddīsha* into a men's club is to be found in Kurdistan only in Amadiya. The *ḥebra* of Zakho occupy themselves strictly with the care of the dead. There is a *shekh khapāre*, chief of gravediggers," and a *shekh khayāpe*, "chief of washers." Each of them has a deputy (Kurd. *rēspi*, pl. *rēspiyāna*, "white beard").[3]

The chief washer has the necessary utensils for the washing brought to the house. They consist of the board (Z. *dargit mīthe*)[4] on which the deceased is washed and whatever is necessary for sewing the grave clothes. In Zakho they are kept in the synagogue, in Amadiya, in the *bēt el miṣwa* at the Bē Ḥazāne, where the *ḥalīṣa* shoe and *malqut* are also to be found. The receptacle for these utensils is called *jillīt mithe* (A.) or *kistet mīthe*.

When these objects are carried to the house, a man runs ahead and calls *Dargit mīthe*! Then the women quickly get the children not merely indoors but into a back room or to the roof. They also take the infants out of the cradle and go into a back room with them. The same thing is done with the sick (Z. and A.). The death utensils, it is said, must not come near a child as they are carried by.

The grave clothes (*khelē'eta*)[5] are made of cotton (*kitān*), which is of a special width and is brought from Mosul. In Zakho the chief washer cuts out the shroud, and his assistants do the sewing. The grave clothes of a woman are made by the women who wash the body. In Amadiya, the grave clothes of the men, also, are sewed by old women.

If anyone fears that there may possibly not be any money at hand for his shroud at his death, he buys the necessary cotton during his lifetime. Old women often provide their grave clothes themselves. They invite the seamstresses and a few women friends to their homes where a meal, called *se'odit khiyāpit kūrākha* is prepared for them. Some of the food is given to children as *segula*, "good luck," and to the *ḥaverim* (A.).[6]

The shroud consists of the same parts as an ordinary garment but is more primitively made. Each hand is thrust into a kind of glove. The corpse receives a *tallit qaṭan*, which, however, lacks *ṣiṣiyot*, "fringes."

The pieces left over from the shroud of a *ḥakham* or a very respected old man are much sought after by mothers. We have told how these pieces are acquired by mothers who have lost several children, and made into a dress for a surviving child who, they fear, may meet the fate of the others (see p. 173). These remnants are also cut into small pieces and hung around children's necks as amulets (A. and S.).

The women gather in the room around the dead man and begin to wail. They bruise and scratch their faces, put mud on their hair, and smear it on their faces and shoulders. They tear out their hair;[7] and if a mother already bereaved of children loses an additional child, she cuts off her braids.

There are also professional mourning women (A. [*bakhtāsa m'*]*adedāna*), who are exceptionally expert in wailing and singing in a heartbreaking manner. In Amadiya and Zakho they receive no remuneration. In Sinne, on the other hand, professional mourners, both Jewish and Muslim, are hired and are encouraged with calls of "Mourn over him well!"[8] The songs that the [*m'*]*adedāne* sing are Kurdish and were taken over from the Kurds. Most of these songs lament the death of a lover or a hero.

Marriage of the Dead

The lamentation for the dead has a special form when the deceased is a youth or a maiden. Then a sort of marriage of the dead takes place similar to the ceremony that, in numerous variations, is performed among many other peoples and has survived even in Europe.[9]

Immediately after his death, the body of a young unmarried man is dyed with henna as though he were a bridegroom.[10] While preparing the henna and during the dyeing, the women sing the same songs as at a marriage ceremony, except that their songs are interrupted by spells of weeping.

If the youth was already betrothed (Heb. *mequddash*), the bride is sometimes brought into the room clad in her wedding garments; and the exchange of rings takes place. The young man's wedding clothes are hung over his body.

If a bride dies, her body also is dyed with henna, her wedding garments are hung over her, and the marriage songs are sung (*Dim ḥamlula*, *Narīke*). The bridegroom, however, is not brought in in Zakho, although this was formerly done in Amadiya.

The customs just described were observed in Amadiya, as well. Nowadays, only the little finger of a dead bride is painted. For a dead bridegroom, on the other hand, a kind of death *ḥuppa* of black cloth is set up. This death *ḥuppa* is sometimes left hanging for years in memory of the dead boy. The parents of a dead bride hang up her jewelry and clothing beside the bed she used to occupy.

In Sinne the wedding clothes and the henna are brought in for both a dead bridegroom and a dead bride, but the bodies are not dyed. The women merely raise the *klīlīlī* amid their weeping. At times the bride is brought in to view the body of the bridegroom; then the lament reaches its climax.

Formerly, youths and maidens already betrothed were buried with all their wedding finery (not the wedding garments); but this custom was abolished as the result of an outrage (A.). A bride had died three days before the time set for her wedding and was buried with all her wedding finery; and a Muslim Kurd stole the jewelry. The thief died, so my informant said, a few days after committing the crime. Nevertheless, to this day, both Jews and Muslims call his family "the graverobber family" (*be ganawit mite*).

Washing the Body

In Zakho a funeral meal (*gurpāla* is served before the body is washed.[11] The ingredients used in preparing this meal are taken from the house of mourning. Therefore, it is a *miṣva* to send supplies for the funeral meal at once to poor people who are known to have none in the house.

The washers of the dead body and all who have assembled in the house of mourning partake of the funeral meal. A portion is sent also to the gravediggers (Z.). In Amadiya, *gurpālit mītha* is intended only for the *ḥaverim*. The funeral meal for a pious man or for an aged man is believed to bring good luck. Mothers take some of it for their children and people come from the homes of the sick to beg a portion for the patient (Z. and A.). In Amadiya, *gurpāla* for an old man or an old woman is sent to sick youths and maidens with the words *Kū khol lā zad'it aiya zubbināle kurākhokh*, "Up and eat, do not be afraid, this has bought your shroud" (A.).

As a *miṣva*, all the friends and neighbors bring some newly drawn water to the house of the dead for washing the body. After the water has been heated, the chief washer requests the women, who are seated about the dead man weeping and wailing, to leave the room so that the body may be carried into the courtyard for washing.[12] The women passionately resist this order; for they know that once the dead man has been carried out by the washers, they will never see him again. The chief washer must finally appear himself and eject the women by force.

The water is heated over a fire in the courtyard. The charcoal that remains is used by young men as a love charm. They take the still-glowing coals and say, *Kudakh mud'ikhli*[13] *aiya palā hādakh dā'akh libit tlubti bā'iyālī*, "As I extinguish this coal, so shall the heart of my beloved be extinguished (i.e., for another) in order that she may love me." The youth then rubs the coals to ashes, which he must throw before the feet of his beloved (A.).

The corpse is taken out and laid on the death plank (Z. *darga*, A. *dāpa*).[14] In former years the men stood around the body of a dead man, the women around that of a dead woman, in order to shield it from the view of the bystanders during the washing; but nowadays the men hold up cloths, making four walls round the corpse. In Sinne there is a special tent for the purpose. [This accords with the custom of the Persian Jews.]

The washers must hold some object in their hands when they enter the death tent (*pardāyit mīthe*), so as not to come "empty-handed" like the dead man. For washing the body they use little bags made of the cotton of the shroud and filled with soap flakes. Mothers who have lost children acquire these *līfe* from the chief washer and wash their surviving child with it (Z., A., and S.). Mothers also use it for washing their daughters on the *lēl benāta* preceding Purim (A.). At the washing of the body of a youth or a maiden, the women sing the songs that are sung at the ceremonial baths of betrothed couples.

The degree of ceremony attending the washing depends on the social position of the deceased. Cold water is poured over the body at the end by way of *ṭevīla* [submersion], and the washers break two new earthenware vessels on the *darga*. In so doing they say, *Jem'a mefaḥlūle*, "Community, forgive him"; and those present reply, *Fēḥel ḥalal hāwe*, "Full pardon be to him" (Z.).

In Sinne the *ḥakham* stands outside the tent and reads *Ana b'khoaḥ* seven times. At each reading the washers break six vessels. Thus, in total, forty-two vessels are broken.

After the washing, the *shekh* is handed the shroud, which is being held in readiness. It is fumigated with *bekhūr* [or A. *bukhāre*, a glue made of acorns] and put on the body. In the dead man's hand is placed the "deed" (*ketāva*) entitling him to four cubits of earth in Palestine (*ketāvit arba derā'e*[15] *qōra*). This "deed" is sold at a high price[16] by an envoy from Palestine and is acquired by almost every Jew.

Weird tales are told of occasions when, through some oversight, the dead man was not given his *ketāva*. In Tchalla, it is said, a man at the time of his death stretched out one arm with a wide open hand. After the washing, the *ḥaverim* tried to put down his arm, but in vain: it was as rigid as iron. Then it occurred to his wife that he probably wanted his *ketāva*. She hurried off to fetch it. As soon as it was put into the dead man's hand, the fingers closed over it, the arm became as soft as wax, and the body was brought into proper position without further difficulty.

In times of persecution, the deceased is also entrusted with a petition from the community, praying for deliverance.

Occasionally, a stone is put into the dead man's mouth to prevent his swallowing his shroud (S.). The men collect the combings from their beards during their lifetime and put them into a little bag which is laid in the grave with them (A.). If the deceased is the second member of his family to die within the year, an egg is put into a little bag and buried with him. This is a very widespread custom (Z., D., and S.).

After being washed and dressed, the body is swathed in bands (S. *shāl*)[17] or sewed into a kind of sack (A.). Then it is carried back into the room. A lighted candle is placed at its head and at its feet. Those present read from the Zohar until the candles have burnt out. The time of burial may depend on the length of time required by the gravediggers (*khapāre*) to dig the grave.

The Grave

In Amadiya, as we have seen, the gravediggers and the *shekh ḥavrāye* proceed at once to the cemetery. The *shekh* chooses a place for the grave, then all the *ḥavrāye* repair to an adjacent spot, where they sit down and eat and drink, one member at a time being sent by the *shekh* to do the digging.[18] In Zakho the corpse is measured, and the chief gravedigger marks out the dimensions of the grave. The office of gravedigger has been hereditary for generations in Zakho. The town now has about thirty gravediggers. Only one at a time does the digging; for it is believed that if two should be in the grave at the same time, one of them would die. As a *miṣva*, each gravedigger tries to work with such intensity that he is covered with perspiration. The relieving digger must not take the shovel from his predecessor's hand; the latter must first lay it down. In Amadiya, the *shammash* of the synagogue stands on the town wall and waits for the signal that the *shammash ḥavrāye* will give from the cemetery in the river valley below. The *shammash ḥavrāye* throws his coat into the air when the grave is ready. The *shammash* of the synagogue then hurries through the streets calling, Miṣva! This is the signal for cessation of work (Z. and A.).

The shape of the grave[19] is uniform among the Kurdish Jews. A pit about a meter deep is first dug, the length and width corresponding to the dead man's measurements; then, within this, a narrower pit is dug, about half a meter deep. Thus, there remain steps, called *berā qōra* (A., brothers of the grave)[20] at the sides. This form of grave obtains among the Muslim Kurds as well.[21] The body is laid in the lower pit; and planks (Z. *farshe*),[22] cut to size, are placed on the steps. In Betanura, Tchalla, and their environs no steps are left in the pit. The grave is of a uniform depth throughout, but steps are formed by piling stones at the two sides. After the body has been lowered into the narrow section, it is covered with a stone, instead of with boards.

Coffins are unknown in Kurdistan. The body is laid on a bier[23] that consists of two parallel poles fastened together with ropes (Z., A., and Betanura). The Jews of Sinne use an open casket with four handles.

The Funeral Procession

The best clothes or the wedding clothes of the deceased are placed on the bier—the *ṣiṣit* being included in the case of old men, the headdress in the case of young girls. In Ushnu the dead man's clothes are carried in the funeral procession by weeping relatives. In Amadiya the bier is covered with a black cloth (*charshabe kasōyit mīthe*).

The funeral procession is far from orderly. About 15 meters ahead of the bier go the *kohanim*, and after them, the aged folk and the *ḥakhamim*. Then comes the bier, followed by the mourners, the washers, and the public (A.). The miṣva of helping to carry the bier is performed by many people in turn, each saying as he takes his place, "With R. Shim'on b. Yoḥai's permission." In Ushnu the body of a bridegroom or a bride is escorted to the edge of the town with *dōla* and *zirne*. If the funeral procession passes a house containing a bridal pair or the mother of a newborn child, all of these, including the child, must be in a back room or on the roof while the procession is passing (Z. and A.) The occupants of every house that is passed by the funeral procession pour a little water into the street (Z.).

The body of a *ḥakham* or other distinguished person is borne first to the courtyard of the synagogue, where the *adōde* or *m'adode* (A. [sermon for the dead]) is pronounced. The women of the family and the dead man's sons are also permitted to come here. Otherwise, the women may accompany their dead only to the end of the street, and the sons only to the city gate. [When the procession reaches the city gate, the *ḥakham*, who walks at the head of the procession, stops and says, "It is the decision of Rabbenu Gershon, the Light of the Diaspora, that *līt rashut min ins min jins dilu birye min dāya nasha maha lā pāyit ila dāir*, that is, "It is not permitted for men or for evil spirits which were born from this man [namely, to do any harm]; they will not go on from here, but will turn back." The "evil spirits" referred to are the spirits who—according to a belief prevalent among the Sephardi Jews and Oriental Jewish communities in general, as well as among the Ashkenazi Jews—are born from the semen involuntarily ejected during the man's sleep.[24] After hearing these words of the *ḥakham*, the sons turn back from the city gate and return home.]

The women must not reenter their homes without washing; therefore, the neighbors pour water over their hands for them when they return. They do not cross the threshold until the men are back from the burial.

At the cemetery outside the town, the bier is set down four cubits' distance from the grave; and the seven *haqqafot* [circumambulations] are performed. The usual ceremonial follows. Then the chief gravedigger and his deputy step into the grave and lower the body into it just as it is. Nothing further is put into the grave. The dead man lies on his back with his feet [west] toward Jerusalem. The cut boards (or stones, as in Sinne, Betanura, and Tchalla) are laid on the steps beginning at the head. Everyone present then recites the verse, *V'hu raḥum y'khapper 'avon v'lo yashḥit, v'hirbah l'hashiv appo, v'lo ya'ir kol ḥamato*—three times—and throws a handful of earth into the grave at each word, making thirty-nine handfuls in all.

After this, Hashkava ["laying to rest"] is recited by the *ḥakham*, a tuft of grass is torn out by the mourners and thrown back over the shoulder, and the mourners are consoled. All this is done in the traditional manner.

The bier must be removed before anyone leaves the cemetery. It is not, however, carried out but is tilted up and pushed over again and again until it is outside the graveyard, where it is immediately taken apart (Z. and A.).

Mourning Customs

When they return from the funeral, the mourners, barefoot and clad in old, dark-colored garments, sit down on mats on the floor.

A light burns in the room night and day, and near it stands a glass of water (A.).

There is no special *se'udat havra'a* in Kurdistan, the first meal that the mourners eat after the funeral being regarded as the *se'ōda havrā'a* ["recuperation meal"]. Morning and evening callers arrive, bringing their own food, which they share with the bereaved family. The *maza* that is brought by the visitors must always include some eggs and, in certain districts, lentils (A. and S.). Some people also practice the custom of bringing the mourners a glass of wine over which the *ḥakham* has said the benedictions (S. and A.).

In Amadiya the *shekh ḥavrāye* decides who is to visit the mourners each day during the week of mourning. He invites wealthy folk for the evenings, if possible, since the evening meal should contain arrack and the well-to-do will include this with the food [they bring] for the bereaved family.

Shaḥarit, *Minḥa*, and *Ma'ariv* prayers are said each day in the house of mourning. On the day when the Torah is read, the mourners are escorted to the synagogue after *Shaḥarit*. The reading is delayed until their arrival. They come barefoot and take places other than those they usually occupy—near the door as a rule.

On Saturday a particularly good meal, including arrack, is brought to them. *Mebōse*, however, is prepared in the house by the relatives (Z.).

During the week of mourning, the house that death has visited is under a taboo similar to that which is laid on the house of a woman with a newborn child. No fire or leaven may be taken from such a house (Z. and A.). In Bijar the mourners are forbidden to eat their own bread. Bread must be brought to them from other houses. In general, no food from the house itself may be eaten during the first three days. Sinne is an exception. Here the rich even slaughter a sheep for the *se'oda havrā'a*.

At the close of the week of mourning comes the *se'ōdit*[25] *resh temanīya* [meal of the head of the eighth (day)], a meal that assumes great proportions among the well-to-do. All the *ḥakhamin* and a fair section of the men of the community are invited, and they spend the night in reading from the Zohar and other sacred works. The son of the deceased often has eight *shammashim* serving tea, coffee, fruit, and cigarettes. *Ma'ariv* is followed by the dinner, then the reading is resumed and continued throughout the night. No one sleeps. Another meal is served in the morning (A. and Z.).

This ends the first part of the mourning rites. The family take off the old black garments they donned for the week of mourning; but throughout the year, they wear only dark-colored clothing. They have this especially made for the purpose. The women even wear dark-colored underwear (A.). They discard all their jewelry; and instead of arranging their hair in the customary seven-to-ten braids, they limit themselves to two or three.

During this year the houses of the mourners are not whitewashed. The family shun all feasts and take no part in the *serane*. It is a general custom to refrain from eating seeds and nuts, ostensibly because cracking them makes a noise and all noises must be avoided at such a time (A.). Thus, the mourners also take care to speak softly and to pick no quarrels.

In Zakho the breakfasts and suppers that would have fallen to the share of the deceased had he been alive *ashāya gedāyit mītha*), are sent to the *ḥazan* or to a *ḥakham* during the year of mourning. When the wife of the recipient takes the food, she says *Matya gō nashāme*, "May it reach his soul" (Z. and A.). [In Amadiya a bowl full of food is sent to the poor every evening during the year of mourning. Whoever receives the food says, *Matya ilnshāme gō qaṣret gan eden*, "may it reach his soul in the tower of the Garden of Eden."] It is further customary for mourners to buy new fruits of all sorts as soon as they appear on the market and to distribute them among the people they chance to meet in the streets, so that they may say the benediction over them. On Rosh Ḥodesh Adar and at Purim (see p. 349), *zelōbīye* [pancakes] are sent to the synagogue for general distribution.

Minḥa and *Ma'ariv* prayers are said throughout the year on the Sabbath eve and the evening the outgoing Sabbath in the house of mourning.

Thirty days after the death of a father, the sons get their hair cut, put on new clothes and go to the *miqve*. People say to the mourners, *Lā khēpētūn ana khiyāpe*, "[May you] not wash yourselves like this washing" (A. and Z.) [or *Ishalla anna khiyāpe lā khēptulo illa b'farhiye*, "So God will, you will not wash again with these washings, but in gladness," (A.)]. The sons must generally be forced by the *ḥakham* to have their hair cut, for they are inconsolable.

After thirty days—and again after a year—the mourners give a meal, called *se'ōdit resh yarkha* [meal of the new moon] and *se'odit resh shata* [meal of the new year], respectively—to which the *ḥakhamim* and a large part of the congregation are invited and at which the Zohar and other sacred books are read.

Aged folk who have no sons, and realize that there will be no one to give the *se'ōdit resh temanīya*, *resh yarkha*, and *resh shata* for them when they die, give these three meals themselves in advance and invite the *ḥakhamim* to read the Zohar.

The Cemetery and Visits to the Cemetery

As the women are not permitted to visit the grave on the day of the funeral, they go to the cemetery on the following day and besprinkle the grave with rosewater. This is done three days in succession by the women of Amadiya. In Zakho these visits (*zartiasa*) take place every day for an entire week, except Sabbath. Accompanied by a large crowd of women from the neighborhood, the mourners go to the cemetery and lay the dead man's clothing on the grave. Many of the neighbors bring along the clothes of their own dead and weep over them.

When they return from the grave, they wash their hands in the river. The people on the way turn aside and hide themselves, for they do not want to meet the mourners (A.).

In Amadiya the graves are visited during Passover and Sukkot, and particularly on the 9th of Abh in Zakho, at every new moon during the first year and thereafter on the eve of Rosh Ḥodesh Nissan and on the 9th of Abh.

The cemeteries[26] of the Jews in Kurdistan are outside the city walls. The old cemetery of Amadiya lies on the slope of the hill on which the town is situated. The newer graves are in the valley. The *ḥakhamim* are buried higher up on the Tepāyit Adōnim [Hill of the Lords].

The cemeteries are not fenced in, and there are no tombstones[27] on the graves. The plots are merely covered with stones or surrounded by a primitive wall of field stones. The whole impression is, thus, one of unrelieved desolation. The cemetery of Amadiya boasts a few nut trees, which belong to the *ḥavrāye*.

Walter Schwarz gives the following description of the cemetery at Sundur near Dehok:

> [The village cemetery is very extensive and occupies an area larger than that of the present village. Exactly like the Kurdish cemeteries, it is totally unattended; in fact, even the distinctive marks of the Kurdish and Arab cemeteries, the trees, are missing here. Small, rectangularly placed stones mark the graves. From a distance the cemetery looks like a stony field. Occasionally one finds stones that are very old, on which one can decipher a few Hebrew letters. The new stones have no inscription. The cemetery is elevated above the village.][28]

Kurdistan, ca. 1947, showing the major Jewish communities.

Arbil, ca. 1940.

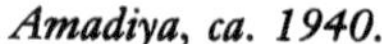

Amadiya, ca. 1940.

The Navi Yeḥezqel synagogue in Amadiya in the 1940s.

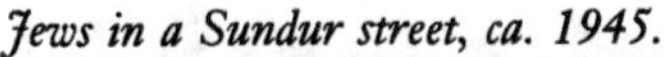

Jews in a Sundur street, ca. 1945.

Kurdish-Jewish Types

Woman from Zakho.

Woman from Dehok.

Man from Arbil.

Man from Barashe.

Man from Diarbekr.

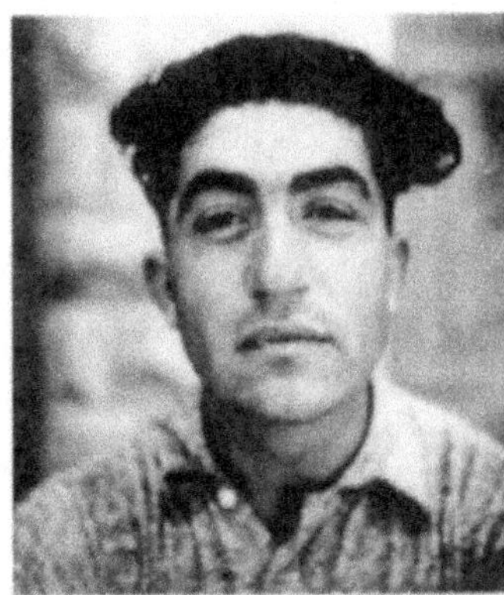

Man from Amadiya.

Man from Tchalla.

Man from Shukho, a village near Amadiya.

Woman from Kurdistan.

Woman from Kurdistan.

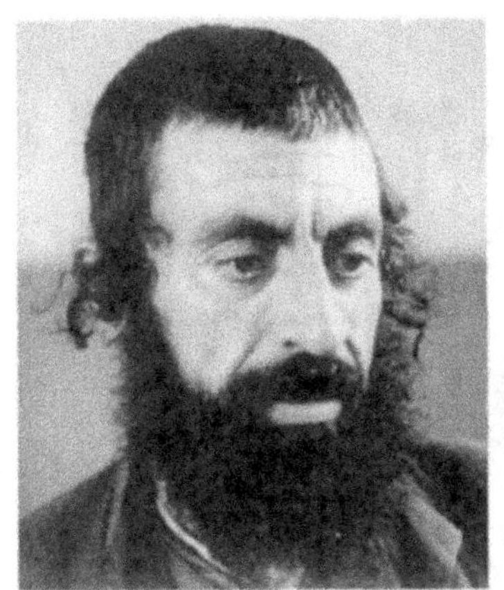

Man from Kurdistan.

Man from Kurdistan.

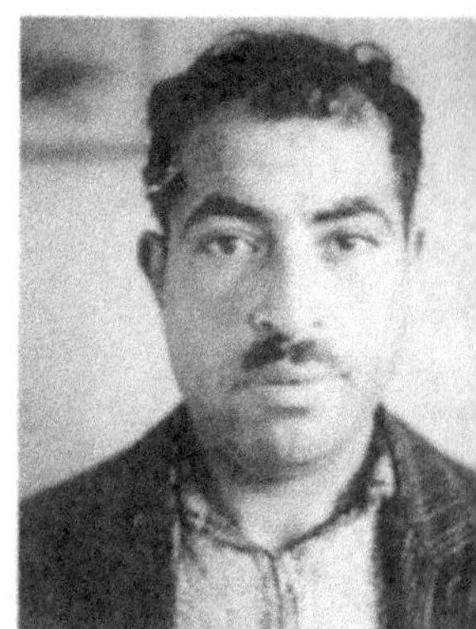

Man from Kurdistan.

[Hakham Alwan Avidani from Amadiya. My chief informant. R.P.].

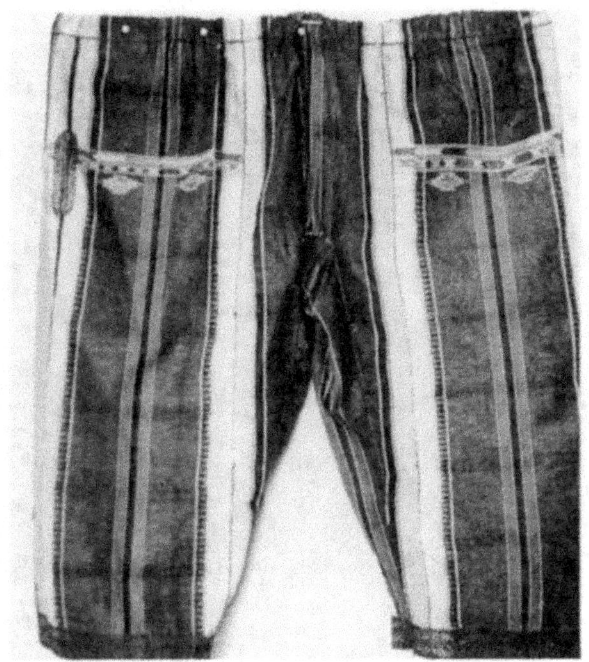

Chāla (pants) and chapuksa (jacket) from Zakho.

Barmale (rugs) from Dehok.

Sāl pesaḥ, tablecloth for the Seder from Sinne.

Kitchen utensils and rug from Sinne.

Dehvet go toqa (gold [pendant] of the chain).

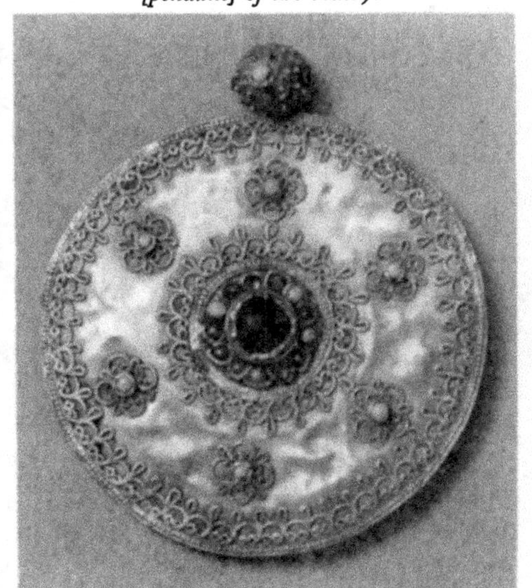

Marvada (earring) from Amadiya.

Kamar malajam (belt buckle) from Amadiya.

Kamar dutabag (double inlaid buckle).

Luaḥ (tablet) from Amadiya, silver, inscribed with the Ten Commandments.

Tāj Torah (Torah-crown) from Barashe, 1863. In the Hebrew University Brauer Collection.

Pointer for reading the Torah, from Amadiya, engraved with the name of the donor, Shabtay Moshe Mizrahi.

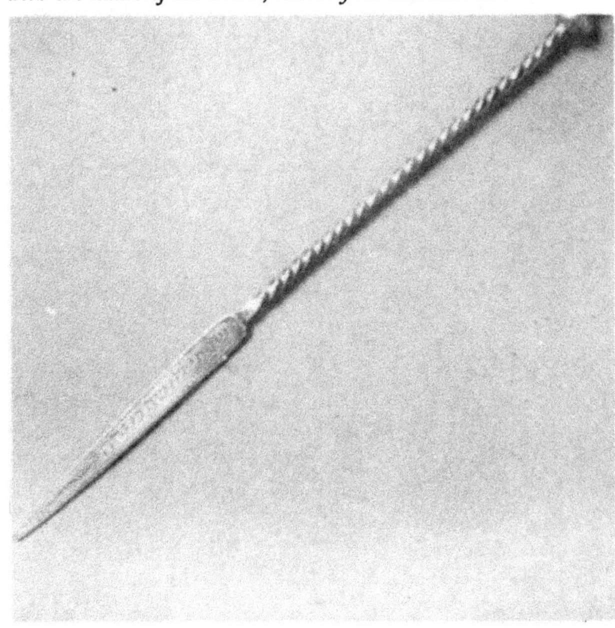

Sepa (sword), amulet for the protection of children. Inscribed with the names of angels.

Mashqas shelōna ("the shelōna-shield"), made of the skin of a gourd and used in the make-believe circumcision of the shelōna (a mummer) in a play performed at Passover. Sketch by Brauer from a mashqas shelōna in the Hebrew University Brauer Collection.

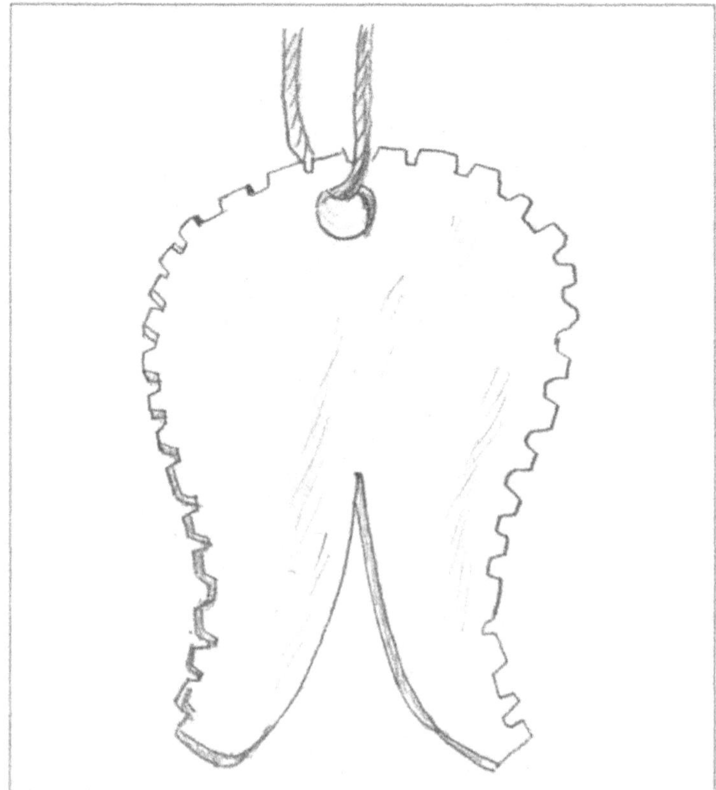

PART FOUR

Economic Conditions

11

Agriculture

Kurdistan is an agrarian country. Its inhabitants are peasants and nomadic shepherds. Trade, handicraft, and the exploitation of natural resources play a subordinate role in its total economy.

If we investigate the position of the Jews in this economy, we find a distinct difference between the Jews of Kurdistan and those of Yemen. In Yemen the Jews form a definite class. They are the craftsmen among the Arab *fellaḥin* and feudal lords; and before the ever-advancing decay of South Arabian autarchy had set in, they were the *only* craftsmen in the country. Not until the last few decades did the Arabs, for lack of other sources of income, begin to encroach on this Jewish monopoly.

The social and economic situation of the Jews in Kurdistan is a much healthier one, since they are not relegated so definitely to a single stratum of the country's economy. The Kurdish Jews live both in the villages and in the towns, however, not merely as tradesmen and craftsmen but also as landowners and peasants. In Kurdistan the Islamic law forbidding unbelievers to own or to build upon land because the *'ushr*—the tithe—may not be collected from them is not enforced.

The danger threatening the Jews in Kurdistan comes from the same quarter as it came in Europe: the steady progress of their infiltration into the tradesman class. There is further danger in the fact that comparatively few craftsmen are found among them. The Jews are not, as in Yemen, the only craftsmen in the country; for the Christians also engage in handicraft. The Jews and Christians together fill the same place in central Kurdistan as the Armenians in northern Kurdistan.

Decline of the Peasantry

It is worthwhile to follow up more closely the causes that led to this progressive transfer of the Jewish peasants to the commercial field. In Kurdistan, the Jews possessed all the qualifications necessary for the development of a vigorous peasant class and were presented there with the possibility of rooting themselves firmly in the soil as farmers. The external obstacles—those independent of the individual—were no greater for the Jews than, let us say, for the Nestorians, who nevertheless succeeded in establishing themselves as peasants.

The causes are to be sought in several phenomena, chief among them being how the economic situation has developed in all these agrarian countries during the last half century [1890–1940]. The immense progress made by the industrial countries and the enormous increase of population that was bound up with this progress caused agrarian countries that were as backward as Kurdistan to decline more and more. The peasant class decreased;[1] and the movement of population to the city, where the tradesman apparently led an easier and better life than the farmer, grew apace.

This process had a very special effect on the Jews, a people adhering to a religion that in the course of the centuries, has been especially adapted to town life. The life of the urban Jew, who can go to a synagogue every day and is regarded as a scholar, looks like an ideal existence to the Jewish peasant living in a village, where there is often no synagogue and it is hard to observe the religious commandments. In the town, so the peasant thinks, one can really live a Jewish life. There is, further, the practical consideration that the town offers the Jew a greater degree of personal safety.

Finally, an additional factor in the gravitation of the farm population to the cities is no doubt to be found in the general insecurity from which the peasantry of Kurdistan suffers. We find this insecurity in all the areas where nomadic and settled populations impinge upon each other. It is possible to live tranquilly in Kurdistan only when one has power behind one.

Saad gives an interesting example of this. While he was in Khaneqin, a certain village was offered for sale there. He decided to acquire this village; but when he consulted the Kaimakam about the purchase, the latter strongly advised him against it. "What will you do there alone?" he asked. "You would have to keep at least thirty men armed with Martini rifles, seeing that you have no following in the country. If you should be robbed tomorrow, then you would come to me. . . . I would send out the tabor aghasi; and you know what he does: when the robbers have gone to the right, he turns to the left."[2]

The Jews, in contrast to the Nestorians, never understood how to build up a political power of their own in Kurdistan. They could exist only by placing themselves under the protection of the aga. And although their position in these circumstances was not very different from that of the Christians and the settled Kurds and although they actually possessed the same political rights as the others, they never succeeded in becoming so bound to the soil as to persist in remaining farmers.

Yet among the Oriental Jews, probably none exhibits so strongly the characteristic qualities of the peasant as the Jew of Kurdistan. His entire being, external and internal, is that of the peasant. The frequency with which the peasant element crops up among the urban Jews rightly leads to the presumption that the movement to the cities was more than a phenomenon of only the last few decades; and we may safely assume that the number of Jewish peasants in Kurdistan was greater in the past than it is at present.

The Jew as Peasant

In Kurdistan there are even today village settlements whose entire population consists of Jews, just as there are purely Christian villagers, such as those in the district north of Amadiya. Among the Jewish village settlements are the following:

Settlement	Location
Tel Kabbar	near Zakho
Sundur	near Dehok[3]
Shandokha	near Dehok
Betanura	near Amadiya
Sündu	near Rekan (one of the oldest Jewish settlements in Kurdistan, numbering seventy families even today)
Kānī Balāwe	near Tchallek (once forty families, now reduced to fifteen)

There are, in addition, villages with a mixed population in which all the Jewish inhabitants—or at least the majority of them are farmers.

Such villages lie in the vicinity of Bashkala (e.g., Qarada, whose eighty families are "all tillers of the ground")[4] and of Amadiya (e.g.,

Barashe, Hōra, Hīr, Herkī, Tchalla, Meza, and Shūkho). Shūkho is situated about one-and-a-half days' journey from Amadiya and was mentioned by R. David d'Bet Hillel as a small village consisting of thirty Jewish families, all of whom were rich peasants.[5]

The Jews raise chiefly wheat (*khiṭe*), barley (*se'āre*), rice (*riza*), sesame (*shishme*), lentils (*tlōkhe*), and tobacco.[6] They also have orchards and vineyards and herds of cattle—whose pasturing is often turned over to the Kurds. Part of their income is derived from oak apples and other "gathered" products and from the cultivation of poplar trees (*spindara*) for building wood. A poplar plantation is called *gininka spindara*.

Rice Culture

Along with grain for bread making, rice is the most important crop in Kurdistan, because it fetches an excellent price; and a rice field, being irrigated, is the most valuable kind of land. The Jews of Barashe were principally engaged in rice culture.

In plowing a rice field, the oldest member of the family must lead the plow, since this is thought to bring good luck. After the plowing, the field is divided into rectangular sections and is flooded, remaining under water several days. For the sowing the oldest member must be present again, with a little rice which he has brought to the field in his hand, not on the mule; and it is he who must begin the sowing. The weeding (*ada*) starts when the seed has sprouted. The part of the field that is not planted but gets the benefit of the flooding is for the oxen.

The ox is addressed during the plowing thus: *Bō wara māla bābēmin Nīso ḥata mürin kerina*, "Go forward, go backward, house of my father Niso; until our death we shall work" (Barashe).

Community Work

For cutting the rice (*jezādit riza*, the people are called together for *zebāre*. By *zebāre* is meant a kind of voluntary labor rendered by Jews and Muslims to the feudal lords of their village or to rich families (including Jewish families). This *zebāre* is evidently no forced labor like the *sukhra* (the aga's feudal right; see p. 225) but a survival of a type of community labor carried out on a voluntary basis for the benefit of people who have large estates.

Still, for the individual, this requisitioning of his labor is no insignificant matter. There are, for instance, the following *zebāre* for the people of Barashe near Amadiya:

1 For breaking up the soil of the vineyard, *khepāra*.
2 For cutting the grain, *jezāda*.
3 For cutting the rice, *jezādit riza*.
4 For cutting twigs for winter fodder, *qeṭāt ṭarpa*.

Since a number of families are entitled to the *zebāre*, and each *zebāre* lasts about eight days, every person gives up approximately forty working days, or a month-and-a-half.

On the evening preceding the date set for the *zebāre*, the servant of the *mukhtar*, the *jezirāya*, calls out from the roof of the highest house that there is to be a *zebāre* at so-and-so's next morning. The people assemble before his house at the proper time and proceed, with *dōla wezirne*, to the field where the work is to be done. The number of participants depends on (aside from the size of the village) the power and importance of the family. There are often as many as 150 workers or even more.

The work is done under the direction of the *resh zebāre*. It is interrupted by intervals of rest, during which the men eat[7] and dance to music. At the close of the day, the workers go to the house of the master of the *zebāre* for *ikhala ashiratī*, "repast of the tribe."

In order that the Jews also may partake of the food, milk dishes only are served. The usual menu comprises rice with sour milk and butter.

The preparation of food for such a mob puts a great additional burden on the women.

Viticulture

Kurdistan is a vine-growing country. Kurdish wine was famous even in ancient times; and up to the present day wine plays an important part in the country's economy. The Kurdish Jews are strongly represented in the vine-growing industry, and still more so in the manufacture and sale of wine, as is natural in a land under Islamic rule. The Kurdish Jews are, in fact, looked upon as experts in viticulture.

A great many vineyards (Targ. *kermit inve* Kurd. *ras terī*) are at present in the hands of Jews; and there is considerable evidence that in earlier times the number was even greater. Not only village Jews but also numerous towndwellers own vineyards, which are passed on in the family from generation to generation. Vineyards in Jewish hands are to be found in Akra[8] and in the Zakho, Dehok, and Amadiya districts. In Ushnu there are twenty Jewish families who own vineyards. The wine made by the Jews of Herki (*khamra herkāye*) and Tchalla (*khamra chalnāya*) is particularly celebrated.

However, it is only in the districts where the Jews are still agriculturalists that they themselves engage in vine growing; elsewhere (e.g., Ushnu), they merely lease their vineyards to the Kurds.

In Barashe every Jewish family owns several vineyards, some of which produce as much as 4000 *rotl* (10,000 kilograms) annually. The work in the vineyard begins in Nissan with the *khepāra*, the hoeing up of the soil. In the case of rich families this is done through *zebāra* (see p. 208); but an ordinary peasant borrows the necessary labor from a neighbor, reciprocating later on when the latter needs similar help. After Nissan (April) comes the pruning (*kizākha*).[9]

In Tammuz (July), when the grapes begin to appear on the vines, a night watchman must be set to guard the vineyards against the depredations not, indeed, of men but of bears and wild boars (*khazūra*), which devour grapes in great quantities. In Zakho the families of the vine growers sit in huts (*kaprāne*) during the vintage to keep watch; but precautions against thieves are almost superfluous, seeing that grapes have hardly any value in the local market and everyone can get whatever amount he wants, in the vineyard, for a negligible sum or for nothing at all.

Only a small part of the grapes is eaten fresh. The greater part is converted into *mē pukhta*, grape syrup, which is an important substitute for sugar (see p. 102) or into raisins (*yibshāsa*, Kurd. *mewīsh*). Raisins have considerable commercial value and are one of the principal export articles of Kurdistan.

For the manufacture of raisins, the vine grower engages Jewish workers, men and women, who get their pay in raisins. A man receives 6 *rotl* per day, a woman 3 *rotl*.

The grapes are first dipped into boiling water to which ashes (*mezaita*) have been added and are then taken to the *mishṭākha*, a flat piece of ground stamped hard, where the women sort them. There are three grades:

1. *Qoshmoshīye*, small and seedless (the most expensive sort, made out of *zerik*
2. *Biyāra*, larger than *qoshmoshīye*
3. *Barat mishṭākha*, the lowest grade

The grapes are spread on the *mishṭākha* for about a week to dry. When the new raisins are brought into the house,[10] the owner of the vineyard climbs to the roof and throws handfuls of old raisins down on the people, saying:

yā brōni mēsun qayim ibōkhun pāsuq:
akhlētun atīqa me'itiqa atīqa min qāmat kāsa palṭētūn
O sons, bring (raisins), in you shall be fulfilled the verse
And ye shall eat old store long kept, and ye shall bring forth
the old from before the new [Lev. 26:10].

One-tenth of the raisins is kept for distribution among the poor (this must be done in the dark; also Z.), one-tenth goes to the government, and a portion of the black grapes is given to the synagogue for the *qiddush* wine (Barashe).

12

Trade

As we have already had occasion to observe, the Kurdish Jews formerly engaged in agriculture and in handicraft more extensively than at present. The transition to business is a comparatively recent phenomenon connected with the progressive concentration of the Jewish population in the town.[1]

The preponderance of tradesmen over craftsmen is especially conspicuous in eastern Kurdistan. Out of 300 Jewish heads of households in Urmia, 120 are shopkeepers and 100 are pedlars. In Kerkuk there are no craftsmen whatever: all the Jews are tradesmen.[2] In Zakho, out of 300 heads of households, 150 are tradesmen. In Amadiya the tradesmen (especially the pedlars) were formerly in the majority, but their numbers are said to have declined considerably since their despoilment at the hands of Mīra Kōra.

We may distinguish three groups among the tradesmen in Amadiya: (1) wholesale dealers, or merchants (*tijāre*); (2) shopkeepers (*dikandāre*); and (3) pedlars (*gadāre* or *baqāle*).

The wholesalers are chiefly dealers in textiles (*bazāzi*) who obtain their goods from Mosul or, in the east, from Urmia and Tabriz. Most of these textiles are imported from Manchester by Baghdad merchants.[3]

Nowadays, [ca. 1940], this buying trip to Mosul is made by automobile in a few hours; but in former times it required weeks, and the departure of the merchants was an affair in which the whole community took part. On the eve and on the morning of this event, the merchants invited their friends and acquaintances to their homes; and when they set out on the journey, everyone accompanied them a short distance.

The merchants gave presents to the water carriers at the city gate and to the schoolmaster and the pupils who formed part of the attendant crowd. The *ḥaverim* also received a gift from each of the travelers and subsequently gathered at their usual meeting place to drink the arrack acquired with this money.

The wholesalers have shops (*dikāna*) in the bazaar or warehouses in their homes. Even in the case of these wholesalers, one must picture conditions as extremely primitive. The smaller merchants and petty shopkeepers likewise have their stands in the bazaar. The number of Jews possessing shops or stands is considerable. In Amadiya nearly all the textile shops are in Jewish hands.[4] In Khaneqin the majority of the Jews are petty shopkeepers.[5]

In Amadiya and Sinne the shops of the Jews are not segregated but are together with those of the Muslims. In Zakho, on the contrary, there is a *shūkit hudā'i* [Jewish market], is adjacent to the Jewish quarter. The same is true of Arbil and Kerkuk.

In addition to textiles, the shops of the Jews carry mainly groceries, drugs, and spices.[6] Some of these are wholesale establishments.

Among the wholesalers are the dealers in grain (*'alāfe*). In Zakho there are four of these. They buy up the grain in the outlying villages and sell it to the townspeople. In the same way, the Jews of Barzan, for example, buy un the harvests of the Kurds. They also buy the entire produce of the orchards and the vineyards on the tree or vine and sell it in Akra and Mosul.

In fact, the business of the wholesaler is very often bound up with money transactions, seeing that the wholesaler usually waits for payment from the Kurd until harvest time or until the time that the Kotchar (the nomads) sell their sheep. It frequently happens, for instance, that the larger villages, in order to avoid the middlemen, make a contract with a wholesaler, who then furnishes every inhabitant of the village with the goods he requires and gets his pay at harvest time. None of the produce may be sold beforehand. At harvest time the *mukhtār* [village head] brings the dealer to the village, where an accounting is made at the house of each peasant. The dealer acts on this occasion as buyer also, because he buys up the grain that has not been paid for in goods and is naturally in a position to receive exceptionally favorable terms (A.).

First and foremost, however, the wholesaler is the banker for the Jewish pedlars (*baqāle*), who form the main body of Jewish tradesmen.[7] Among the pedlars we must distinguish two groups: (1) those who work with a fair amount of capital and (2) those who make the rounds of the villages with small packs. The first deals chiefly in textiles which they load on mules or donkeys; the second supply the village Kurds with much commodities as sugar, spices, matches, coffee, and tea and fancy wares such as needles, thread, mirrors, rings, and so on—that is to say, articles wanting in their otherwise self-sufficient economy. The entire value of the small pedlars stock does not exceed £1.

When the Jews enter a village, they seek out the *mukhtār* and display their wares at his house. They likewise spend the night there, for it is the *mukhtār* who accommodates strangers (Z. and Ushnu). In some districts the *mukhtār* receives a fee from the pedlar (Z. and Barzan; formerly also A.).

Each Kurd is generally a regular customer of one particular Jew, so that, when a dealer arrives, his clients gather about him in the evening at the *mukhtār*'s. If he is an ordinary simple Jew (so Shabtai Yosef informed me), he must regale the Kurds with stories; but if he is one of the richer dealers, the Kurds must regale him with stories.

The pedlars have definite routes and travel for the most part in twos or threes. As their numbers are considerable, a large section of the male population is away from home most of the week. The Jews, while on the road, eat only milk dishes—though the majority of them do not observe the ritual punctiliously and do not, for instance, put on the tefillin (phylacteries). The length of their absence from home depends upon various circumstances. Sometimes it is as much as several months. Thus, in Sinne there are textile pedlars who leave home at Passover and do not return till the beginning of winter (Kislev). They remain at home until Purim, except for minor trips. Hence, most of the children are born in the autumn.

A pedlar from Zakho sets out on Sunday but is not always back by the end of the week. The route of a textile merchant from Zakho, who travels with a mule, may extend as far north as the Lake Van district and as far south as Koi Sanjak.[8]

There are also pedlars who, after Shavu'ot, accompany the Kotchar, the nomadic Kurds, to their pasture lands (*zōzan*), carrying on their mules such commodities as the Kotchar need and returning home by Sukkot (e.g., the Zakho district).

The trade is for the most part barter and consequently dependent on the harvest, the shearing, and so on. The traders accept as payment wool, cotton, oak apples (*apse*), grain, rice, skins, butter, oil, and the like, which form the export goods of Kurdistan.[9] The cash that the merchant gets in loans from the wholesaler must be used to purchase goods that he cannot obtain by barter.

Oak apples (Targ. *apse*, Kurd. *māzi*) are one of the principal export articles of Kurdistan. They are a product of a gathering economy. The oak forests between Amadiya and Rowanduz are the richest oak apple district of Kurdistan, and these two cities are consequently the chief markets for this product.[10] Every village has a special precinct, and watchmen are posted to guard the forests. The harvest always begins on the 8th, 9th, or 10th of Abh (the end of July or beginning of August), when the entire village repairs to the forests with tambourine and flute, drum and trumpet. The Jews also take part. A long stick, bent at the top (*jalāga*) is used for the picking. If the crop is good, one person can gather about 40 *rotl*.[11] The buyers are mostly Jews.

It is difficult to get accurate information concerning the turnover and income of a wholesaler or pedlar. In any case, no comparison can be made between the business of these Kurdish Jewish merchants and that of the merchants of Baghdad or Bombay.

The following case, which made a deep impression on those concerned in it, gives a good idea of the nature of an important business transaction (A.). The mir of Barwilnaye had a quarrel with some other tribes, and the *shekh* of Bamarne arranged a peace between them. For the reconciliation ceremony the mir wished to distribute rich gifts and sent his people with horses and mules to conduct the foremost merchant of Amadiya to Barwilnaye. The merchant took all sorts of clothing and dress material along; and the mir, after a great deal of haggling over the prices, bought about £40-worth of goods; but the transaction would have been a loss for the merchant if he had not been fortunate in the price he received for the cattle that were given him by way of payment.

The earnings of the pedlars are naturally very meager, and only the cheapness of food and the primitive standard of living in Kurdistan enable a man to subsist through peddling. In about 1890 a pedlar in Sinne with an annual income of 20 *toman* (about £5) was considered well-to-do. He could even save 5 *toman* a year out of his earnings.

The pedlars derive their chief profits from their bartering transactions. At harvest time, when the Kurdish peasant is not very particular, they are likely to receive a disproportionate amount of rice, raisins, or the like in exchange for an article of little value. In good times, a dealer with moderate capital can earn about £50 at harvest time through barter (A.).

Money is expensive in Kurdistan. This is especially felt by a merchant who has no working capital, or a dealer who has exhausted his credit and must keep body and soul together by acting as middleman

(Z. *chürikchüye*)—that is by purchasing a little stock from the Kurds who come into town and selling it at once or else by getting employment in the concern of another. A twelve-year-old boy who worked in a shop received a monthly wage of 2 *kran* (1 shilling). My informant from Sinne was, himself, at the age of twenty, a sort of bookkeeper for a *bazāzi* who had a shop in the town and paid him a yearly salary of 18 *toman* (£4.50). He was greatly envied because of this splendid income.

The Jews of Kurdistan occupy about the same position as the Armenians in the Kurdish districts where there are no Jews; and, like the Armenians, they are considered exceptionally shrewd. The Kurds do not see themselves the equals of the Jews as merchants. Once a Jew, so the story goes, came to the house of an aga, who said to him: "Jews are swindlers. Teach me the art of swindling." The Jew was frightened and did not know what to do. He said to the aga, "Get me a large *guṣa* (ball of yarn)." When it was brought, the Jew wound the end of the yarn around the aga's finger, saying, "Hold this firmly until I come back." The aga took a good hold and the Jew went out, gradually unwinding the yarn as he did so. After going some distance, he broke off the thread and tied it to a piece of wood. Then he went to the market place and sold the rest of the yarn very little of which had been used.

The aga in the meanwhile stood and waited. He waited an hour, but the Jew did not return. He waited two hours, but still the Jew did not return. Then he had the matter investigated, and thus it was borne in upon him that the Jew had given him a lesson in the art of swindling. (A.)

13

Handicraft

Besides the tradesmen and peasants, there are the craftsmen, who live both in the towns and in the villages. Although the Kurdish Jews, unlike the Jews in Yemen, are not the only craftsmen in the country (since the Kurds and, still more, the Christians are strongly represented in the manual trades), nevertheless, the role of the Jews as craftsmen is by no means insignificant; and in every village there are Jewish families working as weavers, goldsmiths, dyers, shoemakers, and so on.

In view of the meager cultural development of the country—or perhaps as a result of its cultural decline—Kurdish handicraft today produces only rude work such as will furnish the inhabitants of the country with the most necessary articles of daily use. Occasional specimens of the silversmith's or the weaver's craft which came to my notice were of a higher type. But the political disorders that have visited upon Kurdistan time and again, as well as the unrest consequent on these disorders, have so impoverished the country that the native art, which once evidently existed there, is today almost completely extinct. The Kurdish Jew as tradesman, farmer, or craftsman has so hard a struggle for mere subsistence[1] that his peasant nature is revealed only in its coarser aspect, without being able to serve as the soil from which a native art might spring. Such a native art would have had the better opportunity to flourish, in that many of the Jewish farmers take advantage of the enforced idleness of the hard winter months to engage in some form of handicraft, particularly weaving.

Weavers

Among the Jews of Kurdistan the most widely practiced handicraft is that of weaving. We find Jewish weavers (*zaqāra*, pl *zaqāre*; Kurd. *birkar*, pl. *birkare*)[2] not only in the towns but, even more commonly, in the villages. Among the village Jews are many who practice weaving as a winter profession while engaging principally in agriculture.

There are likewise Christian weavers in Kurdistan, and their work often surpasses that of the Jews in quality. In some places, however, the weaving is entirely in Jewish hands. There are forty Jews working as weavers in Amadiya, but only one Muslim and no Christians at all. In Rovanduz, among sixty heads of households, twenty-five are weavers; Zakho, on the other hand, had only twenty Jewish weavers in 1920, as against twenty-five among the Christians.

Unless the local Jewish peasants supply their own needs or part of them by winter weaving, a village may support two or three Jewish weavers. As a rule, the weavers, a fair proportion of whom are *ḥakhamim*, work at home.

The wool comes from domestic sheep and goats and is prepared and spun by the Jews. The trade in raw wool is largely in Jewish hands, partly owing to the fact (previously mentioned) that the Jews act as bankers among the Kurds. In order to meet the government head tax (*qamjur*) on their herds in the spring, the Kurdish sheep owners borrow from the Jews. The loans are repaid in wool at the shearing, when the *shekh* of the Kotchar invites the Jews to his summer camp (*zōma*) to be present at the weighing out of the wool (*heri bir*). In this transaction the Jew usually gets the added advantage of a very favorable price on the wool.

Grades of goat's wool are generally distinguished. *Mar'az khuwāra* is a fine white wool used for *shāla shapuqsa*. A cloth with a luster almost like that of silk is woven from this.[3] *Mar'az smōqa*, red goat's wool, and *kōma*, black goat's wool, are used for the same purpose. *Sē'era* is a coarse black wool out of which the Kurds make their tents. It is not used by the Jews.

Sheep's wool, *amra* (*khuwāra*, *smōqa*, *kōma*), is used for the manufacture of coarser cloth. *Shāla shapūqsa* for work are sometimes made out of this It is used chiefly, however, for carpets and blankets.

The preparation and spinning of the wool is the task of the women (see p. 181). The wool is first washed, then combed with an iron comb (*masirkit prizla*), during which three grades are sorted out: long hairs *sarshūf*), medium (*nafshāka*), and short (*kulka*).

The loom (Z. and A. *gūba*, S. *charj jolāye*; Kurd. *bir*) is a very primitive model, lying flat and worked either without a treadle or with a treadle sunk into the ground. It is intended for the weaving of simple webs such as carpets.

Tailors

The tailor's trade in Kurdistan is largely a woman's trade. Arbil and Ushnu have men tailors (*khayāṭ*, *khayāṭe*); but in Sinne, Muslims sew for men, and the women make their own clothes.

In Amadiya, on the other hand, tailoring is done entirely by women tailors (*khāyaṭe*). Zakho likewise has forty women tailors to one man. The women tailors both of Amadiya and of Zakho, are patronized by Muslims, as well as by Jews,[4] since there are no Muslim tailors in these towns. However, in places that possess men tailors only, there are always a few Jewish women employed in sewing for Kurdish women.

The work of the Kurdish tailor is extraordinarily lacking in artistic merit—at any rate, today: no antique pieces have survived, since a garment is always used until it is completely worn out. The tailor scarcely troubles to take measurements. The only thing of importance is the embroidery work (*nakish*), which some of these garments boast and which determines their price.

The women tailors also supply dealers with their stocks of ready-made garments, particularly with trousers-and-jackets. In this line, wives of weavers are prominently represented. The women are paid from 3 to 4 rupees for a pair of trousers or a jacket, and somewhat less for a workman's or a shepherds garment (A.).

Raftsmen

Many Jews are engaged in the transport industries. Every Jewish tradesman possesses a mule, or at least a donkey, to haul his goods; but there are, besides, Jews who are employed as mule drivers in caravans (*kartirji*)—for instance in Barzani and in Zakho.[5]

The transportation of goods by water as well as by land is to some extent in Jewish hands. The Jews of Zakho, especially, have taken up this work, as a result, no doubt, of the central position of the town. Zakho is situated on an island in the River Khabor, the main channel for the passage of freight from central Kurdistan to the plain of the Tigris.

Of the four hundred heads of households living in Zakho before World War I, seventy were raftsmen (*ṭarākha*, pl. *ṭarākhe*), a calling closely connected with the timber industry. The fact that one of the oldest Jewish families in the town, Bē Daḥlīka, is a family of raftsmen, attests to the great length of time that this trade has been followed by Jews from Zakho.

There are two kinds of raftsmen: the *ṭarākhit bar ēlī*, upper raftsmen, (i.e., working in the hills) and the *ṭarākhit bar takhti*, lower raftsmen, (i.e., working in the plains). The former transport the timber from the hills to the plains, and the latter (the raftsmen proper) take it on from there to Mosul.

After Passover the upper raftsmen go to the hills and buy up the trees from the Kurds. They are tall white poplars (*spindāre*). The Kurds fell them and cut them into three sections (*iqrā*, root; *naftāya*, central part; and *sartāya*, upper part), which the raftsmen then transport to the riverbank either on mules or on their shoulders. The logs are thrown into the river singly and floated down in masses (*jalab*, herd) by the *trāyit jalab*, "herd drivers"; or else they are transported in a small raft (*karkha*), which is navigated by means of small oars (*garagā).*

The raft proper—the large *kalak*, or *abrā* (pl. *abre*)[6]—in occasionally used for transporting the timber to Zakho; but in general, it is only at Zakho that it is constructed.

In Zakho, the timber, each piece of which bears the owner's brand,[7] is piled up (*singür*, woodpile) and formed into rafts as required. From the top section of the trunk a rectangular frame (*malban*) is built and filled in with other logs. Twigs (*shiwe*) are used for making the joinings. Under the raft the raftsmen fasten 120 to 200 inflated sheepskins (*darfe*, Mosul *jerban*). The raft is then lowered in the water and loaded with goods. From two to four lower raftsmen, depending on water level and drop of the current, handle the oars (*machrefe*).

The timber forming the *abre* is sold when it reaches its destination, but the *darfe* are taken back to Zakho.

[Already Herodotus tells of the putting together of the rafts on the Upper Tigris, of floating them by means of inflated skins, of taking them down to certain places on the Lower Tigris, of taking the rafts apart there, of selling the wood and taking the skins back on donkey-back to the place whence the raftsmen had come (Her. I, 194). It is true that Herodotus relates all this in connection with the *kufa* (the small round boat used to this day on the Tigris); but, as Mr. James Hornell has pointed out to me in a letter, this is a mistake, for the description of Herodotus fits precisely the big rafts, *kelek*].

PART FIVE

Social Organization and Education

14

He Aga and His Jews

In our historical survey we have shown how even today, the farther removed the district from the influence of the central government in Baghdad, the greater the power of the Kurdish chiefs (*agā'e*, sg. *aga*).

Formerly, the power of these chieftains was unrestricted. Benjamin II states quite truly, "Kurdistan belongs more in name than in reality to the Turkish kingdom" and gives the following description of the condition of the Jews about 1840:

> The Jews scattered here and there, and forced to remain in the places assigned to them, are in the true sense of the word, surrounded by tribes of savages. One often finds five, ten, or even twenty Jewish families on the property of one Kurd, by whom they are burdened with imposts, and subjected to ill treatment. Heavy taxes are imposed upon them, which, for the poorest, amount annually to 500 piastres. Finally they are compelled at different periods of the year to perform serf-service, to cultivate their master's field, without receiving or being entitled to demand the smallest compensation for their labor. . . . The master has the absolute power of life and death over his slaves, [and] at his will he can sell them to another master, either in whole families or individually.[1]

The progressive pacification of the territory has resulted in many changes. Nevertheless, even today, there are sections of Kurdistan where the rule of the aga is absolute.[2] For the Jews, however, the agas represent an important political support. Since the Jews are politically powerless, they put themselves under the protection of an aga, who then regards them as belonging to his tribe. He shields them from persecution and punishes transgressions against them according to Kurdish law.

In Amadiya there were three reigning agas, in Sulaimani four; [3] but in Zakho there is only one.[4] In the country districts the Jews frequently take as protectors not the chiefs of the tribes but certain powerful families whose heads are likewise called aga or *pis mīre*, "son of the emir" (Tchalla). In Nirwa, for example, each of the Jewish families, twenty in number, has for generations stood under the protection of one of these family chiefs.[5]

The services rendered by the Jews in return for this protection varies in the different districts. Benjamin II depicts the situation in the gloomiest of colors; and even in the early twentieth century, conditions are described as being very difficult in certain places, Sulaimani, for instance:

> [The Jews are not compelled to give to the agas fixed payments, but they are obliged to send to them presents on the occasion of every feast—whether Mohammedan or Jewish—such as sugarloaves, cloth, dresses. One of the entourage of the aga enters, for instance, a Jewish shop in order to buy something and pays, as he chooses, the half or one-quarter of the price or even nothing at all. The poor Israelite will hesitate to complain. On his return from a business journey, every Jew, whether a poor trader or a rich merchant, must give the aga a part of the money he brought back.][6]

In the country districts, the Jews render services of another kind. On the Muslim feast days they bring their protectors a gift in the form of articles of apparel or food supplies (in Tchalla, thirty eggs and a *manya* of butter). In places where there are Jewish weavers, the latter furnish the aga with whatever garments he requires. The Jew is, besides, his aga's banker and lends him money without interest.

When the Jew marries a daughter, the aga gets one-third of the bride-price (*niqda*);[7] and in districts where the aga is still very powerful (Oramar, Nirwa), he often takes the whole of the bride-price. However, the *pis mīre*—the minor agas—generally give their Jews some rice or other produce from their own harvest.[8] In many districts where the power of the chieftain has declined, particularly those in which the towns are located, the tribute paid by the Jews is actually only symbolic, rather in the nature of a present (S., A., and D.). In Amadiya it takes the form of a gift of seven, nine, eleven, or thirteen eggs. The number given must be odd, never even; for in the latter case, some member of the family would die.

Nevertheless, even after the conquest of Iraq by the British, compulsory labor (*sukhra*) as described by Benjamin II was still in full force.

In Amadiya on the occasions when the *sukhra* is resorted to, the three agas send out their servants every day to fetch their respective Jews. The harvest is the principal occasion for the *sukhra*.[9] Beside his own harvest, each aga has to bring in from the villages the tithe (*ta'ashīr*), which he has bought from the government. Rich agas often acquire the tithe from as many as twenty villages, and much labor is needed for unloading the grain and so on. The same thing occurs at the rice harvest and the vintage. The Jews likewise bring timber (*spindāra*) from the riverbanks for the aga and must give their labor when the aga has some building to be done. Nevertheless, each Jew need work no more than about three hours a day.

Benjamin II states that the aga can sell his Jews at will to another aga either in entire families or singly. Albala reports the same thing from Sulaimani: ["They have divided amongst themselves the Jewish 'clientele'. Each one of them has taken a number of Jewish families under his 'protection'. . . . Recently, when a Kurdish beg sold a domain, he sold at one and the same time the Jews who lived in it."][10]

In the country districts, particularly, where the Jews are at the aga's mercy more than in the towns, they are an asset to the aga. They are handed down in his family from father to son. An aga with three or more Jews under his protection is regarded as powerful and rich, because the Jew is an asset not merely in theory but in actual fact; and his value lies in his salability, rather than in the services he renders.

In former times, the agas carried on a trade in their Jews, and obtained from 300 to 400 *qeran* (£15–20) apiece for them. Whenever they were in need of money, they sold one of their Jews.[11] They could also sell only a part of a Jew. First they would sell a foot saying, *Pi yeki jü ökhō dē ferūshim*, "A foot of the Jew I am selling." One foot fetched about £10.

The following case shows how precarious the existence of a Jew was rendered by his salability. One day when the children of the Jews of Tchalla had gone into the hills to gather wood, the son of an aga came along and tried to hinder them in their task by cutting their ropes to pieces. One of the buys resisted, and in the scuffle the aga's son had four fingers cut off. The boy did not dare return to his house but fled to the hills.

When the aga's son came home and told what had happened, the father was furious. But he could do nothing because the boy's family stood under the protection of another Kurdish *pis mīre*. The aga went to this Kurd and said, "Sell me your Jew." But the Kurd replied, "I shall not sell him."

The aga finally promised the boy immunity (*rāyū bakhad*); and when the boy thereupon returned home, the aga surrounded the house with his retainers and captured him. Nevertheless, he did not yet venture to take his revenge upon him but summoned the *pis mīre* of the family and offered him the sum of 200 *qeran* (£10) for the boy. The *pis mīre* consented, but his wife took pity on the lad and helped him to escape again. He eventually found sanctuary with the Nestorians in Kotshanis.

The aga protects the Jew against injury at the hands of other tribes, as well as of his own.[12] The Jew who travels through the villages will usually limit his trips to districts controlled by his own aga. If he wishes to enter the territory of another aga, he must first obtain his aga's permission.

Not only is the Jew exposed in Kurdistan to robbery and attacks by the Kurdish lords, but—being reckoned among the members of the tribe—he can easily become the victim of a blood feud.

To be sure, a murdered Jew is then avenged in the same way as an actual member of the tribe. The family of Ḥakham Shalom of Zakho stood under the protection of the Tayya, whose settlements lie between Jezire and Zakho. Once, when two of the *ḥakham*'s sons were peddling in home territory, they came upon some Charnakhnaye who happened to be at feud with the Tayya. The Jews were killed and robbed. In the punitive expedition that the Tayya undertook, a number of villages were sacked (Nahum and Z.).

The amount of the blood money (*dimma*) for the murder of a Jew is not fixed. The sum depends on the power of the Jew's protector. According to my informants, there were few cases of murder of Jews in the period preceding World War I.

In the case of the trader Shabo of Zakho, who was murdered near Amadiya, a court of arbitration consisting of two Jews and two Muslims was set up. The Jews demanded 1,000 rupees as compensation and 500 rupees in addition as blood money. But the sons of the murdered man refused to accept any blood money,[13] so a compensation of 1,000 rupees was finally agreed upon, to be paid by the three villages adjacent to the scene of the crime.

In the districts where the Jews are under the protection of great families, the *pis mīre* goes to the aga if an offense has been committed against his Jew and demands compensation from him (*nakhpūsa*, lit., "humiliation"). The aga endeavors to obtain the compensation from the village in question; and if it is not forthcoming, he has recourse to robbery. There are three different classes of robbery:

1. Raids on cattle, mules, donkeys, and so on (*garāne*)
2. Carrying off of plow animals (*jutyāre*)
3. Raids on sheep and goats (*irbit māsa*)

An interesting case of *jutyāre* is reported from Nirwa. Ḥakham Mordekhai, the ritual slaughterer in that town, went on a journey. He carried with him the writing materials that he used in making amulets, which were sought by Jews and non-Jews alike, and some linen out of which he made twisted cords (*gigla ketāna*) to be used as a remedy for fever.

He came to a field where some Kurds were plowing with ox teams. The yoke of one of the teams was broken, and the owner asked the *ḥakham* whether he had some linen with which to repair it. The *ḥakham* denied having any, but the Kurd searched him and took the linen by force. The *ḥakham* returned at once to Nirwa and told his Kurdish protector what had happened to him. Thereupon, the aga called together a few Kurds, who went out, took the teams away from the plowmen, and brought them to the *ḥakham's* house.

The village of the despoiled plowmen at once proceeded against Nirwa; and in the clash that followed, seven Kurds were killed. Hostilities were eventually stopped, and the matter settled by negotiation. The village of the Kurd who had taken the linen was obliged to give the Jew an ox as compensation (Shabtai and A.).

15

THE JEWISH COMMUNITY

[Within each town and village the Jewish community constituted a tightly knit organization whose control extended over all the Jews who lived in the locality. It was unimaginable that a Jew should live anywhere without being a member of the local Jewish community, without participating in the religio-social activities of the community, and without being subject to the rule, and often the whims, of the leaders of the community. The power in the community was in the hands of the *gevirim* (lit. "masters"), and the *gabbai* (synagogue head) chosen by them. Very important were also the roles played by the religious functionary who acted as *ḥakam* (rabbi), *ḥazan* (cantor, prayer-leader), *shoḥeṭ* (ritual slaughterer), *mu'allim* or *istād* (schoolmaster), and *mohel* (circumciser). He was assisted in many ways by the *shammash* (sexton), who functioned as a kind of community factotum. It was the observance of religious rituals and ceremonies and family festivities, always within the framework of the community and with the participation of all its members, that provided the life of the Kurdish Jew with consequence and interest, with enjoyments and satisfactions.]

The *Gabbai*

The head of the synagogue is the *gabbai* [Heb. synagogue head]. This office is sometimes restricted to certain families, in which it is hereditary. These families are generally distinguished by their wealth and position and bear the title Gabbai as surname, for example, Ya'aqov Gabbai (a.) or Yiṣḥaq Gabbai (Z.).

When the office is hereditary, it is, as a rule, held for life. Cases in which the *gabbai* has been deposed because of unsatisfactory performance of his duties are, nevertheless, no rarity. In Amadiya, for instance, the *gabbai* was changed four times in the course of thirty years. One *gabbai* resigned because his business did not leave him sufficient time for directing the affairs of the synagogue. Another proved unworthy of the office, having appropriated the synagogue funds for his private business. When he was discharged, a considerable amount was missing from the treasury.

Since the Kurdish Jews showed no great inclination to assume the office of *gabbai* (a situation arising, perhaps, only in the last few decades), the *gabbai* was chosen by the three *gevirim* and seven *benunim*. The matter was sometimes arranged as follows: these ten men chose three candidates, then these three cast lots among themselves and the one who drew the lot marked *gabbai* was obliged to accept the office (A.).

The rich Kurdish Jews did not seek the office of *gabbai*, which is actually a post of honor, because the management of a synagogue in Kurdistan is no sinecure. The synagogue is the only organization the Kurdish Jews possess the funds of which can be used for defraying the expenses of the religious and social welfare services of the community. There is no taxation other than the payment of voluntary fees, and all of these are in some way connected with the ritual. These fees are administered by the *gabbai*.

The synagogue funds in charge of the *gabbai* come from several sources:

1. Receipts from the sale of posts of honor, usually connected with the reading of the Torah (see p. 267).[1]
2. Contributions to the *quppat arīkha*. Each person gives 1 *grish* per week to this fund. Furthermore, the *shammash* makes a daily collection for it in the synagogue. The *gabēthe ṣadāqa* ['woman-*gabbai* of charity'] makes the collection among the women. Alms for the local poor and for the poor who have come to Amadiya from other places are disbursed out of the *quppat arīkha*. It is used also, for instance, to pay for the graveclothes of the poor and for the grants to the *sheliḥim*, rabbinical messengers coming, for the most part, from Palestine (Z., D., A., and Barashe).

3. Receipts from fines.
4. Receipts from other contributions, such as supplies of oil, wine, firewood, and so on, given to the synagogue. In Sinne they include the cloths presented to the synagogue on Yom Kippur by each member of every family.

The receipts of a synagogue in Amadiya amount to £80–£100 annually in good times—a substantial sum in relation to the standards of Kurdistan. The fees paid by the man called up to the reading of the Torah account for the greater part of this sum.

It is the duty of the *gabbai* to manage the synagogue and all matters connected with it, such as supervising any new building or repairs and safeguarding the synagogue valuables (the Torah. crowns, *luḥot*, etc.). The *gabbai* also administers the houses and land owned by the community.

Sometimes the funds of the congregation are used to defray expenses not connected with the synagogue—from which fact it is evident that the synagogue funds are actually a community fund administered according to the needs of the people.

Thus, the congregation of Tchalla once took money from the synagogue treasury to pay the blood money that was demanded of a certain family.

In the village of Qarda a Muslim Kurd once came to the synagogue and bewailed his lot, saying that he would be sent to prison if he did not immediately pay a debt of 50 francs. The *gabbai* paid it for him out of money belonging to the synagogue, an act that made a great impression on the Muslims.

The *gabbai* receives no remuneration for his work. Even when the *gabbai* of Zakho was occupied almost an entire year in superintending repairs to the synagogue, he received no compensation of any sort. But there are cases in more recent times when a degree of compensation has been paid for services of this kind.

In Amadiya it was formerly customary for the *gabbai* to give a banquet to the congregation after *Sukkot*. This was called *se'ōdit ketāvit fiṣle*, "the meal of recording good deeds," at which the posts of honor acquired at *Simḥat Tora* were registered. In Zakho the *lulav* is kept at the *gabbai*'s house, whence it is brought to the synagogue (see p. 317). The *se'udat kohen haggadol* [Heb., lit., "meal of the high priest"] on Yom Kippur eve is also given by the *gabbai* (Z.).

The *Ḥazan*

Among the Kurdish Jews the performance of all religious services is still concentrated in one hand as of old. The cantor "*ḥazan*," the *shoḥeṭ* [ritual slaughterer], the schoolmaster, and the circumciser are one and the same person.

In Kurdistan, therefore, the *ḥazan* is simply the *ḥakham*. Moreover, he writes the amulets not only for the Jews but for the Muslims, as well.

The performance of religious services being a pious duty, the *ḥazan* gets no remuneration for it[2] but must earn his living as teacher and slaughterer. There are some *ḥazanim* who support themselves by working as weavers.

The *ḥazan* is, however, the recipient of certain emoluments. For instance, he shares with the *shammash* the contributions made by the *olim*, as the Kurds call the outsiders who come to town for the Sabbath and the feasts and who are called to the Torah as *mosif*.

Like the *shammash*, the *ḥazan* is entitled to part of the gifts made when the *haṭṭara* is resorted to (see p. 308), and to part of the receipts from fines. He likewise gets a fee for drawing up *ketubbot* and divorce papers (see p. 125).

The routine duties of the *ḥazan* consist in reciting the prayers and reading the weekly portion of the Law; for (as previously mentioned) the Kurdish Jews are not always able to read the weekly portion of the Law themselves. On weekdays the *ḥazan* often delegates the recitation of the prayers to one of the singers in the congregation.

Furthermore, it is generally the *ḥazan* who delivers the sermon (*drasha*) in Targum on the Sabbath after *minḥa*. These sermons are based on the weekly portion of the Law, except in the period between Passover and Shavu'ot, when they deal with the *Pirqe Avot* [Chapters of the Fathers].

Another duty of the *ḥazan* is the keeping of the community book (*daftar kenishta*) and the register of the dead (*daftar mīthe lehashkava*). On Yom Kippur during the hashkava the *ḥazan* reads out all the names entered in the *daftar mīthe lehashkava*, a process that often lasts about two hours (A.).

In Sinne, the *daftar kenishta* contains only a list of the goods and chattels in the possession of the synagogue. Births are not recorded at all, and there is no death register. Every family merely writes out the names of the dead and the newly born on the flyleaf of the prayerbook.

The *Shammash*

In Kurdistan, as elsewhere, the sexton of the synagogue is called *shammash* (in general A. Kurd.).[3] Since it is he who brings food to strangers and to the poor, he is sometimes called *parnasa* (Z.).

The *shammash* is appointed by the *gevirim* for an indefinite period. Though the salary paid by the congregation is small, the position of *shammash* is much sought after, because its perquisites render it a profitable and carefree one. In Sinne, the *shammash* receives, in addition, free dwelling quarters in the synagogue.

There are some *shammashim* who do their work as a pious duty, accepting, at the most, only the clothes which the *gabbai* buys for them at Passover out of the synagogue funds. The *shammash* distributes the *zewātit shammash* (bread), which they collect on Friday for the poor.

This bread normally represents a considerable part of the income of the *shammash*. In Zakho the *shammash* goes through the streets at midday on Friday, calling out, *Tlumsit shabsa illāha mazidlōkhun*, "Bread for the Sabbath, may God increase it to you."

A loaf of bread is contributed by each family. The *shammash* of the large synagogue collects about one hundred loaves, the *shammash* of the small one twenty five (similarly A.).

In Sinne the *shammash* calls, as he goes through the streets, *Allah mazīz* (for *mezīd*) *ilakhum brākha wāta* (for *zewāta*) *Shabbat*, "May God increase blessing to you; bread for the Sabbath."[4] Some women give two loaves: one for themselves and one for their husbands.

The *shammash* shares with the *ḥazan* part of the money contributed by the men called up to the reading of the Torah or by those for whom *mi sheberakh* is said. In these sums are included the contributions of the outsiders who come as *ʿolim*, pilgrims.

The *shammash* is likewise the recipient of gifts at the time of the feasts. In Amadiya the *ḥaverim* present the *shammash*, who naturally is not one of their number, with a jug of arrack on every Sabbath from Shavuʿot to Sukkot. The *shammash* further receives a portion of the *gurpāla*, the dish of rice and chicken that is sent to the gravediggers at a funeral. This, however, is usually distributed by his wife among the children of his neighbors, because it is looked upon as a potent means of protection.

In Sinne the *shammash* is given the head and the entrails of the very numerous *kappara* fowl (see p. 310).

It is the duty of the *shammash* to call the Jews to prayer, to light the lamps and candles, to provide water for washing the hands, to change the Torah cloaks, to change the Torah crowns, and so on. In some places the *shammash* must make the candles that the synagogue requires for certain purposes or that are distributed among the members of the congregation on stated occasions.

The cleaning up of the synagogue is done not by the *shammash* but by some old women who look upon this task as a *miṣva*. The *shammash* has only to supervise it. It is said of Yiṣḥaq Shammash of Amadiya that he used to test the thoroughness with which the Torah scrolls had been dusted by touching them with his beard. He held his office for thirty years, and distinguished himself during this period by his purity and holiness. In the course of his whole life, he never took anything directly from the hand of his wife; and he invariably washed his hands before lighting any lamp or candle.

The *Shoḥeṭ*

As previously mentioned, the profession of *shoḥeṭ* [ritual slaughterer] is practiced chiefly by the *ḥazanim* and the schoolmasters. Candidates for this profession are taught by a recognized *shoḥeṭ*. Quite often, the calling is hereditary, the sons of *shoḥeṭim* being trained by their fathers. In general, *sheḥīṭa* [slaughtering] is taken up by the sons of the poor, because the sons of the rich engage in trade.

Sündu and Barzani were formerly the main centers of instruction for *ḥakhamim* and slaughterers. Even today people say in Kurdistan: "For from Sündu goes forth the Law, and the word of God from Barzani." Later, first place was taken by Nirwa,[5] and today Zakho has this distinction. Slaughterers are trained in Amadiya, also, and in Akra and Dehok.

Instruction in *sheḥīṭa* was formerly based on the *Sefer Y'min Moshe*, but at present use is made principally of *Sefer Zivḥe Ṣedeq*. There is also a Kurdish work by Ḥakham Shim'on b. Yona Barzani, entitled *Shehīṭat Barzani*, which exists only in manuscript form.[6]

One of my informants had been trained in *sheḥīṭa* in his youth by his father, without, however, obtaining the diploma. Then when he was 27 years of age, he studied for eight months under two *ḥakhamim* in Sinne. A pupil accompanies his teacher for six to eight months for practical training. He must also slaughter several animals in his teacher's presence.

Not all *ḥakhamim*-slaughterers are entitled to grant the diploma. Since a diploma from Zakho is held in special esteem today, Ḥakham Eliyahu of Amadiya sent his son, who already possessed a diploma from the *ḥakhamim* of Amadiya, to acquire, in addition, that of the *ḥakhamim* of Zakho.[7]

Before receiving the diploma, the candidates must slaughter a cow in the presence of the *ḥakhamim*. The flesh of the animal is eaten at the *se'udat semīkha* [Heb. "meal of ordination"], to which the *ḥakhamim* and the members of the community are invited.

Since the demand for slaughterers exceeds the supply, slaughterers who are not yet fully qualified (i.e., who have not yet received the diploma) are sometimes allowed to practice. This is partly due to the fact that the meager earnings possibilities offered by a small community are quite insufficient for a fully qualified *shoḥeṭ*. In such cases, the pupil must either work with another pupil or under the supervision of two *ḥakhamim*.[8]

A slaughterer already possessing the diploma must pass a further examination, given by the messengers from Palestine, who regard this testing of the slaughterers as a matter of great importance.

In addition to the resident *shoḥeṭim*, there are the itinerant *shoḥeṭim* who, from their home town, make the rounds of the outlying villages.[9] They appear at Passover and again at Sukkot, in order to slaughter the animals for the preserved meat (see p. 96) or when a circumcision or a wedding is about to be celebrated. The coming of the *shoḥeṭ* is always a great event for these out-of-the-way places, because the *shoḥeṭ* is also the *ḥakham*, whose duty it is to care for the spiritual edification of such communities.

The *shoḥeṭ* receives a fee for his work and also a portion of the slaughtered animal—except chickens, which he slaughters gratis. In Zakho, the *shoḥeṭ* receives about 6 pence (1 *takka*) for slaughtering an ox, 2 pence (1 *kamari*) and, in addition, part of the flesh and the entrails for a sheep. From the sale of the latter to certain dealers, he derives considerable income. In Amadiya he gets, besides his fee, the tail (*dūma*) of an ox or a cow and the neck (*qedāla*)[10] of a sheep.

The itinerant *shoḥeṭ*, not being in a position to use, or to dispose of, meat or entrails from the slaughtered animals, receives instead a larger cash fee and such provisions as raisins, tobacco, and *mē pukhta* [grape-water]. He is often accompanied by his wife, who acts as *naqdāna*. Her task is to remove the veins from the flesh. In Amadiya the *naqdāne* work without remuneration, for they regard their task as a *miṣva*. In Zakho, on the other hand, the *naqdāna* gets a fee.

Since the profession of slaughtering is a profitable one in the larger communities, the filling of a *shoḥeṭ*'s position in Kurdistan often gives rise to violent quarrels, ending, occasionally, in bloodshed.[11]

There have even been attempts to obtain the position of *shoḥeṭ* by questionable means. Benjamin II reports such a case from the vicinity of Barzani, where a totally ignorant man acquired the coveted position from the Kurdish chieftain in consideration of an annual tribute.[12]

The punishment for transgressing the laws of *sheḥīṭa* are very severe. In this connection the following story is told. A long time ago there lived in Herki a *ḥakham* who was at the same time a *shoḥeṭ*. There were seven other Jews living in Herki, and they too were *ḥakhamim*. One day the *ḥakham* went out to look after his fields, for the Jews of Herki owned much landed property. Thereupon, his sister took eight chickens, slaughtered them with her own hands, cooked them in pots which she had borrowed, and invited the seven *ḥakhamim* to dinner.

In the evening the brother came back and the seven *ḥakhamim* also arrived. The sister set wine and *maza* before them, then brought in the eight chickens. When they ended the meal, she asked, "How did you like the chickens?" "Very much," they replied. The sister continued: "There is nothing peculiar about them, is there? You see, what it took you a very long time to learn, I learned in an hour; for, look you, I slaughtered the chickens myself and cooked them in butter." The *ḥakhamim* cried to the brother, "What have you done?" And the horrified brother replied, "I thought one of you had slaughtered them" So each had thought that one of the others had done the slaughtering.

The *ḥakhamim* imposed twenty-six fasts upon themselves. They broke the vessels, and they locked the girl into a separate house (*judda*) for three months. And it came to pass that in the course of that year all the *ḥakhamim* died, and so the race of *ḥakhamim* became extinct in Herki.

16

The Education of Boys

We have virtually no source material concerning the standard of education among the Kurdish Jews in the past. The Kurdish Jews are an unliterary people, and no work that is in any degree their own creation has yet come to light.

Among the letters published by Mann, a group of five,[1] dating from the first half of the sixteenth century reveal something concerning the school system in Kurdistan. We made use of these letters in our discussion of the Kurdish woman as a teacher (pp. 176–77). These letters show that the school situation of the sixteenth century differed little from that of the present.

The letters were written by Ḥakham Ya'qov b. Yuda Mizraḥi,[2] his wife and his son. Ḥ. Ya'qov had conducted a school in Amadiya; and former pupils of his school were to be found, for instance, in Amadiya, Nirwa, and Sharanish (near Barwilnaye). For reasons not revealed in the letters, he removed from Amadiya to Mosul, leaving behind a large part of his books and manuscripts (letter 5, lines 22, 40). In Mosul he set up a *midrash* (school), which was attended by pupils from Kurdistan itself. Nevertheless, the school was unable to maintain itself unaided; and H. Ya'qov was compelled to spend much of his time in writing begging letters to the Kurdish communities and even to those of Aleppo, Baghdad, Diyar Bekr, and Maraga (letter 1, line 69).

The letters that have come down to us are his petitions to the communities of Nirwa, Amadiya, and Sundur. They had little success; and after the *ḥakham*'s death his widow, who, as we have seen (p. 177), had assisted him in his teaching during his lifetime, was compelled to continue his endeavors to obtain support. When his son, Sh'muel b. Ya'qov Mizraḥi, grew up, he took over, along with the school, the task of sending these begging letters to the Kurdish communities. Evidently, however, the son had no greater success than the father; for in letter 3 he complains that several communities had given him no support whatsoever for twelve consecutive years (line 12).

No precise details regarding the teaching profession can be gathered from these letters. Nevertheless, from their whole tone, we are led to conclude that the Kurdish school of that day was virtually the same as the Kurdish schools of our time.[3]

Teachers and Schools

Although the present-day standard of education is far from high, it is nevertheless worthy of note that in a completely illiterate district over 80 percent of the boys in the towns attend school.

We must make a distinction between urban and rural districts. The rural Jews, who in many cases form only a small group in a village, have no possibility of providing educational facilities for their children. If the father has money, he can send his son to study for a while in the town; or when the *shoḥeṭ* comes to the village, he can detain him for a month or more to give lessons to his son. For the most part, however, the village youth grow up in ignorance, unable to read or to recite the prayers.

The situation is different in the towns, where (as we just noted) the average school attendance is 80 percent. In Zakho and Amadiya virtually all the boys go to school; in Sinne, on the other hand, only 50 percent. None but utterly destitute parents fail to send their children at school. The pupils (*talmīda*, pl. *talmīde*) enter at about the age of four, although some fathers send their sons earlier, even at the age of two-and-a-half.[4] In Amadiya the school (Heb. *bet midrash* called *knishta* by the women) is a communal affair. The teacher is paid by the community. His salary was formerly about £1.10*s*. per month, later about £3. This is supplemented by the customary gifts from the parents. Nirwa, Tchalla, and Rekan have the same arrangement, which was introduced in order that a man without sons might also have a part in the *miṣva* of spreading education.

In the rest of Kurdistan the schools are a private enterprise of the teacher (*mu'allim*).[5] He receives monthly payments from the father. The tuition fee varies from 3 to 10 *grush* per month. In Sinne the father sometimes contracts with the teacher to pay according to sections of the course. For example, for teaching his son from *alef–bet* [the alphabet] to *sof hamiqra* [Heb. "end of the Bible"], he pays about 50 *qran* (about £5).

In Sinne the teacher's earnings are not appreciably supplemented by gifts from the parents. In other towns, the gifts form an important part of the teacher's income. Every Friday, for instance, each pupil contributes a cake (Z. *zuwā'ata*, pl. *zudiātha*); and the teacher sees to it that no child fails to bring it (Z., D., and A.). If a parsimonious mother should try to overlook her duty in this respect and send her son to school empty-handed, the teacher sends him home at once to fetch the cake and teach the mother a lesson at the same time. Besides this, the teacher gets several loaves of bread every baking day; and when an animal is slaughtered for the family, a portion of the meat is sent to the teacher, as well. In Arbil it is customary for the children to go stealing nuts for the teacher.

The custom of sending gifts on feast days further redounds to the teacher's advantage. Each shopkeeper sends him something out of his stock. The draper, for instance, contributes a piece of cloth or an article of clothing, the grocer—rice, flour, or other food products, generally something suitable for the occasion. Another point that is, in effect, an important addition to the teacher's income is his exemption from payment of community dues.

The Kurdish Jewish schoolmaster is usually not merely an instructor but a general community official. In addition to his pedagogic duties, he acts as *ḥazan*, *dayyan*, *shoḥeṭ*, and *mohel*. His work as *shoḥeṭ*, in particular, is hardly conducive to the best results in teaching.[6] He is often called away; and worst of all, on Friday when the Sabbath meat is slaughtered, he is gone all morning. In Zakho the schoolmasters are chiefly slaughterers of chickens and are continually called out not only on Friday but every day in the week.[7]

The teacher's absence is not in itself a great calamity, because the older pupils instruct the younger ones; but naturally, the boys utilize the opportunity for unruly behavior.

The school is either in the teacher's house or in the synagogue (Z., Jezire, A.). The two schools of Amadiya are in two synagogues. In the Knis Navi Yeḥezqel the schoolroom is next to the room of the ḥaverim. The children bring along fur rugs or carpets to sit on. In winter each pupil must furnish one piece of wood a day toward heating the schoolroom, so they come marching in like soldiers, "shouldering arms" with their logs and singing:

sāwun azakhnī nūran ōdakhla
dūkan basmakhla ḥīl istādēnī āse
zavinēni pisrit kisyāsa
tar akhlakhni ta khāṭir qarakhni
shimit illahēni pasnakhle
ta khāṭir naṭerēni
min gālut khalislēni.

Come let us go to make a fire,
To make the room beautiful before our teacher comes.
He will buy us meat of chickens
So that we may eat, so that we may learn.
The names of our God we shall praise
So that he may guard us
And deliver us from the Galut (exile). (A.)

In winter the boys put the good places about the stove up to auction among themselves.

The number of teachers and schools depends on the size of the community. In Arbil there are six schools; in Amadiya (as mentioned) each synagogue has a school. The Bet Midrash Shel Ezra, in lower Amadiya, has few pupils in winter because the snow makes it hard for the children to get there; and in any case, not many Jews live in the lower town in winter. In the summer, however, each school has from forty to fifty pupils. Zakho has only one school, but this school employs four teachers. In about 1920 there were approximately 250 pupils in Zakho. In Sinne, schools were conducted by four *ḥakhamim*, each having from forty to fifty pupils in his house.[8] Concerning the school in Hanekin, whose Jewish population consists chiefly of Kurdish Jews, we quote the following: ["There is no Talmud Torah. Two impoverished rabbis, who are dying of hunger, gather with great difficulty, each in his miserable hovel, some twenty boys whom they impart the rudiments of Hebrew reading"].[9]

Instruction

The school day (*dānā*) is divided into two parts: *dān benōke*, from eight in the morning to twelve midday, and *dān aṣirta*, from one o'clock in the afternoon to four or six. In the interval from twelve to one, the children go home for dinner (A. and Z.).

All the boys study in the same room but are divided into different age groups.[10] When the parents bring the child to school for the first time, the father carries him on his shoulders like a lamb to slaughter. [When a boy comes to school the first time, the teacher writes out for him the whole alphabet in big letters on a sheet of paper. He then smears honey on the letters, and tells the child to lick it. It is then said, *Ribono shel 'olam, yā ilāha mato dusha khilya ile hādaq tora khalia go pumet daya yala*, "Master of the Universe! O Lord, just as the honey is sweet, so may the Torah be sweet in the mouth of this boy!" Then the person who brought the child to school (his father or mother) says to the teacher, *Istādī, pisra tālok garme tālan*, "My Teacher, the flesh is for you, the bones for us." By this is meant, "Do not break his bones, but do beat him so that he should learn" (A.)]. The bitter moment, however, is sweetened with candy. A sugarloaf, candy, and some eggs dyed red are taken along for the teacher (S.). The teacher then pretends that the candy was sent from heaven in a wondrous manner just for the new pupil; and every time the child goes home, he gets an egg or a piece of sugar and runs joyfully to his mother to tell the tale.

The first thing studied in the school is reading. Every child brings a small board[11] to the *midrash*. A sheet of paper is pasted on this board and the teacher, with a reed pen (*qalāme*) and ink (Z. *dewoye*, A. *ḥubra*, S. *marakāv*) writes the letters of the alphabet on the paper in quite the traditional form. The first line contains the letters from *aleph* to *yod*, the second from *kaf* to *'ayin*, the third from *pe* to *tav*. There are several expedients for impressing the letters on the children's minds. The shapes of the letters in the first line are inculcated by means of the following verses (see Pronunciation Guide, p. 408):

ālf itla arba reshawātha	*Alef* has four heads
bē dakh kanūnala	*Bet* is like a stove
gīmel itla dūma	*Gimel* has a tail
dāl dakh dargēla [*maglēla*]	*Dalet* is like a door [a *scythe*]
hē brōna wille gō khepāqa	*He* has a son in her body
vau dakh qaṭi'a ēla	*Vav* is like a stick[12]
zān itla shashta	*Zayin* has a turban
ḥēt dakh ḥōda[13] *īla*	*Ḥet* is like a water jug
ṭet īda willa gū iba	*Ṭet* has her hand in her bosom
yod zurtela mikhwātokh	*Yod* is as small as you (A.)

[The version of my informant, also from Amadiya, agrees with the above only until the letter *he*. The rest of this version runs as follows:

waw dakh ṣuboetala la	*Vav* is like a finger
zayin shashtele bresha	*Zayin* has a crown on her head

ḥet dakh darga illa	*Ḥet* is like a door
ṭet resha lkipa 'lgawa	*Ṭet's* head is bent inside her
yod zurtela mikhwatokh	*Yod* is as small as you

Second Line

kaf ḥor knuna	*Kaf* is like a round hearth
lamed. . . (?)	*Lamed*. . . (?)
mem illa ghlaqta	*Mem* is closed (final *mem*)
nun rēsha illa mumta ilē uduma illa d'ipta ile	*Nun* has a straight head and a bent tail
nun purshaqta	*Nun* is elongated (final *nun*)
samekh jinjoger illa	*Sanekh* is roundish
'ayin trē rēshē illa	*'Ayin* has two heads

Third Line

pē rēsha ille d'ipa 'lgawa ḥor khuwa	*Pe*'s head is bent within her like a snake
pē purshaqta	*Pe* is elongated (final *pe*)
ṣadiq gimshabia il'ēnē unakhira upuma	*Sadiq* is like eyes and a nose and a mouth
ṣadiq purshaqta	*Sadiq* is elongated (final *ṣ*)
qof (resh, shin) illa ḥmilta resh da aqla	*Qof (resh, shin)* stands on one leg[14]
taw akhlta plumtēla	*Taw*'s leg is crooked.]

In addition to this, the letters are associated with words that are within the children's range of ideas. There are two series of such words, one consisting of the names of food, the other of the names of towns or villages. The food list runs thus: *ar'ūra* (manna), *bē'e* (eggs), *gōzē* (nuts), *dō'e* (buttermilk), *hināra* (kurd., pomegranate), *warda* (rose), *zabāsha* (Kurd., watermelon), *ḥabirmān* (pomegranate juice), *ṭaḥin* (dregs of sesame oil), *yavshata* (raisins) (Z. and A.).[15] [My informant from Amadiya substituted *zētē* (olives) and *ḥuna* (henna). The second line goes *kamisrē* or *karṣinē* (a sort of fruit?), *lubye* (a kind of pea), *mshmshe* (apricot), *nimoye* (lemon), *susāne* (a fruit that grows in the hills?), *'aluje* (a small plum). The third line goes *purtakāle* (oranges), *ṣanṣefi* (a kind of fruit?), *qar'e* (vegetable marrows), *rishtenēsa* (dough, like thin noodles), *she'de* (almonds), and *tuse* (mulberries) or *tar'oziye* (a vegetable similar to cucumbers).]

The names of the towns and villages, mostly in the vicinity of Amadiya, are as follows: (1) Urmi, Baghdād, Garago, Dehok, Hīzan,

Vān, Zakho, Ḥebron, Ṭevāria, Yerushalayim; (2) Kerkuk, Līwin (near Tiyāra), Melakhta, Nisēbin, Sabra, ʻAmadiya; (3) Pinyānesh, Ṣīwa (near Amadiya), Qadish (['Eqdish,] an hour and a half from Amadiya), Ravla, Sherānish, Taṣya (near Oramal). [There are different versions also in the third line of place names: Ṣablaq (or more accurately Ṣablagh), Qaro (a village about a day's distance from Amadiya), Rubār (the name of a river and the village that lies on its banks, near Amadiya) or Rulke (a town about two days' distance from Amadiya), and Tiflis.]

After the letters have been mastered, combinations of letters are written on the board. The first letter is combined with the last, the second with the last but one, and so on. Thus, the children read, *Alaf–tau, at*; *bē–shin, bash*; *he–ṣad pashūṭa* (final ṣade), *haṣ*, and so on. The list ends with *Yod mim yam*, *kaf lamed kol*, and the last line reads, *Moshe, ḥazaq, ḥazaq, ḥazaq* (A., Z., D., and S.). In Arbil the children learn the combinations *abgad, hawaz, ḥiṭi, kalman, sa'faṣ, qarashat.*[16]

Amadiya has a special system for beginners. The children learn the benedictions in a practical manner. The teacher puts a certain fruit or other article of food in the child's hand and says, *Brōni bārekh*, "My son, recite the benediction." Simultaneously with this, the children learn the alphabet in the manner just described. The next step is *makhōra* (like this). The child must point out in a printed book the letters that have been learned. After *makhōre* comes *nuqṭe*, "vowel points"—learning the vowels; and finally *hujē* "syllable," combining letters with points to form syllables (A.).[17]

When the boy has finished *hujē*, he celebrates by bringing a bowl of fruit to school for the teacher and the pupils, for now he is to begin reading in a printed book (Z.).

Studying the Bible

The Kurdish Jews begin the reading of the Bible with the book of Leviticus.[18] To signalize the happy moment when his son starts the study of the Torah, the father gives a dinner to which he invites the teacher, several notables, and some of the older pupils. Next morning, the boy brings another bowl of fruit to school for his fellow pupils (A., similarly Z.).

In Sinne, the boy likewise starts with Leviticus; but here, the teacher writes out the beginning—about as far as the second chapter—on separate sheets, and the pupil reads from these. Hence, these lessons are also called *palē*, "sheets." Only when the boy has finished *palē* do the parents buy him a printed Torah, and in honor of this event there is a feast at which a gift is presented to the teacher. Next morning, the father and the women of the family come to the *midrash* and bring several sugarloaves.

The reading of Leviticus is purely an exercise in reading words. The children understand nothing of it, because they read without translating. When the pupil reaches the passage *patōt ōta pittim* (Lev. 2:6), the teacher pulls his ear and says, "What are you giving?" The boy names a sum consistent with his father's means; and with this money, the teacher buys fruit for the pupils (A. and S.).[19] In Zakho, when one of the boys has reached this point, his fellow pupils bring their food to school and eat it there together. During this meal, they break off bits of bread and put them into their soup; this is what they understand by *patōt ōta pittim*. In Ushnu at this stage the father has his son read Leviticus to him from the beginning. The mother then presents the teacher with a sum of money and a *sīnīye* of food and arrack.

When the boys have finished the whole of Leviticus, they proceed with Numbers and Deuteronomy, then with Genesis and Exodus, all still as exercises in reading only. They understand no word of what they read (Z., A., and U.).[20]

In Sinne the sequence is different. Here, only a few chapters of Leviticus are read, till the pupil has attained a degree of facility in reading, then he begins with Genesis.

After Exodus come Joshua and the whole of the Prophets and the Writings. The children still do not understand what they are reading. During this time the pupil brings a bowl of food to school five times—when he starts Leviticus, at the beginnings of Joshua, Isaiah, and Psalms, and finally when he has finished the whole of the Scriptures (Z.).

Not until he has reached approximately his tenth year does the pupil begin with *shar'a*, that is, with the explanation (*perush*) of the biblical text and the translation in Targum, his own language. The translation is not written but has been handed down by word of mouth. Only the Psalms are not rendered in Targum (Z.).

In Amadiya the course is differently arranged. The father gives the *se'ōdit tyāmit tōra* [meal of completing the Torah] after his son has finished the simple reading of the Torah. The boy then begins the reading of Genesis again, but this time with the translation. He has an older pupil sitting beside him to recite the translation to him.

The teaching is not done entirely by the schoolmaster himself. The older pupils assist him; that is, a pupil of a higher class spends about half an hour each day instructing a pupil of a lower class. Then the separate classes (or the separate pupils) finish the studied lesson by themselves. Only the beginners and the oldest boys are taught by the *mu'allim*. Every day there is a test (*tenaya*). The pupil, together with his pupil–teacher, stands before the *mu'allim* and recites what he has learned. If he makes a mistake, the teacher questions the boy who has instructed him, to see who is responsible for the mistake. The guilty party gets punished.

The knowledge acquired by the pupils is very slight. Only a few learn to read fluently, and still fewer attain to an understanding of what they have read. The older pupils study 'En Ya'aqov and Bet Ya'aqov in addition to the Bible. The sources studied for the ritual are the Mishna and Oraḥ Ḥayyim, but the study of the Gemara itself is unknown (A., Z., D., and S.). Since most of the students leave school at the age of thirteen or even earlier, in order to go to work, very few ever get past the Bible.

A little writing and arithmetic are added to the curriculum when the boys are about eight years old, These subjects are studied in the afternoons. In arithmetic (*raqam*) they learn mainly that which will be of service to them in practical life, such as calculation of the prices of goods and the way to write out tradesmen's bills.[21]

Punishments

School punishments are a chapter in themselves. We have often had occasion to observe that the Kurdish Jew has assimilated something of the wildness and harshness of his Kurdish environment. This is evidence also in the teacher and in the nature of the punishments (A. *jiza*; S. *jerima*) he so readily inflicts upon his pupils.

The parents even support the teacher in his brutality. We have seen how the father, when he brings the child to school for the first time, carries him on his shoulder. This signifies that he regards the child as a *qorban*, a sacrifice, and he surrenders him to the teacher with the words, *Mikhwathit qorban ṭā istādit 'olam*, "As a sacrifice for the Master of the world." And to this he adds, *Pisre ṭālokh garme ṭālī*, "The flesh for you, the bones for me."[22] [They believe that those places on a child's body that have been beaten by the teacher will be immune to hellfire. When the child comes home complaining that the teacher has beaten him, his parents comfort him with the words, *Brōni, mil makhēlokh istādokh, ku dūket shebūqet istādokh 'alaklē iba nurī gēhenam lā ghakim ibā*, "My son, let your teacher beat you; wherever your teacher's rod will touch you, the fire of hell will not be able to harm it. (A.)]

Small children are punished by being forced to stand on one foot (A.) or to stand barefoot on the hot ground (Arbil) until they know the lesson. Simpler punishments are pulling by the ear or by the nose, which the boys call *marwāde*, "earring," and *ḥozemta*, "nose ring."

For beating the children, the teacher has various kinds of sticks that inflict varying degrees of pain: a soft stick (A *shebuqa*, S. *ṭūl*) and a hard one (Z. *qaṭi'a*, S. *ṣīwa*). The children refer to strokes on the hand as *das gurke*, "gloves." The pupils take every opportunity of hiding or breaking the sticks.

More severe punishments are *taltō'e* (S. *talō'e*), "hanging," and *falaq* (S. *falaqa*), "block." The *falaq* consists of two boards with holes cut out for the fet, like the appliance used for administering the bastinado. Two boys hold the boards together, and the teacher beats the offender on the soles of his feet (practiced generally). For *taltō'e* a rope is passed over a girder and the delinquent hung up by the heels. In the boys' vocabulary the place where this is done is called *qanāra*, the place where the cattle is hung after slaughtering. They say, *Qanāra wela maḥdarta ṭālokh*, "The slaughtering place is prepared for you" (A.). To make things worse, the boys put a little heap of dung under the culprit's nose and set fire to it. This produces an acrid smoke. Then, as if all this were not sufficient, the victim, while hanging thus, is sometimes obliged to recite the weekly portion of the Torah (A.).

The punishments, however, are not inflicted in a secular manner, (so to speak) but rhythmically, to the verses of the Bible. Thus, the children are beaten to the words of Psalm 78:38, *V'hu raḥum*, and so on (Z., A., and S.). In Sinne, if the teacher beats a pupil of whom he is fond, he recites the verse, "So God give thee of the dew of heaven, and of the fat places of the earth, and plenty of corn and wine" (Gen. 27:28).

It is also customary to punish the children in advance, as a sort of prophylactic measure. Some teachers, for instance, line the boys up twice a day—at noon and in the evening before they leave to home—and strike them lightly on their outstretched hands, rhythmically reciting, as they pass from one to the other, the prayer, ["I give thanks to you, O Lord, our God and the God of our fathers that you gave my share from those who sit in the house of learning and did not give my share from those who sit on street corners" (B. Berakhot 28:6)] (A. and Ushnu). In some places the teacher beats the boys only on Friday, as a sort of "advance payment" for the Sabbath, thus ensuring their good conduct on that day.[23]

Some of the schoolmasters are inordinately cruel. There are cases where boys were so badly beaten that they lay ill in bed for weeks.

When the weather is fine, the boys occasionally go to the riverbank, instead of to school. Then all of them get *taltō'e* (A.). I was told of a small boy who innocently strolled off to a place about an hour's distance from Amadiya, instead of going to school. The teacher hurried after him; and the terrified child, followed by the teacher, ran farther and farther till he reached Bamarne, six hours distant from Amadiya. There, exhausted, he fell into the hands of his pursuer and was beaten till he could no longer walk or even move. The teacher, to his rage, was then obliged to carry the child home on his shoulder When he grew weary of the burden, he simply threw the boy to the ground as though he was a sack. This is the tale as it was told to me.

The teachers also make use of the pupils for their own private purposes. In Sinne, if the teacher was called away in his capacity of *shoḥeṭ*, he had the pupils do the chores, clean the house, do the marketing, fetch building materials—in short, he treated them like workmen.

Instruction is, as a whole, on a very low level. The children never acquire more than a smattering of reading and writing, and there can be no question of any understanding. In an atmosphere of this kind, it is consequently not surprising that such a punishment as the following should exist. A child who can get nothing into his head is put into a corner; and the *me'allim* says, *Rōqun ille tar lāyip*, "Spit on him so that he may learn"—which each child then proceeds to do (A.).[24] To a blockhead the children say, *Amareṣa, torqa lēsa*, "Ignoramus, a bag of resin." [Again, they will say to such a child, *Rēshokh rēsh kēpa ile*, "Your head is a head of stone!".]

Magic remedies are also employed for backwardness in children. As in the case of a sick man, the *ḥakham* writes the names of certain angels on paper or on an egg, washes the ink off, and gives the water to the child to drink.

The remedy is even more efficacious when the names of the angels are written on almonds. The child must put the almonds under his head at night and eat them in the morning. Almonds are considered particularly effective because the almond tree bears fruit earlier than other trees. The choice of almonds, however, also has some connection with the verse "Then said the Lord unto me, 'Thou hast well seen', for I watch [pun on "almond tree"] over thy word to perform it" (Jer. 1:12).

The children themselves also practice this type of magic. For instance, they take the paper that they have used for their writing exercises and throw it into a spring. Thereby, they hope, they will become *ma'yan ḥokhma*, "a source of wisdom." Another practice is the exact reverse of this: the pupils burn up each other's writing exercises in the belief that along with the exercises they are burning up their fellow pupils' intelligence (S.).

When the pupils cut their reed pens, they eat the fibers that jut out from the inside. This will make calligraphers of them (Z.). Licking ink will have the same effect (A.).

The pupils are on terms of good fellowship with each other and give each other nicknames. The strongest among them is called Yo'ab b. Ṣerūya or Avner b. Ner. The son of the *gevir* is dubbed Dawid, and mischief-makers bear the name Titos [i.e., Titus] or Yerov'am ben Nebat.

Student Excursions

The great events of the school year are the student excursions (*serāne talmīde*), on which they feel themselves grown-up and imitate their elders.

The principal excursions take place during Passover (*serāne patīre*), Shavu'ot (*serāne ziyāra*), Purim (*serāne megala*), and Hanukka (*serāne ḥanuka*). Beside these, there are special *serāne*—for instance, on Shabbat Naḥamu, on anniversaries that concern the pupils, and on such important occasions as the birth of a son to the teacher or the completion of the reading of the Torah by one of the pupils (*serāne khetāme tōra*).

The pupils have a chief, *urwit talmīde*. He is assisted by the *shammash talmīde* and two boys whose duty it is to cut the wood (*tewārit ṣīwe*). The shammash and the woodcutters are exempt from contributions to the student fund.

The pupils have a fund that is kept up in various ways. They receive donations, for instance, from the men who are called up to the reading of the Torah, from bridegrooms, "best men," fathers of newborn sons, and so on. This fund serves to cover the expenses of the excursions. Before each excursion, the *urwit talmīde* makes a collection among the pupils. With this money a sheep is purchased—unless the father of one of the boys presents the sheep, as at *serāne khetāme tōra*. The *shammash talmīde* furthermore makes the rounds of the pupils' homes and collects the other requisites for the excursion.

The pupils sometimes invite the grown-ups to their excursion, particularly rich folks who will bring them some arrack. In the place which serves their parents as excursion grounds, the schoolboys have a special corner of their own, *dūke talmide*. There they dance and sing; and the women—chief among them, the wife of the *me'allim*—cook the picnic lunch for them on the spot (A. and U.).

As previously mentioned, the boys arrange a feast if a son is born to the teacher. They collect the food in the same way as for other such celebrations, and the banquet takes place in the teacher's house (A.).

17

The Synagogue

The community life of the Yemenite Jews centers on the *knis*, the synagogue. To the Yemenites, the synagogue is not merely a house of prayer but, we [Germans] may say, a *Männerhaus*, comparable to the clubhouse or community house of the American Indians or the South Sea Islanders.[1] For the Kurdish Jews, on the other hand, the synagogue has no such significance. It is, to them, quite simply the place where they assemble for divine service. The fact that community study of the Torah is virtually unknown to them contributes to this attitude. In Kurdistan, the home is a much more frequent place of gathering for the men than the synagogue; and even when, as in the case of the *ḥavrāye* in Amadiya, a separate room is needed for meetings, they do not resort to the synagogue but arrange for a special room elsewhere.

Age of the Synagogues—Their Names

Before full particulars concerning the synagogues[2] of Kurdistan can be given, there will have to be a thorough tectonic investigation of them, and certain excavations will have to be carried out. Many of the existing synagogues are undoubtedly very old, as attested by several peculiarities in their structure.

The Ṣlōlet Qal'a [Citadel Synagogue] of Old Arbil, that is the part of Arbil that lies on the old town hill, is said to have been built in the sixteenth century. Only parts of the ancient structure have survived, however, since the building has been restored a number of times.

The Knis Navi Yeḥezqel in Amadiya, which was presumably erected in 1250, deserves special attention. On one of its old wooden pillars is an inscription from which the date is taken and reads as follows [in Arabic, written in Hebrew characters]: *Awwal 'imārathā atqn"ṭ aydhan itjadadat fi atq"s, aydhan fi at"r itjadadat ṣufafhā* ["The beginnings of its building [was in] 1559. Thereupon, it was renewed in 1560; thereupon, in 1600, its moldings were renewed."][3]

The *Sefer Pitron Ḥalomot* [Book of interpretation of dreams]—written in 1788 and now in the possession of a *ḥakham* from Amadiya—comments on this inscription: "The beginning of its building was in the year 1559 [of the era] of the documents, and its building was not completed until the second year, which was the year 1560 of the documents. Forty years later they built the galleries around the courtyard, which was the year 1600 of the documents."[4] [The "year such-and-such of the documents" refers to the Seleucid Era, which was the basis of reckoning years during the Second Temple period and remained in use in some Jewish communities down to modern times. It is calculated beginning with 312 or 311 B.C.E., the year in which Seleucos I Nicator returned to Babylon following the Battle of Gaza; that is, the "year of documents" 1559 corresponds to 1248 C.E., and 1560, to 1289 C.E.

It is interesting to note that in folk memory Alexander the Great was substituted for Seleucos I Nicator as the conqueror to whose name is tied the era of documents. One of my informants, who had left Amadiya in about 1925, told me in Jerusalem in 1945 that the wooden capital of the southwestern column, one of the quadrangle of columns standing in the middle of the synagogue courtyard, had this inscription engraved into it: *Awwal amarathā 1549* [sic] *lishtarot Iskander, aḥarē arba'im shana banu et ha'azarot*, "The beginning of its building was in 1549 of the documents of Alexander; forty years later, they built the galleries."]

The synagogues are variously named; some are merely distinguished by size: *knishta rabta* [big synagogue] and *knishta zurta* [small synagogue"] (Z., S., and Arbil). Others are called after the locality in which they are situated such as Ṣlōlet Qal'a of Arbil (mentioned above), and the upper and lower synagogues in Amadiya.

Frequently, the synagogue bears the name of a family or a *gevir*, as in Yemen—although, to be sure, in Yemen the synagogue is established through private initiative more often than in Kurdistan, where the synagogue is a community affair.[5] Ushnu has a synagogue called Kneset Mūsa [Synagogue of Musa] after the Gabbai Musa, and Sulaimani has a *Knishta Me'ir Moshaka* [Synagogue of Me'ir Moshaka].

There are, besides, several synagogues that are held to be extremely ancient and bear the names of biblical characters, presumably because these characters are in some way associated with the synagogues or (at any rate) with the locality.

In Mosul and Betanura there are synagogues named after the prophet Elijah. The following tale is told in connection with Knishta Sayyid Eliya [Synagogue of the Lord Elijah] in Betanura. Many years ago, when there were still about eight hundred Jewish families in Betanura, the community wished to build a large synagogue. The workmen began the building; but when they came to the site the second morning, there was no sign of the work they had done. Elijah had transferred the portion of wall they had built to a spot near the cave where he is said to have rested, which is a celebrated place of pilgrimage in Kurdistan. Since this cave lies outside the town, the notables of the community preferred not to build the synagogue there. But every time the wall was begun, it was found next morning at the spot beside the cave. Then one night, Elijah appeared in a dream to a Jew named Eliya Khudeda and said to him, "If you do not build the synagogue next to my cave, I shall destroy you all." So the synagogue was built outside the cave.

Site of the Synagogue

It is characteristic of the Kurdish synagogue to be situated near a body of running water. This choice of site is evidently connected with the desire to have the ritual bath at the synagogue. A riverbank is the favorite place for a synagogue and is often chosen even though it may be rather far from the town.[6]

Zakho, Dehok, Betanura, and Ora all have synagogues built on riverbanks. In other places, the synagogues are connected with a spring, like those of Nirwa, Tchalla, Bijar, and Ushnu.

The synagogue of Akra was built outside the town in order to be situated at a spring. The water from this spring flows in two branches through the building and out beneath the courtyard. Benjamin II describes the synagogue as follows: "In the middle of the fields, about half an hour's journey from the town, stands a synagogue, remarkable for its great age; near by is a small reservoir, which serves as a bath for the women. . . . Every [Germ. ed. "Friday"] afternoon . . . the Jews go to the river which flows near the synagogue" (*Eight Years in Asia and Africa*, pp. 104–5).

Floor Plan

The Jews of Amadiya say that the floor plan of their synagogues is like that of the Bet Miqdash [Temple of Jerusalem, as described in the book of Ezekiel].

Most Kurdish synagogues resemble each other in one respect, namely, in possessing a walled-in courtyard.[7] This courtyard serves as a summer synagogue. In contrast with the Yemenite synagogues, which generally consist of several rooms in a private house,[8] the synagogues of the Kurdish Jews are always buildings specially erected for the purpose. This fact also attests to the great difference between these two Jewish communities.

As an example of a Kurdish *knishta* we have chosen Knishtit Navi Yeḥezqel in upper Amadiya, which (as previously observed) was built circa 1250. Its ground plan is similar to that of the older Knishtit Ezra haSofer.

The floor plan shows three sections: the courtyard, the synagogue proper, and (connected with the latter) a suite of smaller rooms.

The Courtyard

The synagogue courtyard (*ḥabābel* [gate house]); that is to say, one must pass through two gates in entering the synagogue, a requirement inferred from Proverbs 8:34: "Happy is the man that hearkeneth to me, watching daily at my gates, waiting at the posts of my doors" (also S.). [When entering the synagogue, the people pause for a short while in the *ḥabābel*, leave there their pipes, and so on, then enter the courtyard.]

The courtyard is surrounded by an elevated platform (*dake*, pl. *dakātha*) over which is a roof supported by antique wooden columns (*stūne*). These columns have a step-shaped capital (*gulsa*) very reminiscent of the capitals of Sassanid columns.[9] [The height of these capitals is about 3–4 meters and their width 1 meter; the columns themselves are some 2 1/2 meters high.] The capitals differ in details and seem to belong to different periods. In the middle of the court [which is open to the sky, and surrounded by wooden columns] is a plot of ground containing flowers and trees and surrounded by a low stone fence. [Beneath this central section of the court there is an ancient cistern of considerable size, with a small opening in the center and a hole in the southern side. This cistern has been broken for some years and all the rainwater that enters it is swallowed into the earth.

During prayers, no one sits on its parapet; but on the Sabbath, after the *musaf* prayer is over, the members of the *ḥevra qadīsha* sit there and drink arrack].

The synagogue services are held in the court during the greater part of the year, that is, from Purim to Hanukka. On the west side, the side of the synagogue, the platform is widened to accommodate the reading desk (*side*). The old men also sit there.

From Hanukka to Purim the services are held in the synagogue proper. The building has an ancient substructure of hewn stone. The walls, which are also of stone, are of more recent date. There are no windows, the light entering only through apertures in the ceiling and the three doors that face the court. These doors are called *hekhalot* [lit., "halls"] because they are covered with curtains.

The roof [which surrounds the court in the form of a square frame] is supported by wooden columns, on whose capitals are certain inscriptions and carvings, including a date and some verses from the Psalms. [One of these inscriptions has been mentioned on p. 250. The capital of the southeastern column bears this inscription (in Hebrew): "All nations whom Thou hast made shall come and prostrate themselves before Thee and shall glorify Thy name, Selah" (Psalms 86:9, with slight variations).]

The Jews say that part [of two] of the columns are trees, which still have their roots in the ground.[10] [The synagogue was built on a site where there was previously an orchard of nut and almond trees. When the synagogue was built, it was placed so that two of the trees of this orchard remained in place and served as the central supports of the synagogue. The branches were lopped off and the ceiling was made to rest upon the trunks. These two tree–columns stand in the middle of the synagogue, a little to the north of the *bama*.] The place where the men squat (called *dake* here also) is covered with straw mats (*basīre*). The elite bring along rugs on which to sit, but there are some rugs that belong to the synagogue and are paid for by the congregation.[11]

Everyone has a definite place in the synagogue. This place is handed down from father to son. Only mourners change their places and sit in the southeast corner. The elite sit at the right of the Hēkhal [meaning the Holy Ark], facing the congregation.

In Sinne every family has its traditional place; that is to say, the congregation is seated according to families, not according to age groups. The families of physicians all sit together. In former times violent quarrels would arise in the synagogue if someone sat down in a place belonging to another family. These disputes were even brought before the government authorities. [The floor of the synagogue itself is three steps below the level of the court, in accordance with the verse, "From the depths have I called unto thee."]

In the middle of the synagogue is an elevated platform (*doshka*)[12] on which stands the reading desk (*side*). This is a long table with four sticks (*iqlātha*) at the corners, on which the Torah crowns are set, and seven sockets in which lights are placed at Purim (only A., see p. 350). In Zakho there are no *iqlātha*, because the Torah crowns remain on the scrolls during the reading, and the honor of removing them from the scrolls is not put up to auction.

In Sinne the *seda* stands on an elevated platform, which also provides seatings for several notables. These places are acquired by inheritance.

The *Hēkhal* (Sanctuary)

At the west end of the Knishta Navi Yeḥezqel are three chambers. The central chamber is called *dūke* or *manzal*. It is quite small and contains a cupboard with compartments (*sünduq*), in which the Torah scrolls are kept. The cupboard has a wooden door and is covered with a curtain. The *dūke* further contains the *megilla* [scroll of Esther], the Kursi Eliyahu [chair of Elijah] the shofar, the *malqut* (leather straps) for the scourging on Yom Kippur eve, and a jar of sesame oil.

In the northern wall of the *dūke*, near the ceiling, there is an opening into the second chamber, which serves as *bē genīza* (storage room) for Hebrew manuscripts and books that have become unserviceable.

The third room, the *bē khamra* (wine room), adjoins the *dūke* on the south side. Here is kept the wine required for the use of the synagogue or for the *ḥaverim*. [The floor of the *genīza* is lower than the floor of the synagogue proper. From the synagogue a tiny opening leads into the storage room, which contains some three hundred old Torah scrolls and a considerable number of old prayer books.]

In Zakho also there is a separate room for the hēkhal. It is in the southwest corner of the synagogue and is slightly elevated. The Torah scrolls are set on shelves (*dakanītha*) along the western and southern walls. The scrolls are not protected by special covers. In Zakho this chamber contains also the Chair of Elijah, the *malqut*, and lamps with their accessories and supplies.

In Sinne—that is, in the Persian-Kurdish district—the Torah scrolls are not kept in a separate room. Here the hēkhal consists of niches (*tāqe*) in the western wall. The niches have doors and are covered with curtains (*pardā*)—often several curtains, one over the other, for they are gifts and the synagogue possesses many of them. Arbil, Ushnu, and the village synagogue of Sundur have the same type of hēkhal.

The Torah Scrolls

The antique Torah scrolls are set in heavy quadrangular wooden cases (*tīk*, A. *tika*), often with silver mountings.[13] The newer Torah scrolls have round cases, like those of the Sephardi Jews. In Sinne the round wooden case (*qāp*) is covered with cloth and decorated with metal nails.

The *'aṣe ḥayyim* [Heb., lit., "trees of life"], the sticks on which the scroll is rolled, are called *shebūqa* (Z. and A.) or *'amud* (S.). The scrolls have one or more cloaks (A. *faraji* [or *ḥupo*], Z. *kurtak*, S. *kabā*), which are presented by the wives or female relatives of the donors of the scrolls or by mothers when a child has fallen ill. The women also sew coins, corals (*kisne*), amulet holders (*khiaroke*), and so on, on the Torah cloaks on various occasions in fulfillment of some vow.

On top of the sticks come the Torah crowns (*rimmonim* or *rimonīye*).[14] All the Kurdish *rimmonim* that I have seen are made of silver, in the classic style, with motifs probably deriving from the Turkish. A pair of *rimmonim* from the synagogue of the village community of Barashe,[15] wrought in silver with a design of vine tendrils, is composed of four parts: (1) the stem; (2) and (3) the sphere, which can be separated into two halves; and (4) the screw, which turns to the right. We have seen (p. 155) how water is put into these half spheres, blessed by *ḥakham*, and given as an efficacious drink to a woman in difficult labor.

The upper section of the sphere bears an inscription engraved in a single line along the edge (in Hebrew): "These *rimmonim* are sacred to the Lord, they shall not be sold and shall not be redeemed. [Property] of the Synagogue of the Holy Congregation of Barashe (May our city [i.e., Jerusalem] be built up, amen!) in the year A.D. 1863" Small bells (A. *zāge*, [the bell's tongue, the bell itself being called *zingerogi*]; Z. *zingile*; S. *zangule*) are attached to the *rimmonim*.

In Zakho the *rimmonim* are always left on the Torah scrolls. Only in times of unrest are they removed and placed for safety in the house of the *gabbai*. In Amadiya, on the contrary, only three pairs of *rimmonim* are kept in the synagogue, the others remaining regularly in the custody of the *gabbai*. They are exchanged about twice a month, however, so that all of them may have the honor of serving as a decoration to the Torah scrolls from which the reading is actually done.

The *rimmonim* are also used to adorn the Chair of Elijah, which has special posts on which to set them.

In former times Kurdistan possessed some Torah scribes; thus, part of the old Torah scrolls, written on skins, are home products. But since the passing of these scribes,[16] the scrolls are bought in Mosul, Baghdad, or (in the Kurdish–Persian district) Hamadan.

The number of Torah scrolls to be found in a synagogue varies. In Zakho, the large synagogue has twenty, the small one, ten; in Amadiya the Ezra haSofer has seven, Navi Yeḥezqel, about twelve.[17] The synagogue of Sundur has no fewer than ten.[18]

In or before the hēkhal there burns an "eternal lamp" *sherā'a* (called Heb. *nēr tamīd* only by the *ḥakhamim*). This lamp was formerly made if iron but is now of earthenware, and it usually stands on a wooden chest near the door. In Amadiya it stands on an old iron tripod.

Beside the eternal lamp are generally other lights that are kept constantly burning. Families that have suffered a death sometimes present the synagogue with enough oil to have the *shammash* keep one of these lamps burning for a year. In Sinne there are often from thirty to forty such lamps burning at one time.

On Sabbaths and feast days, in particular, the number of these lamps increases. Sometimes, for instance, a bereaved mother, on bearing another child, will have a "light of the prophet Elijah" lighted for him on every Shabbat, new moon, and feast day for six consecutive years (Z.).

The dust and the remnants of oil from the "eternal lamp" are regarded as valuable remedies. Thus, a person afflicted with a sore will go to the *shammash* and beg for a little *shikhtit benunta*, "dust [dirt] of the shelves," to use as an ointment (Z. and A.).

During the reading of the Torah, the scroll does not lie flat but stands obliquely, leaning against the back of the *side*. The pointer (A. *yad*, A. *mekhūtha*, Sundur *mankhēda*, S. and Arbil *kalam*) used during the reading has not the form—so often met with elsewhere—of a hand with a pointing finger. We have a pointer from Barashe[19] that is made quite simply but shows a fine sense of form and style. Some of the pointers bear inscriptions (e.g., the name of the donor).

During the benedictions, the scroll is always covered with a cloth lest someone think, by any chance, that the benediction is written in the Torah, to which, naturally no jot or tittle must be added. In Amadiya this cloth (*shīshak* or *shīsha*) is hung between the *rimmonim*. In Zakho it is tied around them, whence its name, *kefiye* [Arab., head-kerchief].

In Sinne, on the other hand, it is wound around the cloak like a girdle and is therefore called *khasa*,[20] "girdle."

In some synagogues (Z., D., A., Sundur, Seranis, Bijar, and Sinne) a large brown empty eggshell is suspended from the ceiling and is known as *bēta simorg* or *bēta nishra*, "eagle's egg." The *simorgh* is the wonder bird that occupies an important place in Persian legend.[21] The Jews connect this use of the eggshell (on which several Bible verses are sometimes written) with Exodus 19:4, "I bore you on eagles' wings" and Deuteronomy 32:11, "as an eagle that stirreth up her nest." It is further said that the bird *dūma kaske*, "green tail," which brings earth from the grave of Moses (A.), builds its nest on the roof just over the egg.

The Women's Section

Most of the older synagogues in Kurdistan possess no section for women, since women seldom go to the synagogue. The few who appear (generally old women) either remain in the courtyard or sit, veiled, in the synagogue itself. In Zakho the old women and the girls occupy the synagogue on Yom Kippur, while the men perform the service in the courtyard. The rest of the women, with the children, sit on the roofs of neighboring houses.

In the courtyard of Navi Yeḥezqel Synagogue in Amadiya there is an elevated platform (*dākit avisla* [court of the wine press]), where, formerly, the grapes for the synagogue wine were trampled. Nowadays, the women sit there; being no longer used as a wine press, it is called *dākit bakhtātha*.

In all three synagogues of Arbil the women occupy a closed gallery from which they can look down into the men's room through several small windows. Only a few old women, however, frequent this gallery.

In Sinne, similarly, the women's room (*tūka enshē*) is over the gate house and has a wooden lattice through which the women can look down into the inner room of the synagogue. In the summer the women sit on the roof of a house that stands in the courtyard.

Genīza

We have seen above that the *genīza* in Amadiya at the Navi Yeḥezqel Synagogue is in a separate room, *bē genīza*. At present, however, it appears that only in Amadiya is a special room devoted to the *genīza* (although we may possibly be encountering here an example of a very early arrangement).

In Sinne the platform of the *sede*, *sakū sede*, is hollow and serves as *genēza*. The books, and so on are put in through a hold at the side.[22] Zakho has a similar arrangement, a space for the *genīza* having been left under the stairway that leads from the court to the roof. In Ushnu the *genīza* is in the cellar under the *hēkhal*, and in Dehok, in a space hollowed out of the thick wall.

When the *genīza* is full, the *ḥakhamim* sort out the contents. The worthless pieces are put into sacks and buried in the courtyard of the synagogue, but the old Torah scrolls and all sacred books are returned to the *genīza*.

18

The Sabbath

The Sabbath is the center of the religious life of the Kurdish Jew, and the rigid observance of the law enjoining rest on this day is quite in keeping with the inflexibility characteristic of his peasant nature. Very close attention is paid to the conduct of the community on the Sabbath, and any infraction of the Sabbath laws is severely punished.

In Arbil a father whose son had struck a match on the Sabbath was fined 80 *grush*. In Amadiya the guilty party must pay a cash fine, of which the synagogue gets two-thirds and the *ḥazan* one-third. He must further present the *ḥaverim* with a certain amount of arrack. In addition to all this, he receives forty strokes of the lash, and sometimes has twenty-six fasts imposed upon him.

A vivid description of how the Kurdish Jews deal with misconduct of this kind is given in the story about R. Shemuel Barzani that runs as follows:

The Story of the Healing Pomegranate Tree.[1]

It happened in Kurdistan more than 150 years ago that on a Friday of the Sukkot half-holiday Rabbi Netanel haLevi, who was more than a hundred years old, and his son Rabbi Sh'mu'el, sat in their booth in the town of Barzani. They studied the tractate Ḥagiga of the Talmud and discussed the subject of the *Merkava*, the world of the divine throne. And they got lost in their thoughts, and tried to solve the question of what was *above* the *Merkava*.

Suddenly a green flame descended from on high, and stopped above the Sukka. In that hour the Shekh of Barzani was sitting on the roof of his house, and noticed the green flame over the booth of the Jew. He called his servant, and sent him to find out what was going on in the booth. For he was greatly astonished about the flame, which reached up to heaven but did not destroy anything.

The servant hurried to the place, saw the pillar of fire stand over the Sukka, and the rabbi and his son sit and bend over the books, and the fire did not touch them. Greatly amazed he returned to the Shekh, and reported to him what he had seen. When the Shekh heard him out, he said: "One thing is clear to me: those two are not rabbis but *Sayyid*s descended from the Prophet Muhammad, peace be upon him. For how could a green flame descend from heaven upon the house of a Jew without consuming and destroying it? Go, bring them here, so that I can ask them about their descent."

The servant went and brought Rabbi Netanel and his son Rabbi Sh'mu'el to the Shekh. The Shekh asked them: "What is the meaning of the green fire that stands above your booth?" Rabbi Netanel answered: "We know nothing about a pillar of fire, and we noticed nothing, for we were immersed in studying our holy books."

But the Shekh said: "No, that cannot be true. All of us saw the fire. And this green fire is the fire of the *Sayyid*s. Give me an account of your ancestry, for you must be of the seed of Muhammad."

Rabbi Netanel replied: "You are mistaken. This is the chain of my ancestors." And he enumerated their names.

But the Shekh did not believe him, and said: "You are of the children of Muhammad, and you must convert to Islam, or else you will die."

He imprisoned them in the ***akhura***, the place where they keep the animals, and, in order to torment them he had dry dung burnt next to them. There they sat, and the acrid smoke rose into their eyes. Rabbi Netanel thought: "Let them kill me, but I am concerned about my son. I must save him." He called the Shekh's servant, and asked him to take him to the Shekh. When he was brought to the Shekh, he said to him: "O Shekh, you know that we are forbidden to do any work on the Sabbath, or to leave our houses. Permit us to spend the Sabbath in our house so that we can consider carefully what to choose, your faith or death. On Sunday we will return to you, and tell you our decision."

The Shekh agreed, and Rabbi Netanel and his son hurried home. They recited the prayers and the benedictions, for the Sabbath had already begun, and sat down to the Sabbath meal. When they finished eating, they reflected on their grievous fate. Rabbi Sh'mu'el asked his father: "Does not mortal danger cancel the Sabbath?"

Rabbi Netanel answered: "Mortal danger does cancel the Sabbath." Thereupon Rabbi Sh'mu'el looked at the ceiling from which the *rashke*,[2] the summer shoes, were suspended. He got up, took down the *rashke*, and put them on. Then he grasped the hand of his father, and took leave of him. Rabbi Netanel began to cry. His son said: "Don't cry. Isn't it Sabbath today, and isn't it forbidden to cry?" The father replied: "Let me cry, for that too is a Sabbath joy for me, since it eases the pain in my soul."

The son set out on his way. Because he was afraid that he would be followed, he walked without stopping all night. By dawn he reached the river Zab, and the town of Suriya was before him. But he saw no ferry to take him across. And he lifted up his eyes and saw, on the opposite bank, two Jews who, as was the custom of the Kurdish Jews, had come to the river to relieve nature and to purify themselves. He called out to them, and they were greatly astonished to see Rabbi Sh'mu'el, whom they recognized. They quickly fetched the Muslim ferry-man, who took him across in his *kalak*.[3] The two Jews received him with the words: "My lord Sh'mu'el, it is Sabbath today, how did you come here on the Sabbath of the Lord? We might as well go and seat ourselves at our weaving-looms."[4]

Rabbi Sh'mu'el got enraged. He looked at them with flashing eyes and said: "You perfectly evil men!" Thereupon the two were transformed into dead willow trees with only a few green leaves at the top indicating that they were once alive.

At that time Rabbi Shim'on was teacher and judge in Amadiya. He was a great astrologer, and reading the constellations he concluded that an important visitor would come to him on the Sabbath. Therefore, when his wife was about to cook the Sabbath meals, he instructed her to prepare for the Third Meal two chickens filled with rice instead of one, and two jars of the finest wine.

On the Sabbath afternoon the Jews of Amadiya sat, as was their wont, in the synagogue named after Ezra the Scribe. At that time the Jewish community of Amadiya was still very big, and some four hundred men gathered to hear Rabbi Shim'on's address. Since it was summer, they gathered in the courtyard.

In the very midst of Rabbi Shim'on's lecture a man appeared, covered with the dust of the roads. He crossed the courtyard stealthily, passed all the assembled people, and sat down in the empty synagogue next to the Holy Ark.

All those present instantly recognized the son of Rabbi Netanel Barzani. They were astonished at his sudden appearance on the Sabbath, and they asked each other whether Rabbi Sh'mu'el had stayed with them overnight. But there was nobody with whom he had spent the night.

When they finished the Minḥa prayer, Rabbi Sh'mu'el rose from his place in the synagogue, stepped before the Amadiya community, and said: "I beg you to pronounce sentence over me, for I have violated the Sabbath."

Thereupon Rabbi Shim'on spoke up: "I know your sentence. Come to my house, for the Third Meal is already prepared for you there. I know that you were in mortal danger, and it was only because of that that you violated the Sabbath."

And now we reach Sunday. Early in the morning the Shekh of Barzani sent his servant to fetch Rabbi Netanel and his son. Rabbi Netanel came alone, and told the Shekh about the flight of his son, and his own decision not to convert to Islam, but to die. The Shekh, driven by anger, was about to order Rabbi Netanel to be killed, when an old man, who sat next to the Shekh as his advisor, raised his voice and said: "Why do you want to kill this aged man? Since he already stands at the door of death, it is not worthwhile to shed blood. But make every effort to apprehend his son."

The Shekh let himself be persuaded. He let Rabbi Netanel go free, and sent letters to all the Kurdish Shekhs to inquire whether the Jew Sh'mu'el, who had escaped from him, was staying in their town. Should they find him, they must arrest him right away, and send him to Barzani. Otherwise he would go after them, sword in hand. But the answer came from all places, that no Jew Sh'mu'el of Barzani was found in their area.

However, the Shekh of Barzani was a great sand-wizard. He wrote numbers and formulas for Rabbi Sh'mu'el in the sand, and learned through his wizardry that Rabbi Sh'mu'el was hiding in Amadiya. Thereupon he instantly dispatched a writing to the Shekh of Amadiya demanding that he deliver Rabbi Sh'mu'el.

Since Rabbi Shim'on of Amadiya knew that his guest would be pursued, he took him to the synagogue of Ezra the Scribe, and hid him in the *Geniza*. The *Geniza* is a special chamber next to the synagogue. Three such chambers are attached to the synagogue. In one they keep the wine preserved for use in the synagogue. In the second they keep the Torah scrolls in the winter. From it a window leads into the third, dark room, in which they have been storing for hundreds of years the old holy scrolls and prayer books that had become unsuitable with age. This is the *Geniza*. Into this chamber he brought Rabbi Sh'mu'el, provided him with food and drink, and carefully closed the window on him.

When the Shekh of Amadiya received the letter, and instituted a thorough search among the Jews, the *Geniza* remained hidden to him, and he was unable to find Rabbi Sh'mu'el. And this is what he wrote in answer to the Shekh of Barzani. But the Shekh of Barzani was still not satisfied, and asked the sand magic a second time, and he got again the answer that the Jew he was looking for was in Amadiya. Thereupon he sent another letter to Amadiya, full of even greater threats.

But Rabbi Sh'mu'el in his hiding place knew well that the Shekh of Barzani had used sand magic, which had revealed to him that he was hiding in Amadiya. And he knew that there was no escape for him. He therefore asked Rabbi Shim'on to let him leave his hiding place, and to give him tallit and tefillin, drew a circle around the north-western column of the synagogue, entreated God to take his soul so that he should not fall into the hands of his persecutors, and collapsed dead on the spot.

That is where the Jews of Amadiya found him. They notified their Shekh, who, in turn, informed the Shekh of Barzani. And they buried Rabbi Sh'mu'el in the burial place of the pious and saintly. They erected a monument on his tomb, and round about they sowed pomegranate seeds. Out of the seeds grew thick bushes whose fruit is famous among both Jews and Muslims. But if somebody plucks of the fruit without the permission of Rabbi Sh'mu'el, he falls ill with fever. For this reason the Muslims are afraid of it, and call it *shera din*, the mad lion. But he who suffers of fever and comes to the tomb of Rabbi Sh'mu'el, and asks his permission to take of the fruit, is instantly healed of his fever.

The rural Jews, being few in number, are somewhat less strict. It is said by the Jews of Sinne that their brethren in the neighboring villages know so little of Judaism that occasionally they are in doubt whether or not the Sabbath has arrived. Once, so the story goes, the Jews of one of these villages, being in a quandary on this point, sent a Kurd to the next village to see what the Jews there were doing. The Kurd returned and said: "The Jewish women are sitting on their doorsteps and hunting for vermin. The men are sitting and drinking arrack and eating seeds." "If that is the case," said the Jews, "then it is the Sabbath." (S.) But even in a town like Sinne itself, the people are slack in observing the laws, and some of them were formerly in the habit of going to the marketplace on Saturday to buy fruit. The government has given the head of the community (*rūwat jemā'a*) watchmen whose duty it is to see that no Jews go to the marketplace on the Sabbath.

In the hill districts, the cold is so intense that a fire must be maintained even on the Sabbath; and the contravention of the law is considered justifiable in these circumstances.[5] A Jewish messenger, it is said, once appeared in winter in such a hill community. It was Friday evening, and the people were sitting around the fire which had been lighted before sundown. But the fire threatened to go out and the "Sabbath Kurd," the *nurāya* [lit., "fire man"], whom the village Jews employed on these occasions,[6] was called in to replenish it. Thereupon the messenger sprang up and cried, "It is forbidden to feed the fire on the Sabbath!" The people explained that the cold would be unbearable without a fire; but the messenger would not listen, and the fire went out.

During the night the temperature kept on dropping; and next morning, the people had to wade through deep snow to reach the synagogue. The messenger nearly perished with cold. He shivered and shook, and cried, "Pray faster!" "Why so?" was the rejoinder—"It is the Sabbath." When he returned from the service, he thought he would surely freeze to death; and in the end, he had to allow the *nurāya* to build a fire (A.).[7]

The Day of Preparation

The preparations for the Sabbath take up all of Friday and sometimes even part of Thursday. The women comb their hair with particular care on Friday because it is forbidden to do so on the Sabbath. A frequent question is, *Khewarsi ēnakh kekhīlakh biskakh petilīlakh ṭā shabsa*?, "Friend, have you rubbed your eyes with kohl and coiled your sidelocks for the Sabbath?" But the holiday clothes are not put on till Saturday morning, except in the case of young girls, who deck themselves out on Sabbath eve.

The men also have preparations to make. On Friday morning they must get their heads shaved. In Amadiya the task of shaving heads is hereditary in certain families, and the shaving is done without charge because it is regarded as a *miṣva* performed for the sanctification of the Sabbath.[8] In the afternoon, young and old take their festive clothes under their arms and go to the river for the ritual bath.

This Friday bath (*khiyāpa*) is, like the bridegroom's bath, (see p. 125), a real occasion for public merrymaking, especially for the young people. After the bath, the men don their Sabbath clothes and go home (Z. and A.).

In Sinne, which is under strong Persian influence, the Jews have established public warm baths, like those of their Persian neighbors.

The preparation for the Sabbath food is naturally the task of the women; but the husbands try to do their share. Since women do not go to the market, the men must buy the requisites for the Sabbath. Most of these are already in the house; but such things as fruit, chickens, and so on must be provided. For the men, this is regarded as a *miṣva*; in order, therefore, to make as much work of it as possible, they take each article home separately. My informant from Sinne told me that he often made as many as twenty trips to the market and back.

The bread baked for the Sabbath is ordinary bread, but some strew the *lakhmit hamōṣi* [bread of the *hamōtzi* benediction] with sesame or caraway seeds.[9] Of the contribution of *tlumsit shabsa* for the *shammash* we have spoken (p. 232).

The housewife must prepare on Friday the food for the Sabbath, as well as the Friday evening meal. The *ḥammin* of the Kurdish Jews, the warm Sabbath dish *mebōse*[10] varies with the season of the year and the financial situation of the family; but here, also, we observe the peasant conservatism of the Kurdish Jews.

The favorite kind of *ḥammin* is dumplings (*kutēle* or *kufte*; see p. 100), which are cooked in all sorts of ways but most often in combination with *kāsa*, sheep stomach filled with rice (Arbil, Z., A., Tchalla, and S.). The favorite summer *mebōse* is chicken with rice, *rizā kesēsa*. The Kurds call the dumplings "Sabbath dumplings," *kufte sham'a*, and credit them with healing powers. (See p. 100). The *mebōse* is set on the oven (*kanūna*), which is merely an earthen case without the fourth wall. The fuel used in it is charcoal (*palēt nūra*). To preserve the heat, the fire is covered with ashes, which are called *berēsh dijmine*, "on-the-head-of-the-sinner [enemy]" (Z.). This designation comes from the death custom of strewing ashes on the head of the dead, and the idea appears to be that the ashes here strewn should strike not a member of the family, but a sinner. After the ashes have been covered, an earthen slab (*sedōde*) is placed over the open side of the oven, and the space between the pot and the *kanūna* is sealed with clay. Eggs are stuck into the clay. An oven sealed in this way is actually called *mebīsa*.

In contrast with the Yemenites, to whom the importance of the Sabbath oven lies largely in the need of keeping their coffee (*gish*) hot,[11] the Kurdish Jews are not accustomed to warm beverages on the Sabbath. It is doubtless for this reason that the men indulge so freely in arrack on this day. The women drink only water. In Amadiya the Muslim Kurds sometimes send hot tea to their Jewish friends, and in Arbil the Jews even order coffee from the Kurdish coffeehouses, paying for it in advance.

Friday Evening

Nowadays, there is no public announcement of the approach of the Sabbath. In Amadiya the shofar was formerly blown as a signal.[12] Betanura had a special shofar for this purpose. The first signal warned the people in the fields to cease work and go home; a second signal was given for those who worked in the gardens, nearer home; and a third was for the lighting of the lamps. Today, the call of the Muslim *malla* [mulla] from the minaret of the mosque apprises the women that it is time to end the Sabbath preparations (Z. and A.).

Before the husband leaves for the synagogue, he exhorts his wife, *Māleq ma'liq sherā'a meshave duksa mābes mebīsa*, "Light the lamp, spread out the carpets, warm the *mebīsa*" (A.) [or *Mobislokhun ma'alkun sherā'a khabcha haya mrozdiglokhun shulḥan d'vuqula shabsa haya*, "Have you made the *ḥamin*? Light the candle a bit quicker! Have you set the table? Catch the Sabbath a bit quicker!" The husband issues these orders in a gentle manner.]

The Sabbath lamp was, in former times, made of iron or earthenware and was oval in shape, like those found as far back as the paleolithic age.[13] Such earthen lamps are used in Nirwa even today. In Sinne there were earthen lamps with handles, whose name, *sherā'e hamdāni* [lamps of Hamadan], points to their Persian origin. The commonest type of lamp at present is a glass bowl filled with caster oil and provided with several wicks.

After lighting the lamps, the housewife arranges the Sabbath *sīnīya*. She puts four, six, or twelve loaves of *lakhmit hamōṣi* on the *sīnīya* or in a basket[14] (among the poor). Formerly, a dish of salt was placed on the bread. The *sīnya* is then covered with a cloth (A. *mēda*), which is made up of a great many square bits of colored material. Sometimes a verse like "Remember the Sabbath day to sanctify it" is embroidered [in Hebrew] on the Sabbath cloth. In Sinne we find some especially beautiful covers richly embroidered with ornaments and Hebrew inscriptions. These covers resemble those placed over the Passover dish.

The goblet for the benediction is set beside the Sabbath bread. This goblet (*kanīna*) is not, as a rule, exceptional in any way but is an ordinary brass or earthen beaker. Nowadays, a simple glass serves the purpose, though some people use silver goblets engraved with their names.

After the service in the synagogue, the people greet each other with the words *Shabbat shalom*. In summer the family spends Friday evening on the roof of the house. The benediction is said over the bread and the wine, then the men sit down to their arrack and *maza* and sing Sabbath songs. The meal follows later on.

The Kurdish Jews are not accustomed to eat fish on Friday evening. One should eat something sour, they say, on this evening, because the planet Mars is in the ascendant (*gelāwesh*). the almost universal Sabbath eve dish is therefore *khamusta* (p. 100). In Zakho, especially, there is no family without *khamusta*—hence the following tale. A Jew of Zakho, having spent the whole week peddling in the villages, as was his custom, returned home late on Friday. He asked his wife what she had cooked; and when she answered, "*Yiprakh*" (p. 100), he said, "Then give me my pipe so that I may smoke." "What!" cried the wife, "You want to smoke—and it is Sabbath eve " "No," replied the husband, "if you haven't cooked any *khamusta*, it can't be Sabbath eve."

After dinner, the people seldom go out into the streets; they read a little from the Zohar and retire early; for they must be up next morning at about four o'clock. On Sabbath morning they sing *pizmonim* [liturgical songs] and proceed to the synagogue without breakfast. Every man is present at the service, but no women (except a few of the aged).

Sabbath Morning

On Sabbath morning the reading from the Torah takes up a great deal of time, since the individual member of the congregation (who on other occasions has only a passive role) can take an active part in the service. The honor of being called up to the Torah is of such outstanding importance to the Kurdish Jews that they have developed a special procedure for this part of the service.

In Zakho and Amadiya (likewise D.) the posts of honor[15] connected with the *'aliya* (summons to the Torah) and the services bound up with it are sold by auction once a year, on Simḥat Tora (p. 320). In Sinne they are sold twice a year: on Simḥat Tora and on the last day of Passover.

As an example let us take an auction sale at Amadiya. Frequent quarrels accompany the proceedings, because the posts of honor are much desired, and there is great rivalry over their acquisition. The privilege of opening the Torah shrine (*petīkhat hēkhal*) is sold to two persons. Husbands of barren women make a particular effort to obtain this function, seeing in it, evidently, a magic remedy. Other posts that are sold to two persons are the *qāpit sēfer*, who removes the scroll from the hēkhal and places it on the *sīde*; the *moqdōre*, who opens the scroll and shōws it to the congregation; and the *shushbin*, who stands at the right of the *ḥazan* and lays the silken cloth (*shīsha*) over the scroll when the men who have been called up pronounce the benedictions. At the left of the *ḥazan* stands the *somekh* with a printed Torah in his hand, to see that the *ḥazan* reads correctly. This function is also sold to two persons, who, like the former, perform their duties alternately. If the *ḥazan* makes a mistake, the entire congregation, which is on the look out for such occurrence, raises a great outcry, till the *ḥazan* goes back and repeats the passage correctly. The *'aliya* of the Kohen is not sold by auction because there are few Kohanim in Kurdistan. [In Amadiya there was only one Kohen in the last few years.] On the other hand, there are many Levites; and to avoid clashes, all of them are called in turn. [In Amadiya more than half the community were Levites. The *shammash* rises and announces, *Ilāhā mazedbokhun, Levi*, "God multiply you, Levi!" With this, the selling of the Levite begins; and everyone proceeds to bid.] Only half of the third *'aliya* is sold. This post is divided into four sections—termed *aqlasa* like the four sections of a slaughtered animal.[16] The four men who acquire them are called up on Monday, Thursday, Saturday morning, and Saturday afternoon, respectively. The remaining half of the third *'aliya* is reserved for bridegrooms, fathers of newborn sons, guests, and so on. The Kurdish Jews have a further custom, that of calling the *'olim* ["those who go up," strangers] to the Torah. At weddings, circumcisions, or occasions when outsiders are in town, all who have no *'aliya* or whom it is desired to honor are called to the Torah, one after the other, as *'olim* before the "third." The section for the "third" is in this case divided into several parts and, if necessary, is repeated. In consequence, the reading sometimes stretches out interminably.

[In Sinne the strangers are called up to the Torah as *mosifim* (those who are added), following the *samukh* (i.e., the sixth *'aliya*). An attempt was also made to introduce this custom in Amadiya, but it failed to take root. In Amadiya, the strangers for whom the verse of the third *'aliya* did not suffice are called up before the *samukh*, and the first three verses out of the section of the *samukh* are read for them. The same three verses are repeated again and again until all the guests have been honored by an *'aliya*, and only then comes the turn of the *samukh*.]

The fourth *'aliya* (*revi'i*) is likewise divided into four parts so that each holder of the post is called up every fourth Shabbat. Quarrels are frequent at the sale of the "fourth"; and it brings a high price, for many are eager to acquire it. On the other hand the "fifth" (*ḥamishi*)—also in four parts—is not greatly sought after, so that it is cheap and is usually sold to poorer members of the congregation.

The greatest of the posts of honor is the "sixth" (*samukh*), which, like the "third," "fourth," and "fifth," is divided into four. Half the yield from the sale of the "sixth" goes to the synagogue and half to the *ḥaverim*. The "seventh" (*mashlim*) is likewise divided into four but is sold to mourners only.

The post of *maftir*, who reads the section from the Prophets, is not sold for the whole year at once but on every Sabbath separately. It is often acquired by mourners who are observing *yahērṣiyāt* (*Jahrzeit*). Fathers also like to buy the *maftir* in order to give their sons practice in reading.

[The original name of the *Jahrzeit* among the Jews of Kurdistan is *ṣōmit bābā*, "the fast of the father," and *ṣōmit yima*, "the fast of the mother." The anniversary of the death of a father or a mother is a day of fasting. If the anniversary falls on a Saturaay, they do not, of course, fast; but those who are strictest will fast the day after (A.). The word *Yahrzeit* (*Jahrzeit*), despite its Yiddish origin, is widespread in the Jewish world, and is found in Sephardi religious writings, as well.]

Nowadays, the *Hafṭara* is read in Hebrew only; but in former times—in Amadiya, for instance—it was read exclusively in Targum.[17] In the synagogue of Amadiya there are some ten "tablets" of silver in which a carved the ten commandments. If it is desired to call someone up to the reading of the Torah, the *shammash* approaches him with one of these tablets, a sign that he is invited to read the Torah. If the one invited does not wish to have the *'aliya*, he kisses the tablet but does not rise from his place. If, however, he does wish to be called up, he kisses the tablet, rises, and goes up.]

After the service, the people go to the houses of bridegrooms, *shushbinim*, or fathers of newborn sons or to other places where it is usual to assemble.[18] In Amadiya the *ḥaverim* gather at the Bē Hazāne (see p. 63) for the great Sabbath drinking party, at which bridegrooms, new fathers, guests, etc., are entertained.

The men go to the synagogue without having eaten and do not eat the "second meal"—that with the *ḥammin* (*mebīse*)—until their return from drinking party. To a person who comes to the service only on the Sabbath, it is said, *Nekhiplokh min mebīse sēlokh ṣelosa* "You respected the *ḥammin*, therefore you came to prayer," that is, "You were ashamed in the presence of so-and-so" (A. and Z.)

Before eating the second meal, many people, as a sign of mourning, practice the custom of eating the eggs that were put into clay on the oven (A. and S.).

Of the women, only a few of the aged attend the service. After doing the strictly necessary housework (washing floors is forbidden), the women don their Sabbath clothes and spend the rest of the morning paying calls on brides, mothers of newborn children, or mourners.

The maidens deck themselves out in holiday garments and much jewelry and either assemble in the courtyards of certain houses to dance or else sit on the roofs, singing and joking. The boys and younger girls play games but only such as require no ball or other instrument.

After the second meal, the men go to the homes of mourners in order to read *mishmara*, the weekly portion of the Prophets, Hagiographa, and Mishna. The schoolboys go to the *bet midrash* for the same purpose.

Then the men lie down and take a nap until it is time for the *drāsha* (A. and Z.; S. *dārūsh*, *dārash*)—the interpretation, by the *ḥakham*, of the weekly portion of the Torah [and of the precepts or customs]. The *drāsha* often occupies two hours. It is the only field in which the Kurdish Jews do any original writing.

While there is hardly a man who misses the mourning service, the attendance at *minḥa* is far from perfect, even though the *shammash* goes through the streets and summons each one personally by knocking on the doors and calling, for instance, *Shammo minḥa*![19] At this hour and after *minḥa*, the Kurdish Jews are, as a matter of fact, assembled at one of their characteristic affairs. The men sit in groups on the roof or, in winter, in the rooms, singing, telling stories, and partaking liberally of arrack and *maza*. The songs they sing are also of a secular nature—Kurdish songs of heroic exploits, for instance—and the young people often begin to dance to the singing of the men. This contrasts with the Yemenites, whose *ḥakhamim* see to it that the people engage in no worldly pursuits on the Sabbath.

If the husband has not himself taken the "third meal" along to the drinking party, his wife brings it to him. The meal consists of fish, chicken, and *yiprakh*; and the husband eats it in the company of his friends—all being, by this time, well heated with arrack. These hours, lasting till dusk, are sometimes spent in promenading on the town wall or walking to the river; and for the Kurdish Jews it is these hours that actually represent the [enjoyment of the] Sabbath.

The closing Sabbath ceremony, *havdala*, seldom takes place at home. A few perform the *havdala* in the synagogue; but for the most part, the men go for *havdala* to the houses of mourners, where it is recited for a period varying from a month to a year, in accordance with the importance of the dead man.

The *havdala* candle in the synagogue at Zakho is an ordinary tall candle, made out of the ends of the candles used at Yom Kippur. It lasts till Purim. The candle that is used after Purim is made by the *shammash* from the ends of the *sham'it megalla*. This candle is also used for reading from the Torah on dark winter days. There are, in addition, ten small candles, which are held by boys.

Myrtle (*āsa*) is used instead of spices and is kept over from Sukkot for this purpose. Everyone present gets a bit of dried myrtle. When the myrtle is all gone, carnations, sewed up in a little bag, are substituted. *Rēkhan*, wild thyme (basilicum), is also used; and for this reason, mourners often sow *rēkhan* on their roofs (Z.). The custom of scanning the fingernails by the light of the *havdala* candle is universal. In Sinne one spits sideways several times after scanning the nails. It is customary in this town to sit during *havdala* and to strike the folded hands upon the knee in such a way as to produce a sound as of jingling coins.

When the words *borē m'orē ha'ēsh* are recited during the benediction over the candle, the children call out:

kate dijminit yisra'el lā pāyis—
od pāyis rēse yāwis

May none of the haters of Israel survive—
Who survives, may his head dry up. (A. Z. being similar)

After the close of the Sabbath, the men sit with their friends late into the night over arrack and *maza*. This is also the hour at which many of their family celebrations take place—*lēl kesēsa*, the "night of the chickens," for instance and the hour when song, dance, and arrack combine to raise their spirits and stir their emotions.

PART SIX

Holidays

19

Pesach

Among the Kurdish Jews, as among Jews elsewhere, Passover or Pesach [Heb. Pesaḥ] is one of the major feasts. Isolated Jewish families living in the villages stream into the towns at this time in order to celebrate the feast in the midst of their brethren.

Thus, to Amadiya come villagers from Bamarne, Inishk, ʻAradan, Eqdish, Beʻenatan, and Hamdhiye [all in the vicinity of Amadiya]. They appear three or four days ahead of time and bring with them cattle and wine.

The Kurdish Jews commonly call the Passover feast *patire*, [or *ʻedet patire*. The feast of Passover (A.)], the term used in the Targumim for unleavened bread;[1] but during the days of the feast itself, the usual designation is *pisha*.

The Kurds use various expressions to describe the Jewish feast, for example,

ʻaīda bohāre	feast of spring (A.)
ʻaīda māne bē k'we	feast of bread without salt (A.)
ʻaīda taḥlishke	feast of bitter herbs (A.)
ʻaīda nissāne	feast of Nissan (Z., D., and A.)

Since many heads of families cannot read the Haggada, the Seder is not celebrated in every household separately, but several families (often as many as forty) assemble for a joint Seder in the household of a *ḥakham* or some other man who can read well, who is called *merē pisḥa* [master of the Passover].[2] Since it is considered a great honor to be *merē pisḥa*, some aspirants to this distinction have a *ḥakham* prepare them for the task of conducting the Seder. There is great rivalry over the Passover guests; and all sorts of pretensions and disputes must be settled before the *merē pisḥa* knows definitely whom he is to entertain. It is generally an all-year struggle.

Shabbat Hagadol

Shabbat Hagadol [Heb. Great Sabbath], the Sabbath preceding Passover, marks the end of this struggle; for on this day the *merē pisḥa* learns definitely whom he may expect at the Seder. In Zakho the Shabbat Hagadol is called Shabthit Baṭīye, Sabbath of Joy.[3] [In Amadiya it is Shabsa Yaqurta or Shabbat Hagadol.] A special kind of cake, called *farnīye*, made of eggs and sesame, is prepared at the home of the *merē pisḥa* two or three days before the Shabbat Hagadol; and the *merē pisḥa* sends some of it by his wife to all the people whom he desires to have as his guests at the Seder. A refusal may be due to some disagreement with the *merē pisḥa* or to a preference for some other invitation. At the Seder evenings (as we shall see) there are often dramatic performances of a burlesque nature; and families that enjoy a special reputation for the success of these performances exert a great attraction.

Nevertheless, the *merē pisḥa* pays a personal call on all who have refused his *farnīye*, and makes a final effort. In order to lend weight to his visit, he has some important personage accompany him. Then, on the Shabthit Baṭīye, those who have accepted his invitation appear at his house; and he knows the number of Passover guests (*pisḥāye*) for whom he must provide.

After the service on Saturday morning, the guests come to the house of their *merē pisḥa*, where they eat, drink, and make merry. The young people don their new Passover clothes and go with the musicians to the river to dance and sing.

In Amadiya [and Zakho] the Shabbat Hagadol takes its name from these new Passover clothes: Shabthit Makhwōyit Jile, Shabbat of Dress-Display. [In Amadiya it is also Shabthit hirgē, Sabbath of Clothes.] Here, the *merē pisḥa*, having exerted himself throughout the entire year to acquire desirable guests for his Seder evening, already knows who is coming. On Friday morning the wives of his *pisḥāye* come to help in the preparations for the Shabbat; and next morning all the *pisḥāye*, both husbands and wives, are entertained at a festive meal in his home. It is a very jolly affair; and at the close, the guests, both men and women, stick a flower in their headdress as a sign of their joint participation in the coming Seder and go thus to the excursion grounds. The Shabbat Hagadol is the Sabbath of Joy in all of Kurdistan.

Preparing the Matzot—Procuring the Grain

The making of the matzot (sg., matzo; Heb. *maṣṣot*) occupies an important place in the Passover preparations. Formerly, the Kurdish Jews engaged in agriculture to a greater extent than now (a fact that we have constantly stressed in the course of this book), and every head of a family went to the fields in order to cut the grain for the matzot himself. He chose as distant a field as possible, one that the chickens would not be able to reach; for it was customary to say, *Mosēlan shemūra lashmēla qālit dikilit māṣa tā māṣa*, "We brought *shemūra* [guarded)grain)] that has not heard the voice of a chicken from the town, for the matzot."

He threshed the grain himself with the *khatōre*, on freshly washed carpets, (A.). Nowadays, the grain for Passover is bought directly after the harvest. Only the best grade is chosen, and it is kept in the house in tightly sealed earthen jars. However, a distinction is made in most districts between wheat for ordinary matzot *lakhmit pisḥa* or *lakhmit patīre* and that for the *maṣṣot shemūrot*, "guarded matzot." In Amadiya the wheat for the latter is bought in the summer on the stalks and threshed at home, whereas the rest of the Passover wheat is bought in the market place in Abh, after the harvest. In Ushnu all wheat to be used for matzot is cut under supervision, but only that intended for *maṣṣot shemūrot* is threshed in the house.

The manner in which the Jews of Zakho and Dehok ạcquire their Passover grain is very interesting. During Shavu'ot, about thirty Jewish families from among the poor of Zakho go out into the fields of the Muslim Kurds to glean. Gleaning is an occupation practiced almost exclusively by Jews, and each family (for the women and children share in the work) glean year after year on the same farm.[4] The people say *Faqīrīm pēzē il shublē*, "The poor are going out to the ears." The gleaners are called *shublāye* ["spikers" or "earers"]. each family gathers about 10 *rotl* (25 kilograms) a day. The women spread out a cloth and thresh the grain then and there with the *mekutke*. The gleaners spend about thirty days in the fields.

When they return to Zakho after completing their task, both children and adults stream out of the town to meet them, because they know that the *shublāye* are bringing something for them, namely, *kilōrē* (Ger. *Kringeln* [doughnut-shaped bread]), made out of the grain they have gathered. Each of their acquaintances, not excepting the rich, receives one of these.

The gleaners are also accustomed to bringing with them for distribution as gifts a kind of comb made by braiding fresh ears of wheat and called *mesirqit khite* [wheat comb]. This is hung over the door as an amulet. The gleaners know that the wealthy Jews will give them a rich present for a *mesirqit khite*. The use of such a harvest amulet is very widespread.[5]

The wheat gathered by the gleaners is sold to the Jews of Zakho, who use it for making their *maṣṣa shemūra* or for their Passover baking in general.

The greatest care is given to the sorting and cleaning of the wheat. Since the Seder (as we have seen) is celebrated only in certain houses in Kurdistan, it is chiefly the *merē pisḥa* who must make these preparations; for he alone has need of a large quantity of matzo and of *maṣṣa shemūra*. The *pisḥāye* eat with him on the first two and the last two evenings of Pesach; and in any case, much meat but little matzo is consumed during the Passover period. The amount of matzo baked by any ordinary family is consequently small.

The burden falls almost entirely on the *merē pisḥa*; and the quantity of grain that he must get cleaned and sorted is very large. Hence, in Amadiya, it has become the custom for the *merē pisḥa* to invite the *pisḥāye* to his house at Purim to take part in the *bedāqit khite*, "sorting of the wheat." The *merē pisḥa* gives them all a meal on the first day; and on the next, the women come to clean the wheat and other requisites. First, the grains are cleaned. They pass through the hands of three women, the last of whom must be particularly sharp-sighted. Then come the legumes. Rice must pass from three to five inspections, sesame even as many as ten, because its grains are very small. With the exception of certain ultrapious individuals, the Jews of Kurdistan, unlike those of Persia, eat rice during the Passover feast.[6]

Grinding the Grain

In former days the grain was ground with a handmill, as is done now in Sulaimani. But at present it is more common to use the public water mill, which is worked by Muslims. In order to be able to use the mill for grinding the Passover grain, the Jews rent it for a certain period and have it thoroughly cleaned. About fourteen days before Passover the *gabbai*, the *ḥazan*, and the *shammash* go to the mill to see that the cleaning is properly done. The millstones are newly trimmed, all vessels most carefully scoured, and the floor covered with mats. On the day when the grinding is to begin, the *ḥazan* cleans everything again with meticulous care. The grinding, while not done entirely by Jews, is under very strict Jewish supervision.

The Baking of the Matzot

Matzo has a variety of names: *lakhmit ēza* (Z. and A.), *lakhmit pisḥa* (A.), and *lakhmit paṭīre* (A.). [In Amadiya the "guarded matzot," which are specially prepared for being placed on the Seder plate and eaten during the Seder are called *maṣit sālā*, "matzot of the basket," (i.e., the Seder plate). All other matzot, which are eaten during the Passover are called *lakhmit 'eda*, "bread of the holiday." The Muslim Kurds are fond of eating matzot, which they call *nanē aidē*, "holiday bread."] The baking of the matzo begins on 2nd Nissan, because the Kurdish Jewish women do not work on the day of the new moon. Two kinds of matzo must be prepared: the ordinary unleaven bread, which is baked by the women, and *maṣṣa shemūra*, which is baked by the men, on the day of the Seder.

A number of new ovens are constructed, and the women do their baking in turn, according to a prearranged plan. Several families collaborate, because there must be no interruption in the work. Not for a single moment may the dough remain still, lest it ferment. Therefore, the women keep on shaking not only the vessel containing the dough but also any lump of dough that they happen to be holding. The amount of dough that may be held in the hand is also fixed. In Amadiya there is a special vessel for measuring out this amount. It is called *'ajna* and is used only for the baking of matzot. The Jews of Sinne have another system. They divide the flour into half-rotl quantities before the baking is begun, and knead only a half-rotl quantity (called *'omer*) at one time. The matzot made from the first *'omer* is termed *sala* and is preserved until Shavu'ot.

The sprinkling flour used in baking the matzot is made out of rice or lentils. Every woman has her allotted task, and each loaf passes quickly from one hand to the other till it reaches the oven rolled out and is clapped on the oven wall with the baking cushion.

The matzot are almost exclusively *lakhmit tanūra* [oven bread], not *lakhmit doqa* (i.e., bread baked on the *dōqa* or baking sheet; see p. 94) In Tchalla *lakhmit dōqa* is also baked for Passover. The matzo does not differ from ordinary *lakhmit tanūra* in shape, but in certain localities it is a little larger.

The women declare that matzot baking is a very strenuous affair. They say, *Liban qidle*, "Our heart is burnt up." Therefore, in Amadiya, a special drink, seldom used on any other occasion, is prepared for them. This drink, *shahmiza*, consists chiefly of sour ingredients such as *mayit smōqe* and onions mixed with *ṭākhin* and harks back, so they say, to Ruth 2:14: "And Boaz said unto her at mealtime, 'Come hither, and eat of the bread, and dip thy morsel in the vinegar'."

The *ḥakham* and the *ḥazan* are present at the baking to make sure that the women have observed all the regulations. The matzo is carried home to the singing of hymns[7] and is suspended from the ceiling in a basket so that no mouse or other creature may be able to get at it.

Purifying the Kitchenware; the Search for *Ḥameṣ*

Several days before Passover, the *shammash* makes the rounds of the houses and collects wood from the women for the *'agāla*, the scalding of the vessels. This is done in the courtyard of the synagogue. A large pit is dug, and over it is set one of the great copper kettles (*magila*) that certain rich Jews possess.

On the day appointed for the scalding, the *shammash* climbs up the roof of the synagogue and calls loudly in all directions, *'Agāla, 'agāla*! The summons is answered by a stream of women bringing the vessels they expect to use during Passover. Two large cauldrons necessary for the task in hand are first made *kasher* [kosher] by being filled with water that is brought to the boil and into which three heated stones are thrown. During the work, one on the cauldrons is kept boiling constantly while the other is filled with cold water. In the scalding of all the other vessels no heated stones are used.

Just before the *bedāqa* [A. *bedāqit ḥamīra*], the search for *ḥameṣ*, the housewife puts, [at her husband's behest,] some bits of bread or other *ḥameṣ* in various corners of the house. As a reminder of the ten plagues, there are ten such pieces, whence the ceremony is also called *bedāqa isra pirtīqit ḥāmeṣ* [search for ten pieces of *ḥameṣ*]. On the eve of 14th Nissan, the master of the house takes one of the candles made by the *shammash* for each family from the wax belonging to the synagogue (Z.), and proceeds to do the searching. In Sinne the *ḥameṣ* must not be touched by hand but is picked up with the firetongs. In some places it is put into a vessel containing salt[8] A.). The searcher has a knife with which to probe the corners. In Ushnu the *ḥameṣ* that is found is out into the *doqa*, the baking sheet. The *ḥameṣ* is kept in a safe place during the night so that no mouse or other animal may approach it. On the morning of 14th Nissan it is burnt with the *etrog* and the *lulav*, which are kept over from Sukkot for this purpose.

On the eve of 14th Nissan a man who is to have a Seder at his house must go to draw water for the baking of the *maṣṣa shemūra*. In Amadiya there are only five ovens; and the various *merē pisḥa* form five *khurawātha*, groups, the heads of which carry out this duty.

These men are escorted by the youths and the boys. They all walk quietly to the spring; but during the drawing of the water and on the way back, the men sing the "Alef-bet Song." This is based on reciting up to the letters of the sacred name YHWH, arranged HHWY. It begins, *Alef, bet, gimel, dalet, he*, then *he, dalet, gimel, bet, alef*; then forward again as far as *he* and back, then as far as *vav* and back, and finally as far as *yod* and back. [In Amadiya they sing another alphabet song that has no connection with the name YHWH but contains all the letters of the alphabet. It runs *alef, bet, gimel, gimel, bet, alef*, then *alef, bet, gimel, dalet, dalet, gimel, bet, alef*, and so forth, each time adding one letter until they recite the entire alphabet back and forth.] The men take the jar on their shoulders and sing; the others clap their hands. When the men have finished singing, the boys begin their "Halleluya Song":

Hallelūyah, hallelū 'avdē Adony
Hallelū adir adirim, adir Adonay

[Praise, praise, servants of the Lord,
Praise the most mighty, the mighty Lord]

When the group passes through the Jewish quarter, the girls step out of the doors and sing *Hallalūya wehallalūya bakhlakh idlēl be'e shlīqē pisra tūya*, "Hallelujah, we shall this night eat hard (boiled) eggs and roast meat."

In Sinne and in Sulaimani this custom does not obtain. In these towns the water is drawn not by the men but by the girls—indeed, even by Muslim Kurdish women who in Sinne nowadays sometimes serve as domestics in Jewish homes. In both Sinne and Sulaimani the *maṣṣa shemūra*, also, is baked by the women, instead of by the men.

Ḥameṣ may be eaten on 14th Nissan up to nine o'clock in the morning; but the food is cold (bread and *masta*)—for no cooking is allowed—and it is eaten in the courtyard, instead of in the house. After the last *ḥameṣ* meal the mouth is washed and rinsed. The *ḥameṣ* is burnt in the yard. In some places the fire for the burning of the *ḥameṣ* is kindled with the *etrog* and the *lulav* from Sukkot (A.). The

Jews of Sinne occasionally dispose of their *ḥameṣ* by throwing it into the river, [which is reminiscent of the *tashlikh* rite].

Merchants who have *ḥameṣ* in stock close their shops during the feast. In Kurdistan (as elsewhere) it is also customary to sell any remaining stocks of *ḥameṣ*; but here, the sale is an actual, not a fictitious, one.[9]

Although at other times, Muslims are constant visitors among the Jews and often eat with them, no Muslim is permitted to enter a Jewish home during Passover lest he introduce *ḥameṣ* on his clothing.

The women dye their hair and hands with henna before Passover since henna is considered *ḥameṣ*. On 14th Nissan everyone bathes, cuts or trims his hair, and dons his new clothes. Those who are especially pious take the ritual dip in the river.

At ten o'clock in the morning, the *shammash* calls out from the roof of the synagogue that all work must cease; thereafter, only tasks essential to the Passover celebration may be performed. The men set about baking the *maṣṣa shemūra*.[10] The five *khurawātha* (groups) go to their respective ovens (A.), bearing the water they have drawn and singing the "Alef-bet song." They take over from the women the whole work of baking except the final step, at the oven, which is retained by an old woman.

In Betanura and Tchalla, where every family bakes its own matzo, the wife helps her husband. If she happens to be *nidda* [menstrually impure], a neighbor acts as substitute.

The oven is stoked with the willows and the lulav kept over from Sukkot. During the baking, the words *kohen*, *kohen* (or *levi* or *yisrael*, as the case may be) are constantly repeated to prevent mistakes (Z. and A.), because among the Kurdish Jews the *maṣṣa shemūra* of these three classes is distinguished by certain signs.

In Amadiya and Bamarne diagonal lines are drawn with a myrtlewood stick across the matzot, one line signifying Kohen, two Levi, and three Yisrael. In Hīl, Barzāna, and Sündu one, two, or three impressions, made in the matzot with a thimble, serve the same purpose as the lines. This sign was formerly used by a few families in Amadiya also. The most usual sign, however (Z., D., S., Barashe, Betanura, Nirwa, Rekan, Tchalla, Ushnu, and Sulaimani), is a small protuberance resembling a nipple, at the side of the matzo in the appropriate number—whence its designation, *chichikyātha* (Barashe).][11]

For the *afikoman* two particularly large Levi matzot are baked. The *pishāye* sing pizmonim [liturgical songs] as they bring the *maṣṣa shemūra* to their *merē pisḥa*.

Blood Libel

Blood libels in connection with the baking of matzo are known only in the Persian–Kurdish area. R. David d'Bet Hillel, who traveled through Kurdistan in 1827–28, writes that in 1821 such a case occurred in Urmia.[12] A Muslim boy disappeared, and the Jews were accused of using his blood for the baking of their matzot. All the Jews, including the head of the community, Mulla Rafael, were imprisoned. One Jew was cut to pieces at the city gate, another beaten into insensibility. The Jews were finally released through the intercession of Abbas Mirza of Tabriz, but only after payment of a fine of 1,000 *toman* to his brother, the governor of Urmia.

A second case from Urmia is reported by Grant, who was, with some interruptions, missionary in this town from 1835 to 1840. Grant writes, "During my residence in Ooroomiah, a Jew was publicly burned to death in that city by order of the Governor, on an allegation of the pretended crime! Naphtha was freely poured over him, the torch was applied, and the miserable man was instantly enveloped in flame!"[13]

Finally R. David d'Bet Hillel reports a case that occurred in Maraga about the year 1800.[14] With the intention of bringing the blood accusation against the Jews, some Muslims stabbed a Muslim boy until the blood flowed. The Jews were attacked, several of them died as a result of their wounds, and their houses were looted. When the governor of Tabriz, under whose jurisdiction Maraga came at that time, heard what had happened, he at once issued an order to let the Jews depart in peace. They were brought to Miandoab, where they settled.

The Seder Dish

The men repair early to the synagogue for *minḥa* and *ma'ariv* and for the purpose of placing the *'eruv maṣṣa* in the Hēkhal.

While the men are at the synagogue, the wives of the *pisḥāye* go to the house of their *merē pisḥa* to help in the preparations for the Seder. The room is festively lighted with candles. The women get the Seder dish together without attempting to arrange it; for this task is reserved for the *merē pisḥa*. He himself will put everything in its proper place later on. In this matter there are no differences throughout Kurdistan.

On the Seder dish (Z. *mēdū pisḥa*, A. *sal pisḥa*) is set a separate plate (*farkhasēni maṣṣe*), containing the *maṣṣot shemūrot*. Seven matzot of each kind are put in this plate, because of the large number of guests. The *marōr* (Z. and A.; S. *marūr*)[15] occupies the center of the Seder dish.

Earlier in the morning the *merē pisḥa* has sent a boy to cut the *marōr* and the *karpisa* [celery or parsley], which is found in large quantities at the river near Amadiya. Round about the *marōr* come the hard-boiled egg (*be'ta*), which is boiled in water instead of being cooked in hot ashes as usual; horseradish (Z. and A. *khasē*, S. *kāhū*); and two green onions (Z.) *Ḥaroset ḥalīq* (A. and S.), or *ḥilīq* (Z.),, is provided in considerable quantity in view of the large number of participants.[16] It is made by soaking raisins for two days, boiling them down to a syrup, adding sesame (*shushme*) and finely pounded nuts, then boiling the whole again until it has the consistency of honey. Some people use honey instead of raisins. Finally, the Seder dish contains the bone (Z. and A. *zerō'a chachiksa*, S. *baska*), which is from the preserved meat (*qalya*) made at Sukkot. These bones are salted down at the time and kept in a separate room. A day before Passover they are taken out, soaked in lukewarm water, and roasted. The bone that is laid on the *sal pisḥa* is for the master of the house; the others are served to the *piṣḥāye*.

The Jews of Sinne take a piece of roasted meat without bones and season it with special spices as a reminder of the meat roasted by Joshua in the desert, the odor of which lured all the Jews.

Near the Seder dish stands a vessel containing water mixed with *smōke*. The Seder dish is covered with a cloth called *qaramtit pēsaḥ* (not *pisḥa*), made of many patches in the manner described earlier. The use of beautifully designed tablecloths for the Seder in Sinne is probably due to Persian influence. [These tablecloths are used also in Amadiya.] "Elijah's cup" is unknown in Kurdistan.

The type of *sal pisḥa* used in Betanura and Tchalla is worthy of mention. It is a wickerwork dish, set on a three-legged stand and adorned with a bough (*sēpe*). On it lies a book. Each guest, as he enters, lifts up the dish and kisses the book, saying, *Salōkhun berīkha*, "Your Passover dish be blessed." Then he kisses the beard of the *merē piṣḥa*.

The Seder Evening

In Amadiya the Zohar is placed on the Seder dish. When the master of the house returns from the synagogue, he blesses his family. The guests, on entering, kiss first the Zohar, then the *merē pisḥa*, after which they seat themselves on the floor around the Seder dish.

Everyone stands while pronouncing the benediction over the first glass of wine; but as they drink, they let themselves down slowly to the floor, leaning sideways on the cushions that lie on either side. Each time the glasses are drained, they are collected and rinsed by the *shammash*.

When, at the first washing of the hands, the guests say, *Belō berākha*, the *shammash* adds, *Darenokh gō mizākha*, "I shall put you in the grain case (of the mill)"—which brings the retort, *Qōrünokh lā korākha*, "I shall bury you without grave clothes" (Z.).

Some *karpisa* with a bit of onion is sued for the benediction over the fruits of the earth. When serving the *karpisa*, the *shammashim* throw it before the guests as though it were "feed for cattle." A great quantity of it is consumed.

In Betanura and Tchalla there is an interesting custom. After partaking of the *karpas*, all the *merē pisḥa* with their *pisḥāye* go to the home of the *gevir*. On entering, they kiss the book that is lying on the Seder dish and the beard of the *gevir*. They read the Haggadah as far as *dayyēnū*, and drink three glasses of wine. Then they proceed to the house of another *merē pisḥa*, read the Haggadah once more as far as *dayyēnū*,and regale themselves again with three glasses of wine. In this manner they visit four or five households, and when at length they return to the house of their own *merē pisḥa* to finish the reading of the Haggadah, they are generally quite drunk.[17]

Afikoman

When the *merē pisḥa* sets about distributing the middle matzo, he asks, "Do you know why the middle matzo is divided into two parts?" And he begins the recitation of the story of the Jews from Abraham to the Exodus from Egypt. If he himself is not qualified to do this, he has the *ḥakham* write it out for him beforehand. On reaching the passage about the parting of the waves, he breaks the matzo (S.).

The middle matzo is broken in such a way as to form the letters *dalet* and *vav*. The *dalet* is put back on the Seder dish, the the *vav* serves as *Afikoman*.

In Sinne the *vav* is sprinkled with salt, folded up, and wrapped in a silken cloth, which the father binds around the right upper arm[18] of one of his sons, saying: "May it please God that you bind the *ketubba* around the arm of your bride thus." Sometimes the child falls asleep and the other youngsters untie the *afikoman* and hide it. Not until he has given them a chicken as a forfeit, will they surrender it.

In Amadiya, on the first night, the *merē pisḥa*—and on the second night, his son—binds the *vav* on his shoulder in a cloth, girds his loins, comes into the room from the outside with a staff in his hand, and recites Exodus 12:11 and 34. The following dialogue then takes place:

Whence do you come (*me'ēka sēlokh*)?
From Egypt (*min miṣr*).
What are you bringing with you (*lēka bāzit*)?
The dough of our fathers from Egypt. They had no time to bake it. Come, I will tell you the story of the miracle which God performed for our fathers.[19]

The custom in Zakho is similar. There a boy takes the *afikoman shemūra*[20] over his shoulder in a cloth and walks up and down the room a distance of four cubits. Then he gives it to the *ḥakham*, who passes it on to one of the guests for safekeeping. The *afikoman* must have a *chichine*. The *ḥakham* admonishes the guest to take good care of the pearl, *jauwāher*, which is on the matzo; and the guest receives it as one receives a pledge, saying, "I take this pledge *amanita*, in the head of which is the pearl,[21] and lay it in this red cloth." To the witnesses he says, "What does the pearl resemble?" "It resembles the *chichine* on the breast of a woman," is the reply. Then he puts the *afikoman* under his garment, because the people will try to steal it from him (Z.).

At the words *hā laḥma 'anya*, which the Kurds pronounce *hē laḥma* on the analogy of the words *hē lakhem zera'*, (Gen. 47:23), the men draw close to the Seder dish and grasp it with their hands. Behind them sit the women and children in several rows and grasp the shoulders of the men. When the reading begins, the men move the dish back and forth; and the women move with them. All are in good spirits, and at the words *b'ne ḥorin* the men lift the dish high up and the women rise their *klīlīlī* (Z.). In other places the *sal pisḥa* is merely lifted up.

Hā laḥma is recited six times: first by the *merē pisḥa* in Aramaic and Targum, then by his brother and his son in Aramaic and Targum.

Ma Nishtanneh

In Sinne the ceremony known as *shalshalakān*, "like a limping man" precedes *ma nishtanneh*. Two or more boys leave the room, put on appropriate costumes, wind a large turban around their heads, and take a staff in their hands. One of the boys wears a beard and carries over his shoulder, in a cloth, the utensils that the Jews bore with them when they came out of Egypt. A second boy rides on the shoulders of the first. The latter knocks on the door and is asked, "Who is there?" "I." "Who are you?" "A Jew." "Come in!" The boy enters, limping. Several other boys limp in after him. The limping is explained by the twofold meaning of *pasaḥ*—"to limp" and "to pass over." The guests proceed to question the boys further: "How do we know that you are

Jews?" "We know Hebrew." "Have you brought with you provisions for your journey?" "Yes." "What are your provisions?" And the boys begin *ma nishtanna*. Then one of the boys reads out the passage. He is rewarded with an egg.

In Amadiya all the youngsters are eager to read *ma nishtanna*. So when this point is reached the son of the *merē pisḥa* and several other boys are chosen and told to "go out and beat their heads against the wall." They go out and knock on the door with their heads. They are encouraged to vie with each other in the force with which they do so: the one who knocks hardest, they are told, will be allowed to read. They say, *Inkan lā makhētin rēshokh bāsh illit tar'a lā yiwakhlokh bē'e*, "If you don't beat your head against the door harder, no egg will be given to you." the boys do their part manfully; but the man within say only, *Lā smē'elān*, "We don't hear you." This is repeated several times—often until the youngsters' heads are bleeding. Finally, the door is opened and the boys are questioned in the same way as in Sinne. When doubt is expressed as to their being Jews, they show their earlocks; and to the question, *Mayle zawādok*, "What are your provisions (for your journey)?" one of the boys answers, *Itli zawāda: ma nishtanneh*, "I have provisions: *ma nishtanneh*" (also Z.). Therewith, he points to a sheet of paper on which the *me'allim* has written *ma nishtanneh*. [Another version of this dialogue is *Meka keset*?, "Whence do you come?" "From Egypt." *Eka bazat*?, "Where are you going?" "To Jerusalem." *Mayle zawādokh*?, "What are your provisions?" *Ma nishtanneh* (A.)]

But as the Kurdish Jews are eager to enhance the joy of the feast of liberation with jests that are, after their peasant fashion, sometimes exceedingly coarse, they profess to be dissatisfied with these proofs and demand a stronger one. Whereupon the youngster either jestingly permits himself to be examined or is overpowered and forced to do so as is done in the *shelōna* skit.[22]

Then the boy recites the *ma nishtanneh*. He holds a glass of wine in his hand but does not drink of it; for it is to be used later on, at the enumeration of the ten plagues. The promised egg is given to him at the eating of the eggs before the meal.

The Ten Plagues

The Seder customs in connection with the "ten plagues" are essentially alike throughout Kurdistan, but there are nevertheless some minor local differences. In Ushnu the finger is dipped in wine at the mention of each plague, as is customary elsewhere; and the drop is shaken off into an empty eggshell. A little arrack, tobacco, and some bitter herbs (*marōr*) are added. One of the men takes the egg and in silence throws it on the doorstep of one known to hate the Jews, returns in silence, and washes his face and hands before taking any further part in the Seder.

The practice of "ritual" silence[23] and the use of the vessel containing the drops for the purposes of black magic are fairly general in Kurdistan. The silence sometimes extends to all those participating in the Seder.

Before the ceremony of the ten plagues is begun—specifically, when the passage *asher ta'ase bō* is reached—every vessel in the house that contains food must be covered (Z., S., and Dehok). In Sinne two special earthen vessels are provided before Passover and are produced at the command, "Bring food for Pharaoh and the Egyptians," which precedes the ceremony of the ten plagues.

It was formerly customary to dip the finger in wine and shake the drop off into the water jar; but as this is liable to bring a curse upon the man who does it, the drop is nowadays poured directly in. Twenty-six drops in all (ten for the Hebrew names, ten for the Targum, and three for each of the abbreviations) are poured into the jar.

When asked the meaning of the abbreviations for the ten plagues, *dṣakh–'adash–b'aḥv* the *ḥakham* jestingly explains that they stand for *ṭlōkhe mebushlē gō qōqā*, "lentils cooked in a barrel" (Z.).[24]

The jar containing the wine drops is taken out and emptied on the doorstep of an enemy of the Jews or at some remote spot (Dehok). In any case, great care is taken not to spill any of the water at the door of a Jew, for all are convinced that this would result in a death in that house during the coming year. The same baleful influence is ascribed to the water in which the wine glasses are rinsed after each drink. The Muslim Kurds have an equally firm faith in the power of this water, and Kurdish women buy the water in order to pour it on the doorstep of some enemy (S.)

Dayyēnu

Kamma ma'alot ṭovoth is sung alternatively by two men. At the word *dayyēnu* ["it would be enough for us"] the Seder dish is raised aloft. In Zakho all present raise their arms. In Sinne it is the custom for the guests to strike each other with onions at the word *dayyēnu*; [the Jews of Persia do the same].

After the reading of *dayyēnu*, an old man who has the reputation of being a good storyteller is invited to relate the history of *dayyēnu* (Z., A., and S.); and he begins the following tale. A *ḥakham* was so poor that he had not enough money to buy what was necessary for the Seder evening. So his wife said: "Go to the marketplace. Perhaps you will find some work there and earn a little money." The *ḥakham* did as she bade him, and in the marketplace he heard that the king had been robbed and was looking for a magician who could discover the thief.

The *ḥakham* plucked up courage, went to the king and said that he would find the thief. The king agreed to give him four days in which to make good his undertaking; but if by that time he had not found the culprit, he must die. The *ḥakham* received an advance payment from the king and bought himself new clothes and provisions for the feast days.

In the evening, as the *ḥakham* sat at his table reading the Haggadah, the king with several of his attendants came to the house incognito. The king bade his army chief, who was among his attendants, to climb to the roof and look down the chimney to see if he could make out what the Jew was doing to discover the thief.

The *ḥakham* had just reached the passage *dayyēnu*. When the general heard the *ḥakham* call out several times, *Dayyēnu*! he concluded that this must be the name of the thief. He climbed down and reported to the king that the Jew was calling out the name of the thief and that it was Dayyēnu. Now a man by this name happened to be living in the town; and when a search was made in his house, the stolen goods were actually found there.

In Sinne there is another version of the story. A Jew was falsely accused of stealing from the king and was sentenced to be hanged. As a last favor he begged to be allowed to celebrate the Pesach feast. His petition was granted. In the evening the real thieves came to see what the Jew was doing. When they heard him saying, *Dayyēnu*, they thought that he knew the name of one of them; and they made haste to return the stolen goods.

In Amadiya it was formerly the custom for the *merē pisḥa*, when he reached the passage *b'khol dor vador ḥayav adam*, to draw in his trousers at the ankles with a piece of rope, tighten his belt, and take some matzo in a cloth over his shoulders and a staff in his hand (as described earlier). Then he would go out a distance of four cubits; come back quickly; point to the staff, the dough, and the girded loins, and say, "Thus our fathers departed from the land of Egypt."

The Passover Meal

Before the meal, the *shammash* brings in the hard-boiled eggs; and the *merē pisḥa* distributes them, one to each of the *pisḥāye* except for the boy who has read the *ma nishtanneh* and is entitled to two. The guests, however, are not content with a single egg, so they bring along some of their own and often consume as many as ten or a dozen.

The children play a game called *hilka shekāne*, "egg breaking" (Kurd. and S.) or *hēkānē* (A. and Z., from *hēk-kānē*) with their eggs. They bump them against each other and the one whose egg breaks must surrender it to his opponent. Another game is called *jizirkī* (A.). Two players, A and B, put up a certain sum of money, half of which is invested in eggs, the other half being the stakes. The eggs are bumped against each other as in the other game. The young man who has an unbroken egg at the end is the winner. (A., Betanura, and Barzani). It is a real game of chance that is played in the intermediate days between the beginning and the end of the feast and in which, at times, a thousand eggs are involved.

The children have another amusement that should be mentioned. They take *sepe* leaves and weave them together to form what they call "steps" (Heb. *ma'alot*, Targ. *darājit mala*. With these they decorate the Seder dish, while they sing *Kamma ma'alot tovoth* (A.). In Betanura the "steps" are made on the second evening, and young and old fasten them in their headdress to signify the completion of the Seder evenings.

The Passover meal consists chiefly of rice and meat. Rice, indeed, is the basis of all the meals served during Passover. Even people who can seldom afford it during the rest of the year have it at Passover and would feel greatly humiliated if they were without it at such a time. Meat, also, is never eaten in such quantities as on Passover. Matzot, on the other hand, are little used and matzo is therefore baked in considerable quantity only by the *merē pisḥa*, as explained earlier.

Burlesque Plays; *Shelōna*

In order to raise the festive spirit of the Seder evening, the Kurdish Jews introduce, at given points in the ceremony, burlesque skits, which may be regarded as the beginnings of a dramatic art. Their present form seems to be a degeneration of some forerunner. At all events, it is difficult to believe that they represent burlesque scenes pure and simple.

One of these skits is called *shelōna*.[25] A man is dressed up as a *qāshā*, Nestorian priest, by being clad in women's clothing, with a woman's *abāye* on top and his abdomen padded out.[26] Some families have a special garment for their *shelōna* performance. One kind of *shelōna* garment, for example, is woven in Rekan of black and white or black and yellow material. The *shelōna* winds a huge turban around his head, puts on a beard, takes a staff in his hand, and goes into the women's room. There he chooses the wives of some of the men guests and a few girls. The women and the girls—and sometimes a number of small children—follow him into the men's room creeping on all fours.

The *ḥazan* then asks the *shelōna* where he comes from and is told, "From Egypt." "What are you bringing with you?" "I am bringing a herd of sheep. Buy it from me." "If it is good, we shall buy it. Have you some good ewes that we may slaughter and use for making *qalya*, preserved meat (see p. 96)?" "I have a few." With these words, he takes the wife of the man who has asked the question then throws her on his chest, or else the woman crawls up to him on all fours; and the *shelōna* bids the man feel of the "sheep" to see how fat it is. As the man does so, the *shelōna* raps him sharply on the hand with his stick. The *shelōna* throws the girls to the young men in the same way. All manner of variations—and not infrequently some rough byplay—are introduced into the performance. In some districts (e.g., Tchalla and Nirwa) the Muslims come to witness the *shelōna* performance and Kurdish women then take part playing the roles of ewes and are thrown at the men by the *shelōna*. The performance gives the children a good opportunity for mischief. They stick pins and splinters into the *shelōna* and his sheep, whereat the *shelōna* flies into a rage and strikes out wildly in all directions. This adds to the hilarity, since the rougher the performance, the better pleased is the audience.

Presently, the *shelōna* goes out, returns in a short time, and points to the Seder dish with his staff. "What is that?" he asks. The master of the house replies, "That is *pisḥa*." He tells the story of the Exodus and explains the meaning of the Seder dish. The *qāsha* expresses a desire to take part in the Seder, but the guests will not allow it unless he proves that he has been circumcised. A pretended examination takes place, the man is pronounced to be uncircumcised and is invited to submit to the operation. After some hesitation, he consents. He is laid on the floor and the *ḥazan* is summoned to act as *mohel*. He calls for "the big knife." An axe is brought in. A special clamp (see p. 167), *mashqas shelōna*, made of a piece of pumpkin rind[27] and of a monstrous size is used for the *shelōna's* circumcision. During the sham operation, the guests sing the hymn,

Elī haqshēv lī
ush'ma' l'qōlī
yiḥye nimōlī
uv'ne hēkhal,[28]

which it is customary to sing at a real circumcision. Having thus become a Jew, the *qāshā* is allowed to sit down at the Seder table and the dinner begins. After the *shelōna* performance or on the second evening, the guests play the game "selling the skin"; A.).

Felling the Trees

Another burlesque scene of a different type acted on Passover is *qeṭā'at gōza*, "felling the walnut tree." In the version here described it has been performed in Betanura for generations by the same family.[29]

Several young men arrange themselves in a row or a group to represent trees. Then the two chief players appear each with an axe, and proceed to test out the trees by striking them on the back and listening at the seat for a hollow sound. Finally, one of the woodcutters finds a tree that satisfies him and calls to the other, *Birra, birra, shakhna dūsha*, "Come! Come! Honeycomb!" His colleague comes, listens, and tells him to go to the aga and buy the tree.

He goes to the house of the aga; but there, the servants refuse to admit him and he must force his way in. At first, the aga does not wish to sell; but when the youth makes a rush at him crying, *Buuuh*!" he yields immediately. "Come," he says, "sit down and eat." "Your food be on your head," is the reply.

An agreement is finally reached, and the youth goes back to cut down the tree. But no sooner has he begun than a swarm of bees, buzzing loudly, issues from within the trunk and attacks the second woodcutter. He screams. More and more bees swarm out to attack, and at length he falls unconscious to the ground. His companion, who is engaged in sawing the tree, is frightened. He rushes to the unconscious man, lifts up his leg and speaks into the seat of his trousers: *Birra, birra*, "Come, come." But the man remains motionless. His colleague weeps and wails and begins to sing a song for the dead. Then he brings the victim's wife and children and these join in the mourning.

As the man still shows no sign of life, the aga is called and blood money is demanded of him. The aga tries to restore the man to consciousness in the same manner as the others, but without success.

When this has continued for some time, the man suddenly sneezes. The people are overjoyed. They wash him and bring him food. They drive away the bees and take out the honey. A second wrangle with the aga's servants follows, but this is finally settled through the interveniton of another aga.

One can easily imagine what boisterous hilarity a performance of this type arouses in an audience composed of Kurdish Jews.

Stealing the *Afikoman*

We have told above how the *afikoman* is given to one of the guests for safekeeping. After the meal this develops into a burlesque skit of the same class as those just described. The *ḥazan* demands the return of his pledge, the *afikoman*; but the man to whom it has been entrusted denies ever having received it. Still more, he turns the tables and accuses the *ḥazan* of having stolen it. A merry quarrel follows, in the course of which an attempt is made to force a "confession" through "torture" from either the *ḥazan* or the real offender. Sometimes, the *afikoman* is actually stolen; and a fine in the form of a few chickens is demanded of its guardian. If he refuses to pay, he is hung up by the heels in the manner previously described (see p. 245) until he yields.

In Zakho the joke is sometimes carried so far that the *afikoman*, after being stolen, cannot be found again. In such a case, the Kurdish *ḥakhamim* have decreed that one must start again at the beginning of the Haggadah and repeat the entire ceremony. There have been a number of instances of this kind.[30]

On the second evening the *merē pisḥa* gives each of the *pisḥaye* two small pieces of the *afikoman*. One piece is eaten, and the other kept as an amulet. The housewife, for example, puts a little of it in her various stores (rice, flour, salt, etc.), since it is believed that if this is done, the stores in question will not be exhausted for a whole year (S.).

Special powers are ascribed to seven-year-old *afikoman*: it is, for instance, claimed that a piece of seven-year-old *afikoman* renders its possessor bulletproof and that if it is thrown into a swollen stream, the waters immediately subside (Z.).

The seder evening ends at about eleven o'clock. In Zakho the men have still to go to the river to dispose of the bones.

The Feast Days

The two main feast days are the occasion of reciprocal ceremonial visits. After the morning service, all the *pisḥāye* go once more to the house of their *merē pisḥa* where a meal "better than a wedding feast" is set before them. Their wives and daughters do not appear, but some of the good things from the feast are brought home to them by the women of the *merē pisḥa's* household.

After the meal, each *merē pisḥa* with his guests pays a formal call on the other Passover groups. The *gabbai* is the first to be visited, then come the others in the order of rank. Half the calls are paid on the first day, the rest on the second day.

In Sinne a bowl of fruit stands prepared in every home for these visits. When the guests arrive, each of them takes a fruit or a flower and gives it to one of his companions, who sniffs at it, kisses the hand of his friend, says the benediction, and returns it to the donor. Then the guests sit down and are regaled with fruit and arrack. While the men are paying these visits, the young people, accompanied by the musicians, go to the river or some other place outside the town to dance. In the afternoon, the adults join them.

Next evening, at the house of each *merē pisḥa* the whole Seder ceremony is repeated as prescribed by tradition. Work is suspended throughout the entire eight days of Passover.

In Zakho, the third day of Passover is a general excursion day. The excursion is named after its "aga" (e.g., *serānit bē Zākin*)—the title bestowed upon the Jew who bears the expenses of the *serāne*, pays the musicians, and provides the refreshments served in his *diwān*.

There is dancing and singing. The women prepare the food for the men. The girls and young women go about the hills dancing the *deranga* in groups. In their hands they carry *ṭarashta* (pl. *ṭarashyāsa*) boughs [*Quercus sterilis*?]; and when one group comes upon another, they beat each other with the boughs. If they chance upon a young man, they surround him and beat him, too, with the boughs.

In the evening, they all return to the town, accompanied by the musicians.

During the half-holidays, the people call upon each other and go strolling in the outskirts of the town. In Betanura and Tchalla and their outlying districts all work is suspended throughout the whole Passover period, but there are no *serāne*. The time is spent in making rounds of calls. *Ḥalīq* (see above, p. 284) and arrack are served in each house; and both men and women, who pass from one house to another, become intoxicated.

On the last two days the *pisḥāye* visit their *merē pisḥa* again, bringing with them arrack and *maza*. At the close of the feast, they greet each other with the words *Rēsh shatokh berikhta*, "The beginning of your year be blessed," and kiss each other (Z.) Their Kurdish friends send them bread, milk, and eggs. Even the aga was accustomed to send baskets of bread, eggs, and so on to the Jews, because the Kurds regard these acts of friendliness as a good omen for the coming year (Z. but not A.).

20

Shavu'ot

The Kurdish Jews call Shavu'ot, the second of the three pilgrims' festivals, *Ziyāra*, Pilgrimage, because Shavu'ot is their time for making pilgrimages to the holy places.[1] The most important of these pilgrimages are those to the grave of the prophet Nahum ha-Alqoshi in al-Qosh near Mosul, where the symbolic ascent of Mount Sinai also takes place; to the graves of Ḥazan David and Ḥazan Yosef in Bē Ḥazāne at Amadiya; to the grave of R. Netanel Halevi Barzani at Barzan; to Elijah's cave at Betanura; and to the tomb of Daniel at Kerkuk.

The Kurds of Amadiya call the feast Ja Zera [or Aida Jahzra, Feast of the Yellow Barley"]—a distortion of the word *ziyāra*—and the Kurds of Zakho call the pilgrimages to the grave of Nahum *'ida sayyid Naḥum.*

In Sinne the feast is termed Asarta (Heb. 'Aṣeret, Aram. 'Aṣarta) by the Jews, and Jashen Kalāna—Baking of Kalana, the typical Jewish Shavu'ot pastry—by the Kurds.

The popular custom of eating dairy dishes at Shavu'ot obtains in Kurdistan also. Hence, part of the preparation for the feast consists in providing a great deal of butter and cheese. The Jews who trade in the outlying villages barter their goods at this time chiefly for these products. On Shavu'ot eve, the meal does not differ in general from an ordinary supper; but in Tchalla, Rekan, and certain other places, a dairy dish called *madīra* is eaten on this evening. *Madīra* is made of pounded wheat, cooked in sour milk with dumplings (*kutēle*) that contain a filling of butter and flour instead of the usual meat.

After the meal, the people go to the synagogue for *ḥatīmat ziyāra*, as they term the reading on the first Shavu'ot night.[2] This night ranks even higher among the Kurdish Jews than the night of Hoshana Rabba. The people likewise gather at the houses of mourners, where it is customary to ask a minyan of *ḥakhamim* over to read in honor of the dead.

Whereas in Zakho only a few old women come to the synagogue, in Amadiya nearly all the woman and girls participate in the nocturnal readings. Some of the women also take part in the readings at the houses of mourning.

In the synagogue are hundreds of lights, for everyone has a light burning in honor of his dead. Nowadays these lights are for the most part oil lamps with wicks, but in some places wax candles are also used (D. and Betanura).

In remembrance of their dead, families bring bowls of fruit into the synagogue, so that the benedictions may be said over them. If a close relative had died within the year, the mourners endeavor to obtain as many *new* fruits as possible, since over these the blessing of *sheheḥeyānū* is pronounced. Wealthy folk have fruits specially sent from Baghdad for this purpose.

In the morning, the pious go to the river again for the ritual bath, because they wish to receive the Torah like a bridegroom, who takes the ritual bath before the *qiddushim* [wedding].

In Zakho the *'aliya* of the "ten commandments" is bestowed on the *gevir*. In Amadiya it formerly fell to the man who had succeeded in acquiring "the fourth" for the entire year. Today, this *'aliya* is put up to auction separately in Amadiya[3] and in Sinne.

In Amadiya, after the service, the women bring *yiprakh* (see p. 100), arrack, and three-cornered cakes (*kāde*) from the homes of mourners and set them before the *shekh* of the *ḥaverim*; for these are gifts connected with the death cult. The *shekh* distributes the *yiprakh* to the *ḥaverim* only but the *kāde* to the other members of the congregation, as well.

Similarly, in Sinne, on the first day of the feast, mourners give a dinner at which *yaprakhe* is served. Here, instead of *kāde*, there is *kalāne*, a baked dish peculiar to the Jews and consisting of a three-cornered crust filled with onions. It is from this dish that the Kurds have taken their name for the feast, *jashen kalāne*.

[In connection with the *kāde* that is eaten on Shavu'ot, the following tale is told in Amadiya. The Christian Pentecost, called *sulāka*, falls several days before the Jewish Shavu'ot; and it is the custom of the

Christians to bake *kāde* for their feast. These *kāde* are rolls made of flour and butter. One day a dog owned by a Jew saw that another dog, owned by a Christian, was holding a *kāda* in it mouth. The Jewish dog, wishing to have some of it, said to the Christian dog, "Give me some." "No," said the Christian dog. The Jewish dog said, "In a few days' time it will be our feast; and if my master gives me a *kāda*, I shall give some to you." But the Christian dog answered, "I am not giving you any." The Jewish dog thought to himself, "What should I do?" He asked the Christian dog, "What is the name of your feast?" "Sulāka," said the Christian dog; and as he said so, the *kāda* fell out of his mouth. The Jewish dog snatched it up and ate it. The Christian dog said, "You just wait! Soon it will be your feast!" When the feast of Shavu'ot arrived, the Jews prepared *kāde*; and the owner of the Jewish dog gave him one *kāda*. When the Christian dog saw him, he said, "Give me some of it!" The Jewish dog answered, "You would not give me any of yours, I won't give any of mine either." The Christian dog said to him, "What is the name of your feast?" The Jewish dog dug his teeth firmly into the *kāda*, and answered between his teeth, Ziyāra, and finished eating his *kāda*.][4]

For the Kurdish Jews the true significance of the feast of Shavu'ot lies in the great pilgrimages to the holy places, to which the Jewish population streams from far and near.

The pilgrimage to Bē Ḥazāne in Amadiya brings together a great mass of people, and many a Jewish household is obliged to provide quarters for as many as fifteen families. The *ziyāra* of the men takes place on the first feast day, after the service—that of the women on the second day. Before proceeding to the grave, the pilgrims take the ritual bath and put on new clothes. Then they file past the grave and each one kisses it.

On the second day, in particular, at the *ziyāra* of the women, there is great hilarity. The women dance and sing, and the girls bring their swings (*zanzōke*). The *gabbai* sits at the entrance to the tomb, serving wine or sherbet to the visitors. Then the latter approach the grave, kiss it, make their personal petitions and distribute among the various collection boxes the money they have saved for this purpose during the year.

After the visit to the tomb the women gather again to sing and dance and wish each other *ziyāra berīkha*, "a blessed pilgrimage."

The most celebrated of the Shavu'ot pilgrimages is the one to the tomb of Nevi Naḥum at al-Qosh, in which many thousands of Jews from Mosul, Baghdad, Basra, and the whole of Kurdistan participate.[5]

A significant feature of this *ziyāra* is the Ascent of Sinai, which takes place on both feast days.[6] Near the grave is a hill called Har Sinai, Mount Sinai. The people climb this hill, and the ten commandments are read at the top. Each community holds its own service. The *'aliyot* are sold by auction, and the prices are often forced very high up by the participation of some Jew from another congregation in the bidding; for it would reflect little credit on the community to allow the *'aliyot* to be acquired by an outsider.

After the reading from the Torah, the crowds descend the hill with great jubilation. Bands accompany them, and the strongest men go in front dancing the sword dance.

On the second day the reading on Har Sinai is repeated. On the third day every one again files past the tomb, makes a donation, and is presented by the *gabbai* with *tubarke*, some of the sweets and fruits which had lain on the grave over night.

After the morning service and the *ziyāra*, which immediately follows it, the people return home for the Shavu'ot dairy meal. In Amadiya this meal consists of butter (*kā'de*), honey, and milk drinks; but in the country districts the women cook *madīra* (see p. 296).

After food, everyone proceeds to the house of the man who has secured the *'aliyot* of the "ten commandments," there to dance and sing and partake of arrack and *maza*, which are lavishly served.[7] In some places the winner of the *'aliya* of the "ten commandments" gives a dinner to several of the notables of the community. When the men sing halleluya, they add, in their exuberance of spirits, *Hallelūya, hallelūya, bakhlakh bē'e shlīke pisra tūya*, "We want to eat hard-boiled eggs and roast meat" (A.).

The custom of dousing one another with water is still practiced among the Kurdish Jews. In Zakho the young men pour water over the girls. In Sinne, where the custom has survived in its pristine vigor, water is poured from the roof on passersby. Even the non-Jews are not spared; and as a result of these attentions, they are forced to change their clothes several times.

21

9TH AV

We have often emphasized that in an investigation of Jewish feasts among the Oriental Jews, the difficulty lies in the impossibility of determining which customs are indigenous. There is no community so isolated as not to have some connections with other Jewish communities.

This difficulty exists also with regard to the customs associated with 9th Av. In some places (e.g., Sinne) the national mourning begins as early as 17th Tammuz; but in most places it does not begin until Rosh Ḥodesh Av. The interval between 1st and 9th Av is called *ḥizīne*, "mourning" (A.; Z. *ḥazīne*). The customs practiced during this period are the usual ones. Thus, it is forbidden to eat meat. Anyone who has meat in his house cooks a Sabbath meal on Rosh Ḥodesh Av in order to use it up; and after the meal, the meat pots and dishes are put away in one of the little-used side rooms. The market is converted into a strictly meatless one, and butter and cheese have enormous sales. Any action associated with festivity (such as drinking wine or donning holiday garments) is avoided, and no one commences a new task. The weaver will not begin a new web; the women do not knit or wash clothes.

The teacher refrains from punishing his pupils during this period, but he does not neglect to assure them that everything will be fully made up in the future (Z. and A.). Since all pleasures are forbidden, the children are not allowed to visit each other or to go out walking. The teacher also sees to it that the boys should not go bathing in the river, as they usually do at midday. In order to remind them of the penalty that awaits any transgressor, he writes the word *falaq*, "block" (see p. 245), in red ink on the calves of their legs twice a day (Z.).

The teacher explains to his pupils that this prohibition is due to the fact that Lēl Hūza, a demon (lit. "Night of the Jews,") is in the water during the period of mourning.

The children are convinced that they themselves have often seen Lēl Hūza. They declare that he followed them and that he is broad and tall. They sing the following song about Lēl Hūza:

Lēl Hūza *lē gō māya hā*
ēmid azil gō māya
mahile Lēl Hūza

Night of the Jews is in the water.
Whoever goes into the water
Him the Lēl Hūza seizes. (Z.)

The final meal before the fast generally consists of rice. In Sinne a dish of rice and lentils is eaten, followed by an egg sprinkled with ashes; but this custom is not practiced in other places in Kurdistan except by the *ḥakhamim*. The pious have only rye bread with water. After the meal, which each person eats alone, ashes are strewn on the dishes, and they are put away like the meat dishes. A portion of this meal is sent to the *ḥakhamim* and to the poor, so that these may say the *hashkava* over it.

As far as possible, old and dark-colored clothing is worn on 9th Av. In former times the head cloth (*jemadāne*) was put on wrong-side out (A.). It was further customary to rend the garments as for the dead (A. and S.). The people go to the synagogue barefoot, or else they wear only black stockings or (most frequently of all) the Kurdish cloth shoes *reshike*.

The synagogue is suitably prepared for the time of mourning. The evening before, the carpets and cushions are removed and the Torah cloaks and the curtain of the Ark of the Covenant are replaced by black or worn-out ones. The silver Torah crowns are also taken off the scrolls. In some districts (Zahok, Dehok, Tchalla, and Hora) *rimmonim* of black wood are substituted for those of silver; and a freshly broken myrtle bough takes the place of the usual silver pointer (Z. and A.).

The Reading of *Ēkha*

Since the summer services are everywhere held in the courtyard of the synagogue in Kurdistan, Ēkha (the Book of Lamentations) is also read in the open. The heat is at its height at this season in the continental climate of Kurdistan; hence, 9th Av is sometimes referred to as Ṣōmit Ṣehwin (Z.) or Ṣōmit Seḥyon (A.), the "Fast of Thirst"; and it is customary to make a fan (*marwākha*) for use during the service (Z.). [In Amadiya 9th Av is called Ṣōm Seḥyon Urwa (Fast of the Great Thirst). The fast of 17th Tammuz, which precedes it, is called Ṣōm Seḥyon Z'ora (Fast of the Little Thirst).]

The people do not occupy their usual places in the synagogue on 9th Av; and no lamps are lit, each group of worshipers having only a small candle beside them. When the congregation is large, it is customary throughout Kurdistan for the *ḥazan* to stand up and read the Ēkha by the light of a small candle, which a child holds for him. In Amadiya the *ḥazan* stands up and reads the first verse of chapters 1, 2, and 3 and the first three verses of chapters 4 and 5, in Hebrew. After each reading, he sits down; and a member of the congregation finishes the chapter in Targum. Most of Ēkha is thus read in Targum.

In Zakho there is a remarkable custom connected with the reading of Ēkha. It is called *kheṭakh nashe*. Two old men who are sitting next each other and are absorbed in prayer will have their garments sewn together by the youths so that one cannot get up without the other. At the end of the service, there are often twenty such pairs in the synagogue. The custom is practiced in the night, as well, the people being sewn to their beds. No explanation of this peculiar custom could be given.[1]

After the reading of Lamentations, all the lights are extinguished—not only the lights in the synagogue but every light and every fire in the entire Jewish quarter. When the mother goes to Ēkha with her grown daughters, she warns her small daughters who remain at home to put out the lights later on. No fire may be kindled throughout the community until the slaughterers come next day at noon to slaughter the animals for *kappara* or for the evening meal (A.). Then, in accordance with the custom that obtains in all Oriental communities, the *ḥazan* announces in Hebrew and in the vernacular the number of years that have elapsed since the destruction of the Second Temple; and the congregation prostrate themselves on the ground, bury their faces in their hands, weep and wail, and beat their heads. In Zakho, when the *ḥazan* calls out *Oi lānū* (woe to us) at the end of his announcement, the *shammash* strikes the wooden door of the Ark of the Covenant loudly with a large key, and the young men, their heads still on the ground, cry out, *Hūhūhū qamqatālē lēl hūza*, "He, he, he killed the Lēl Hūza!"[2]

After the service, the people go silently home. The usual greetings are omitted. The men generally go to sleep, in order to avoid engaging in worldly conversation. The bed is made as hard as possible, and a stone is put under the pillow.

The women gather at the house of a woman who can sing *Halāla*, a song in Targum portraying the destruction of the Temple (A.). In Zakho the women sit on the roofs and sing the song *Lēl hūza* (see p. 301).

The Morning Service

The pious rise early and bind on the tefillin (phylacteries) at home. No one washes; the fingertips are merely dipped into water and the eyes moistened.

When the *ḥazan* takes out the Torah, he does not put it on his right arm but on his left; and during the reading, the scroll is held by two men (Z. and A.), instead of being set on the *sīde* as at other times. A myrtle bough serves as pointer (see p. 256).

After the reading of the Haftara (the section from the Prophets, every verse of which is accompanied by a long paraphrase in Targum), Ēkha is repeated in the same manner as on the previous evening and is followed by Job in Targum.[3] Most of the congregation leaves before the reading of Job, only the old men and the schoolboys remaining.

When the husband returns home after the service, the wife says to him, "Go and buy me *berakha* (blessing)." Then it is customary for the husband to go to the marketplace and buy a sack of rice or wheat (Z.) or fruit (A.) from the Muslims. The Kurdish Jews explain this custom by saying, "The Temple was destroyed, but now we are sitting in new houses and are bringing in new food."

Everywhere in Kurdistan, animals are slaughtered at midday on 9th Av. Since the beginning of the month, the meat-hungry Jew has gone meatless; and he has a craving to indulge in his favorite food after the fast. The *shoḥeṭim*, however, refuse to set about the slaughtering. They object to disturbing their own mourning mood; so they put off the work from hour to hour until the people, fearing that there will not be time enough to prepare the meat, begin to murmur; and finally the *urwat jemā'a*, the head of the community, forces the slaughterers to do their duty.

The *shoḥeṭim* dip their fingers four times into the blood, and sprinkle it in the direction of the four winds. Then, in remembrance of those who died at the destruction of the Temple, they make a sign with the blood on their necks, faces, and foreheads (A.). In Zakho, when the *shoḥeṭim* go to the river where the slaughtering is done, the boys hurry after them; for they are again permitted to go bathing after the long interval of abstinence. As the blood of the slaughtered animals flows into the river, the boys call out that it is the blood of Lēl Hūza. They swim after it and smear themselves with it.

Children's Games Played on 9th Av

The boys play certain games which, as the Kurdish Jews say, have their origin in the miṣva of occupying oneself with dust and ashes on 9th Av.

In Sinne the children play a game called *kākla mushān*, "mice game," in order to get their hands soiled with earth on the occasion of 9th Av. They heap up a little mound of earth, pour water over it, and make holes on top of it and on three sides. It then resembles an oven, and the children sometimes proceed to cook on it. One has the impression that this game has lost its original significance.

In Zakho the children play a game called *shanshalōtkat*. They choose sides and each party is assigned a section of field or street that has as many places as possible that are fairly well screened by fences, and so on. Each child has brought along a bag of ashes from home. The parties withdraw to their respective territories and proceed to make rows of small ash heaps, each row containing at least ten heaps; for otherwise, they will not be sufficiently visible and in the end will not be counted. The children try to put the ash heaps in places that are hard to find. When these preparations are finished, the boys repair to a spot previously agreed upon, usually the wall of the synagogue. After the groups have all arrived at the meeting place, group A proceeds to the domain of group B, group B to the domain of group A. It is the task of the groups to find all the *shanshalōtkat* of their opponents and demolish them. In order to check the results at the end of the game, groups A and B repair together to field A and go over the ground. The heaps that were overlooked are counted. The same is done in field B. If the number of "misses" is equal on both sides, the result is a draw, *rēsha berēsha* [lit., "head for head"]. But if, for example, group B, which numbers twenty members, failed to find one hundred of the *shanshalōtkat*, the average number of "misses" for each child in that group would be five. The boys of group A would then have the privilege of riding on the backs of their opponents five times back and forth to the heaps that were overlooked.

Kappara

In Sinne, money is collected from the members of the congregation for the purchase of a cow, which is slaughtered before the gate of the synagogue as *kappara* (atonement) or *qorbani* [sacrifice]. The flesh is distributed among the poor. A bit of it, however, is taken home to the children by their mothers, because it is believed to bring good luck.

The eyes of the *kappara* animals are thought to possess special powers. They are therefore sold by auction and bring high prices. These eyes are worked up into amulets for children. One such amulet[4] shows an eye set in a silver hemisphere and, stuck on top, a blue button containing seven holes.[5]

After the *kappara*, it is permissible to prepare the evening meal and to put on shoes.

When the master of the house returns home after the evening prayer, his wife breaks a vessel [an old earthenware pot] before his feet and says, *Mikhwasit twirī* (pronounced *twizī*) *aya āman qam aqlokh hadakh napli düshmünokh qam aqlokh tōri*, "As I broke this vessel at your feet, so shall fall your enemies, at your feet shall they be broken" (A. and Z.) [or, more briefly, *Naple dujminokh kam aqlasokh*, "May your enemies fall before your feet" (A.)] In Zakho the wife stands on the roof during this ceremony.

After this, the family eats the evening meal, which (as mentioned) consists of a meat dish. The pious, however, refrain from eating meat even on this evening, preferring to dine on lentils.

22

The Days of Awe

[*Yamim nora'im* (Days of Awe) is the general Jewish term for what in English are usually referred to as "the High Holy Days." They are most solemn days of the Jewish calendar, comprising the two days of *Rosh haShanah* (New Year) on the 1st and 2nd of Tishri, and *Yom Kippur* (Day of Atonement), which follows them after an interval of eight days on the 10th of Tishri. They are preceded by a month of penitence, beginning with the New Moon of Elul. In their general approach to the Days of Awe the Jews of Kurdistan differed in little from the other Jewish communities of the world.]

The Penitential Days—*Seliḥot*

Among the Kurdish Jews, also, the days of penitence and abstinence begin with the New Moon of Elul, called *rēshit sehērit rakhamīme*, "beginning of the month of mercy" [A.].

On the day of the New Moon, food is distributed to the poor; and on every day until Yom Kippur, bread is sent to the poor by three families (A.). The recitation of *seliḥot*, the penitential prayers, is begun on the third night—in Amadiya, however, on the first Sunday of the month Elul.

In order to wake the people for the nocturnal devotions, the *shammash* goes through the Jewish quarter before midnight, knocks on all the doors, and calls everyone by name. He summons even newborn babies who have not yet any names, calling them *bōna* (*brōna*) *zōra*, "little son." In Zakho he likewise summons those who have recently died. The Muslim neighbors of the Jews of Zakho believe that it is lucky to be awakened at midnight; and they consequently pay the *shammash* to wake them, too.

The Jews call to each other, for example, *Moshe kumlokh*, "Moshe, are you up?" From this, the Kurds term the *seliḥot* nights *kumlōkhe*; and for them, *kumlōkhe* is the time for irrigating the rice fields (Z.).

The children likewise exhort one another to get up; and if a child lingers, they douse him with water. In Amadiya nearly all the women attend the *seliḥot* services.

The *seliḥot* are intoned by the *ḥazan* or any member of the congregation who is a good singer. Certain *seliḥot* are assigned to the boys; this often leads to violent quarrels as to who should have the privilege of singing (A. and Z.). In Kurdistan it is not customary to blow the shofar after the *seliḥot*. This was, indeed, formerly done in Amadiya; but the custom was abolished about 1920 because it was argued that this frequent blowing of the shofar detracted from the value of the true shofar blowing on the New Year and the Day of Atonement.

For the boys the *seliḥot* nights are nights of special joy, and they have certain games that they play only at this time. In Zakho, as soon as the *seliḥot* are over, shortly before dawn, the boys rush to the riverbank to play until the sun rises.

One of the games peculiar to the *seliḥot* nights is called *mehināsa* (sg., *mehinē*), "mares." The boys start preparing for weeks in advance. They pick out the strongest of their comrades in the school and try to secure them as their *mehināsa* with gifts of money, sweets and raisins.

Often, a boy will entice away his comrade's chosen "mare" by promises of finer presents. This leads to violent quarrels among the boys in the weeks preceding Elul. But when, at length, a youngster has secured his two "mares," he sets about making them strong for the *seliḥot* nights. He gives them all the sweets he can save up and invites them to his home. "These are my *mehināsa*," he says to his mother; "see how lean they are. I must make them strong for Elul. Give me some food for them." The mother must then serve the two boys with *yiprakh*.

The boys make bridles for their "mares," and on the *seliḥot* nights furious contests are fought out between the various teams.

Another game is known as *taktakoshkat*. For this, the boys begin collecting camel's dung weeks before Elul. Out of the dung they make little bombs, which they explode at the riverbank (Z.).

The New Year

On the eve of the day of preparation for the New Year's feast, at the time of the *seliḥot* services, the *haṭṭarat nedarim*, "release from vows," takes place. Everyone must first give the *gabbai* a gift of money, *pārit haṭṭara*, half of which goes to the *ḥazan* and half to the synagogue; then ten *ḥakhamim* pronounce the *haṭṭara*. The women and girls also come to the synagogue for *haṭṭara*; but among them, the money is collected beforehand. If a woman cannot attend the service in the synagogue, the *haṭṭara* is said in her home.

In Kurdistan (as elsewhere) it is customary to fast on the day of preparation. Work is not suspended till midday; but the men go to the market in the morning to buy the requisites for the feast, especially the fruits and other kinds of food that serve as "a good omen."[1] In Amadiya each householder buys the fruits himself. Since the *shoḥeṭim* do not slaughter enough sheep to provide everyone with a sheep's head, each purchaser gets only part of a head. In Zakho, on the other hand, a number of people assemble at the house of the *merē pisḥa*; and only he buys the fruits and the sheep's head.

At midday everyone gets a haircut and proceeds to the river to bathe and to don the white garments that are worn on the New Year and the Day of Atonement.

The customs practiced by the Kurdish Jews at Rosh haShana[2] exhibit no special features. This is a feast at which great care is taken to carry out the traditional commandments. Undoubtedly, local peculiarities have been weeded out in favor of traditional forms. Indeed, much of the difficulty in investigating popular customs among the Jews at festivals arises from the fact that through the supervision of rabbinical messengers, special local usage is forced to give way to the rigidly traditional customs.

Among the Kurdish Jews it is usual to recite the prayer *aḥot qetanna* [a little sister][3] before the evening prayer and to do so with tears. The prayer is read both in Hebrew and in Targum and, in some places (Herki), in Kurdish.

After the service, the worshipers greet one another with the words *Tikkatēv besēfer ḥayyim tovim*, "May you be inscribed in the book of the good life." In Zakho the people go to the house of the *merē pisḥa* to eat of the fruits whose Aramaic name or whose taste is considered a good omen for the coming year and of the sheep's head. Nuts are to be avoided, and it is forbidden to eat anything sour; but sweet foods should be indulged in as much as possible. After the meal, the men sit long at their reading of Mishna and Zohar. The very pious take another ritual bath on this morning.

In Amadiya there is a special sale of the functions of honor connected with the reading of the Torah. Mothers buy the privilege of setting up the *rimmonim* for their small sons; and the father holds the child on his arm while he performs his task. During the service, two assistants (*somekhim*) stand at the *ḥazan*'s side; and several songs are sung by the three together.

The climax of the service is the blowing of the ram's horn, the shofar (Z. and A. *teki'a*, A. and S. *shofar*). Great care is taken of the shofar throughout the year, so that it may have a good tone at Rosh Hashanah and Yom Kippur. Various expedients are resorted to for preserving the tone: it is customary to keep a bird's feather, soaked in oil, in the shofar (A. and Z.)[4] and before the New Year to lay the horn in vinegar water (Z.) or pour some arrack into it (S.). The *ḥazan* usually does the blowing. He practices a great deal beforehand in order worthily to fulfill the difficult task that he is to assume in behalf of the community.

In some districts the Kurds forbid the blowing of the shofar. This is probably due to fear of magic. The Jews of Zebar (east of Rekan) assemble secretly in a cave and there carry out the precept.[5]

After the morning meal the people go to *yeshiva* [sitting] in the houses where a death has occurred within the year. Here they are served coffee and fruit so that they may say the benedictions for the soul of the departed.

After *minḥa* the men, young and old, go to the river for *tashlikh*, "cast (out the sins)." Of the women, only the older ones take part. The people stand in a row on the riverbank—the *ḥakham* in the center—and shake their coats and trousers without, however, turning out their pockets. While shaking their garments, they hold the four fringes (Heb. *arba' kanfoṭ*) in their hands. Benjamin II gives the following description of the *tashlikh* ceremony in Rowanduz: "An other curious custom is that on New Year's day, after the ceremony of *Tashlikh* (prayer at the waters). This ceremony is practiced likewise in many parts of Europe. It is a more symbolical act. They go to the stream flowing at the foot of the mountain, recite there the prayer, and throw themselves into the water and swim about. They imagine that by this bath they are cleansed from all their sins, quite forgetting the new sin they commit in taking the bath itself; such an act is forbidden on festival days" (*Eight Years in Asia and Africa*, p. 122).

None of my informants could tell me whether the ceremony was actually ever performed in this manner.

In Zakho, nowadays, the Jews stand on a raft in the river. The ignorant even wade into the water, believing that in this way they can the better get rid of their sins. In Akra it is customary to stand with the feet in the water.

[In Amadiya the *tashlikh* is performed on the town wall. On the wall is a place where there was once a well, which is now completely filled in. They stand upon the well, whence they can see, at a distance of some 4,000 cubits, a waterfall that drops from a great height and, in falling, turns three mills. While they say the *tashlikh* prayer, they look at this waterfall. At the words *Mī Ēl kamōkha* (Who, O God, is like unto you?), each one of them lifts the hem of his clothing; and at the words *tashlikh bim'tzullot yam* (cast into the depths of the sea), they shake the hem three times.]

The Day of Atonement

Between the New Year and the Day of Atonement come the Ten Days of Repentance. Pious men and women are accustomed to fast during this period, that is, to eat only the evening meal.

The more general practice, however, is to refrain at this time from eating *khuwarūsa* ("white"). By "white" is meant, strictly, milk and butter; but eggs, onions, and garlic are also avoided. Some explain the custom as being due to the fact that milk products come from non-Jews and that nothing coming from non-Jews should be eaten during the days of repentance.[6]

The Kurdish Jews call the Day of Atonement Kippur or ṣōma Urwa, (Great Fast, S. and A.) or *ṣōma arīza* (Dear Beloved Fasting, Z.). From this, the Kurds sometimes call it Roya Mazana Jihiyana (Great Fast of the Jews, Z.); but their more usual designation is *'Īda Dikla* (Feast of the Chickens). Even the Jews use the term Yom Zebāḥit Dīkila (Day of the Chicken-Slaughtering).

The Kurds bring a great many chickens to the market on the days preceding Yom Kippur, for they know that the demand will be great.

In the night preceding the day of preparation for Yom Kippur, the *shammash* wakes the people for *seliḥot* an hour earlier than usual. Even small children are awakened, because it is considered unlucky to be asleep during the *kappara*. For the *kappara*, a white animal is chosen, if possible—generally, a cock for a man and a hen for a woman. There must be a bird for every member of the family; but among the poor, an egg is often substituted for the hen.[7]

Wealthy families take a sheep as *kappara*; and this then serves as a general *kappara*, such as the Kurdish Jews are in the habit of resorting to on other occasions (e.g., in case of illness).[8] Each family comes to the courtyard of the synagogue with its sheep. The *shoḥeṭ* leads the sheep around the family three times, and every member of the family lays his hand upon it before it is slaughtered.

The *kappara* chicken, on the other hand, is slaughtered at home. The *shoḥeṭ* begins his work at midnight in order to finish in time. He lets the blood flow into a *doka* filled with wood ashes, after which the master of the house recites the benediction over *kissuy ha-dam*, "covering the blood."

For the *kappara*, as on other occasions, chickens are slaughtered gratis; but the pupils of the *shoḥeṭ* sometimes give him the fowl as a gift. The heads and the entrails are put on the roof as food for the birds, and the meat is distributed to the poor.

In the morning the great wax candle, *sham'a mevōrakh*, "blessed candle," is conveyed to the synagogue.[9] This candle, which is about 2 meters high and 30 centimeters thick, is made by the *shammash* at the expense of the synagogue. In Amadiya the wax is purchased out of the money that is collected at the scourging (*malqut*) on the Day of Atonement.

In Zakho the *shammash* brings the candle to the *gabbai*'s house a few days before Yom Kippur. This transfer must be effected after dark. On the day of preparation preceding Yom Kippur, the candle is decorated with kerchiefs and a wreath of roses. Then about midday the congregation come to the *gabbai*'s house, where they are served refreshments. The sale of the candle follows. With the object of forcing up the price as high as possible, the sale is conducted with much clamor and hilarity.

The successful bidder takes the candle on his shoulder and, escorted by the crowd, brings it to the synagogue. The women standing on the roofs pelt him with wheat and raisins and sound their *klīlīlī*. The candle is set up opposite the Hēkhal; and some of the parents have oil lamps lighted for their children, wives, for their husbands (Z.). In Amadiya a candle is lighted for every member of the family.

The *sham'a mevōrakh* is extinguished the day following the fast and the portion that remains is used as *havdala* candle in the synagogue (see p. 271). It is regarded as a bad omen for the community if the candle goes out prematurely.

In Sinne a thick wax candle, 1 meter in height, is set up in the synagogue by every family that has lost one or more of its members through death within a certain number of years (sometimes for a period of ten years); and the synagogue is brightly illuminated by the mass of these memorial candles.

The scourging (*malqut*) takes place in the synagogue after *minḥa*. This custom is carried out by the Kurdish Jews with the greatest seriousness and zeal; for it is entirely in keeping with their rough nature, and they attach great importance to it.

For the flogging they employ a special whip, made of oxhide and ass's skin. This practice is explained by reference to Isaiah 1:3, "The ox knoweth his owner and the ass his master's crib." But this is a recent explanation, since we are unquestionably dealing here with a very ancient instrument of flagellation. The Brauer collection at the Hebrew University possesses a particularly fine old piece[10] from Sinne. It has a wooden handle 20 centimeters long, into which is inserted an oxhide strap, folded into four thicknesses and sewed together at the edges with a narrow oxhide thong 33 centimeters long 6.7 wide, and 1.2 thick. (HUBC 37:11). Handle and lash are embellished with impressed lines. Down the length of the lash, in the middle, on both sides, is a strip of ass's hide 1.4 centimeters wide, sewed to the strap through the middle with a narrow thong of oxhide. A strip of ass's hide projects at the end and is formed there into a little roll.

Every synagogue possesses a scourge, which is kept in the Ḥēkhal. A scourge of this kind is likewise a treasured heirloom in the families of some of the *ḥakhamim*. But in Zakho there are only two specimens in all.

One of the pillars of the synagogue serves as whipping post in Amadiya. The penitent strips to the waist and faces the pillar, throwing his arms around it. One of the pupils binds his arms with an old prayer shawl. The lashing is administered by the *ḥazan*; and (as we might expect from what we have learned of the Kurdish Jew) the strokes are anything but gentle. The *ḥazan* stands on a stone behind the penitent and often grips the whip with both hands in order to be able to deliver stronger blows. He gives either three strokes or, if the penitent so desires, "forty but one," reciting the thirteen words of Psalm 78:38 three times. The Kurdish Jews utter loud cries during the lashing—not, however, on account of the pain, but rather from inner agitation.[11]

After the flogging, the penitent distributes alms. The poor surround him, crying, *Mamo, mamo*, "Uncle," and will not allow him to dress until he had satisfied them (Z.). Then he goes to the river for the ritual bath. In Amadiya it is customary to immerse oneself five times, but the ultrapious do so "forty times but one" (Z., A., and S.).

The women put the food for the close of the fast into the oven and tell the children that at this time the oven is guarded by a serpent and must be left strictly alone. The last meal before the fast usually consists of chicken and rice. Young and old fast; and the mother admonishes her daughter, *Ṣōmin berāti nāpiklakh khā kākit dēhva*, "Fast, my daughter, then you shall grow a golden tooth" (A.).

As the precept demands, the people go to the synagogue without shoes. Many wear the *reshke*, the footgear woven from goat hair (p. 88); and, as a substitute for sackcloth, they bind around their bodies, next to the skin, a rope made of goat hair called *dalke*.

All the men who are away from home return for Yom Kippur, and everyone attends the service at the synagogue, so that the courtyard, where the service is held, is filled to capacity. The women and girls stand on the roofs of the neighboring houses.

Kol Nidre is sung three times in the original and three times in Targum. During the singing, the whole congregation weeps; and the girls and women on the roofs weep and wail. The mother says to her daughters, *Bekhe berāti tekhātir illāha yāwil khāye ṭa bābikh akhawāsakh*, "Weep, my daughter, so that God may give life to your father and your brothers" (A.).

The very pious take upon themselves a vow not to speak until the blowing of the shofar next day. Many remain standing during the entire eve and day of Yom Kippur.[12] In order to render this self-inflicted ordeal a little easier, they wind bandages around their bodies. Some of the *ḥakhamim* spend the night in the synagogue so as to avoid coming into contact with women or non-Jews or occupying themselves with vanities. In Zakho there are a great many girls who take the vow of silence. This, they believe, will win them the boon of a good husband.

Next morning, everyone is in the synagogue before sunrise. The reading of the prayers is divided among three *ḥazanim*. An especially large number of worshipers is called up to the Torah on Yom Kippur, because many men spend the whole year traveling in the villages and are at home with their families only during the Days of Awe and Passover. Furthermore, all who can do so come from the villages into the towns for Yom Kippur.

Before pronouncing the priestly blessing the Kohanim go to the wash basins, and the Levites pour water over their hands. This water is given as a healing drink to the sick or to barren women (A. and Z.).

Yom Kippur is observed with peasant fervor by the men, to whom fasting is no great hardship; but among the women, there is a continual coming and going. During the *piyyutim* [liturgical poems], which are sung in Targum, the women weep copiously. But there are also many men who do not spend the whole day in the synagogue but go home after the morning prayer and sleep until *minḥa*.

In Sinne the men sit on the elevated platform of the *sīde* during this interval, and every boy and girl in the community presents them with a kerchief for the Torah scrolls. These cloths, numbering more than two hundred, are later sold for the benefit of the synagogue.

A man to whom a son is born on Yom Kippur is subjected to severe treatment. It is asserted that he sinned in having illicitly slept with his wife on the fast of the Tenth of Tevet, the day when Nebuchadnezzar laid siege to Jerusalem. The sinful father is wrapped in a mat, laid on the ground, and trodden upon three times by each of those present. He must spend the whole of Yom Kippur in this mat (A.). In Zakho, however, he is released when his punishment is over.

After the blowing of the shofar at the evening prayer, the women hurry home in order to light the lamps and take the *mebose* out of the oven for the *fetartit kippur*. The dish most frequently used for breaking the Yom Kippur fast is a sweet-and-sour one: dumplings (*kufte*) of wheat and meat cooked in the juice of unripe grapes *mebīsit khumsa* (A., Z., and Sulaimani).

23

Sukkot—Tabernacles

Among the Kurdish Jews, the feast of Sukkot [Booths] is called Sukka or Sukkot. In Sinne the term Ēlanē, Feast Time, is also used; for Sukkot is regarded in the Persian-Kurdish district (as in the talmudic writings) as the feast par excellence. The Muslim Kurds call Sukkot Blue Hut, Kapra Shīne (Z., A., and Ushnu).

There are places where every family builds itself a booth (S. and Sulaimani); but for the most part, the booths are erected only by a few families, who invite the others to celebrate with them, as at Passover.

In Zakho about a fourth of the families build *sukkot*. In Arbil there is generally one booth in each courtyard; in Amadiya only seven families out of eighty erected booths, in Barashe two or three out of twenty-five. In Ushnu, likewise, there were only four booths for a hundred families; and these were built at the homes of the *ḥazan*, the *gabbai*, and two rich men.

The Booth

In Kurdistan, as in other countries, the building of the booth is begun directly after the close of Yom Kippur. The booth is erected in the court or, very often, on the roof. In Zakho it is an old custom for the timber merchants to lend the wood for the *sukkot*. In the evening, therefore, the men repair to the river, where the timber yards are located; and each one obtains the wood he requires and takes it home himself. Then he digs out the four corner holes and sets up the corner posts.

Next morning, groups of people go to the forests with mules to get the *khilapta*, "osiers," for the walls and ceiling. Since the osiers are put up on the eve of Sukkot, the day is called *yom gezālit sukke* (Z.) or *yom kasōyit sukka*, "day of covering the *sukka*" (A.). No nails are used in the building of the *sukka*. Everything is tied with ropes or willow withes.

The *sukka* is decked out with carpets and gaily colored cloths, except in the country districts like Barasha, where the osiers are left uncovered. To the ceiling are attached bunches of fruit of as many different kinds as can be obtained; little bundles of salt, pepper, and so on; a "Jonah's gourd," *qara maye* (A., watermelon; also S.); and an egg with the Hebrew inscription from Leviticus 23:42, "Ye shall dwell in booths seven days" (A. and Ushnu). The children fold up pieces of paper to resemble birds, *chuchikyātha* and hang them in the *sukka*. These, they say, are the souls of the *ḥakhamim*.[1]

The people sit on the ground on rugs, around the low table (*kursi*) on which is set the *sīnīya* with the food. According to the Kabbalistic custom, a chair called *kursi babawātha*, "chair of the fathers," is also placed in the *sukka* for the *ushpizin* "the celestial guests." Every day, a bowl of food is prepared for the *ushpizin* and is later given to the poor.[2]

When the owner of the *sukka* returns from the synagogue on the first evening of the feast, he does not immediately enter the booth but waits until all his guests have assembled so that all may enter together. Women are not included among the guests at this time. The mothers climb up to the roof and throw candy down to their children as the latter step into the booth. A bridegroom is also pelted with candy of this occasion (Arbil).

The meal is not provided by the host. Each guest brings along his own arrack and *maza*; later on, the wives arrive with the food.

Lulav (the Sukkot Bouquet)

In Kurdistan only the synagogue has a *lulav* [and *etrog*. The *lulav* consists, as it does in all Jewish communities, of a palm-branch, flanked by twigs of myrtle and willow. The *etrog*, popularly called *trinja* among the Kurdish Jews, is the citron. These "four kinds," as they are usually referred to, are held together in both hands, the appropriate benediction is pronounced over them, and then they are shaken up and down and toward the four winds. This benediction and shaking, performed on each of the eight days of the Feast of Booths, is an essential part of its ritual.]

Myrtle (*āsa*) and willow (khilapta, *Kurd.* bīl) grow everywhere in Kurdistan; but individuals cannot afford[3] the *lulav* and the *etrog*, because these must be imported from Baghdad or Jerusalem, or, in the Persian district, from Rasht.

In Amadiya two old men used formerly to go to Baghdad to get the *lulav* and *etrog*. When it was learned that the caravan with the bearers of the palm branch and citron was approaching the town, the teacher, the pupils, and all who could leave their work—even Kurds—set out joyously to meet it (Z. and A.).

The *etrog* and the *lulav* are first taken to the house of the *gabbai*, where they are sold by auction. On the day preceding the eve of Sukkot, the people, in procession, singing the song *Dē khamlūla* (p. 125), bring them to the house of the *merē lulav* [*lulav*-master], the successful bidder for the *lulav*. From the roof of her house the wife of the *merē lulav* throws candy and nuts at the people in the procession, and in the house refreshments are served to all comers.[4]

Next morning, even before the sun is up, the people are awakened by the *shammash* in order to bring the *lulav* from the house of the *merē lulav* to the synagogue, whence it is returned to the house of the *merē lulav* after the service. The honor of being *merē lulav*, seeing that it involves serving refreshments to about sixty persons daily, is a very costly one. The *lulav* is wrapped in a silken cloth. There is no box for the *etrog*.

In the synagogue the *merē lulav* gives the *lulav* to everyone, in order that each may say the benediction over it. In former times old women also held the *lulav* and said the benediction.

Before *minḥa* on the first day, the congregation gathers in the *sukka* of the *gevir*, on the second day in that of the *ḥakham*. There is singing and dancing, and a few of the old men perform the sword dance with wooden ṣwords. For *minḥa*, a procession proceeds to the synagogue, the youths in front, dancing with kerchiefs, and the old men behind them, dancing with swords (A.).[5]

Hoshana Rabba

The night preceding the Hoshana Rabba [Great Hoshana] is called *lēl arāva* "night of the willows." On the *lēl arava* the men take the ritual bath and don white clothes, as on Yom Kippur.

In Amadiya the men assemble for the nocturnal readings in the synagogue, in Zakho and Sinne, in the *sukka*. The *gabbai* of Amadiya has a large quantity of grapes brought to the synagogue, and people in mourning bring a bowl of fruit and cakes (*zelōbiye*). The fruit and the cakes are distributed several times during the night. Women also come to the synagogue for these readings, but they sit silently in the courtyard (A.). With the rising of the moon, the reading of the Psalms commences. The men form groups of ten and assign a portion of the Psalms to each group. In Sinne the shofar is blown after the reading of each book. No one must fall asleep during the reading. The *gabbai* walks through the rows of readers to see to this. The worshipers, in their brutal way, used to wake a sleeper by treading heavily on his leg; but since this not infrequently resulted in broken bones, they limit themselves nowadays to stepping on his toes (A.).

Examining the Shadow

In Kurdistan, too, we find the old popular belief that on this "night of the sealing of one's fate" the head of a man who is destined to die within the year casts no shadow. Before the reading of the Psalms some of the men, especially the *ḥakhamim*, go out to examine the shadows cast by the head, arms, and legs.

In Arbil it is said that only certain persons are competent to examine the shadow at night. They go out unobserved and study the shadow cast by their own bodies in the moonlight. From specific signs they can detect whether anything untoward will overtake themselves or other members of their family. They reveal nothing to others of what they have observed but attempt to avert the threatened evil through vows.

A Jew of Sinne told me that on Hoshana Rabba, while taking a walk with some other young men, he suddenly noticed that the shadow of one of his companions was headless. He beckoned to a friend and drew his attention to this disquieting fact. The friend confirmed his observation. And, in fact, the youth died within a short time.

Beating the Willows

It is customary to fetch the willow branches for the *lulav* during the night or at dawn. In Amadiya the privilege of doing this is reserved to the family Bē Hūda. Several members of this family go to the river at midnight, but the osiers, *hoshanot*, and bring them to the synagogue. In Zakho all the men from the various *sukkot* get the osiers and deliver them to their *merē lulav*. Each person takes seven boughs but beats only with five (A.).[6] The women, who nearly everywhere go to the synagogue for Hoshana Rabba—and even little children—get themselves willow branches.

The ignorant pick out branches that are especially large and strong, under the impression that the larger the bough, the better kept is the precept. In Zakho some of the young men tie several branches together forming a pole that reaches to the ceiling of the synagogue. At the top they fasten a large nosegay of roses or some apples or pomegranates. Others chose particularly strong branches and bend the tops into a sort of club with which they go about beating the people (also A.).

Although Hoshana Rabba is the feast at which the fate decreed for men receives its legal force, nevertheless, even on this grave occasion, there is no lack of the burlesque among the Kurdish Jews. Thus, in Ushnu, the youths in the synagogue steal the cloth in which the men bring their food for the nocturnal reading. They take it to their victim's wife and tell her that her husband wants some more food and a bottle of arrack. Deceived by the cloth, she does as she is bid; and the youths then proceed to consume the food and drink in the synagogue.

In Sinne the young men go to the fields before sunrise and play all sorts of tricks there. The steal fruit, prepare it in the open, eat it, and wash it down with arrack.

In the morning the *lulav* is taken from the house of the *merē lulav* and brought in especially festive procession to the synagogue, this being the last time that this ceremony is to be performed. The seven circuits are distributed among men who bear the names Abraham, Isaac, Jacob, Joseph, Moses, Aaron, and David.[7]

Those who make the circuits are beaten with the willow boughs. The people also beat each other with the boughs, sometimes not too gently. All attempts to abolish this custom have been in vain (Z. and A.).[8] The beating of the willow branches takes place in the courtyard.

No special customs are practiced in Kurdistan on Shemini Aṣeret [the eight day of Sukkot]. Simḥat Tora, on the other hand, is a true popular feast; and there are many processions, in addition to the circumambulations on the eve and the morning of Simḥat Tora.

Simḥat Tora

The circumambulations on the eve of Simḥat Tora are made after *minḥa* and after *ma'ariv*; but these are not very festive, and the seven circuits are consequently sold all together instead of separately, as on Simḥat Tora itself.[9]

On the morning of Simḥat Tora, the privileges and functions of honor for the entire year are sold by auction (see p. 162). In Amadiya the honor of being *ḥatan Tora* (i.e., *ḥatan me'ōna wayā'al*) and the honor of being *ḥatan bereshit* are also put up to auction; but both are always acquired by the same man.[10] In Zakho these functions are not put up to auction: the successful bidder for the privilege of being "sixth" becomes *ḥatan me'ōna* as well, while the two who are to be the "seventh" become also *ḥatan wayā'al* and *ḥatan berēshit.*

In Amadiya the notables solemnly escort the *ḥatan* to his house, where he entertains them at a meal. The remaining members of the congregation come also; but they bring along their own food, the *ḥatan* merely furnishing the arrack. The *ḥatan Tora* must furthermore present several bottles (*betuna*) of arrack to the *ḥaverim*. The honor of being *ḥatan Tora* is thus a rather expensive pleasure. In Zakho part of the congregation escort, in joyous procession to his home, the *ḥatan Tora* (*wayā'al*), the other part, the *ḥatan berēshit*; and both these *ḥatanim* serve their escorters with festive refreshments.

After the meal at the *ḥatan*'s house, the people go home; and several hours before *minḥa* the *shammash* summons the congregation to Simḥat Tora (A.). In Amadiya, when the circumambulations in the synagogue Navi Yeḥezqel are finished, everyone repairs to the synagogue Ezra Hasofer, where the circumambulations are delayed until their arrival. In Sinne the circuits are made in one synagogue after the evening prayer and in the other after midnight. The young men usually take part in the circumambulations in both synagogues, but they are especially fond of the midnight circumambulations. They follow up the latter with a gay night of eating, drinking, dancing, and singing.

In Zakho the main circumambulations take place at about eleven o'clock in the morning. It is customary in Kurdish communities to make the circuits also a third time, namely, after the evening prayer.

Circumambulations

All the Torah scrolls are taken out of the hēkhal for the processions. The scrolls are decked out with flowers; and the most beautiful scroll, adorned with roses, is carried to the *sīde* by a group of dancing men (Z. and A.) In Sinne each scroll in turn is placed on the *sīde*, so that all the scrolls may enjoy the honor of having the circuits (*hakkafot*) made about them. Two old men stand beside the scroll as *shushbinim.*

The privilege of carrying the Torah scrolls in the circumambulation is sold by auction, and each *hakkafa* is put up to auction separately.

This sale of the *hakkafot* is one of the richest sources of income that the synagogue possesses (A., S., and Arbil; in Z. there is no sale). A joyous spirit reigns in the synagogue throughout the ceremony. The fathers who have succeeded in getting one of the scrolls take their small sons on their shoulders while making the circuits. Behind the men with the scrolls come the children. Flags are unknown in Kurdistan, but in some places, the children are given candles to carry. In Amadiya [rights to carry] the *lūḥot* [silver tablets inscribed with the Ten Commandments] are put up to auction, and the fathers acquire them for their children. There are about sixteen of these; and the youngsters, with the *lūḥot* in their hands, follow the men in the circumambulation. In Ushnu the boys take part with the prayer book on their heads.

The circuits are accompanied by the singing of hymns. The young men lift the *ḥazan* and the other singers on their shoulders, and the singing is done from this elevated station.[11] While the circumambulations are going on, the men and youths dance; but the dancing must not take place too near the processions lest the young men, who dance with considerable abandon, should accidentally knock a Torah scroll out of the hands of its holder. The dances are enlivened by variations of all sorts. For instance, four youths will form a group, two dancing while each carries on his shoulders one of the others, the upper two joining hands. Or else three will form a group, two dancing while the third stands with a foot on the shoulder of each. Others build a pyramid three men high, the topmost of whom wears an enormous turban, made out of a number of head cloths (A., A., and S. *poshīye*). Sometimes the "village simpleton" is wrapped up in a shawl and carried on the shoulders of the dancing youths like a bundle (Z.).

Arrack is drunk freely during the ceremony, and many drink to excess. The women clap their hands, raise their *klīlīlī*, and sprinkle the procession with rose water. The ceremony of the circuits often lasts two hours.

In Amadiya, when the circumambulations are over, the schoolboys bring the people at home bunches of grapes from the synagogue as *tūbarke*, sweets. The time after *minḥa* is occupied in making calls on the *gevirim*. After *ma'ariv* there are often further processions.

The children greet the close of the feast by calling, *Nūne nūne kudkha qam kanūne*, "Nūne, nūne, each individual to his oven!" (A.). [This greeting shows that in the opinion of the Jews of Kurdistan, the winter begins after the close of the feast, for it is usual to sit around the oven in winter.]

In the evening the *sukka* is dismantled and taken apart. The master of the house first removes some of the fruit that has been hanging there, then the guests follow suit. Many people go to several booths in order to participate in the removal of the fruit. The bottle of oil that hung in the *sukka* is kept for the sick.

Numerous customs are connected with the *lulav*. The *etrog* and the *lulav* are preserved for other uses. The *etrog* is kept until 15th Shevat, the New Year of the Trees, and then eaten with benedictions (Z., Arbil, and S.). Pieces of it are also given to pregnant women as a protection against the "evil eye." (Z. and A.).[12]

The *lulav*, as well as the *etrog*, are credited with magic powers. For barren women or sick persons the *ḥakham* writes the names of certain demons on a leaf of the *lulav*. Then the leaf is burned, or else the patient drinks the water in which the writing has been washed off. The *lulav* is likewise used for burning the *ḥameṣ* before Passover and stoking the oven for the baking of the *maṣṣa shemūra* (see p. 277).

The willow boughs are put to the same uses as the *lulav*. In Zakho they are collected from all the guests by the owner of the *sukka* and carefully preserved.

If a cow falls ill, she is taken to the *ḥakham*. The *ḥakham* strikes her on the head, shoulders, and back with a willow branch, then he takes a small piece of wood from it and fastens it to her horn (A.).

In Amadiya, on the day after Sukkot there is one of the biggest *serāne* of the year; for, according to the Talmud (B. Sukka 45b), one must be joyful on this day.

24

THE "CONTROL OF RAIN"

[Since the rainy season in Kurdistan, as in most places all over the Middle East, normally begins in the fall shortly after the Sukkot holiday, the proper place to discuss the rites performed in case of drought is between a presentation of the Sukkot observances and that of the 15th of Shevat (January–February) ceremonies. Brauer collected material on this subject in Jerusalem in interviews with Kurdish Jews, and presented his findings in a paper (in Hebrew) in the *Sefer Magnes* (jubilee volume in honor of Dr. Judah L. Magnes, president of the Hebrew University; see Publications).[1] What follows is my translation of this study.]

Visitation of Tombs

Among the various customs performed by Kurdish Jews for the purpose of putting an end to drought, only the visitation of tombs comprises, in addition to magical elements, also a religious one, and it is the only one that the Jews did not adopt from the neighboring population elements. Customs paralleling it can be found also in other Jewish communities.

In Arbil, in case of drought, a Thursday is designated as a fast day. On Wednesday night they gather in the synagogue, and make donations of money for the offering up of sacrifices. Next morning, nobody is absent from the Shaharit prayer. They blow the shofar, and after the prayers go to the cemetery, where the *shoḥeṭs* slaughter the sacrificial animals. On one occasion, for instance, they "sacrificed" an ox, two cows, and three sheep. Before the sacrifice, the rabbi and the slaughterers lead the animals around the tombs seven times, the number corresponding to the seven *ushpizin* [saintly guests] who are symbolically invited to the *sukka*, Abraham, Isaac, Jacob, Moses, Aaron, Joseph, and David (see above, p. 316), and blow the shofar. Then they take the animals to a nearby place, slaughter them, and distribute the meat among the poor. According to their accounts, rain begins to fall the moment the *shoḥeṭ* takes the knife into his hand. They remain standing in the rain until Minha time, and then they return, singing and jubilant, to town, where the Muslim Kurds receive them with due honor.

On this custom we have information also from the *Teshuvot* (responsa, i. e., authoritative opinions on religious questions) titled *Rav Po'alim*, written by the Baghdad rabbi R. Yosef Ḥayyim, who died in 1909: "There is a custom in the town of Arbil (may our city be rebuilt) at the time of drought: they take five or six heads of cattle, and lead them to the tombs of the saintly men buried in the cemetery, and they slaughter an animal on each tombstone.[2] Then they pray for rain, recite the "Thirteen Attributes" of God, blow the shofar, return in peace [to the town], and distribute the meat among the poor." Rabbi Yosef Ḥayyim's opinion is that it is strictly forbidden to perform this custom, and that they must discontinue observing it.[3] Nevertheless, my inquiries have clearly shown that the custom described, and other customs in connection with drought, have remained alive to this day. The statement that the animals are slaughtered on the graves is doubtful, and one must rather suppose that the slaughtering took place somewhere outside the cemetery.

A similar custom is practiced in Sinne, in Persian Kurdistan. They proclaim a fast, and collect donations for sacrifices. In the morning all of them go to the synagogue, and slaughter the ox or the sheep in the synagogue courtyard. The whole congregation stands around the "sacrifice," and they cry, "*Kapparah* (atonement)!" Every one tries to put his hand on the animal. The meat is distributed among the poor. The people remain in the synagogue and recite Psalms. After noon they go to the cemetery, taking along a Torah scroll and a chair to place it on. Next to the graves they recite the prayer for drought, and then usually read these passages from the Pentateuch: for the Kohen, Exodus 32:11–14; for the Levi, Exodus 34:3–4; for the Yisrael, Exodus 34:4–10. Then they circle the tombs of the saintly seven times, blow the shofar, and everybody cries and laments.

In Amadiya they proclaim a fast for Monday, and go to the tombs of Ḥazan Yosef and Ḥazan David, which are located in the courtyard of the Navi Yeḥezqel synagogue (see. above, p. 63). If no rains fall despite these observances, they impose a fast on the community. They fast on Monday, Tuesday, Wednesday, and Thursday, observing also the other four prohibitions constituting a fast: they refrain from washing and anointing themselves, from putting on leather sandals, and from marital intercourse. Instead of sandals they wear the *rashke*, the Kurdish summer shoes, mentioned above (p. 261). Next Monday they recite *seliḥot* (penitential prayers) after the Shaharit prayers, and blow the shofar. If their prayers have still not been answered, they take out the Torah scroll from the Holy Ark, put a black mantle on it, and the rabbi strews ashes on the Torah and on his own head.[4] Seeing this, the congregation bursts into tears. Then they go to the cemetery, to the section in which the sages and saintly men are buried, which is called *tāfiya adōne*, mound of the masters. Near those tombs is a stone, not unlike a table, called *kēfat sefer torah*. They place the Torah scroll on this stone, and pray, recite *seliḥot*, read the passage Deuteronomy 4:30–5:30 from the Pentateuch and the Book of Jonah as the *Hafṭara*, and blow the shofar. In Amadiya the slaughtering of animals is not customary; instead they make charitable donations.

If, despite all this, no rains come, they impose a fast on the congregation, and on Monday take out three Torah scrolls, put ashes on them and on the heads of the seven elders of the community, and go to the cemetery. If even this has brought no results, they proclaim a fast for Tuesday and Wednesday, and the elders observe a *mahbūsa*, that is a fast of two days and two nights. Wednesday night they sit and recite *seliḥot*. On Thursday they take out seven Torah scrolls, and put ashes on them. Seven elders, each of them aged eighty or more, put ashes on their heads, and the whole congregation daubs ashes on their foreheads. On the way to the cemetery they raise a big lamentation, and the elders undertake not to leave the cemetery until rain falls.

In Dehok the custom of going to the cemetery is known, but other rain-making customs have a more important role. In Zakho they don't go to the cemetery at all.

In Akra they fast three consecutive days. They pray in the synagogue, which is located outside the town, and they blow the shofar. They study the Torah all night long, in the House of Study located in the town itself. If all this has brought no results, they go to the cemetery with the Torah scroll.

In Mosul, if no rain falls after the fast and the blowing of the shofar in the synagogue, they go to the cemetery. Mostly they visit the most famous among the tombs, that of R. Sh'mu'el Barzani, styled "*adoni.*" Sh'mu'el Barzani lived in Barzan, and was forced to flee from there in his old age and seek refuge in Ashur (that is, Mosul). He was the father of R. Shim'on Barzani, called *shera din*, that is, mad lion, who fled from Barzan to Amadiya and died there. His tomb is visited by Jews and Muslims alike, with respect and adoration. The circumstances of his flight from Barzan are recounted in the story about the healing pomegranate tree, presented above (pp. 259–63).[5]

Such a visitation to the tomb of R. Sh'mu'el Barzani in Mosul was carried out during Passover in 1937. In those days there was a prolonged drought. The Muslims performed all their rain-making ceremonies, but to no avail. At that juncture the government [*sic*] sent word to the chief rabbi and requested that the Jews should perform their own rites. The Jews recited *seliḥot* and Psalms, blowed the shofar, and read the passages from the Bible appropriate for the alleviation of drought. But no rains fell. During Passover it was forbidden for them to fast, or to go to the cemetery. But after the holiday they went to the cemetery to the tomb of R. Sh'mu'el, accompanied by soldiers and Muslims.. They stood there all day, praying, and after the Minha rain began to fall.

In Ushnuya (Ushnuiyeh, near Lake Urmia) they perform the slaughtering of sacrificial animals, not near the cemetery, but on the banks of the river. In general, rivers have an important place in the rituals of the Kurdish Jews. Thus, for instance, it is their custom to erect the synagogue on the bank of a river, and the bride and groom must perform immersions in the river. These customs are connected with their beliefs in the purifying power of flowing water. If no rains fall, they take out two Torah scrolls and go with them to the river. The sacrifices, too, are taken to the river. To begin with, the men immerse themselves in the river, then they slaughter the animals, and the children and adults draw a line on their foreheads with the blood. The remaining blood is poured into the river. The meat is distributed among the poor.

Since we are interested here primarily in the magical-popular customs, we do not discuss in depth the custom of visitation of tombs. In these rain-making customs we find many old traits. But, as is often the case in Jewish ethnology, we are here, too, unable to establish whether these traits are truly old, or are new and resemble old traits only by coincidence.

An old custom, for instance, is the removal of the Torah scroll from the Holy Ark, and the strewing of ashes on it and on the head of the rabbi.[6] The custom used to be to take out the Torah scroll from the synagogue to the street, and to read from it in the open air.[7]

Subsequently, this custom became combined with another. They appealed to the Fathers, the great saintly men who possess "power," in order to make rains fall. For this purpose they used to visit their graves. The custom of turning to the saints and visiting their graves is mentioned in the Talmud.[8] The custom of reading the Torah in the open air became combined with the custom of visiting the saints' tombs, even though it is forbidden to read the Torah in a cemetery.

However, among the Kurdish Jews this custom became combined with yet another one: that of presenting a real sacrifice to the Fathers. That these sacrifices are not atonements but gift sacrifices is evidenced by the type of animals slaughtered. For atonement only cocks and hens or sheep and rams are slaughtered, but never cattle, which to slaughter as a rain sacrifice is the custom of the Kurdish Jews. And even though the Gaons and the early decisors permit the laying of the hands on the animals offered as atonement and their instant slaughtering thereafter, one must emphasize that the laying of hands and instant slaughtering are actually characteristic features of real sacrifices.[9]

The Rain-Bride

Apart from the visitation of tombs, there are among the Kurdish Jews several magical customs for the purpose of ensuring rainfall which they, it would appear, adopted from the Muslim Kurds. It is, of course, also possible that the Jews brought them along to Kurdistan from their old places of habitation. Even though it is difficult to decide among the two possibilities, the first seems to be more probable, since the songs which accompany the customs are in Kurdish, and not in the neo-Aramaic language of the Kurdish Jews.

Let us begin with the custom of the rain-bride, since this custom is widespread among other peoples, and thus requires no special clarification.

In Zakho, the *būk barāne*, that is, rain-bride, is a young man dressed in torn clothes, with a chain made of cattle bones around his neck and a basket on his head. He is accompanied by four other young men, and is followed by a crowd of youngsters and children. They wind their way through the streets and dance. Two of those who accompany him clap hands and two others sing:

Our bride is beautiful, beautiful,
And where is the remedy for the bridegroom?
Our bride seeks rain.
O, God, she wants food,
Lov, lov, lov.

As they pass from house to house, each house-owner pours water on the rain-bride, and gives food as a gift to her company.

The custom of *būke barāne* as performed in nearby Dehok is similar. A young man takes off his clothes and puts on only short trousers. He smears his legs with grape honey, and sticks on them tufts of cotton wool. In the same manner be acquires a beard. Around his neck he puts a bridle, and he is also tied with a rope with which a large group of young men pull him all over the streets of the town. They enter the houses, singing: "*Būke barāne, būke barāne*" (Bride of Rain, bride of rain). The others respond: "*Barān dawet, barān dawet*" (She wants rain, she wants rain).

Here too the house-owners pour water on the rain boy, give raisins and some money to the other youngsters, who divide the booty among them after the completion of the procession.

This custom belongs to the type of the most widespread custom called "Rain bride." In the original form of this custom the ritual rules demanded the participation of a naked girl, who was led around in the street and the people poured water on her. At a later stage she was covered with a shirt made of tree leaves.[10] This custom is a typical example of sympathetic or imitative magic. The girl represents the vegetation, or the god of vegetation, which (or who) comes to life again by being doused with water, which is an imitation of rain.

As among the Kurdish Jews, so among other peoples, the place of the girl is frequently taken by a boy. This is the case in southern Europe, for example, in Macedonia and Dalmatia.[11] Also in Poona in India they dress a young man in tree leaves, and lead him around in the streets as the Rain King and the householder and his wife sprinkle him with water, while the children receive presents.[12]

In Amadiya, on the other hand, they dress up a woman in man's clothing. She attaches a beard made of goat's hair to her face, ties a kerchief around her head, and thus attired walks the streets of the town.

In some localities the human being representing the spirit or the god of rain is replaced by an image or effigy. Thus, for example, in Sinne they make an image out of two beams, and dress it up in clothes and veils. They call it *būke barāne*. A young man carries the image in his hands, and the children pour water on it. Accompanied by young people, among them Muslim Kurds, the young man marches along the streets with the image and sings:

"*Būke barāne hawu hawu*" (Bride of the rain, he, he). And the children respond: "*Ya khwa voāre*" (O God, give rain).

Here too the owners of houses pour water on him, and give gifts. If anybody refuses to pour water and to give gifts, they break the vessels in which he keeps water. Upon the conclusion of the procession, the figure is thrown into the river.

The same ceremony is performed in Ushnuye, and there too the figure is thrown into the river.

A performance with such a figure is known also in Armenia. There [the children dress up a broomstick as a girl, carry it from house to house, and sing:

Nurin, Nurin is come
The wonderful maiden is come...
Bring water to pour on her head,
Give butter to smear on her hair,
Let the blessed rains fall,
Let the field of your father grow green...

They pour water on Nurin, receive presents of butter, eggs, rice, and so forth. Afterwards they take Nurin to the river and throw her into the water.[13]

The same custom obtains also in Egin, Armenia, where the boys carry about an effigy which they call "Chi-chi Mama" or "the drenched Mother."[14] In Urfa in time of drought the children make a rain-bride which they call "Chimché-gelin," which, they say, means in Turkish "shovel bride." Here too the effigy is thrown into the river.[15]]

A different form of the custom is found among the Jews of Arbil. There, next to the bride a bridegroom also appears, represented not by images but by live people, that is, by young men. The youth who represents the bride, *būk barāne*, is dressed in women's clothes, and the bridegroom wears, as in Zakho, only short trousers. He too smears his body with a glue and attaches tufts of cotton wool to it. His face he smears with black clay, and sticks to it a beard of goat's hairs. On his head he has a tall hat made of cardboard, and around his neck a chain of rags. Here, too, he is led around in the streets by a rope tied to his neck. The entire ritual has turned into a burlesque. Although the basis of the dramatic performance is the representation of demons for the purpose of magic, as a rule comic features play an important role in it. Thus, for example, while they march along the street accompanied by a large crowd, the "bridegroom" tries to embrace the "bride." She pushes him away. He stumbles and falls. Thereupon the "bride" sits down next to him and cries over him in the manner of mourners crying over the dead. Then the "bridegroom" and the "bride," accompanied by the crowd, go from house to house, and the people pour water on them and give presents to them.

The burlesque performance of death and mourning is undoubtedly based on a magical-dramatic representation of the death of the vegetation god, the mourning over him, and his resurrection.

It is of interest to mention here that a bride and bridegroom appear also in the circumcision rites of the Kurdish Muslims. In Zakho, for instance, two boys get undressed, smear themselves with grape honey, and stick tufts of colored cotton wool to their body. They put on high hats which cover their faces, as well, with holes for the eyes. They hold swords in their hands, and thus they march along the streets, next to the horse on which is carried the child to be circumcised. When they pass the houses of rich people, they are given presents, and especially the father of the child is lavish with his gifts.

Robbing the Flocks

A characteristic custom observed by the Kurdish Jews in case of a drought is the one called "robbing the flocks." It seems that this custom, too, was adopted by the Jews from the Muslim Kurds, but the Jews perform it in their own special manner, and the Muslims seem to have given over its observance to the Jews.

I have collected information on this custom from several sources. In Zakho three women dress up in men's clothes, and wind kerchiefs around their heads until it is not possible to recognize that they are women. They borrow weapons from the Muslim Kurds, and arm themselves with rifles, bullets, and daggers. They get up early in the morning, go out of the town, and lie in wait for the shepherd of Zakho or of the neighboring village, in order to rob him of his flock.[16] They fall upon the shepherd, tie him with ropes, and bring him, together with his flock, to the town. Zakho is located on an island in the Khabur river, and a bridge leads to it from the river bank. Next to the bridge a great crowd of Muslims, Christians, and Jews awaits the women. Some men fall upon the shepherd and push him into the river three times. All this takes place in silence, without any accompaniment of singing or of speaking. They talk only in sign language. They say that they act in this manner in order not to reveal that the robbers are women. However, it would seem that we have to do here with a kind of ritual violence, as is known, for instance, from the water-drawing rite at Easter-time in southern and eastern Germany.[17] After the shepherd has been thus submerged, they take him, dripping wet, together with the flock, to the fortress, to the governor, who receives them with joy and gratitude. He gives presents to the women, and the shepherd too gets from him damages, after which he can go back to his place with his flock.

In Dehok, located near Zakho, there are women experienced in the performance of this ritual robbery. They, too, dress up in men's clothing, and borrow weapons from the Muslims, who are notified in advance. At the break of dawn the women go out of the town to lie in wait for the shepherd of the nearby village and his flock. They fall on him, tie him up, and bring him back to town together with his flock. They announce their coming by shooting off the rifles and sounding their "*klilili.*" The men gather in throngs and wait for them. Even soldiers and government officials participate in the reception of the women. All of them together go to the governor, who gives gifts of cash to the women, to which the heads of the Jewish community add their own presents. The governor orders the bonds of the shepherd to be released, gives him damages, and permits him to return home with his flock.

The "robbing of the flock" is known also in Amadiya. However, its observance has been discontinued in recent years. The women used to dunk the shepherd into the river, to douse the flock with water, and also to pour water on each other and on the men who came to take the flock back.

In Ushnuye the rite is observed somewhat differently. A large number of women—about fifty—disguise themselves in men's clothing and provide themselves with sticks as arms. They go out of the town to rob the nearby village of its flock. They fall upon the shepherd, and beat him with their sticks. The shepherd cries for help. Some of the women drive away the flock, others hold the shepherd and the men who come to help him. The encounter degenerates into serious beatings, and some of the women sustain injuries. They take the flock to the governor, and the affair concludes in the manner described above.

The basis of this custom has been explained as follows: they take the flock to the town so that the young animals, separated from their mothers, should begin to bleat, and thereby augment the crying and moaning of the people begging for rain.[18] This explanation, which is a literary one, has some support in a passage in the Jerusalem

Talmud (tractate Ta'anit 65b [chapter 2, Halakha 1], [which elaborates on the account found in Jonah 3:7–8 of the repentance of the people of Niniveh, and] which reads: "What did they do? They put the calves inside and their mothers outside, the colts inside and their mothers outside," so that the young animals should cry, and their cry reach God. Such a custom is still found among the Bedouin,[19] and also among the Muslim inhabitants of Mosul, as a Kurdish Jew, who had participated in it, informed me. Still, I find this explanation unsatisfactory.

In Frazer's *Golden Bough* no trace is found of this custom, or of any other like it. Nor did Abeghian find it among the Armenians. The form in which the custom is practiced in Ushnuye indicates quite clearly one thing, which does not appear in the other versions. It is told with special emphasis that fighting takes place, and that the women sustain injuries. Also, the essential form of the custom involves the abduction of the flock of the *neighboring* village. The purpose, therefore, must be the fighting, which constitutes an important part of rain magic in several places. Thus in Egghiu in Ethiopia the custom is to engage in bloody fighting in January, for a whole week, between neighboring villages, in order to ensure the falling of rain.[20]

But even with this we have not yet got to the real basis of the robbing of the flock. And since it is not yet known to which *Kulturkreis* this custom belongs,[21] we must be careful in offering an explanation. But the impression is gained that it belongs among the customs surrounding the ancient gods of fertility and vegetation. Such a fertility-god is Hermes, who is, at one and the same time, also the god of rain.[22] In addition, he is also the patron of shepherds, and is a robber of flocks, who robbed part of his brother Apollo's flock.[23] It is quite likely that such mythological beliefs underlie [or did originally underlie] the "robbing of the flock" of the Kurdish Jews.

The Skull Custom

Rain can be withheld also as a result of magical manipulations. In Kurdistan, the responsibility for drought is often attributed to the grain merchants and the bakers. These two professions are in the hands of the Muslims and Christians in Kurdistan. Both have an interest in lack of rain, since at times of drought the price of grain rises, which brings great profits to both of them. The Jews usually bake the bread in their own homes, and the bread they bake suffices for them for a whole month at a time. They buy the grain at harvest time for the whole year, and only in case of drought are they forced to supplement their supplies with additional purchases.

In Sinne, when there is a drought, and the bakers expect that there will be a shortage of grain, they instantly raise the price of bread, and let their customers wait for hours, in order to show to what extent the people are dependent on them. And if suddenly rain begins to fall, the Muslims, Christians, and Jews together engage in a joyous demonstration with an orchestra of flute and drum, in front of the baker's house, to show how glad they are at his misfortune.

The bakers and grain merchants figure also in the verses sung in connection with requests for rain by the Jews and the Muslims. The following lines, from Sinne, refer to a conversation between the baker and his daughter:

My daughter, go out and see whether rain is falling.
Yes, Daddy, rain is falling drop by drop.
O, my daughter, drop by drop it blinds the eyes of your father.

Another song, also from Sinne, refers to the plight of the grain merchant's mother:

Rush of rain, rush of rain,
The grain merchant's mother goes down into the grave.

In the view of the Jews the grain merchants and bakers are able actually to withhold the rain by their magic. The magic they resort to is very powerful, and is performed especially by the Christians. The bakers take dough and put it around their feet, like shoes, tie it around with rags, to prevent it from falling off, and thus equipped go out into the streets (Amadiya).

Even stronger is the magic performed by the Christians in the environs of Zakho. They too make themselves shoes of dough, and with them on their feet go out to the fields to plough.[24]

As a counter-magic the Jews and the Muslims perform this rite. At midnight three to five strong young men go to the Christian cemetery. They dig up a body from its grave, cut off its head, go with the skull to the river and throw it into the water. It seems that the basis of this rite is imitative magic: by producing bubbles which rise up when they throw the skull into the water, the magic that withholds rain is annulled (Dehok and Zakho).

In Amadiya such a rite is performed somewhat differently. Two Kohanites, four Levites, and four Israelites go to the Christian cemetery. Two of the Israelites remain outside as guards at the gate. One Israelite opens up the grave of a Christian who died recently, and one of the Levites cuts off his head. An Israelite puts the skull on top of a stick, and thus they go with it to the river. At the riverbank the Israelites hands the stick with the skull to a Kohanite, who dips it into the water and then throws the skull into the river. Immediately rain begins to fall. In Turkish days the Jews used to receive permission from the Kaimakam (the governor) to perform this rite.

The counter-magic with the skull is, as mentioned, resorted to also by the Muslims. Thus, for instance, in Akra, the Muslims dig up the skull of a Christian and put it into water for three days—this causes rain to fall.

This custom is known also among the Armenians. They, too, throw a skull into the water, or slaughter a lamb and throw its head into the water.[25] Mostly they use the skull of a person of another faith. The Christians of Urfa, for example, throw the skull of a Jew into "Lake Abraham."[26]

In Sinne they practice yet another rain-making magic in which a skull figures. The Jews performing it use a donkey's skull. They take the skull up to the roof, place it at the edge of the flat roof, then pour water into it so that the water flows through it as through a spout down to the ground. The children pass by and gather wood from the people. They arrange the wood in a pile on the roof, light it, and throw the skull into the fire. Once the fire has engulfed the skull, they pour water on it and throw the skull down to the ground.

This otherwise unknown use of a donkey skull is of special interest, for it undoubtedly is a survival of the mythological role played by the donkey. Among the Sidonians and Syrians the donkey was an animal sacred to the god of nature.[27] The connection stems from the insatiable lust attributed to the donkey. Thus,for example, the medieval German mystic Saint Hildegard (1098–1179) said, "The donkey is a fool, and is almost blind due to its lust." In ancient Greece the donkey had a role in the cult of Dionysus and the Bacchants, and was depicted in an ithyphallic state.[28] In Greek homes they used to set up in the garden the skull of a she-ass that had given birth to young, believing that the power of fertility emanated from it.[29] This explains the use of a donkey's skull in the rain-making ritual. The rite undoubtedly belongs to the *Kulturkreis* which attributes powers of growth and fertility to the donkey.

The informants who told me about the Kurdish rain-making rituals repeatedly emphasized that the Muslims and Christians would first attempt to put an end to the drought, and when they did not succeed they turned to the Jews with the request that they perform their own traditional rites. Thus, on one occasion, the Muslims and Christians of Ushnuye sat for five days praying, beating their heads against the ground, and drumming for hours on end,[30] but no rain fell. Then the Muslim mullah appealed to the Jewish rabbi, and the rabbi organized the visitation to the cemetery. Immediately rain fell. In many places in the Muslim world the Jews had the reputation of being masters of rain magic.[31]

A recurrent motive in all the Kurdish Jewish stories about rain-making is that while the efforts of the Muslims and Christians remain unsuccessful, the ritual performed by the Jews is crowned with success so rapidly that a strong downpour surprises them while they are still out of doors. The Jewish cemeteries of Kurdistan are mostly found outside the towns, on mountain slopes. The rain comes so suddenly that the Jews who participate in the rain-making ceremony arrive back in town drenched from head to foot.

It is related, for instance, that in Ushnuye, after the animals were slaughtered and the meat given to the poor, they put the meat in baskets which they carried back to town on their heads. While they were still underway, such a strong rain fell that it washed the blood of the pieces of meat down through the baskets onto the faces of the men. When they arrived back in town, and the Muslims and Christians met them with a joyous reception, they were surprised to see the Jews with their bloodied faces, and asked them whether it was the Jewish rain-making custom to engage in bloody battles among themselves.

The belief that the power of rain-making was primarily in the hands of the Jews contributed significantly to the position of honor and respect the Jews enjoyed in many places in Kurdistan. A Kurdish governor once expressed his thanks to the Jews by saying: "You have the true faith. The Kurds desecrate their faith, and are sunk in fornication."

25

Hanukka

Among the Kurdish Jews Hanukka is not one of the major feasts. This is evident from the fact that work is not suspended during Hanukka, although the Kurdish Jews never miss an opportunity to declare a holiday. The [traditional Jewish] law likewise does not make stoppage of work obligatory on this half-holiday. Women, however, do not work during Hanukka; and this applies not merely to the evenings, in accordance with the general custom (i.e., while the Hanukka lights are burning), but to the whole period. Needlework, in particular, is forbidden. The following verse refers to the fact:

ḥanuka darzē bē nūka
nuk nūki chafta

Hanukka, the needle is without a point,
Its point is crooked. (S.)

The general designation for the feast is Ḥanuka; but there is, in addition, the name *Ḥanukāye*, which is connected with the Hanukka lamp. The Kurdish terms have reference to the Feast of Lights: ʻĪdat Chera Hurka, Feast of the Small Lights (Z.) and aʻīdat Shirʻa, Feast of the Lights (A.).

For the Muslim Kurds, the Hanukka feast of the Jews marks the beginning of winter. They say, *Chera hurka juhiyāna sere zevistāna*, "Little lights of the Jews, beginning of winter" (Z.). The Kurds of Amadiya also call Hanukka Sire Zevistāne, Beginning of Winter. In

Sinne they call it Shāw Chera Zōsan, Night of the Winter Light; in Sulaimani, Cherā'i zistān, Light of the Winter.

For the Kurds of Amadiya, Hanukka is the time for the beginning of the snowfall, just as Sukkot is the time for the beginning of the rains. This notion also finds expression in the following children's rhyme from Amadiya:

ḥanūka
talga duka

Hanukka
Snow on the ground.

Hanukka has actually been incorporated in the popular sayings connected with the weather. In Zakho, which lies in the plain and has rain, instead of snow, the people sing [in Hebrew], *Ḥanukka, b'mayim, b'rakha mishamayim*, "Hanukka with water, blessing from Heaven." In Amadiya they sing,

ḥanūka māye
brākhā bāse min shimme
ḥanūka pokhe
brākhā gō khokhe

Wet Hanukka—
Blessing comes from Heaven.
Windy Hanukka—
Blessing in [plums].

Hanukka is a feast that requires no special preparations. In the evenings the men go to the synagogue as on every weekday, and the *ḥazan* lights the candles. The Hanukka lamp[1] in the synagogue is just like the one in the home. In olden times the Kurdish Jews had no candlestick or Hanukka lamp at all, and this is the case in certain places even today (Z., D., Nirwa, Rekan, and Betanura; formerly also A.). In place of the Hanukka lamp, they cut a long, thin wax taper (Kurd. and Arab., *finda*; Jaba, *Dictionaire* p. 295) into small candles and simply stick them on the wall in a row. The *shammash* [servant light][2] is placed in the same row, instead of a little higher as is the general custom. This kind of Hanukka lamp is called *findat hanuka*.

The oldest type of Kurdish Hanukka lamp is made of iron. In Amadiya it is in two sections with four oil holders in each. A wax candle serves as *shammash*. In former times, a simple iron bowl with wicks was also used as a Hanukka lamp (Z.).

There are likewise Hanukka lamps of clay. Those made by the women of Amadiya consist of nine separate lamps, each shaped like a Roman lamp. In Sinne the clay lamp was formerly merely a lump of clay in which depressions were made with the finger for oil and wick. The most primitive—and at the same time the most typically Kurdish—lamp is simply a row of nutshells filled with oil and provided with wicks. This kind of lamp is still very popular in Kurdistan (Z., D., Rekan, and formerly S.). Eggshells were also used for this purpose.

Since there is no olive oil in Kuristan, all sorts of oils are used for the lamps, such as sesame oil, caster oil, sheep fat, melted butter, and so on.

The *shammash* is generally a separate candle, not joined to the lamp. In Ushnu it consists of a reed containing tallow and a wick.

The candles were formerly stuck on the wall facing the door. The custom of having the lamp in the doorway is of late date. Here, the lamp is put on a small projection or shelf on the doorpost (Z. *benunta*, A. *dukit ḥanuka*), opposite the mezuza. In Sinne it may also be in a niche (*taq*) inside the room.

If the whole family lives in the same house, the married sons assemble in the father's room, and only the father lights the candles. The married sons, however, light candles for their own families. Sometimes, the father surrenders the *miṣva* of lighting the candles to one of his sons (who must likewise carry out this duty if the father is absent).

For cases in which the head of the family is away and there is no one else in the house to light the candles, or when the man cannot recite the necessary benedictions, schoolboys go through the Jewish quarter to perform these services. After the benedictions, the Hebrew hymn *Ṣur y'shu'atī 'anēnī-Adonay 'anēnī*, "Rock of my salvation, answer me, O Lord, answer me," is sung; and Psalm 30 is recited. The boys who light the candles get a present either at once or at the end of the feast. They are therefore accustomed to say, after the recitation of the last words of Psalm 30, *Kha janga fēka*, "A handful of fruit" (Z. and A.).

In Kurdistan there is no special food peculiar to Hanukka. The Jews of Sinne eat pumpkin (*shewītya* Kurd. *banī*) on the first Hanukka evenings, a practice taken over from the Kurds, who eat pumpkin for the last time in the season on *shāw cherā zōsan* [i.e., at Hanukka].

Every evening after supper the people visit a different house, where they dance, sing, and play games till late in the night. In Amadiya they go to the house of a *gevir*[3] on the first and the last evening. There are no special Hanukka games. They play the usual winter games, a favorite being the "ring game" (Z. and A. *esiqsa*, see p. 353), which corresponds to the "stocking game" (*gurva bazī*) of Sinne.

The children likewise gather in a separate room and imitate their elders. They have a *shammash* serve them tea and fruit; and they play games, especially *mīra, wazīra uqezirāya*, "king, vizier, and policeman," which they play with knucklebones. On this occasion, they do not light another Hanukka lamp; but they bring along as many wax candles as possible and stick them on the wall so that the room may be festively lighted up.

At home, the girls make themselves new wax candles out of candleends; and they light their candles while reciting the benedictions. The boys also try to get a supply of wax, and they light their candles next morning at the school.

The custom of lighting the Hanukka lamp in the morning at the synagogue still obtains in Zakho, Rekan, and Betanura but no longer in Amadiya or Sinne.[4]

If the weather is fine, the schoolchildren make a *serane*; but they are even happier when it snows or rains, for then they go to the synagogue and celebrate *qormō bīqā*.[5] They make merry in the same way as at other feasts, but on this occasion they sing,

qormō bīqā
dikila khenīqa[6]

[Firewood and a bottle]
The chicken is strangled (or drowned). (Z., formerly also A.)

The adults, as well, celebrate *qormō bīqā* when it rains; it is possible that this function has some connection with Hanukka as marking the beginning of winter.

In Kurdistan the *Megillat Antiochus* is read at home during Hanukka, whence has arisen the custom of the burning of an effigy.[7] A figure is made out of wood and rags; it has a beard, a pipe in its mouth, and a large candle in its hand. A child takes this doll, which bears the name Ḥanūka, and goes through the streets with it, calling for gifts. The other children run after him, singing songs.

At the close of the Hanukka week the children tear off the beard, pour petroleum over the doll, and set fire to it, crying, "Antiochus, Antiochus!"

In Sinne the name Antiochus has failed to survive in connection with this custom. At Hanukka a youth is dressed up like a *shekh* with a long white beard and is led from house to house.[8]

The oil that remains from the Hanukka lamps is carefully preserved. It is regarded as a medicine, especially for chidren. Pregnant women anoint their bodies with it in the synagogue, and barren women mix it with the water in which the Kohanim have washed on Yom Kippur and drink it. (Z.)

The ends of the wax candles are also looked upon as possessing curative powers (Z.). Women and girls mix the wax from Hanukka candles with the *qachke*, a sort of chewing gum, in the belief that this will bring them blessing (A.).

The remains of oil, wicks, and so on are collected during the week. At the close of the feast a great bonfire is made of them in the courtyard, and the people dance round about it (S.).

[Some generations ago, there lived in Amadiya a rich Jew whose name was Ḥanukka. On the first day of the feast of Hanukka, one would rise and say to him, *Ḥanukka, mā bōda? Talga mpilē 'lduka*, "Ḥanukka, what are you doing? The snow has fallen in its place." Ḥanukka would answer, *Mā bōda? Bakhla ubshatya ubdamka bakhavod kulūkhun kislēni*, "What I am doing? Eating and drinking and sleeping, with the honor of all of you at my house" (i.e., I am inviting you all to me). In the evening they would all go to dine at his house. In former times it was customary, between Hanukka and Purim, for most of the men to gather after the evening prayer in the house of one of the members of the community and to enjoy themselves until midnight. They would drink arrack; eat *maza* and all kinds of "dry" fruit, such as raisins, walnuts, almonds, peanuts, and so on; and sing religious and secular songs.]

26

15TH SHEVAT

Among the Kurdish Jews 15th Shevat is, in a very peculiar degree, a feast of fertility—from which it is evident that the Jews of Kurdistan were in former times more closely associated with agriculture than at present and placed great emphasis on the practice of fertility customs, like other peasant populations. At all events, they observe customs that—although they may have undergone a partial transformation—certainly originated in magic practices designed to increase the vegetation.

Among the Jews of Sinne 15th Shevat bears a name that points to its origin: Mizdāni Ilāne, Good Tidings for the Trees. The Kurdish term is Dar Awus, Pregnant Tree.[1] In Sulaimani the feast is called Simḥat Ilāne, Joy of the Trees; in Zakho, Ēz Ilāne Tree Feast; [in Amadiya, Edet Ilāne, Tree Feast. In Amadiya it is said that on 15th Shevat, *ilāne gimzarwari ugṭani māye*, "the trees begin the bear water."]

The general Jewish custom of eating as much fruit as possible on this day obtains in Kurdistan also. The people send each other bowls containing thirty different kinds of fruit, and in the streets there is a lively movement of boys and young men delivering these bowls to the houses. The Muslim Kurds also send fruit to the Jews, in the hope that the Jewish benedictions may have a favorable effect on the fruit trees. The Jews say that their benedictions make the trees "pregnant" on this night.

There is no uniformity in the manner of reciting the benedictions over the fruits. Sometimes the master of the house invites a minyan [ten adult males] to his home, and each member of it recites the benediction over a different kind of fruit. There are, however, people who believe that each person must bless all the fruits together at least once a year; and this may be the only opportunity to do so.

In order that everyone may say the benediction over each fruit, it is customary in Suqqis to set the bowl of fruit in a side room and bring one fruit after another into the room where the men are assembled; then all present recite the benediction in unison over each fruit.

For the women, 15th Shevat is, first and foremost, a day for the practice of magic customs connected with fecundity, because the women associate their fate with that of the trees.

If it rains or snows during the night, the women says, *Ilāne tvīla kolī*, "The trees are taking the ritual bath"—that is to say, as the husband cohabits with his wife after the ritual bath and the wife hopes to become pregnant, so, according to their belief, the trees will be fertilized after their "ritual bath."[2]

The women take raisins and candy and strew them around the base of the trees, in the conviction that this will promote the fertility both of the trees and of themselves.

Barren women also seek to become fruitful through the fruitfulness of the trees by attempting to transfer to themselves the pregnancy that the trees acquire on this night. To accomplish this, the women must go to a fruit tree in the darkness, embrace it, and say,

dār auwis tō na auwis
min auwis bō nīta
ai shatā kāsa dīdī zamṭa

Pregnant tree, you shall not become pregnant,
I shall be pregnant in this intention.
This year my body shall be filled. (S.)[3]

In Amadiya the women say as they embrace the tree,

yā ilāna semakhisokh tālī
semakhīsi tālokh
ashataṭ ana samkhan
dak ahit yewit fāke
ana yāwan fēke

O tree, your pregnancy for me,
My pregnancy for you.
This year I shall become pregnant.
As you give fruit,

So shall I give fruit.[4]

The women also take their grown daughters to the trees and give each to one of the trees to wife.[5] After a few weeks, they go to see whether the tree has put forth blossoms; and from this they decide whether or not the daughter will marry within the year (S.).

After the benediction over the fruits, some women, in order to make their hair grow more luxuriantly, have another woman pour water over their heads with the words:

kudakh ana ilāna masqē piqkha
hādak mistakh yā brāti paqkha

As the trees pur forth blossoms
So your hair, daughter, shall flourish. (A.)[6]

The children, too, have a rhyme applying to this night; but its import is somewhat obscure:

wayiqra qorqōra
tabāqa shilānē
rēshokh qaṭenew
bāqa lēle mizdani ilāne

And he spoke *qorqōra(?)*[7]
A sheet of apricots[8]
Your head I cut off
For the night of "good tidings" of the trees. (S.)

[In Amadiya the men gather on 15th Shevat in the courtyard of the Bē Ḥazāne, bringing with them all sorts of dried fruit and bread, and make *zulubiye*, small pancakes. The *ḥakham* preaches a sermon on the text "Then shall all the trees of the wood sing for joy" (Ps. 96:12).]

27

Purim

[As in all other Jewish communities, so among the Kurdish Jews, Purim is primarily the holiday of the children. In keeping with the rough character of the Kurdish Jews, the reading of the *Megilla* (the Scroll of Esther) in their synagogues is turned into a veritable bedlam, with the shooting off of various kinds of guns and pistols, with the explosion-like bursting of bladders of slaughtered animals, and with cries such as "We have crushed Haman's testicles!" Outside the synagogue, too, the holiday is characterized by wild behavior of the children and youths, with beatings, obscene masquerades, fire games, peltings with filth, and the like.]

Customs of Adar

In the month of Adar one should be gay, says the Talmud: "When Adar enters, one multiples gaiety" (B. Ta'anit 29a). Hence, the holiday spirit of Purim begins with the New Moon of Adar. The Jews of Amadiya call this day Iseherit Benātha, Girls' First of the Month. On the morning of this day, the head of the family invites his married daughters with their husbands and children to a dinner at his house.[1]

In Zakho, Rosh Ḥodesh [New Moon of] Adar is called Ghelāqit Tar'e[2] Locking of the Door. When the father returns home after the morning service in the synagogue, he finds the door locked. The children will not open it until he has given them a present, which must be in the form of money. It is put in their hands which they extend through the hole in the lock. In Amadiya, where the custom likewise obtains, the fathers give their daughters a piece of jewelry [*khezemta*], sometimes even a golden ornament. [On this occasion, it is customary to pierce the ears and the nose of the girls.][3]

In Ushnu the custom is practiced on the eve of Purim. Here, too, a locked door confronts the fathers on their return from the reading of the *Megillat Ester* [scroll of Esther, in the synagogue]; and only a gift will gain their right to enter.

The dead are not forgotten in the joys of Adar. Families whom death has visited within the year or in the last few years send *zelōbiye*, a kind of cake containing nuts and dates, to relatives and to the poor, as well as a large portion to the school for the teacher and the pupils, in order that these may say the benediction for their dead (z. and D.). [Together with the *zelōbiye*, they send the teacher five to ten eggs in fat (A).] In Amadiya, where the *zelōbiye* is not distributed until 13th Adar, Yom Ta'anit Ester [Heb., Day of the Fast of Esther], the pupils, on receiving their share from the teacher, say

ilāhā mabikhlū
ilāhā maqrū
wa'adū mijālū

God give them comfort,
God bring near
Their time and their hour.

In Arbil on each day from the first of Adar to Purim a different family, chosen in accordance with a definite scheme, distributes cakes among acquaintances and schoolchildren for "the souls of the dead."

Shabbat of the Girls

Like the first day of Adar, so the first Sabbath of that month, takes its name from the girls, Shabthit Benāthā, Girls' Shabbat, or Zutyāthit Kālo, Bride's Cake (A.; Z. *zūdiath kālo*). The customs peculiar to this Sabbath are substantially the same in Zakho, Dehok, and Amadiya.

The girls form groups, *khūlewāthā* (A.), each with its leader, *istatta*. Beginning with the first of Adar these groups go about soliciting contributions of wood, as is done in parts of Europe (e.g., in Switzerland *Holzheischen*) for the bonfire at Easter or other celebrations. One of their "begging songs" runs thus:

pātike bīnā bīnā
maḥla jūme pīr ḥajūme

ishalla ilāhā yawilōkhun
khā berōnā
halūlan khā ṣīwa.

[Patike (a woman's name), bring, bring,
Mahla (a woman's name) in the weaving pit[4] an old wrapped-up woman
May it please God to give you a son,
Give us a piece of wood.] (A. and Z.)

The following song is addressed to the head of the house:

bēl bēlāwa, bēl bēlāwa
inshalla khōde Avraham biket zāva

[May the house always stand, may the house always stand,]
May it please God, may He make Abraham a bridegroom. (Z. and A.)

A corresponding song is addressed to the housewife:

bēl belūka, bēl belūka[5]
inshalla khōda Gazāle biket būka.

[May the house always stand, may the house always stand]
Please God, may He make Gazale a bridge. (Z., also A.)[6]

If in some house a contribution is refused, the girls proceed to sing lampoons. they also display considerable ingenuity in diverting the attention of the occupants while one of the girls steals some wood. This indulgent attitude toward thieving that is done for ritual purposes is fairly widespread. We find it, for instance, among the Jews of Tripoli, when they gather wood for the Purim fire;[7] and it is by no means unknown in European folklore.[8]

The girls pile up the wood in a house that is put at their disposal. They sell part of it and use the rest for their ritual baths.

The girls of Amadiya take these ritual baths on the Shabthit Benātha and on *lēl Purim*, (Heb., "eve of Purim)"; the girls of Zakho only on *lēl Purim.*

For the Shabthit Benātha in Amadiya the girls get together whatever is needed for baking, and take it to the *istatta* in the courtyard of the house which has been chosen as a meeting place. There they build themselves a new stove and set about baking the *zutyāthit kālo*, the bride's cakes, with the new cooking utensils acquired for the purpose. Old utensils will not do, because some woman may possibly have used them at the time of her impurity. The girls decorate the cakes by making impressions in them with a wedding ring, *esiqsit qadōshe*.

Khiyāpit Kalewātha (The Brides' Bath)

On Friday the water for the bath is heated over a fire made with the wood they have collected. The *istatta* is bathed first. The girls wash her and dress her hair in the numerous plaits that the women of Kurdistan affect. During the process they sing,

ṣoṣiyāsakh yarīkhe khamūsit ister hamalka asya ṭālak
ishalla shō'a brōne hawēlakh ze'ōrit kulo makhelakh

Your braids shall be long. The maidenhood[9] of Queen Esther shall be for you.
God grant that you have seven sons, and may the youngest of them beat you.

At the last word they strike the *istatta* on the back. The other girls then bathe, one after the other; and each one is struck on the back by the *istatta*. After the bath, the girls don their holiday attire and go home. In the evening they assemble again in their house to dance and sing.

Saturday morning the celebration at the house is resumed. The girls all bring fruit, and the *istatta* has it distributed. Then the *istatta* assigns a task to each girl: one is to dance, another to sing, and so on; finally, the girls are sprinkled with rose water to the words of the following verse:

rikhōkhun hāwa maya rēkha
maskirtūlū ṭelibōkhun baya rēkhit kadyawathōkhun

May your fragrance be of this fragrance,
Make your bridegrooms drunk with the fragrance of your breasts.

After this, the girls repair to the fields outside the town and play games (e.g., games like *buselman*) until the time of the afternoon prayer, when they return to their house. There, the *istatta* hands one of the *zutyāthit kālo* to each girl, who wraps it in a silken cloth and takes it home and hides it. But when the girl's friend or fiance arrives shortly after to pay her a visit and asks where the *zā'tit kālo* is, she answers bashfully that she has none. The young man, however, knows better. He hunts until he finds it, whereupon he kisses it and exclaims, "What a beautiful bride!" Then the girl cuts the cake and divides it among her parents, sisters, brothers, and friend. The latter, as he eats his portion, says, *Kuddakh khilāli aya zā'atakh khādakh ilāha awidlakh rizqi*, "As I ate this your cake, so may God make you my lot" (A.; similarly Z.).

Collection of Wood by the Boys

Beginning with the first of Adar the boys and young man also go about collecting wood for their Purim amusements. In Dehok they even store this *pātike delonke*, "Wood of the children," in the synagogue.

The boys of Amadiya roam through the streets, and call out their "Wood for Haman!" in the appropriate language. To the Jews they cry, *Qadit Hāman*!, to the Muslim Kurds, *Dar'ē Hamāni*!, and to the Christians *Ṣīwit Hāman*!

Neither the Muslim Kurds nor the Christians hesitate to give "Haman wood" to the children. Even when (as used to happen) the boys were not content with collecting wood but proceeded to steal chickens, their victims did not resort to harsh measures. "Haman's children (*bichīkit Hamāni*) have done it," they said indulgently.

In Amadiya there was a certain Nestorian family of the Ṭalnāye sect, whom the Jews looked upon as descendants of Haman; for when the children came to their house and called, *Sīwit Hāman*, they answered, *Sīwit Mordekhai* and gave nothing. The children would consequently make a terrific racket in front of the house with their various Purim noisemakers.

[During the two weeks from the first of Adar until Purim, the children used to collect not less than 1 or 2 centners [110–220 pounds] of wood. When they had enough wood, they would sit down with their wood along the street and cry "We have wood!" Then the people would come and buy wood from them and give them a good price. With the money the children got for the wood they would buy beer or chickens or a lamb for their Purim meal. (A.)]

The Girls' Second Bath

The second bath that the girls prepare with the wood they have collected takes place on *lēl purim* [Heb. Purim eve]. As a result of this additional bath, the maidens, it is said, become as fair at Purim as Esther when she appeared before King Ahasuerus. Hence, this bath is called *khiyāpit benātha, āse ilēnī shiprit Ister*, "Bath of the maidens, may the beauty of Esther come to us."

For this bath the girls assemble, as before, in their meeting place (which is always, for obvious reasons, the house of a rich man); but this time, their mothers accompany them. Henna is prepared. The prettiest of the girls pours the water over it before the kneading, and the company sings *Dē mesūlū*, "Come now, bring." Then each girl is dyed with henna (A.).

After the dyeing, the mothers bathe their daughters, singing *narīke* as over a bride, and pelt them with roses and nuts. Thus, all the girls are bathed in turn in a prearranged sequence (A. and Z.).

Purim or Megalla

The Kurdish Jews seldom use the name Purim for this feast. Their most usual designation is Megilla or Megalla or Mo'ed Megilla [feast of the Scroll] (Z., D., and A.). Then, too, there is the expression Feast of Haman, Jiznā Haman (Ushnu and Sulaimani); the Kurds consequently refer to the Jewish feast as 'Ida Hamāni (A.). In the south (Sulaimani) and in the Persian district (S.), Purim is called Lelangē.[10]

We have discussed the preparations made in the weeks preceding Purim. On the last day before the feast itself, Ta'anit Ester, the Fast of Esther, is everywhere observed. Boys and girls of seven or more take it upon themselves to fast—not, to be sure, without an eye to a reward in the shape of a finer Purim gift.

Part of the Purim preparations consists in the baking of different kinds of cakes, *zelōbiye* (Z., D., and A.) being the most popular. The *nāḥale deHāman*, "ears of Haman," are favorites in Ushnu, while in Sulaimani cookies of various shapes (e.g., *kalda*, "bride," *khīwā*, "snake," etc.) are preferred.

Reading of the Megilla

In the evening everyone, young and old, men and women, come to the synagogue for the reading of the *megilla*. Even infants in arms are brought along for the express purpose of listening to the reading. The women sit in the courtyard.

The young people are full of the holiday spirit. The girls are decked out like Esther when she was summoned to the presence of Ahasuerus. In Amadiya the young folk sing as they go to the synagogue—marriage songs, for the most part, such as the Kurdish song *Harē khezeme jarē khezeme ta bachin blinde*, "You(?) Khezeme, poor Khezeme, you of the tall figure" (A.).

Everyone who can read owns a *megilla* written on parchment. In Amadiya the *meqilloth* were written by the scribe Ḥayyim b. Ya'qov Hagabbai and cost 10 rupees (13 shillings) apiece. The Kurdish *megilla* is entirely devoid of ornament.

For the reading of the *megilla*, as for Yom Kippur eve, the *shammash* in Zakho makes a large, thick wax candle with seven wicks, *sham'it megalla*. This candle is extinguished as soon as the reading is over and is used throughout the year (till Rosh Hashana) as the light for the reading of the Torah. The honor of holding the *sham'e* during the reading of the *megilla* is sold by auction and brings a substantial price (about £4); but the purchaser retains the right of holding it when it is used during the rest of the year. In addition to the *sham'it megalla*, the *shammash* makes about a hundred smaller candles for distribution among the people. Every group that has a *megilla* gets a candle, and it is given to one of the children to hold.

In Amadiya, the *shammash* makes a *misrāja*, a large wax candle surrounded by smaller candles—which is just like the *sham'it khitna*, the bridegroom's candle (see p. 129), except that the small candles are not colored. The privilege of holding it is put up to auction here, also. The *shammash* further makes a number of small candles for the possessors of *megilloth* and seven additional candles that represent the seven pillars of the world and are placed on the *sīde*, reading desk, in the sockets made for the purpose.

In some places, the honor of reading the scroll is sold by auction (Z. and D.). In Amadiya, it is always bestowed on the *ḥazan*. If the successful bidder in the other towns cannot read, he, too, surrenders his privilege to the *ḥazan*. The latter reads the *megilla* aloud, the congregation reading with him—but softly, except for certain passages that all must read aloud.

Before the reading of the *megilla*, a special *pizmon* by Yefet Benaya is sung, whose first stanza goes

[Give song and chant, O chosen people,
  To God supernal and read the *megilla*.
Friends, praise him who performs great deeds,
  Who is found to be much help in troubles,
And saved his servants from evil decrees
  In every generation—I cannot count them.
And the root of the son of Agag he totally destroyed
  And changed his plan to a joy for me.[11]

In Kurdistan not only the *ḥazan* (as is the general custom) but also the owners of individual *megilloth* unroll the entire scroll before the reading.[12] The passages read aloud by the congregation, in addition to the usual ones (i.e., Esther 2:4–5, 8:15–16, and 10:3) are verses 6:1 and 7:6. The congregation reads these verses first, and the *ḥazan* repeats them. In Zakho the congregation reads aloud from 9:30 to the end, 10:3 being repeated three times. In Amadiya, the congregation reads aloud the whole of chapter 10. [On the eve of Purim, the *megilla* is read in the original Hebrew; next morning, however, it is read only in Targum; that is, the *ḥazan* follows the Hebrew text with his eyes but pronounces the Targum translation. (A.)]

At verse 2:16, "So Esther was taken unto King Ahasuerus," the girls pass both their hands over their faces (A.). At verse 3:5, "Haman was full of wrath," the congregation in Zakho says, *Khümā tāle tā yime*, "Heat for him and his mother." At verse 9:26, the *ḥazan* raises the *megilla* and shakes it.

Popular Customs at the Reading

Among the Kurdish Jews, as in all Jewish communities, the public reading of the *megilla* is the occasion for special outbursts of joy. The people bring to the synagogue all sorts of appliances for creating a din; and whenever the name of Haman or his sons is mentioned, these are used to the full. At the mention of Haman's name in the evening prayer, the people make such a deafening noise by clapping their hands that order can scarcely by restored.

The boys and young men have various kinds of pistols (Z. and A. *debancha* S. *tapancha*), with percussion caps that they either make themselves in a primitive way or (more recently) buy in the marketplace. Formerly, the young men in Sulaimani borrowed guns from the Kurds.

There are also different sorts of detonating balls[13] that can be bought in the marketplace. In Sinne, the people bring small hammers to the synagogue; and at the mention of Haman's name, they bang on the floor.

The Kurdish Jews also have rattles (A. *rashrashinqa*, Arbil *rashraje*), which are made by the carpenters; but in Amadiya these have leather tongues, instead of [the usual] wooden ones.

The effect of all these devices is supplemented by stamping on the floor at the mention of Haman or his sons—with a special fervor if the names of those archenemies of the Jews have previously been written on the floor with charcoal and are blotted out by stamping on them (A., Arbil, and Sulaimani).

Similar to this is the custom of writing the names of Haman and Amaleq on two stones and knocking them together (S.). This resembles the practice of the men of Amadiya at their Purim drinking parties. They take two pieces of wood, on which they write in Hebrew, "Accursed be evil Haman" and "Accursed be evil Zeresh." Then they pour arrack over them and blot out the names, saying in Hebrew as they do so, "Give strong drink unto him that is ready to perish" (Prov. 31:6).

The most characteristic noisemakers of the Kurdish Jews are the *bambāle*, "bladders."[14] At Sukkot everyone begins to collect the bladders of slaughtered animals. These are blown up and suspended from the ceiling. At Purim the family take to the synagogue as many as they can carry and distribute any surplus among less fortunate friends. In Zakho, several hundred of these *bumbāle* are brought into the synagogue. When the *ḥazan* reaches the last word of Esther (9:6, "five hundred men," everyone explodes his *bumbāle*. [In Amadiya the children explode their *bambāle* when the words "Haman was filled with wrath" (Esther 5:9) are read and again at the words "Nevertheless Haman refrained himself" (5:10) and "Vaizatha" (9:9).] The result is not unlike the thunder of guns on a battlefield. The children add their bit by firing off their pistols and crying, *Peqe'īlan ishkāsit Hāman*, "We have crushed Haman's testicles!" In Amadiya this sentence is said at the close of the *megilla*. This continues about a quarter of an hour; and when the last *bumbāle* is burst, the *ḥazan* proceeds to restore order by banging on the *sīde*. Then the reading of the *megilla* is resumed. Finally, the customary curses and blessings are recited.

In Sinne (also A.) the following song is sung at the end [in Hebrew]:

[Those confident in my hopes,
and all the seed of my blessed ones,
Say, all of you, "Blessed, blessed, blessed is Mordecai."

In the snare that he [Haman] prepared
In it he himself got caught,
Say, all of you, "Cursed, cursed, cursed is Haman."

Great pride had he who dwelt in secret [Mordecai,]
He brought up Hadassah [Esther] with a crown,
Say, all of you, "Blessed, blessed, blessed is Esther."

They spoke in stealth,
The branch and root of Agagi [Haman],

Say, all of you, "Cursed, cursed, cursed is Zeresh." (translated from Heb. by R.P.)]

After the reading of the *megilla*, the boys read *hashkavat Haman* ['the laying to rest of Haman'], a parody on the *hashkavat hameth* ['the laying to rest of the deceased']. The grown-ups generally read this parody at the Purim dinner. There are several versions of it, one of which, from Dehok, has been published by Joseph J. Rivlin.[15]

As soon as they return from the synagogue, the people sit down to the Purim dinner, thus ending the fast. This dinner is a sumptuous affair. Even the poor permit themselves the luxury of two chickens for the Purim feast (Z.). There are, however, no dishes or delicacies special to Purim.

If the head of the family, through illness or some other cause, cannot attend the reading of the *megilla* at the synagogue, he invites a *ḥakham* to his home to read it for him.

After the dinner, the master of the house reads the *megilla* to the women of the family in Targum. In Zakho, the women of several families assemble in one house and hear the *megilla* read both in Hebrew and in Targum. In other places, it is usually read to the women in the evening in Hebrew and in the morning in Targum. In Sinne it is read in Hebrew before the dinner and in Targum after the dinner.

Evening Games and Amusements of the Young

The evenings and nights are given over to merriment. We have already described the "bathing of the maidens" on Purim eve. The grown-ups gather on this night (or on the two Purim nights) at the home of an especially respected relative; bring their arrack along; and sing, dance, and joke till past midnight. They also play games; but this form of Purim entertainment is not as popular among the adults in Kurdistan as in Eastern Europe, for instance. The Kurdish Jews content themselves with cards, dice, or knucklebones is called *chige Haman*, "Haman's knee joint."[16]

The Jewish children of Amadiya also play the *esiqsa* [ring] game. [The children divided themselves into two teams, which sat down opposite one another. A big copper bowl was brought, and two upturned copper cups were placed upon it. Under one of the cups a ring was hidden. One of the children then lifted up one of the cups, and if he found the ring under it, his team began the game, that is, hid the ring for the first time. Now they placed seven upturned copper cups on the bowl, and the team beginning the game hid the ring under one of the cups. Actually, only one child of each of the two teams took an active part in the game, the others being mere spectators. The child representing the opposite team now had to lift up the cups in turn, first guessing whether or not the ring was there. Before he lifts up the cup, he can say *puch*, "nothing," or *dastgul*, "hand to the flower" (meaning the ring). If he said *puch* and the ring was nevertheless found under the cup he raised, he lost seven points, and it was now the turn of the opposite party to try its luck. If he said *puch* and the ring was not found under the cup, he was allowed to lift up another cup. If, at this second time, he again said *puch* and the ring was found under the cup, he lost six points, for now only six cups remained on the bowl; and so forth. If he said *dastgul* and the rig was found under the cup which he raised, he gained seven points; if he said *dastgul* and the ring was not found under the cup, he lost seven points. If he said *dastgul* when there were only six or five cups on the bowl, and the ring was found under the cup, he gained six or five points; if not, he lost the same number of points. If he said each time *puch*, *puch*, and the ring was not found under the cups, until only two cups were left on the bowl, he gained all the seven points, that is he gained the whole bowl, and was entitled to hide the ring a second time. When the loss of any team reached a hundred, the game was brought to a close, and the losing team had to pay its opponent four or five bottles of arrack. In this manner the children generally lost all the money they got as the price of the wood (see p. 348), and on the day of Purim they would go to their fathers and ask for some money. They also would go to the houses of the rich and steal from the food prepared for the poor. When they were well provisioned in this way, they arranged a *serāne* (excursion) to the river. This going to the river took place on Shushan Purim, the day following Purim.

On the eve of Purim the children also would sew the clothes of those among them who fell asleep to the four corners of the rugs on which they lay (compare the similar custom practiced on 9th Av).]

The real Purim merrymakers are the young people. Purim is in the true sense of the word their holiday; and in Kurdistan, as elsewhere, we see in this fact the kinship between Purim and the customs practiced in Europe at Shrovetide.

While people are still at their dinner, the children, especially the children of the poor, go through the streets, climb up to the roof of a house and drop a string through the chimney into the room. In Amadiya a *bambāla* is tied to the end of the string. A gift of some sort (money, cakes, candy, or the like) is tied to the string or laid in the *bambāla*. [If, however, the landlord wishes to play a trick on the children, he will put a piece of burning coal into the *bambala*. (A.)] The youngsters on the roof also sing "begging songs." The following begging song from Amadiya resembles the one sung during the wood "campaign" in Zakho (see p. 346):

bēl belāwa bēl belāwa
kha mindi bēya kāwa
'azo odakhlē zāva
mal yāva

[May the house always stand, may the house always stand
A thing in the window,
Azo (a man's name), let's make him a bridegroom,
May the house always stand.]

For a girl they may sing,

bēl belōke bēl belōke
kha mindi bēya bezōke
istēr odakhla bōke
mal yavōke

[May the house always stand, may the house always stand,
A thing in this hole,
Esther, let's make her a bride,
May the house always stand.]

In Sinne the children sing the following Kurdish song:

hatātē matāte
kurru kanishtan nimrāte
lēila jenē birsīya
hawar akah qlujah nīyah

[*Hatātē matāte*
Sons and daughter will not die
The demon's mother is hungry
She cries "There is no cake."]

We have told how the young men, as well as the girls, collect wood for Purim. They, too, sell part of it; and with the proceeds they purchase chickens, arrack, and other supplies. The young men and the boys also form *khūlewātha*, "associations," like the girls, and choose a meeting place where they assemble on the eve and the day of the feast to eat, drink, dance, and sing. The games that add such hilarity to their weddings (e.g., "selling the skin") are played here, too.

Masquerades

The most popular of the Purim masquerades is that called *lebōke*. For this an exceptionally fat youth is chosen. He is padded out and dressed up like a pregnant woman[17] with enormous bust and abdomen. His face is painted; and he is further adorned with a beard, a mustache, a pair of horns made of felt, and a cowbell around his neck. Thus, he is led through the streets by a rope, while his "escort" sing boisterous songs.[18]

When the *lebōke* stops before a house, he is asked, "Where do you come from?" He answers, "From Babel:"

hā lebōke, tā chī īnā?
min Haman īnā
bō chi īnā?
dā ritlētwi[19] *paqīnin*

Leboke, what have you brought?
I brought Haman.
Why did you bring him?
To crush his testicles. (A. and Kurd.)

The children dance about the *lebōke* and call *Haman harasha*ʻ [evil Haman]. In each house he is given meat, eggs, raisins, and also some money; but instead of being pelted with nuts like a bride, he is pelted with pebbles and doused with water (A.).

The Jews of Sinne have a similar masquerade. They dress up a youth like a Muslim *shekh*, with a long beard, a huge stomach, a sash wound many times around his middle, and an immense turban. But he does not venture into the streets in this getup. It is an indoor masquerade only.

The Jews of Sinne have another grotesque figure, however, which they lead through the streets at Purim, with a band, to collect money. This figure, like the *lebōke* of Amadiya, is provided with horns. The Jews say that it was taken over from the Muslims, who used masks, *kala dīyū* (demon's head) at their *nauruz* (New Year's celebration), which almost coincides with the Purim feast. The *nauruz* masqueraders stick a long pole in their belts, then a boy climbs up the pole and performs acrobatics at the top. The Jews either borrow the horned masks from the Muslims or make some of their own out of paper. Then they go through the streets with music playing and collect money.

Fire Games

Among the games played by the young people at night or by day are also fire rites similar to those that obtain in Europe in great number during Shrovetide. Such fire rites are found likewise among the Jews of Yemen.[20]

Some time before Purim the youth associations in Zakho begin digging out tree roots (*qormüksa*). They lay in a goodly store, and on Purim eve they burn them in a fire until they are red hot. These roots, which are as round as balls, are called *rēsh Haman*, "head of Haman." The boys take the glowing *qormüksa* to the river, where they drive them to each other with sticks resembling hockey clubs, indulging in loud and picturesque cursing of Haman as the sparks fly from the burning balls under their blows. They also write the names of Haman and Amalek on pieces of paper and burn them on the glowing wood. The game is kept up until nothing is left of the *rēsh Haman*,. then they exclaim, *Halāṣ—mepishpishle rēsh Haman*, "Finished—Haman's head is dashed to pieces."

In Amadiya similar chunks of wood, *reshit Haman* [Haman's head] are beaten until they are soft and fibrous, then set on fire. The boys form two teams which throw the burning balls to each other with calls of *Lo-lo-lo-lop-lopke.*

The boys use ordinary balls (*tape*) in much the same way. They write *Haman harasha'* on the ball and strike it with a bat. Whoever catches the ball becomes the batter (A.). Even the *ḥakhamim* play this game for half an hour or an hour on Purim eve (A.). The Muslims, too, are lured to the river by the fire games; but there are no women or girls among the spectators, because they might not be altogether safe there on this night of freedom.

Burning of the Haman Effigy

The Haman effigies are usually burned on Purim eve; but there is no uniformity in this respect throughout Kurdistan, for some localities stage several of these spectacles during the Purim festivities. The custom is now for the most part purely an amusement of the young people, because the mythological background has been crowded out by the burlesque element. In Arbil a large wooden cross is wound around with rags so that it resembles a life-sized human figure. This figure is dressed in old clothes, with a *masbaḥ*, a cap worn by the Christians, on its head. In its mouth is thrust a pipe filled with dung, and on its neck is hung a chain made of the excrement of an ass. The effigy is doused with petroleum and set afire. When it is completely burnt, the crowd throws stones on the remains. This represents a stoning and a burial together.

In Ushnu the children of every Jewish neighborhood prepare two or three Haman effigies of wood and rags. These are burnt in the evening before the reading of the *megilla* and on Purim morning after the service. During the buring, the children sing verses in which they insert the names of various families:

Haman zilē bēl khanāna
mindēlū elew gā adabkhāna[21]

Haman went to the family Hanan,
They threw him into the latrine.

or

Haman zilē bēl 'azīza
belew teqīr benūra
min īla hulā'i lefarkekh be'ai shūla

Haman went to the family Azizah,
His house was burnt with fire.
From the hands of the Jews you will not save yourself in this affair.

or

Haman zilē bēl mezala
hiwlū ba'īlew mesāla

Haman went to the family Mezala,
They put a scale(?) in his hand.

In Sulaimani the girls set about making a Haman and a Zeresh figure out of wood and rags a week before Purim. The faces are painted with charcoal. Haman gets a beard, Zeresh a grotesque necklace. The girls of every courtyard prepare these effigies, so that the burning ceremony staged by the girls alone is performed in about twenty places throughout the town. The burning of Haman (*maqlīle Haman*) comes on the first night, that of Zeresh (*maqlīle Zeresh*) on the second. Even the Muslim Kurds take part. The figures are stuck into the ground, soaked with petroleum, and set afire, while the girls sing songs similar to those sung in Ushnu.

In Sinne, also, the children of each district prepare Haman and Zeresh effigies, Haman being adorned with chains of goat's dung by way of necklace and rosary. The verses sung are of the same type as those of Ushnu and Sulaimani, for example,

Haman zilē bē yōkhē
metūlo kame telōkhē

Haman went to the house of Jochebed,
They set lentils before him.

In Amadiya the girls make figures intended to represent Vashti and Zeresh. That of Vashti has a tail—hence the (general) term of obloquy used by the women, *Vashti marē dūma*, "Vashti with the tail." Some of the girls' associations burn the effigies during the preparations for the bath on *lēl Purim*, others the next day before the meal.

In Amadiya, as in the other towns, the figure of Haman consists of a wooden frame wrapped in rags and dressed in women's clothes but provided with a beard, thus representing a hermaphroditic being here also. The burning of Haman (*makōdit Haman*) takes place on the morning of 14th Adar, on the excursion grounds. Muslim Kurds, including notables, are among the spectators. The *kaimakam* asks "What have you done with Haman? Have you burned him?" This is the signal for the burning.

Before the figure is set afire the children pelt it with filth and thrust into its mouth a lighted pipe filled with dung. The women bring their children's urine and pour it over Haman, saying, *Shekulokh māyit warde mārikhlū*, "Take your rose water, smell it."

The wood that the boys have gathered is heaped about Haman, and he is burned at the stake while the women and girls sing the song *Miltāsha* to the accompaniment of tambourines (*tambelushka*) made of old pots with a piece of leather stretched over the rim, which are gripped under one arm. The children scatter Haman's ashes to the winds or throw them into the water.

14th Adar

With the burning of Haman's effigy in Amadiya, we have reached 14th Adar, the actual day of Purim; and we must return to the customs practiced on the morning of that day.

The young people have spent half the night at their sports and games, and the adults, as well, have been up until the small hours; but morning finds them all in the synagogue once more, and the scenes we have described in connection with the reading of the *megilla* are repeated.

In Zakho the various groups of girls again assemble on this morning in the house where they had gathered for their ritual baths. They bring along rice and cook the chickens purchased with the proceeds of the sale of part of their wood. Then all the groups go on a *serāne*, and the young men join them at the excursion grounds after the service.

Toward midday, the groups return to their respective houses. If any group happens to have among its members a wealthy girl whose home serves as the meeting place, her father generally provides an assistant to prepare the chickens and rice for the group. The girls sit down on the veranda (*birbanke*) to eat their meal. But in the meantime, the young men have returned from their excursion, and climbed up to the roof of the house. They start teasing the girls, who retort, and a lively badinage follows. The girls, each of whom is afraid of getting a reputation for gluttony, pretend to be bashful and refuse to eat before the boys. Time and again, the father drives the intruders away, but in vain—no sooner has he disappeared than they are back and at it again. Finally, the girls primly takes a few bites of the food, wrap the rest in a cloth, and go home. Each young man thereupon hurries after the girl of his choice, escorts her home, and eats the Purim meal with her—a thing unheard of at any other time.

Purim Presents

After the service comes the hour of the Purim presents. In some places (Z. and Ushnu) the poor stand in front of the synagogue and receive a coin from each member of the congregation as he comes out. In Sinne, the poor go about in the synagogue after the reading of the Torah and make a collection, while their children stand at the entrance and receive alms from the people as they leave.

The traditional Purim gift consists of a dish of food. In Zakho everyone must send such a dish to two of his friends. Besides this, it is customary to remember the children of one's relatives with a gift of money. The children themselves receive only a few pennies out of this money, for it is actually intended to be spent on new clothes provided for them at Passover. These gifts are, in fact, a formality or, at most, a friendly gesture, since everyone gets back in gifts as much as he gives.

The *shedōrit keleyāthā*, "sending of gifts," in Amadiya consists in sending a plate of meat and dried fruits to one' acquaintances. They also send *sanbūsak*, a dish prepared only for the *shedōrit keleyāthā*. The ingredients are *ḥurtumāne*, "peas," ground in a handmill, meat that has been pounded in a mortar, and about twenty eggs. These are mixed, seasoned with pepper and other spices, and baked in tail fat.

In the case of close friends, a piece of jewelry, such as a pair of gold earrings, may be included with the *sanbūsak* for the daughter of the family—or a ring for the son.

In Sinne and in Sulaimai, the sending of Purim gifts is termed *lelangāna*. Here it is customary for relatives to send to each other a bowl of fruit, cakes, and chocolate. The children get colored eggs. For each schoolboy, moreover, the teacher prepares a sheet of paper on which he has written both in Hebrew and in Targum in ornamental characters, the benedictions that are recited before and after the reading of the *megilla* and the *pizmon Tenū shīra wezimra*, which is sung before the reading of the *megilla*.[22] In Amadiya, also, such ornamental sheets are presented to the schoolboys.

After the morning service, the people sit down to the *se'ūdat Purim*. Except for *sanbūsak*, which is prepared also in Sulaimani (where it is called *sumbuske*), there are no special Purim dishes; but the feast is made as sumptuous as possible. Drinks are plentiful; and the men, in obedience to the talmudic injunction, drink to excess—not an unusual occurrence, to be sure, among the Kurdish Jews, who are quite partial to arrack. The name of Haman is written on a piece of paper and the paper pasted on the bottle. Then the name is blotted out with wine or arrack (Z.). Moshe b. Yiṣḥaq Baglugnaya's Purim song gives us a picture of what goes on at a Kurdish Purim celebration:

[Let us come and drink important wine,
and also without the wrath of a viper,
But with happiness we shall return to the heart,
To rejoice in the joy of Purim.
Let the faithful friends sit
Each one with bottles in his hands,
With fat cocks,
To rejoice in the joy of Purim.
Send gifts to the man of destitution
Then drink sweet things
Empty your glass with joy
To rejoice in the joy of Purim.
Be ready for the meal
With harp and violin and dance
For the sake of mitzva rejoice, trembling
To rejoice in the joy of Purim.

From morning to evening hurry,
Return, and a second and a third time
And tear the beard of Haman,
  To rejoice in the joy of Purim.][23]

The young people of Amadiya go on the excursion in the morning and prepare their Purim meal on the excursion grounds. The *ḥaverim*, however, eat their Purim feast in the Bē Hazāne, then proceed to the excursion grounds to witness the buring of the Haman effigy as described earlier. The people sing and dance; and toward evening the girls, moving in rhythmic step, bring out the *zelōbiye*. *Minḥa* is said at the river, and the evening prayer at the city gate.

In Arbil, Betanura, and Sinne the *megilla* is read both on the eve and on the morning of 15th Adar, because these are believed to have been walled towns even in the time of Joshua.

28

Shabbat Beshallaḥ and Shabbat Naḥamu

Among the special Sabbaths observed by the Jews in Kurdistan is the Shabbat Beshallaḥ (Exod. 13:17), usually called by them Shabsit Shīra, "Sabbath of the Song (of Moses)." It is the end of winter—hence the peasant saying, *Shabsit beshalakhīla süswa beshalikhla shilukhte*, "Shabbath Beshallaḥ: winter is shedding its skin" (Z.).

In Zakho this is in particular the Sabbath of the *mijlis*—the representative of the Jews—who is usually also the wealthiest man in the place. On this Sabbath he gives a great banquet for which he has long since begun his preparations because he must provide great quantities of arrack and *mazat shira*. For the *maza* he needs principally chickens and fish. There is therefore a tacit understanding among the Jews to refrain from buying chickens at this time lest the *mijlis*, who must buy about fifty chickens, be forced to pay a prohibitive price. Furthermore, when the fishermen bring fish to Zakho for this Sabbath, they are exempted from paying the usual import tax; for they say, "We are bringing fish for the *mijlis* of the Jews."

On the Shabbat Beshallaḥ the *mijlis* is called up as "forth." In Amadiya, where this *'aliya* is likewise bestowed on the richest and most important man in the congregation, the reading is done by the notable himself; but in Zakho the *mijlis* merely pronounces the benediction. Everyone stands up, and some of the men imitate the *klīlī* of the women. It was formerly the custom in Amadiya for the women to bring timbrels to the synagogue and, on hearing the verse "And Miriam the prophetess, the sister of Aaron, took a timbrel in her hand; and all the women went out after her with timbrels and with dances" (Exod. 15:20), to strike their timbrels, raise their *klīlīlī*, and pelt the *merē shīra*, "master of the song," with sweets.

After the service the people go home to eat *mebōsa*, which on the Shabbat Shīra consists everywhere of *harīsa*, a porridge made of ground wheat (*girse*). The use of wheat porridge is explained as having its basis in the Hebrew phrase *B'shabbat shīra' leḥem ḥiṭṭa*, "On the Shabbat Shīra bread of wheat" (S.), [whose initials spell *BS*h*LḤ*, which stands for Beshallaḥ]. As an "offering to Pharaoh," a chicken (*fūrūch*)[1] is laid on the *harīsa*; and the custom is explained, *W'nahagu Yisraēl, Hashēm yishm'rēm, b'shabbat shīra l'vashel ḥiṭṭim parug rokhēv 'al harīsa*, "And it was the custom of israel, the Lord preserve them, to cook wheat chicken on Shabbat Shīra, riding on *harīsa*," [whose initials spell *WYHY BS*h*LḤ PR'H*, which stands for *Way'hi b'shallaḥ Par'oh*, "And it came to pass, when Pharaoh had let go . . . (Exod. 13:17)].

Then the people go to the house of the *merē shīra*, where they sing and dance and are liberally served with *maza*, arrack, and *harīsa*.[2] On this occasion, also, the families of the sick send for some *mebōsa* to the home of the *merē shīra*, since it is credited with special healing powers.

The *merē shīra* sends gifts on the Shabbat Beshallaḥ to the *shekh khayāpe*, the *shekh khapāre* (see above p. 193) and the *shammash*.

Rekan had a special custom. On this day there was a performance representing the drowning of Pharaoh and his men. My informant saw this "puppet show" performed in Rekan by a man named Ezra. The people came to him and said, "Ezra, let Pharaoh ride." Ezra had a large dish of water; and over this, he and his wife held a cord on which several figures were strung. While Ezra sang a song, the figures were made to slide back and forth, and were finally dropped into the water. In this performance we detect the influence of the obscene play of *Ashuraga*, with which certain Kurds travel through Iraq and Syria and in which the figures of a man and a woman are strung on a cord.

The Sabbath following the Ninth of Av, [generally] called Shabbat Naḥamu, "Sabbath of Consolation," from the opening words of the portion of the Prophets, also bears the name Shabsit Yakulta, "Great Sabbath," in Kurdistan.

An especially good meal is prepared for this Sabbath, the *mebōse* being made of carefully chosen chickens. Some of the *mebōse* is sent to the poor and to the sick.

At the close of the Ninth of Av, new clothes, to be worn on the Shabbat Naḥamu, are cut out, especially for the children. Everyone must have at least one new garment. If the people of Tchalla are asked why they have new clothes made for this Sabbath, they reply, "Because we are descended from the snow slide (*ranīya*)." The *ranīya* is called the *ranīya* of *nevuzar-addan*.

The privilege of reading the *hafṭara* is sold by auction and brings a high price.

The Shabbat Naḥamu is regarded as a beneficent time for betrothals *qiddushim*, a fact that may have some connection with its being the girls' Shabbat.

On the morning of the Shabbat Naḥamu the girls, festively arrayed in their new clothes, assemble in a courtyard and dance there until the men have finished the service. Then they proceed to the synagogue, often even with the musicians, in order to meet the bridegroom and escort him home (A. and Z.).

Next day comes the *serāne naḥamu*, which is mainly a *serāne* of the young people. Youths and maidens repair to a give place outside the town and dance and sing. The schoolboys also go on a *serāne* with their teacher (see p. 247), and the *gevirim* are invited to accompany them (A.).

NOTES

Preface

1. Cf. Erich Brauer, *Y'hudē Kurdistan: Meḥqar Etnologī*, ed. and trans. Raphael Patai, Studies in Folklore and Ethnology, vol. 2 (Jerusalem, 1947).

2. Abraham Ben-Ya'agov, *Q'hillot Y'hudē Kurdistan* [Communities of the Jews of Kurdistan], (1961; reprint, Jerusalem, 1981).

3. Joseph J. Rivlin, *Shīrat Y'hudē haTargum* [Poetry of the Targum Jews] (Jerusalem, 1959).

4. Edith Gerson-Kiwi, "The Music of the Jews of Kurdistan," *Yuval* 2(1972): 59–72.

5. Irene Garbell, *The Jewish neo-Aramaic Dialect of Persian Azerbaijan: Linguistic Analysis and Folkloristic Texts* (The Hague, 1965).

6. Yona Sabar, *The Folk Literature of the Kurdistani Jews: An Anthology*, (New Haven, 1982).

7. Yitzḥaq Ben-Zevi, *The Exiled and the Redeemed* (Philadelphia, 1961); Raphael Patai, *Israel Between East and West: A Study in Human Relations* (Philadelphia, 1953), s.v. "Kurdish Jews" (index).

8. *Encyclopaedia Judaica* (Jerusalem, 1972), 10:1296.

9. *Encyclopaedia Judaica* 8:1449.

10. Raphael Patai, *The Seed of Abraham: Jews and Arabs in Contact and Conflict* (Salt Lake City, 1986), pp. 131–37.

11. Cf. Rivlin, *Shīrat*. Cf. also Abraham Ben-Ya'aqov, *Shīrah uFiyyuṭ shel Y'hude Bavel baDorot haAḥaronim* (Jerusalem, 1970).

12. Cf. Edith Gerson-Kiwi, in *Studia Musicologica* 7 (1965): 61–70.

13. Idem, "Kurdistan," *EJ* 10:1299–1300.

14. We know, e.g., from Kurdish amulets published in T. Schrire's *Hebrew Amulets* (London, 1966) that the Kurdish Jews believed in Lilith, Satan, and a large number of angels.

Preface to the Hebrew Edition

1. As to the special problems in Jewish ethnology, see my "Problems and Tasks of Jewish Folklore and Ethnology," *Journal of American Folklore* 59, no. 231 (Jan.–March 1946):25–39.

2. My translation from the German.

3. Cf. Clyde Cluckhohn, "Some Reflections on the Method and Theory of the Kulturkreislehre," *American Anthropologist* 38 (1936) 157–196 and W. Schmidt's appraisal of Cluckhohn in his *Culture Historical Method of Ethnology*, trans. S. A. Sieber, (New York, 1939), pp. 63–69.

Chapter 1

1. Carl Ritter, *Die Erdkunde von Asien*, vol. 9 (Berlin, 1840), p. 8.

2. The older material on Kurdistan is collected in C. Ritter's *Die Erdkunde von Asien*, vols. 9–11 (Berlin, 1840–1844). For bibliography see *EI*, s.v. "Kurdistan"; E. Banse, *Die Türkei*, 3rd ed. (Braunschweig, 1919), pp. 417–21.

3. *Sefer Massa'ot shel Rabbi Binyamin*: *The Itinerary of Benjamin of Tudela*, ed. M. N. Adler (London, 1907). Quotations are from this edition. In connection with the travels of Benjamin, we must not forget that from the seventh century on, Nestorian missionaries penetrated as far as China. At all events, Asia was not as unknown as the Europeans supposed.

4. In connection with the question of Benjamin's itinerary, see the introductions and notes to the editions cited; also Paul Borchardt's "Der Reiseweg des Rabbi Benjamin von Tudela und des Rabbi Petachia aus Regensburg in Mesopotamien und Persien. Ein Versuch," *Jahrbuch der jüdisch-literarischen Gesellschaft* 1924:137–62. See also *EJ*, s.v. "Benjamin von Tudela," (by Borchardt).

5. All the mss. give the population as 25,000 (p. 77). Yet it is curious that Joseph ibn Virga in his *Shevet Yehuda* and Joseph Kohen in *'Emeq haBakha* mention only 1,000 families.

6. *Sibbuv ha-Rabbi Petaḥya* (many editions). Quotations are from *Travels of Rabbi Petachia of Ratisbon*, ed. and trans. A. Benisch (London, 1856).

7. Jacob Obermeyer gives 1173 as the date of Petaḥya's sojourn in Nisebin (*Die Landschaft Babylonien*, Frankfurt a.M. 1929, p. 130).

8. Obermeyer writes that Petaḥya ["came through the then important town of Hisn–Kaifa (this is the proper form of the name, today a miserable village, called Ḥasan Kõf), on the banks of the Tigris, above Diarbekir, that is from the north, to Nesibin" (trans. from Germ. by R.P.)].

9. *Iudae Harizi Macamae*, ed. Paul de Lagarde (Göttingen, 1883). See also K. Albrecht, *Die im Tahkemoni Vorkommenden Augaben über Harizis Leben, Studien, und Reisen* (Göttingen, 1890).

10. Of the *Book of Instructions* only fragments have thus far been published; see Abraham Ya'ari, *Sh'līḥīm meEretz Yisrael L'Aseret haShevatim*, Jerusalem, 1940, p. 6, n. 1. Mss. are in Sassoon Collection, no. 995, Hebrew national Library, Jerusalem (Ms. Heb. 8 637) and Schocken Collection, no. 13207. For a detailed analysis of the book see David Solomon Sassoon, *Ohel Dawid*, London, 1932, pp. 1021ff.

11. The communities in Kurdistan had the following funds (*quppot*), which were administered by special *gabbaim*: Quppa of R. Meir Ba'al ha-Nes (The Miracle Worker) in Tiberias, Quppa of R. Shimon b. Johai in Safed, Quppat 'Avodat ha-'Olam; and Quppat Raḥel Immenu.

12. Jacob Mann, *Texts and Studies in Jewish History and Literature* (Cincinnati, 1931), vol. 1, p. 537.

13. Ibid., pp. 487, 529. Part of the letters published by Mann are evidently copies of letters that had been dispatched. The Kurdish Jews were accustomed to keep a copy of

every letter they sent and, for reasons of economy, made use of old letters for this purpose.

14. Simḥa Assaf, "Nosafot le-Toldot ha-Yehudim b-Kurdistan" [Further notes on the history of the Jews in Kurdistan], *Qiryat Sefer* 13 (1936–37): 266. On more recent *sh'līḥīm* who visited Kurdistan, see Walter Fischel, "Iggerot Kurdistan," *Sinai* (1939) 6ff.

15. On R. Yehuda Diwan, see *EJ*, s.v. "Diwan"; Ya'ari, *Sh'līḥīm*, pp. 17ff.; Assaf, "Nosafot le-Toldot," p. 86. R. Yehuda also visited the Jews of Yemen; see *EJJ*, p. 8.

16. R. Yehuda Diwan also mentions other *sh'līḥīm* who came from Palestine to Kurdistan; see Yehuda b. Amram Diwan; Constantinople, 1739, *Huṭ ha-M'shullash*, T'shuvot 4; Assaf, "Nosafot le-Toldot," p. 86.

17. Assaf, "Nosafot le-Toldot," p. 269; see also Fischel, "Iggerot Kurdistan," p. 7.

18. Thus, an emissary from Hebron and Jerusalem writes from Amadiya to one of the neighboring communities, "[If you fail to send a suitable contribution,] I shall put you under a ban here in Amadiya; and know further that you will not prosper in anything, for in Jerusalem before the Wailing Wall and in Hebron before the Cave of Makhpela you will be banned from the community of Israel so that your city will be cast off and misfortune will be your lot in this world and in the next" (Assaf, "Nosafot le-Toldot," p. 269.

19. Before R. David, Joseph Wolff had been in Kurdistan. In 1825 he visited the Jews of Salamas and Urmia (see p. 45).

20. On R. David d'Bet Hillel, see Abraham Ya'ari, "Massa'ot R. David" [Travels of R. David d'Bet Hillel], *Sinai* 2:4–5.

21. In this connection, see also the request for subscriptions that R. David printed in Madras in Ya'ari, "Massa'ot R. David," *Sinai* 2:24–33, p. 6.

22. The title of this rare volume is *The Travels of Rabbi David d'Bet Hillel: From Jerusalem through Arabia, Koordistan, Part of Persia, and India, to Madras*, (Madras, 1832). This book was unknown, also, to Carl Ritter, though the ninth volume of his *Erdkunde von Asien*, which deals with our area, did not appear till 1840.

23. A Hebrew translation of the section on Kurdistan was published by Walter Fischel, *Sinai* 6 (1939). The names in parentheses reproduce R. David's spelling.

24. This is evidently the same village that Joseph Israel Benjamin (Benjamin II) designates as Zelma (*Acht Jahre in Asien und Afrika von 1846 bis 1855* [Hannover, 1858], p. 74). He declares that it was named after its founder, "a Jew famous in the whole vicinity for his riches, his noble character, and his heroism in war." This is probably the village of Salabag.

25. R. David describes Sukho as a village of thirty Jewish families, all of whom are rich peasants and own large herds: "They have also a multitude of fine white adar trees, which are planted round about the village, and with these they supply Assyria and Baghdad: (*Travels*, p. 59). The village, he says, was inhabited only by Jews. Sukho, or Shukho, which Mann also failed to identify (confusing it with Zakho; see *Texts and Studies*, letter 2, esp. line 214) is reached in a day-and-a-half from Amadiya by way of Barwilnaya to the east. Today, thirty-five Jewish families live in Sukho as peasants, weavers, and traders. However, there are, in addition, twenty Christian and twenty Kurdish families. Up till now, no Jew has emigrated from Sukho to Palestine.

26. R. David wrote the names as he heard them pronounced. Arbil is often pronounced Arvil.

27. R. David writes Sabblagg in accordance with the native pronunciation of Kurds and Jews.

28. Turkish Bashqalan.

29. On the travels of Ker Porter and C. J. Rich, resident of the East India Company

in Baghdad, see C. J. Rich, *Narrative of a Residence in Koordistan* (London, 1836). See also Ritter, *Erdkunde*, vol. 9, esp. p. 425. Unfortunately, I could not obtain Rich's book.

30. See Ritter, *Erdkunde*, vol. 9, pp. 641ff.

31. [Surai are the Nestorians, concerning whom cf. *ERE*, s.v.]

32. Eli Smith and H. G. O. Dwight, *Missionary Researches* (London, 1834). See also Ritter, *Erdkunde*, vol. 9, esp. p. 11.

33. Justin Perkins, *Residence of Eight Years in Persia Among the Nestorian Christians: with Notices of the Muhammedans* (Andover, 1843).

34. Asahel Grant, *The Nestorians: or, The Lost Tribes.*

35. Badger (see note 37) describes the political changes that enabled Grant to make his journeys into the mountain region.

36. William F. Ainsworth, "Account of a Visit to the Chaldeans Inhabiting Central-Kurdistan," *JRGS* II (1841): 21–76; idem, *Travels and Researches in Asia Minor, Mesopotamia, Chaldea, and Armenia* (London, 1842).

37. George Percy Badger, *The Nestorians and Their Rituals: with a Narrative of a Mission to Mesopotamia and Coordistan*, 2 vols. (London, 1852).

38. The reports of the missionaries of the London Society are scattered through the files of its journal, which first bore the title *Jewish Expositor* and, later on, *Jewish Intelligence and Monthly Account of the Proceedings of the London Society for Promoting Christianity Amongst the Jews.* From 1861 the journal had a supplement entitled *The Jewish Records.*

39. On the adventurous career of Joseph Wolff, see *Dictionary of National Biography*, s.v. "Wolff, Joseph"; and H. P. Palmer, *Joseph Wolff, His Romantic Life and Travels* (London, 1935). Wolff's real purpose was also to find the ten tribes in order to convert them to Christianity. Wolff likewise visited Yemen. See *EJJ*, pp. 5–6.

40. The original reports of the first journey appeared in the *Jewish Expositor*. They were later collected in Wolff's *Missionary Journal and Memoirs of Rev. Joseph Wolff*, 3 vols. (London, 1827–29). These volumes were not at my disposal.

41. Joseph Wolff, *Researches and Missionary Labours* (London, 1835), p. 491.

42. *Dictionary of National Biography*, s.v. "Stern, Henry Aaron"; A. A. Isaacs, *Biography of H. A. Stern* (London, 1886). Stern also visited the Yemenite Jews (see *EJJ*, p. 6) and the Falashas.

43. On Stern's journey, see also H. A. Stern, *Dawnings of Light in the East*, pp. 206ff.

44. *JI* 1848: 295, 297–98, 316.

45. Concerning these journeys, see *JI* 1859: pp. 212 ("Many towns have been visited in connection with this mission in Persia, Koordistan and Lower Assyria"), 405ff.; "Journal of Bruhl," *JI* 1864: 89ff.; *Jewish Records*, Oct. 1865, p. 38; J. M. Eppstein, "Visit to Kerkook," *Jewish Records* Oct. 1893: 167ff.; idem, "Journey to Kurdistan," *JI* 1893.

46. See *JI* 1893: 1.

47. J. J. Benjamin, *Acht Jahre in Asien und Afrika von 1846 bis 1855*, (Hannover, 1858), p. 392. A French edition appeared earlier: *Cinq années en Orient (1846–1851)* (Paris, 1856); but it contained only the section on Asia. A Hebrew translation by David Gordon, *Sefer Massa'e Yisrael*, appeared in Lyck (Elk, East Prussia, later Poland) in 1859. [This Hebrew version, however, is much shortened. An English translation, too, was published, the second edition of which (Hannover, 1863) contains notes and emendations by the author made during his stay in America.] On Benjamin II, see "Necrology," *Jewish Chronicle*, May 3, 1864; *Allgemeine Zeitung des Judentums* 1864:352; *EJ*, s.v. "Benjamin, Jos. J." See also the portrait in his *Drei Jahre in Amerika* (Hannover, 1863).

48. "[Obeying] a long and deeply cherished wish of my heart, a wish harbored from my earliest youth, . . . I determined . . . to make first a journey to those parts, where once my forefathers dwelt in the days of their glory and of their misfortune, and thus, as

in a vision, seek the traces of what remained of the ten tribes of Israel" (*Eight Years*, p. 7).

49. Benjamin writes that the village of Zelma lies two hours northeast of Nisebin and that the mountain range Jebel-Sanjack is an hour's distance from Zelma. This can only refer to Tur-Abdin, which is inhabited mainly by Jacobites, who speak a language akin to the Targum of the Jews. Today there are no villages in Tur "inhabited mainly by Jews," and it is doubtful whether there were in Benjamin's time. At all events, Benjamin's account of this district is inaccurate.

50. Barzan seems never to have been visited by a European traveler before Benjamin II.

51. A. H. Layard's *Niniveh and Its Remains* London, 1867, p. 200, also reports the existence of nomadic Jews in Kurdistan.

52. Among Benjamin's contemporaries were some who doubted the authenticity of his book. But these doubts were unfounded, for it is beyond question that he actually visited the regions he describes. His journey was the undertaking of a person entirely devoid of scientific education.

53. See reports from Khoi-Sanjak (*BAIU*, 1889, p. 48 and 1896, p. 52), Sulaimani (1895, p. 64), Urmia (1892, p. 53), Rowanduz (1897, p. 84), and Urfa (1896, p. 54).

54. See under N. Albala, J. Bassan, and Sassoon in the Bibliography.

55. For bibliographies of Kurdistan, see *EI*, s.v. "Kurdistan"; Banse, *Die Türkei* 3d ed. (Braunschweig, 1919), pp. 417ff.

56. Henry Binder, *Au Kurdistan en Mésopotamie et en Perse* (Paris, 1887), with excellent illustrations.

57. A. M. Hamilton, *Road Through Kurdistan* (London, 1937). Hamilton built the Arbil–Rowanduz highway and published important photographs of landscapes and cities.

58. Lamec Saad, *Sechszehn Jahre als Quarantänearzt in der Türkei* (Berlin, 1913).

59. Ephraim Newmark, "Ereṣ ha-Qedem" [in Hebrew], *He'asiph* 1889:39–75.

60. Zev Wolf Schur, *Maḥazot ha-Hayim* [Scenes from life] (Vienna, 1884). The account of his journey first appeared in *haShahar*.

61. A. J. Brawer, Mi-Parashat Massa'otay be-Faras, *Sinai* 6 nos. 9–10 (1930):239–50; no. 11 (1938):430–38.

62. A. Z. Idelsohn "Sippurim ba-Lashon ha-Aramit ha-Ḥadasha" [Tales in the neo-Aramaic dialect], *HaShilo'aḥ* 29(1913):121ff.; idem "Aramäisch sprechende Juden," *Die Welt* 30 (1912), 906–7).

63. *Hebräisch–Orientalischer Melodienschatz*, vol. 2 pp. 31, 128–40.

64. Albert Löwy, "Notes on the Jews in Kurdistan," *Sixth Annual Report of the Anglo–Jewish Association* (London) 1897:94–99; "On a Unique Specimen of the Lishana shel Imrani," *Transactions of the Society for Biblical Archaeology* (London) 4 (1876):98–117; "On Kurdish Folk Lore in the Kurdo-Jewish Dialect," *Transactions of the Society for Biblical Archaeology* (London) 6 (1878):600-602.

65. Jacob Mann, *Texts and Studies in Jewish History and Literature*, (Cincinnati, 1931), vol. 1, pp. 477–549.

66. Simḥa Assaf, "Le-Toldot ha-Yehudim be-Kurdistan u-Shkhenoteha" [On the history of the Jews in Kurdistan and the neighboring countries], *Zion Me'assef* 6(1934): 85–112; idem, "Nosafot le-Toldot" (see n. 14), pp. 266–71.

67. Walter Fischel, "Bei den Juden im Kurdischen Bergland," *JR*, Jan. 8, 1937; *EJ*, s.v. "Kurdistan."

68. R. Duval, *Les dialectes néo-Araméens de Salamas* (Paris, 1883); I. Gottheil, "The Judeo-Aramaic Dialect of Salamas," *JAOS* 15(1893):297ff.

69. Franz Rosenthal, *Die Aramäistische Forschung seit den Arbeiten Theodor Nöldekes*. Leiden, 1939.

70. J. J. Rivlin, "Sippur Dawid ve-Goliat bi-L'shon Targum" [The story of David and Goliath in the Targum dialect], *Zion* 4(1930):109-20.

Chapter 2

1. "Often enough these ravines are not straight clefts; they wind in the most curious fashion and have endless ramifications. The Rowanduz is the best known and perhaps the grandest of them all. It has no less than five branches through which tributary streams flow to join the Rowanduz River, and each of these is itself an imposing canyon" A. H. Hamilton, *Road Through Kurdistan* (London, 1937), p. 110. Hamilton makes frequent mention of the inaccessibility of the Zagros; e.g., in referring to the Berserini, he says, "There were few sections where one could ride even on mule-back" (p. 161).

2. From May to October, it is rainless. Annual rainfall: Zakho 1,026, Amadiya 1,097, Rowanduz 1,053, Akra 936, Sulaimani 836, Arbil 462, Kerkuk 394, and Mosul 350. Dov Ashbel, *Rainfall Map of the Near East*, Jerusalem, 1940.

3. Our area has only two meteorological stations, namely, at Mosul and Kerkuk. Figures for mean maximum and minimum temperature in 1938–39 (in centrigrades) are

	July 1938		January 1939	
	Minimum	Maximum	Minimum	Maximum
Mosul	20.7	42.4	2.8	12.9
Kerkuk	25.1	41.1	4.6	13.7

(Data is from Dov Ashbel, *Annual Report: The Climate of Palestine and Adjacent Countries* Tel Aviv 19(1938/39). On the temperature of the mountain region, Hamilton writes, "August is one of the hottest months in Kurdistan, and in that country means a temperature of 110 degrees (43.33 C.) in the shade"; again, "An icy wind out of Turkestan swept through the black gorge and froze everything it could find to freeze" (*Road Through Kurdistan*, pp. 240, 263).

4. This is true. Thus, Hamilton writes: "One day. . . . I was returning from Arbil (to Spilik) when I heard that there had been a brush between the local Surchi tribes of Spilik and the Hurke nomads, who nearly every year came into conflict with the villagers of the foothills. Several women were engaged in this fight, for they are just as warlike and as good shots as the men" (ibid., p. 90).

5. Eugen Prym and Albert Socin, *Der neu-Aramäische Dialect des Tur Abdin*, Göttingen, 1881, vol. 2, index, s.v. "Eichhörner."

6. In laying out this road, the builders did not have in mind merely the principles of highway engineering; they made a point of passing as much as possible through territory occupied by insubordinate Kurdish tribes: "Once highways have penetrated a region the wildest people are pretty sure to become peaceful simply by copying civilized modes of life" (Hamilton *Road Through Kurdistan*, p. 73).

7. Witness the Royal Air Force attacks on Rowanduz.

8. See illustration by Henry Binder [and W. A. Wigram in Binder's *Au Kurdistan en Mésopotamie et en Perse* (Paris, 1887), facing pp. 96, 209].

Chapter 3

1. Albert Löwy, *Transactions of the Society of Biblical Archeology* 4 (1875): 98.

2. On the attempts at identification of this area see J. Obermeyer, *Die Landschaft Babylonien*, Frankfurt a.M., 1929, pp. 10ff.

3. [Dr. Brauer did not live to write this chapter.]

4. On the various places mentioned in the Talmud, see Obermeyer, *Die Landschaft Babylonien*; cf. also Jacob Mann, *Texts and Studies in Jewish History and Literature* (Cincinnati, 1931), vol. 1, pp. 477ff.

5. See the material in Obermeyer, *Die Landschaft Babylonien*; also Mann, *Texts and Studies*, vol. 1, p. 477, where he attempts to sketch the history of the Jews of Mosul.

6. On the exilarch of Mosul, see Jacob Mann, *Livre d'hommage a la mémoire du S. Poznanski*, Warsaw, 1927, Hebrew sec., pp. 23–27.

7. On the David Alroy episode see Mann, *HaTequfa*, 24:341ff.; idem, *REJ* 87:257.

8. Benjamin always writes Amariya, instead of Amadiya. This is an instance of the same error (on the part of the copyist) that occurs in connection with the name Alroy.

9. Benjamin gives the names of the men to whom the exilarch applied as Nasi Zakkai and R. Josef Burhan al-Mulk [or al-Falak], the astrologer (*Sefer Massa'e* [ed. D. Gordon, 1859], p. 80).

10. In a third source, the *megilla* of Obadya the Proselyte (cf. J. Mann, "Obadia le Prosélyte,", *REJ* 71 (1920): pp. 90–91) he is called al-Dūgi (or Dōgi). The three variants follow easily from the Arabic or Hebrew script. The form Dūgi or Dōgi is interesting in view of the fact that Dōga דוגא is the name of a family living in Amadiya today. From some of the letters published by Jacob Mann (*Texts and Studies*, vol. 1 (1931), letters 7–8) we learn that a certain Simon Doga was head of the Jewish community of Amadiya.

11. Jacob Mann, "Ha-T'nu'ot ha-M'shihiyot," *HaTequfa* 24(1928):345.

12. Ibid. No tradition about Alroy has survived among the Kurdish Jews. All that they know about him comes from recent sources.

13. *EI*, 1st ed., s.v. "Irbil" by Streck.

14. For Arbil see *Maq*. 18.4.144–46, 20.2.15, 24.3 (*Judae Harizi Macamae*, ed. Paul de Lagarde [Göttingen, 1883]).

15. For Mosul, see *Maq*. 24.1, 29.1, 47.7, 48.8.18, 50.128.

16. *Maq*. 46.9, 47.8, 50.43–44 and 107.

. I came to Mosul in the month of Tevet (January), when storm swept through the land.

The season was cold; who can withstand its cold?
The rain gathered its warriors, and the snow hoisted its banners on the mountains.

18. [Dr. Brauer intended to publish a special paper on these Jewish places of pilgrimage.]

19. [I am indebted to A. Ben-Ya'aqov of Jerusalem for the text of this inscription.]

20. Assaf, "Le-Toldot." *Zion Me'assef* 6(1934):85.

21. [Folk-tales of this type are very widespread. Cf. Stith Thompson, *Motif-Index of Folk Literature* (reprint, Bloomington and Indianapolis, n. d., ca. 1989), vol. 4, p. 251: "K.185.1. Deceptive land purchase: ox-hide measure . . . Type 2400: As much land bought as can be surrounded by an ox-hide. The hide is cut into very small strips."]

22. For our text, the ms. of the Hebrew University has been used (Hebrew octavo, 637).

23. This is a Bible quotation (2 Kings 4:10). Its use is noteworthy, in view of the fact that today neither beds nor tables nor chairs are used in Arbil.

24. Mann, *Texts and Studies*, vol. 1 p. 485.

25. Maragha—today an utterly insignificant town—is mentioned also in one of the seventeenth-century letters published by Assaf, *Le-toldot*. Justin Perkins visited Maragha in 1854 and found that the town had 15,000–20,000 Muslim inhabitants, as well as twenty to thirty Armenian families; Jews are not mentioned. (*Residence of Eight Years in Persia Among the Nestorian Christians; with Notices of the Muhammadans* (Andover, 1843), p. 196.

26. Mehmed was blind in one eye.

27. See *EI*, 1st ed., s.v. "Rawandiz" (by B. Nikitine). On the continual raids by the Kurds, see *EI*, 1st ed., s.v. "Kurds" (by V. Minorsky).

28. H. A. Stern writes, "The Jews, who formed a great part of the population, were treated with merciless cruelty and oppression; many of them migrated to other towns; and those that were not so fortunate, submitted to the yoke of the tyrant" (*Dawnings of Light in the East* [London, 1854], p. 225).

29. Henry Binder, *Au Kurdistan en Mésopotamie et en Perse* (Paris, 1887), pp. 197–98. See also *EI*, s.v. "Kurds" (by Minorsky).

30. In this connection Lamec Saad's *Sechszehn Jahre als Quarantänearzt in der Türkei* (Berlin, 1913), which describes the situation at about the year 1880, is most illuminating.

31. R. S. Stafford writes as follows in his excellent book, *The Tragedy of the Assyrians* (London, 1935): "There is no reason to think that the Assyrians had greater regard for the sanctity of human life and property than the Kurds, nor that the Kurds generally had a lower standard of conduct—admittedly a rough-and-ready one—in their many raids and fights, than the Assyrians" (p. 22).

32. Instances are the uprisings of Shekh Said Naqshbandi, in 1925, in Turkish territory; Shekh Maḥmud of Sulaimani in 1930; and Shekh Aḥmed of Barzan and Nuri of Rowanduz, both in 1932.

33. [The Turkish–Iraqi boundary line runs somewhat to the north of Amadiya in an east-to-west direction for some 250 kilometers.]

34. The Assyrians question has been dealt with in detail by R. S. Stafford, administrative inspector in the Ministry of the Interior in Iraq, 1927–33, in *The Tragedy of the Assyrians.*

35. [Cf. also the hard judgment of George Percy Badger on the Jacobites (*The Nestorians and Their Rituals; with a Narrative of a Mission to Mesopotamia and Coordistan* [London, 1852], vol. 1, pp. 44, 61ff.) and Prym-Socin, *Tur'Abdin*, vol. 1, p. X.]

36. It is interesting that Stafford does not mention the Jews at all.

37. The reason given by the Jews is that the Turks forbade emigration to Palestine and that they, the Jews, declined to live in such a country.

38. Yitzḥaq Ben Zvi, *Okhlosēnu ba-Aretz* Jerusalem, 1929, vol. 1, p. 67, writes that the Kurds were the first Oriental Jews to settle in Palestine. This was in 1812.

39. Between 1920 and 1926, nineteen hundred Kurdish Jews emigrated to Palestine (ibid.) p. 67.

40. There were times when Kurdish Jews earned £1–£2 a day—as teamsters, for instance, a calling that they had followed in Kurdistan also. This was an unheard-of sum for a Kurdish Jew. Since their wants are few, they soon accumulated £100, bought lots, and set about building houses.

41. For example, the Jewish inhabitants of the village of Barashe near Amadiya, emigrated to Palestine en masse and built a synagogue there.

Chapter 4

1. Even in Jerusalem the Jews settle in districts according to places or origin. The Jews of each Kurdish community generally erect their own synagogue and live in its vicinity.

2. The Christians, on the contrary, settle at some distance from the Muslim Kurds. Thus, the Kurdish village Guzarash (not, as in Binder, Guzareck) lies 50 meters from the Nestorian village Gundik (Binder, *Au Kurdistan*, p. 182). The same is true of the Kurdish village Jessi and the Nestorian village Berj (p. 186). In Amadiya a considerable number of Kurds live in Jewish houses rent-free. In return, they perform the necessary tasks for the Jews on the Sabbath.

3. In Amadiya there are two Jewish quarters, one in the upper city and one in the lower: *she'utha ilettha* [upper quarter] and *she'utha ketetha* [lower quarter].

4. [That is, "Street of the House of Zābin," etc.]

5. My informant from Ushnu sold his house, which he estimated at £100, for £10.

6. In Binder's day upper Amadiya lay half in runs: "La ville n'est qu'un monceau de mines, dans lesquelles vegete une miserable population" (*Au Kurdistan*, p. 117; see also illustrations pp. 202, 207).

7. On the Kurdish house, see Basil Nikitine, "La vie domestique Kurde," *RETP*, pp. 334–35. But this section, also, is very inexact. Concerning the condition of the houses in Zakho, Lamec Saad writes, "The poverty is general and the dirt unbelievable; also the houses are miserably built" (*Sechszehn Jahre*, p. 254). [R. David d'Bet Hillel describes the houses of Zakho thus: "The houses are built of hewn stones; but their appearance is bare, and the streets and the *sūqs* are narrow" (Walter Fischel, trans., "Massa' l'Kurdistan." [in Hebrew], *Sinai* 3 [1939]:218.

8. Good illustrations of older houses in Amadiya, made of stone (from the year 1886), in Binder, *Au Kurdistan*, pp. 202, 207; see also pp. 168, 182.

9. On the manufacture of mud bricks in the Aramaic villages round Damascus, see S. Reich, *Les villages Araméens de l'Anti-Liban*, Damascus, n.d., p. 56.

10. Benjamin II mentions the fact that the houses in Kurdistan consist, for the most part, of wickerwork: "The houses constructed of wicker-work have a very bare appearance, they are tolerably high, have one story, and inside and outside are daubed with a kind of mortar" (*Eight Years* p. 130).

11. Old structures have copper roofs, e.g., the Bē Ḥazāne in Amadiya.

12. Cf. the similar verse sung by the Yemenite Jews, *EJJ*, p. 73.

13. A description of a village house, which in general resembles the houses in Zakho, is given by Walter Schwarz, "Bei den Kurdischen Juden," in *JR*, July 12, 1935.

14. Formerly only one floor, without a courtyard but with a veranda *qedāne*, the roof of which rested on wooden pillars.

15. New Kurdish immigrants in Palestine receive expensive presents (particularly household articles) from their friends, in order to facilitate their acclimatization.

16. The rich sometimes use a low wooden divan (Z., A., and Arbil *takhte*)

17. See illustration of these sleeping platforms in Binder, *Au Kurdistan*, p. 102. He saw them in the Urmia Lake district, where they were 1.50 meters above the ground (p. 101). [According to Banse, *Die Türkei*, p. 232, they were 5 meters high.] They are much used in the Armenian district.

18. *Kish, kish*! is the expression used for shooing away chickens.

19. A specimen is in HUBC 39:40. This mezuza, it was explained, was turned round when a non-Jew entered(?).

20. HUBC 39:80 (from S.).

21. HUBC 38:100 (from A.).

22. Specimen in the private possession of E. Brauer. [Its fate after Brauer's death is unknown.]

23. HUBC 39:42.

24. Concerning the power of the wolf to ward off demons, see also p. 171.

25. Z. *kabaniyeth bētha*, "(female) cook"; A. also *kabāni*; S. *khemāla*; Ushnu *ama*.

Chapter 5

1. In Yemen, for instance; see *EJJ*, p. 79.

2. The Kurds of the Amadiya region were taken as a sample.

3. See illustration in Binder, *Au Kurdistan*, p. 123; see also the description of the costume of the Hartoshi Kurds in *Geographical Journal* (1894:86). Today it is replaced by the *chokhik* (Targ. *chukhta* or *pastak*). See Max Tilke, *Studien zu der Entwicklungsgeschichte des Orientalinchen Kostüms*, Berlin, 1923, pl. 80: "These peculiar, sleeveless jackets are made of strongly fitted woolen stuff, 1 centimeter thick. For this reason only the edges can be sewn together" [trans. from Germ. by R.P.].

4. Cf., e.g., Georges Marçais, *Le Costume musulman d'Alger* (Paris, 1930), pp. 31–36 on Turkish influence on costume in North Africa and *yelak*.

5. *Chakme* are mentioned by Mann, *Texts and Studies*, letter 12, which was sent from Amadiya to Yona of Mosul and deals with business transactions: "You will receive 35 *sāke* (long woolen stockings) for *chakme* through Abdul Rahman (lines 5–6). There are also *sāke* for *kalke*, i.e., for low shoes. Mann did not understand this passage.

6. Binder also gives a list of the gala garments of a Christian peasant of Julamerk. For some old and valuable pictures of Nestorians (which are, however, somewhat in the style of illustrations in children's books), see Perkins, *Residence of Eight Years in Persia*, facing pp. 6, 262, 414.

7. *Chāla chapuksa* (some also say *chapukta*) are likewise called *berguze* in Amadiya, Rekan, and their vicinity. There are, for instance, red-striped *berguze garamūsi* that come from Garamus. The jacket is open at the armpits—a feature of Persian, Indian, and Caucasian garments also. See Tilke, *Kostüm*,. pl. 27 and p. 13.

8. Some pictures that reproduce in excellent fashion the colorful impression made by this costume as worn by the Assyrians of Tel Tamer on the Khabur are to be found in the *National Geographic Magazine*, December 1938, pll. 4, 7. The garments depicted probably come from Zakho. The basic color of the garments worn by the two men in plate 4 must be visualized as being somewhat darker than in the picture—less violet. The *chāla chapuksa* appears also in the older pictures in Perkins. The "Nestorian of the mountain" on the plate facing p. 6 is wearing it (the confining band below the knees is not understandable), as is the Nestorian priest from the mountains on the plate facing p. 414. In Perkins, the garments have blood-colored stripes; but this is probably due to the primitive style of the pictures which were designed for Perkins by a Persian artist.

9. For Kurds of today in *shalo chapek*, see Hamilton, *Road Through Kurdistan*, illus. 12, 16, 25.

10. See illustration in Friedrich Ratzel, *Völkerkunde*, 2d ed. (Leipzig and Wien, 1894), vol. 2, p. 738, unfortunately without indication of place.

11. A specimen from the Aissors is in the Caucasus Museum in Tiflis; see Tilke, *Kostüm*, pl. 79.

12. The long sleeves are called: *buchkiyata* (A.; Barasha *lebandiya*, which the Surai also use; Kurd. *lebhandi* [*buchik bōtani*, "sleeves from Bohtan," i.e., Western Kurdistan). The collar is embroidered by the bride. The sleeves of a specimen are 87 centimeters long and 1 meters wide (HUBC 37:1 a). The area in which these shirts (with long, wide sleeves ending in a point) are worn stretches from Eastern Asia to the Southern Caucasus.

13. H. Naumann, *Grundzüge der deutschen Volkskunde* (Leipzig, 1933), p. 7.

14. "Nearly every one of these Persian Kurds had some weird garment of European origin. Such treasures were all greatly prized and kept in neat repair by their owners, who wore them day and night for the better part of a lifetime. [They also wore old uniforms of all varieties.] But where the coolie who appeared in a morning coat with long tails of a cut popular about 1850 had secured it no imagination could discover" (Hamilton, *Road Through Kurdistan*, p. 142; see also illus. 19).

15. See, for instance, the relief of the King of Sam'al from Sendshirli (Berlin) and the procession of musicians (Constantinople) in Weber, pll. 25 and 37, respectively.

16. Kurdish stockings and specimens of colored stockings made by Oriental Jews of various countries are [were] to be found in HUBC.

17. Maclean, *Grammar*, p. 297: *reshike*, "shoes of felted wool." See illustration in Binder, *Au Kurdistan*, p. 150 (the ones hanging up); to the left are *kalke sorani*, to the right, *chakme*. See also Grant, *The Nestorians, or the Lost Tribes*, p. 70.

18. In the winter there are also snowshoes, which consist of a round frame with a rope net.

19. [But they make use of slippers that are open at the back.]

20. For example, *yifraḥ al-qaranful min jaybiha*; see 'Omar b. Abi Rabi'ah, *Diwan*, ed. Schwarz (Leipzig, 1901), 51, 21a.

21. R. P. A. Dozy, *Dictionnaire detaillé des noms des vetements chez les Arabes*, Amsterdam, 1845, s.v. *fisṭān*. The *fistien* is also the outer garment of the Palestinian peasant woman; see, e.g., Mulinen, *ZDPV* 30: 168.

22. Tolke, *Kostüm*, pp. 40ff.

23. Such a shoulder wrap is seen, e.g., on the immigrant Semites in the mural painting at Beni Hassan (Middle Kingdom). It is of woven, figured material, the design having "straight, diagonal, and serrated stripes, as well as dots, mostly red and blue on a white background. Regretfully, the painting gives no clue as to the technique used in producing these ornaments" (Tilke, *Kostüm*, p. 42; [trans. from Germ. by R.P.]).

24. A specimen of the *abāye ketāwa* consists of four widths of cloth, each 29 centimeters wide and 1.30 meters long (HUBC 38:106). The cloth is of red-dyed wool with vertical and horizontal stripes of green, and the sewing is done with green woolen thread. The weave of the cloth is coarse and uneven.

25. Also, for instance, the Chaldaeans of Qaraqosh (near Mosul); see Henry Field, *Arabs of Central Iraq*, Chicago, 1935, pl. 139ff. Field does not give name of the wrap. He describes the costume of the Chaldaeans as follows: "Dressed in black heavy robes (*izar*) which hang down to the ground, the older women cover their heads with a black cloth (*kaffiyah*) so that only the face, hands, and poorly shod feet are visible" (p. 433). Neither Badger nor Perkins mentions the *schräge Emporwurf*. A good illustration of a Kurdish woman wearing the shoulder wrap, from the Hilprecht Collection, is to be found in Franz C. Endres, *Die Türkei* (München, 1916), p. 48.

26. "The Persian shirt is characterized by the neck-opening with a side-split" (Tilke, *Kostüm*, p. 25; [trans. from Germ. by R.P.]). The Persian shirt also has no wide, hanging sleeves (Ibid., pl. 82).

Chapter 6

1. See *EJJ*, pp. 105–6.

2. A. and Z. *kewāra*, pl. *kewarāre*; S. *kuwāra*.

3. In Rekan and Tchalla ashes are strewn on the sack.

4. A. *tashta*, S. *markan*.

5. The separate stages in the making of a loaf are *lēsha*, *gūṣa*, *patōḥit gūṣa*, *dauwarta* and *ṭlumṣa* (Z. and A.).

6. A. *marzag*, S *mazraga*, and Ushnu *refēda*.

7. A. Jaba, *Dictionnaire Kurde-Français*, St. Petersburg, 1879, p. 94: *teptepe, pain rond*.

8. Jaba, *Dictionnaire*, p. 309.

9. A. *kethētha*, pl. *kithyātha*; a cockerel is *warke* or *fūrūj*. Cocks, *dikīle*, are little eaten.

10. *Qiqwāna* or *quqwāna* (Arthur J. Maclean, *Grammar of the Dialects of Vernacular Syriac*. . . , Cambridge 1895, Oxford 1901, p. 284) and *quqwanta* (Mark Lidzbarski p. 557), the Asiatic red-legged partridge.

11. Z. *chuchiktha*, pl. *chuchikyātha*; A. *sikhandoke*; and S. *merijī*.

12. A. *tapiksa* (pitfall) or *farhakiyatha* (springe). The Jews are forbidden to trap birds with lime twigs because the birds are liable to get their legs broken.

13. In Barashe and Rekan it is also called *pisra qadīt*. It may be eaten uncooked.

14. See, e.g., Brauer, *Züge aus der Religion der Herero* (see Publications, p. 31), pp. 48–49, 55.

15. Maclean, *Grammar*, p. 186.

16. Jaba, *Dictionnaire*, P. 239: *ser-tu*, "crème de lait d'autre betail que de la vache."

17. On the Kurdish churn, see, Martiny, *Kirne und Girbe*, p. 97 (communicated by F. von Luschan); see also illus. 81, tripod with churn. Martiny does not mention the term *mashqa*.

18. *Mishkha* (Z. and A. Kurd. *rüni*, Ushnu Kurd. *rom*) is melted butter.

19. See Maclean, *Grammar*, p. 61; Jaba, *Dictionnaire*, p. 191; J. de Morgan, *Mission Scientifique en Perse*, Paris, 1895, p. 143. "This is curds and whey watered to the consistency of milk, slightly sour, and always cool, for they keep it in porous skins—it is the most refreshing drink possible" (E. B. Soane, *To Mesopotamia and Kurdistan in Disguise*, London, 1912, p. 168).

20. Ushnu *dolma* (Maclean, *Grammar*, p. 62), Turk. *ṭulme*, Arab *vibrag*, A. Kurd. *iprakh*, Z. Kurd. *dolama*. *Kusa* or tomatoes filled with rice.

21. In Sinne, the Muslims actually call the *kufte kufte musā'i kān*, "Jewish dumplings," or "*kufta sham'a*, "Sabbath dumplings"; likewise A. "*kutilkit shambiye* or *jüba*. The Kurds come to beg *kutele* for their sick, since they are considered a remedy for fever (A.).

22. Maclean, *Grammar*, p. 101; *hamüsta* (Alqosh), "a sour dish dressed with vinegar."

23. Jaba, *Dictionnaire*, p. 350: *kuwi*, "sauvage."

24. Maclean, *Grammar*, p. 165: *maza* (Pers. and Turk.), an appetizer, a whet before dinner. On *maza* at Turkish drinking bouts, see Arminius Vámbery, *Sittenbilder aus dem Morgenlande*, Berlin, 1876, p. 78.

25. ["To the arriving guest, to the hero of the day, to every one who has to be congratulated, whole sugarloaves are given as a present; and on top of the big wooden trays (*gonja*) on which the long line of servants transports the gifts for the bride on the occasion of weddings, several dozens of such sugarloaves stand erect" (Vámbery, *Sittenbilder*, p. 74; trans. from Germ. by R.P.)]

26. [Cf. Fischel, trans., *Massa' l'Kurdistan*, p. 17.]

27. ["Especially liked is the *baklava*, a dough saturated with fat and butter, in whose consumption the Turkish stomach performs miracles" (Vámbery, *Sittenbilder*, p. 74; trans. from Germ. by R.P.)]

28. [Cf. Prym-Socin, *Tur Abdin*, vol. 1, p. x.]

29. Today the women sit there during the services (see p. 257).

Chapter 7

[For a comparative perspective, cf. Raphael Patai, *On Jewish Folklore* (Detroit, 1983), pp. 202–37, based on interviews conducted in 1944–45 with elders of the Meshhed community residing in Jerusalem.]

1. Customs that are found also among the Muslim Kurds will be designated Kurd. My main source for these cases is a description of marriage ceremonies among the kurds of Zakho, which I noted down as communicated by a Jew of Zakho.

2. I found this custom only in Amadiya.

3. Even in Palestine the Kurdish Jewish girls marry exceptionally early—at fifteen or sixteen years of age.

4. Z. and A., *ṭalobāya*, pl. *ṭalobāye*.

5. [Cf. Raphael Patai, "Marriage Among the Marranos of Meshhed," *Edoth* (Jerusalem) 1947:173.]

6. The marriage customs of Sinne are briefly described by A. J. Brawer, "Mi-Parashat Massa'otay b'Faras," *Sinai* vol. 1, no. 11, (1939):433-36.

7. Kurd.–Pers. *shir*, "milk." See Morgan, *Mission*, p. 143.

8. See Assaf, "Le-Toldot ha-Yehudim," which also describes another case in which parents sell their daughter in a time of need. This case, however, may come from Persia where conditions are often still worse.

9. Mann, *Texts and Studies*, vol. 1, letter 19, p. 542; see also p. 489.

10. This does not refer to Zakho (as Mann thought) but to the village of Sukho, which is a day-and-a-half distant from Amadiya.

11. Mann, *Texts and Studies*, vol. 1, letter 9, p. 525; see also p. 486.

12. The marriage processions always return by a different road from the one they came by. This usage is based on magiç. It is called *chape bulke* "at the left of the bride," since the procession comes from the right and turns to the left on leaving. [Another explanation of this term is "the lengthening" of the bride.]

13. [The *shirinī khorān* is observed in practically all the Jewish and non-Jewish communities of Persia.]

14. The custom of throwing wheat at marriage ceremonies is very widespread.

15. Some families in Amodiya have no *qadōshe* at all, because the betrothal ceremony brings them bad luck. Some celebrate the *qadōshe* together with the seven benedictions.

16. In Amadiya it often takes place directly after the *ṭlāba*.

17. Betrothal rings of various kinds are [were] found in HUBC. Rings with black stones are especially favored as symbolizing the beauty of the bride (cf. Sons of Sol. 1:5).

18. Brawer, "MiParashat Massa'otay," p. 17, speaks of *qiddūsh ērūsīn* also; but this is a mistake.

19. The custom also exists among the Muslim Kurds and was probably taken over from them.

20. Mann, *Texts and Studies*, vol. 1, p. 521.

21. Which month is meant is not clear from the letter. Perhaps it is Nissan, i.e., the month of Passover. Shortly thereafter (line 33), 1st Adar is also mentioned. My informant stated that the seven benedictions usually take place on 14th Nissan before sundown.

22. Similarly Kurd., *fēkīya zawā'i* and *fēlīya būke*.

23. Old Syriac *Dagālā*, "liar, cheat." Maclean, *Grammar*, p. 60.

24. Jaba, *Dictionnaire*, p. 384.

25. Also among the Kurds, the *leliye* is the night preceding Sunday.

26. Whether this the only reason or we are dealing here with a taboo is difficult to judge. Worthy of mention, however, is the fact—from an entirely different *Kulturkreis*, namely, the Polynesians—that in Samoa, for example, the mourners must not put the food into their mouths themselves but must be fed by others (Georg Buschan, *Völkerkunde*, Stuttgart-Berlin, n.d., vol. 2, p. 239).

27. Jaba, p. 272: *roubar*, "riviere."

28. Such a *lifit kālo* is [was] in HUBC (36:61).

29. This makes her light of foot and orderly. Wheat is thrown in Ushnu also, [as well as in many other places all over the world.]

30. Jaba, *Dictionnaire*, p. 351: *koumyk*, diminuhve of *koum* "coiffure, bonnet, tout ce qui sert a couvrir la tête." See illustration in Binder, *Au Kurdistan*, p. 168.

31. The old clothes are bestowed upon the leader of the musicians. It may happen that he is thrown into the water in these clothes, as a joke.

32. A. *baska pechā'i*, pipe stem covered with cloth. See Mann, *Texts and Studies*, vol. 1, 530, text XII, line 11; he could not explain the term.

33. In Zakho the bridegroom who has enemies and is afraid of a spell has the seven benedictions recited in secret on the *lēlīye*, after midnight. Nevertheless, he goes to the river next day for the immersion and the dressing and then to the bride's house, where, however, only the reading of the *ketubba* takes place.

34. Cf. Brawer, "MiParashat Massa'otay," p. 18.

35. Cases have occurred in which the bride would not permit the bridegroom to put his foot on hers.

36. Jaba, *Dictionnaire*, p. 79: *pisht der*, "les traverses d'une porte."

37. See also Brawer, "MiParashat Massa'otay," p. 18

38. The edge of one such crocheted cover is adorned with two clasped "hands" made of beads, supposed to represent the bride and groom (HUBC 39:67).

39. Old Syriac *gnuna*, "a bride chamber." Maclean, *Grammar*, p. 54 [cf. talmudic גננא, bridal chamber].

40. See the similar customs, (p. 125).

41. See the similar custom, (p. 123).

42. [Israel Davidson, *Thesaurus of Medieval Hebrew Poetry* (New York, 1930), vol. 4, p. 210, no. 82.]

43. If the bride is found to have been deflowered, the people say, *Pāsit bābakh yummakh kumta*, "The face of your father and mother became black." [This expression is in conformity with the general usage in Near Eastern lands, where "to blacken the face" of somebody means to bring disgrace upon him, while "to whiten his face" means to bring honor upon him.]

44. Morgan, *Mission*, p. 140: Kurd. *kassu*, "belle-mere, mere de la femme".

45. See Jaba, *Dictionnaire*, p. 43; *berbuk*, "commere de noces."

46. In Arbil the following *pizmon* is sung on the way:

> Assemblies of people, bless God
> And raise a voice of strength and power
> Let Israel rejoice and be happy.

[Cf. Davidson, *Thesaurus*, no. 2196; trans. from Heb. by R.P.]

47. The description that follows is based on the customs of Amadiya.

48. Cf. Maclean, *Grammar*, p. 229: *sipūwā*, "a mouthful."

49. [Cf. Davidson, *Thesaurus*, no. 8775.]

50. Some families celebrate the bridegroom's breakfast not on Sunday morning but on the morning directly following the seven benedictions. Rich families, in particular, do so. There are, besides, some families who do not observe the breakfast at all. The fact that the bridegroom's breakfast takes place on the morning following the seven benedictions gives the impression that this is the original custom. Still, it is possible that the bridal pair formerly consummated their marriage on the night preceding Saturday, as in Yemen (see *EJJ*, p. 162) and that the breakfast consequently did not take place until Sunday.

51. There is a very similar custom in Bavaria. It is called *Ehren* (honors): "Each guest approaches the table, drinks to the health of the couple a glass of wine, and 'indicates' in a loud voice the amount that he wants to donate. A scribe keeps an accurate ledger about this" (Georg Buschan, *Die Sitten der Völker*, vol. 4, p. 162; see also illus. 128; [trans. from Germ. by R.P.]. Records of the gifts are kept in precisely the same manner in Kurdistan. [This custom can be found also among other Oriental Jewish communities.]

52. Maclean, *Grammar*, p. 301: *shoda*, "Joy."

53. Among the Muslim Kurds, the father keeps half the bride-price for himself.

54. There are said to be cases in which the aga had the bride sent back. My informant tells of a case in which such a bride, before being taken back to her home, was kept a prisoner by the aga for three days. Perhaps it was such occurrences that gave rise to the report of Benjamin II that the *jus primae noctis* obtains in Kurdistan: ["Besides this, the bride, before she enters the house of her husband, must place herself at the disposal of her master. . . Only within the last few years has this odious abuse been reformed, and changed into a monetary payment. A sanguinary event was the cause of this. A young girl, after a desperate encounter, having killed her master" (*Eight Years*, p. 127)]. None of my informants had any direct knowledge of the practice of the *jus primae noctis*, the existence of which is in any case doubtful.

55. Brawer, "MiParashat Massa'otay".

56. See p. 87, 181; also Kurd.

57. Jaba, *Dictionnaire*, p. 115: *ğerde[-jerde]* bande (de voleurs)"; cf. Arab. *jarīd*, "detachment of cavalry."

Chapter 8

[Much comparative material from Middle Eastern (and other) Jewish communities pertaining to the subject of this chapter is collected in Raphael Patai, "Jewish Folk-Cures for Barrenness," *Folk-Lore* (London) 55 (Sept. 1944): 117–24) and 56(Dec. 1933 and Mar. 1945): 208–18; idem, "HaLeda baMinhag ha'Amami" [Birth in popular custom], *Talpioth* (New York) 6 (1953): 226–68, 686–705); 9 (1965): 238–59; idem, *On Jewish Folklore* (Detroit, 1983), pp. 337–443.]

1. Shabtai Barashe saw this custom practiced in Rekan about 1910.

2. A *sudra semaka kameta* from Herki is [was] in HUBC.

3. HUBC. 39:43; *birwana* (Pers. *birwān*) see Maclean, *Grammar*, p. 39.

4. Alfred Wirth, *Anhaltische Volkskunde*, Dessau, 1931, p. 134.

5. On rules of conduct during pregnancy, see Ploss-Bartels, *Das Weib*, 11th ed., Berlin, 1927, vol. 2, pp.461ff.

6. In Amadiya, on the contrary, it is precisely fish whose use is forbidden.

7. In Brandenburg, pregnant women tie a snake skin round their bodies. Ploss-Bartels, *Das Weib*, vol. 2, p. 455.

8. Ibid., 449 has examples of amulets carried in the girdle.

9. Ibid., pp. 470ff.

10. [In another version the newborn child is a daughter; and the old woman, afraid, takes a wax candle and from it fashions a male member and attaches it to the newborn in order to mislead the demons.]

11. [Erich Brauer, "Bräuche der kurdischen Juden" (see Publications, p. 32). Translation from Germ. by R.P.]

12. In Upper Austria and in the Salzburg district, it is believed that delivery is facilitated if the wife is wearing something from her husband's wardrobe. This custom is reported from Slavic countries also and from France (Ploss-Bartels, *Das Weib*, vol. 3, p. 28.

13. While we possess numerous examples from Asia—e.g., from Persia (Ploss-Bartels, *Das Weib*, vol 2, pp. 759–60—of elevated squatting during delivery, I could find nothing corresponding to these wooden bars.

14. A specimen is [was] in HUBC (39:55).

15. In Zakho it was customary for a woman who was in pain and feared a miscarriage, to tie one of her husband's shoes round her body (Ploss-Bartels, *Das Weib*, vol. 3, p. 34.

16. Ibid.

17. Ibid., p. 36.

18. On salt as a magic expedient, see H. Pfannenschmidt, *Das Weihwasser im heidnischen und christlichen Kultus* (Hannover, 1878).

19. For example, in Greece the midwife says, "If I don't sprinkle your child with salt, it will be a miserable creature and will be good for nothing" (cf. H. Ploss and B. Renz, *Das Kind in Brauch und Sitte der Völker*, 2 vols., Berlin, 1911–12.

20. A good survey of the extent to which the custom of washing the child in salt water has spread is to be found in S. Reich, *Études sur les Villages Araméens*, Damascus, n.d., p. 74, n. 1.

21. "Infants, immediately after birth, are washed in cold water; and, after being rubbed all over with a quantity of fine salt, are wrapped in swaddling-clothes (usually a quantity of old rags)" (Grant, *The Nestorians or the Lost Tribes*, p. 247).

22. See examples in Ploss-Renz, *Das Kind* and O. von Hovorka and A. Kronfeld, *Vergleichende Volksmedizin*, Stuttgart, 1908–9, vol. 2, pp. 638–39.

23. "For the first six days, the child, well wrapped up, is placed on a biejing" (B. Nikitine, "La né domestique Kurde," *REPT* 3 (1922): 340). For *biejing* we must read *beying*, "sieve."

24. "The forty days following childbirth are called 'zystani' for the mother, that is 'wintery'" (ibid.; [trans. from French by R.P.)].

25. ["In Swabia nothing must be borrowed from the house in which there is a woman in childbed" (Ploss-Bartels, *Das Weib*, vol. 3, p. 165; other examples also given). Among the Muslim Kurds, "during this time, neither the 'dapirk' nor the other women who were present at the childbirth may leave the house nor remove any object which was brought in for the childbirth(?)" Nikitine, 340; trans. from French by R.P.)]

26. See, for instance, the similar use of garlic among the Yemenite Jews (*EJJ*, p. 189).

27. Nowadays, instead of this, a piece of sugar is moistened with spittle and put into tea, which is then given to the infant to drink.

28. Spittle is used as a remedy against the "evil eye." The face and hands of the child are rubbed with the spittle of those who are presumably guilty of having cast the "evil eye" (S.). Compare the use of spittle in magic Frazer, *Golden Bough*, index, s.v. "spittle." On saliva as the bearer of the soul, see Wilhelm Wundt, *Völkerpsychologie*, Part IV: *Mythus und Religion*, Leipzig, 1920, vol. 1, pp. 98–99.

29. The children are told of the birth in the words *Laglag qam meseleni o brona (e bata)*, "The stork has brought us this boy (this girl)" (Z.).

30. If a family has already lost several children, ten *ḥakhamim* will be invited to the house to read the Zohar. In the homes of the poor they sit only a few hours, in those of the rich, often throughout the night (Z.). The *ḥakhamim* receive a fee.

31. In rare cases, guests are entertained also after the birth of a girl.

32. The reason given for prohibiting the bringing of meat into the mother's house before the third day was that on the first and second days she would still be too weak to walk round the meat.

33. Maclean, *Grammar*, p. 100: *ḥilyuta*, sweetness, sweetmeats.

34. In Sinne, on the other hand, he is called up as *revīʿī* (fourth).

35. If the father knows how to read, he recites the *shaharit* [morning prayer] and *musaf* also; otherwise, he leaves this to an acquaintance (A.).

36. In Barase, where the *ʿaliyot* are sold every Sabbath, the father buys all of them on this Sabbath.

37. The ordinary word for breakfast is *gadaya; fetarta* applies only to the funeral feast or the meal given for a bride or for the father of a son.

38. See M. Zobel, "Bräuche nach der Geburt eines Kindes," *Almanach des Schocken Verlags* (Berlin) 1938/39:103.

39. Kurd. *shesh*, six.

40. *EJ*, s.v. "Bagdad"; cf. also *ERE*, s.v. "Birth," where further examples are given.

41. Nikitine, "La vie domestique Kurde," *RETP* 3(1922):340; [trans. from the French by R.P.]

42. Lilith is the queen of the demons, who lies in wait for women in childbed.

43. In connection with the wolf's teeth, see also p. 171 on the first tooth.

44. Cf. p. 212.

45. So. termed throughout Kurdistan; Kurd. *sonat kar*.

46. Ḥakham Abraham of Sinne told me that he had circumcised about five hundred Kurdish boys. A Kurdish circumcision clamp is [was] found in HUBC (38:104).

47. There are [were] several specimens in HUBC. One is apparently two hundred years old and bears the inscription [in Hebrew], "Presented in honor of the Prophet Elijah—may his merits protect us! Amen."

48. On the power of the *Umbelliferae* (caraway seed, dill, fennel) to ward off demons, see Hovorka-Kronfeld, *Volksmedizin*, vol. 1, p. 98.

49. As they gaze, they say to one another, *Ishalla hal ich'ah yarkhe hawēlakh ābitkhā brōna gazrakhle*, "God willing, may you have a son circumcised in nine months."

50. In Zakho the long sleeves of the dresses are termed *duluksa*.

51. A good illustration of a rocking cradle (from Armenia) is found in Ploss-Bartels *Das Weib*, vol. 3, p. 205, illus. 870. This picture gives a good idea of the position of the mother while nursing. See also Pflug, "Die Kinderwiege," *Archiv für Anthropologie* 19, illus. 21; Hans Virchow, "Die armenische Wiege," *Zeitschrift für Ethnologie*, 1924:208–9. [Similar hanging cradles can be seen in the Palestine Folk Museum in Jerusalem.] In Sinne there is, besides, another kind of swinging wooden cradle, *lülü*—a cross between a hanging, and a standing, cradle.

52. The use of the urine pipe is widespread in the territory in which this type of cradle is used. Thus, we find it in Armenia, Kurdistan, and Turkestan and among the Kirghiz and certain Arab tribes. [It is used also in Iran and other Middle Eastern countries.]

53. Ploss-Bartels *Das Weib*, vol. 3, p. 195.

54. The Nestorians of Kurdistan have the same custom: "They are nursed while reposing in their cradle, which is just high enough to enable them to obtain their nourishment, while the mother sits upon the floor, with her side towards the cradle" (Grant, *The Nestorians, or the Lost Tribes*, p. 248).

55. HUBC. 39:54, from Herki.

56. A. *farkhiye kake bronakh*, "feast of the teeth of your son"; S. *kāke palote*, "cutting of the tooth."

57. Sometimes she buys only the first dress, as a symbol.

58. *Gedah bula koleh bakef.*

59. See HUBC 38:135.

60. See HUBC 38:153.

61. Jaba, *Dictionnaire*, p. 307: *qarāch*, "nomade", Turk. Pers. *qarāchī*, "Bohémien."

62. Two specimens [were] in HUBC (39:56 and 39:62).

Chapter 9

1. L. F. Clauss, *Von Seele und Antlitz der Rassen und Völker*, München, 1929, pp. 16ff.

2. Mann, *Texts and Studies*, vol. 1, pp. 507ff., letter 4; cf. Assaf, "Le-Toldot," p. 93.

3. The name Mizraḥi does not prove that the man was a native of Baghdad, as Mann assumes (*Texts and Studies*, vol. 1, p. 480). In Jerusalem, for example, the name Mizraḥi is one of the commonest family names among the Kurdish Jews. In Kurdistan itself the name scarcely ever occurs.

4. Ibid., p. 483, also allows for a light doubt ("if it be her own composition"). We must remember that the Kurdish Jews, who, moreover, keep a copy of every one of their letters, possess a series of model letters—a sort of guide for letter writers—according to which the various begging letters, etc., are composed.

5. Quite recently, there was a girl in Bijar, who helped her father in his teaching. After her father's death, she also said *qaddish* for him in the synagogue.

6. It is said that the families of *ḥakhamim* formerly spoke only Hebrew. This is how the women of these families happened to learn the language (A.).

7. In Jerusalem there are two Kurdish Jews who have three wives. H.Z. of Nirwa has three wives and twelve daughters. In Kurdistan, some of his children died; and it was chiefly his grief at having no son that caused him to take new wives. Now, at last, a son has been born to him.

8. In Sinne, a man with three wives is much sought-after. A person suffering from fever goes to him and says, *Marde seh janan che khasa bo darman* (Kurd.), "Man of three wives, what is good as a remedy?" Usually, however, it is difficult to find a man with three wives, so the sufferer must be content with a man who has only two, saying, *Marde du jonan*, "Man of two wives."

In Amadiya the wife of a man who is ill with fever (Kurd. *shaw-ta'e*, night fever) goes to a man with two wives at the time that he is eating and says, *Khōdane dū jenā kōrabin dūjminā* (cf. *dujmen*, Jaba, *Dictionnaire*, p. 183) *darmāne shaw tā'e chinā*? (Kurd.), "Man of two wives (may your enemies go blind), what is the remedy for fever?" The twice-married man then gives her some of the food he is eating as a medicine for her sick husband.

9. In Jerusalem, where the rabbis refuse to give permission for a second marriage without the consent of the first wife, I learned of the following case. A Kurd wished to marry a young woman; and as he could not do so without his first wife's consent, he gave the latter a divorce. Despite this, the first wife did not wish to give him up and went so far as to turn over to him all her scanty earnings as a laundress.

10. Actually *'amra*.

11. Jaba, *Dictionnaire*, p. 2: *egêl*, [=*ejel*] "dernier moment, heure de la mort," Arab. *ajal*. It is explained as "His days went." It is said, for instance, of a man who was killed in an accident on the way, *Ajala zikwale lau zille*, "His days went, because he went."

12. Also among the Nestorians and Kurds, the men and women eat separately (A.). Concerning the Nestorians, Grant writes: "The women did not eat with the men, but, instead of receiving what they left, as is very common in the East, a separate portion was reserved for the females." In Sinne they eat together, but only when they are alone, i.e., when there are no guests. (*The Nestorians, or the Lost Tribes*, p. 75).

13. The women of Sinne know it as far as *'al mezuzot betekha uvish'arekha*. In Amadiya the women add a prayer of their own in Targum—"whatever their hearts suggest."

14. S. Kurd. *klaf ko*.

15. The comb for carding wool (*masirqa*) is made of iron, or of wood with iron teeth.

16. Specimens are [were] to be found in HUBC from Amadiya, Sinne (*tashī*), and Rekan (37:5C, 38:96, and 38:151, respectively).

17. In Sinne many women made caps (*'araqchin*) out of patches. This was the most profitable of the crafts practiced by the women. They were able to earn 2 *qaran* daily, a sum with which they could defray the entire expense of the household.

18. See also Zalman Rubashov, "Urmia," in the Tel Aviv daily *Davar*, Sept. 6, 1940.

19. In Sinne the woman puts on the worst clothes she has. They are kept in a cloth made of many bright-colored pieces and called *chehil tītā*, "forty patches."

20. Although according to the law cooking is permitted, usually, the wives of neighbors and others do the cooking for them; but if the wife can get no substitute, she

does it herself (A. and S.). However, she must not taste the food or salt it with her hand (A.).

21. If the wife does not expect the husband to come home, she defers the immersion until his return, since she is afraid that the demons may notice her purity (S. and A.).

22. In Sinne, other garments belonging to the husband may serve the purpose (e.g., his belt).

23. The custom was probably taken over from the Kurds. The cutting off of the braids as a punishment for adultery was practiced among the Germans also (Tacitus, *Germania* 19).

24. The whole affair was concluded only after some very involved transactions. The young woman's beauty had attracted a rich Jew, who married her immediately after the legal interval of ninety-one days. Previous to this, however, the young woman's father had married a young daughter of the rich admirer. The divorcee thus became the stepmother of her stepmother.

25. An unmarried woman is almost an unknown phenomenon—except, perhaps, in the case of an elderly widow with grown-up children.

26. At the seven benedictions of a *tolaqta*, a person who is suffering from a cough, *shoba*, should drink some water out of a ladle (*itrāna*); then he will recover (A.).

27. Assaf, "Le-Toldot," pp. 92–93 is of a contrary opinion: "There are some who decide that the commandment of levirate marriage takes precedence over the commandment of the *ḥalīṣa*, even if the levir [the brother-in-law] already has a wife and children." My informant from Sinne said that the cases of *ḥalīṣa* greatly outnumber those of the *yibbum*.

28. Mann, *Texts and Studies*, vol. 1, p. 543 (fol. 2, recto) line 4.

Chapter 10

[This chapter contains many remarkable details showing the basic identity of the customs observed at birth, marriage, and death. Despite the existing studies devoted to this phenomenon, it requires additional intensive investigation, especially from the psychological point of view. For intra-Jewish comparison, cf. Raphael Patai, *Historical Traditions and Mortuary Customs Among the Jews of Meshhed* [in Hebrew] (Jerusalem, 1945.]

1. Specimens [were] in HUBC (39:38–39) found only in Amadiya. This kind of armlet was also worn by the mourners during the week of mourning.

2. Actually, there should be eighteen.

3. In Sinne there is no *ḥevra*. There are the *roḥēṣ* or *mīla khelāna* (washers of the dead) and *qabār*, gravedigger.

4. A. *dāpit mīthe*, S. *taḥta*.

5. A. *khelē'eta*; Z. *khelēta* (Maclean, *Grammar*, p. 100: *ḥal'at*, *ḥalat*, *ḥleta*, "robe of honor, present, gift"); S., Rekan, and Tchalla *kurākha* (also A. *khelē'eta* being a euphemism); S. and Bijar *malbūsh* or *labūsha*.

6. In Sinne one buys the material during one's lifetime.

7. In Sinne, women whose hair is falling out are accustomed to stick false hair on their heads with wax. As a sign of mourning, they tear this hair off and lay it on the grave.

8. Also in Mosul, Muslim women are hired.

9. O. Schrader, *Die Totenhochzeit* (Jena, 1904). O. Laufer, "Totenkronen," *ZVV* 26: 16ff.

10. In Ushnu, flowers are laid on this body, and roses, on his face.

11. Hence their curse, *Yā rabi gurpālokh akhlane*, "God grant that we eat your funeral feast" (Z. and A.).

12. The men mourners do not sit with the dead but in a separate room. Often, they are even taken to the synagogue, since they must not hear the wailing of the women.

13. Maclean, *Grammar*, p. 68, according to Lidzbarski, it is *dā'i*, to extinguish.

14. In this connection, see the curse used by women (above p. 176).

15. Maclean, *Grammar*, p. 70, *drā'a* or *drāya*, the Persian yard or meter, about 39 inches.

16. In Dehok the price is 1–2 dinars, in Amadiya, about £4.

17. In Ushnu, the band is wound seven times around the corpse. At each winding a stone and a coin are put on the band. These are thrown away during the *haqqafot*.

18. The burial plots are not bought. There are, however, some old women who buy a place during their lifetime from the *shekh ḥavrāye*, in order, for instance, to lie at the side of a dead son. The payment is not made in money but in arrack (A.)

19. Generally *qora*; S. also *ziarta*.

20. Z. *bira qōrā*; S. *alḥad*: Ushnu *miangor*.

21. Nikitine, "La vie domestique Kurde," *RETP* 3 (1922): 342.

22. Actually "stone." This points to the probability that originally, the use of stone was general. In Sinne, this stone is called *kēpa alḥad*.

23. Z. *miṭa*; A. *shaqlit mīthe* (if the body is lying on it, *miṭa*); S. *tavūt*; Kurd. (Jews also) *darbaste*.

24. [Cf. J. L. Zlotnik, ed. *Ma'ase Yerushalmi* (Jerusalem, 1946), pp. 32, 102.]

25. [The variants *se'udat* and *se'ōdit* seem to be due to variations in the pronunciation of the word by the informants.]

26. A. *bātē ḥayyim*; for women, *ṭapāya*, "shoulder of a mountain" [*tappe* is a Persian word meaning "hill"]; S. and Ushnu *bēt haḥaimē*; Z. and D. *qorātha*; S. and Bijar, *ziaryē*; Z. and Rekan, *ziartiātha*; Kurd. *siāratan*.

27. In Amadiya there are said to be graves that are seven hundred years old; and some of these have stones with [Hebrew] inscriptions, which read thus ["This is the grave of X, son of Y, who departed in the year ———, in the month of ———, on the day ——— to his house of eternity, and left life to his sons. May his soul be tied into the bundle of life."] Also, in Sinne, there are graves with inscriptions. For a long time past, the Kurds have refused to permit inscriptions on Jewish graves.

28. Walter Schwarz, "Bei den kurdischen Juden," *JR*, July 12, 1935, p. 3; [trans. from Germ. by R.P.].

Chapter 11

1. Schwarz writes as follows concerning the Jews of Sundur: ["Although the fields and the vineyards are well kept and yield good crops, although these Jews have unbelievably modest requirements, they are rather poor because they find no market for their products" (Walter Schwarz, "Bei den Kurdischen Juden," *JR*, July 12, 1935; trans. from Germ. by R.P.)].

2. Saad, *Sechszehn Jahre*, p. 177.

3. This village was also visited by R. David d'Bet Hillel (see Fischel, "Massa' l'Kurdistan," p. 10). Walter Schwarz gives a good description of a visit to the village of Sundur. ["The village Sandor is inhabited only by Jews. Thus it was as far as one can remember" (see note 1; trans. from Germ. by R.P.)].

4. Anglo-Jewish Association, London, 6th Annual Report, 1897, p. 97.

5. Fischel, "Massa' l'Kurdistan," p. 11.

6. E.g., in Barashe. In Ushnu twenty-five families were formerly engaged in tobacco growing; today there are only five.

7. These "snacks" are the subject of the verse, *Mammi khul ikhalt kalba qū qiyamtit arye*, "Little brother, eat the eating of a dog and arise the arising of a lion," i.e., eat as quickly as a dog in order to be able quickly to continue your work but continue it with the strength of a lion (Barashe).

8. "Around the town are fruitful and well-cultivated fields. Olive and date trees, as well as vines, grow upon the declivities; a considerable proportion of them belong to the Jewish community" (Benjamin II, *Acht Jahre*, p. 74.

9. Grades of grapes are

zerik, the best grade, round and white (for raisins)
rashme'u, black and long (for raisins)
selōpi, good and white
mīrani, white
sa'dani, long and white
ta'alik, black (for wine).

10. In Zakho this is done in the dark for fear of the "evil eye."

Chapter 12

1. We have no historical information concerning the economic and social position of the Jews in former times. We can only say that the urban Jewish settlements are very old. For similar migrations from the country to the town and their accompanying phenomena, compare, for instance, the migration of the Babylonian Jews of the Gaonic period.

2. "In Kirkuk, as in all Kurdistan, the chief occupation of the Jewish inhabitants is that of drapers and mercers, the cotton cloth and print trade is entirely in their hands"; in the caravan with which Soane left Kirkuk, there were two Jews who were going to Kurdistan with printed cottons for sale (E. B. Soane, *To Mesopotamia, and Kurdistan in Disguise*, 2nd. ed., London, 1926, pp. 123, 164). Apparently the situation is similar in Halabya: "There are in the Halabya bazaar fifty-two such shops, and probably twenty of these are occupied by linen drapers and cloth merchants, chiefly Jews, who are the principal part of the commercial population" (ibid.) p. 232).

3. Ibid., p. 123.

4. For illustrations of shops in Amadiya, see Binder, *Au Kurdistan*, p. 206.

5. Albala, *BAIU*, 1911:74. The Jews possess many large shops also: "In the bazaars, many stores belong to Israelite notables" [trans. from French by R.P.].

6. Cloth merchants, haberdashers, grocers, publicans, ambulant moneychangers, etc." (in Khaneqin, *BAIU* 1911:74; [trans. from French by R.P.]. These merchants are still called *baqāle* (A.).

7. Eighty to 100 peddlers out of 300 tradesmen; A. 40 out of 200; S. 120 out of 400; Urmia (about the year 1900) 100 out of 300.

8. Concerning the dangers to which the peddlers are exposed in these mountain districts, see p. 226. It is said that the peddlers of Zakho never die at home: they meet either a natural or a violent death on the road.

9. These goods figure also in the business letters dating from the middle of the eighteenth century, which were published by Mann (*Texts and Studies*, vol. 1, letters 6 [pp. 520–22], 12 [pp. 530–31], and 13 [p. 531]). From these letters it also appears that the transactions involved were small affairs.

10. Banse, *Die Türkei*, p. 230.

11. A *batman* (4 *rotl*) brings from 5 to 10 rupees (A.).

Chapter 13

1. Walter Schwarz "Bei den kurdischen Juden," *JR*, July 12, 1935, on the Jews of Sandur: ["Chiefly the artisans in the village are in a very oppressed state." Trans. from the German by R.P.].

2. Benjamin II also speaks of the Kurdish Jews as weavers: "The different woolen stuffs, which are manufactured by the Jews in Kurdistan, are likewise exported into foreign ports. This is a branch of trade which many of them cultivate most industriously. They likewise make carpets. Their looms are extremely simple: on two pieces of wood, which are placed in the ground, at a certain distance from each other, they make good and even splendid stuffs." (*Eight Years*, pp. 129–30). In S. the weavers are called *jōla*, e.g., *Ezra jola*.

3. In order to obtain the silky luster the wool yarn is dipped into an extract of a sort of onion call *gilke*.

4. In Z. this even led to complications, for the Kurds made up to the Jewish dressmakers.

5. Lamec Saad, *Sechszehn Jahre*, p. 254. "The Jews (of Zakho) are mule drivers between Mosul and Jezire."

6. [This word seems to be of the same root as the talmudic name for raft, *mabbara*; cf. Raphael Patai, *Jewish Seafaring in Ancient Times* [Hebrew] (Jerusalem, 1938), p. 148.]

7. The brands have such forms as the following, for instance: [brand symbol] or [brand symbol].

Chapter 14

1. *Eight Years*, p. 126.

2. On the status of the agas in our epoch, see, e.g., Hamilton, *Rood Through Kurdistan*, pp. 93ff., 105, 122, about Hamada (aga of Kala Tchin), Sayid Taha, and Ismael Beg of Rowandus.

3. *OW* 1909: 575.

4. In order to maintain their power, the agas had to send a heavy tribute to the Sultan at Constantinople. They consequently despoiled their subjects—believers and, still more, unbelievers, both Jews and Christians—not stopping even at murder. When, in Khoi Sanjak, the Jews once refused to pay the tribute to the aga, he had their *ḥakham* attacked and murdered in order to cow the rest of the community. Cf. *BAIU* 21 (1896): 54.

5. [Cf. also the Wigrams' vivid description of Jews "domesticated" by Kurdish agas (W. A. and Edgar T. A. Wigram, *The Cradle of Mankind* [London, 1914]. pp. 317–18).]

6. [N. Albala, *OW* 1909: 579; trans. from Germ. by R.P.]

7. In these districts it is the bridegroom who must furnish the bride-price, *niqda* (see pp. 110–13).

8. My informant told me that when a Jewish housewife is out of rice or *masta* (sour milk), she goes to the wife of the *pis mīre* and is supplied with what she needs.

9. Three families in Amadiya were exempt from the *sukhra*, among them the Bē Yosef Barashe. Rich families could also acquire exemption by supplying a substitute.

10. Albala, *OW* 1909:579; [trans. from Germ. by R.P.].

11. The Christians are in the same plight. The Kurdish mayor of Zakho said to Saad: "Lately one of the Kurdish *begs*, who owes me an amount of money, wrote to me that at the moment he had no cash. He will, however, sell in the near future his Christian, that is, he will transfer him to another Kurdish *beg*; and then he will pay" (*Sechszehn Jahre*, p. 255; [trans. from Germ. by R.P.].

12. In the demoralized state of many Kurdish tribes, the contrary also occurs. Albala reports the following from Sulaimani: ["Thefts during the night are frequent in the

Jewish quarters. Several individuals, armed to the teeth, break down the door of a house and carry away whatever they chose to. . . . The thieves are the agents of the agas and act on their behalf" (*OW* 1909:579; trans. from Germ. by R.P.]).

13. There is a saying among the Kurds: *Dimmit bābokh khilokh*, "The blood money of your father you ate."

Chapter 15

1. The people who acquire posts of honor often pay not in cash but in kind. The *gabbai* must sell the goods and administer the funds.

2. In more recent times, there has been a special *ḥazan* in Zakho; but he must not act as *shoḥeṭ*.

3. S. Kurd. *khadam*.

4. The Muslims of Sinne also have this custom.

5. The family Bē Avidāni, to which the four *ḥakhamim* of Amadiya belong, comes from Nirwa. In the letters published by Mann, (*Texts and Studies*, vol. 1) it is chiefly *ḥakhamim* from Amadiya who granted diplomas, e.g., Ḥ. Shim'on Sh'muel Doga (letter 8) and Shim'on ben Binyamin Halevi (letter 15)—both probably from the middle of the eighteenth century.

6. Concerning this book, see Assaf, "*Le-Toldot*," pp. 109–11. A copy of this ms. dated 5420 (=1660) was brought from Kurdistan by Walter Fischel.

7. A slaughterer's diploma of the year 5525 (1764), drawn up by Shim'on b. Binyamin Halevi, is published in Mann, *Texts and Studies*, vol. 1, p. 533.

8. Ibid., letters 14 and 20 are pertinent.

9. In Sinne there were ten such itinerant slaughterers.

10. The *shoḥeṭim* of Sinne (who are also schoolmasters) have so much meat, especially on Fridays, that they send their pupils around to sell it for them. Meat is extraordinarily cheap. In Sinne the price of a *rotl* is about 2 pence.

11. Ibid., letter 21, pp. 545ff. acquaints us with an incident of this kind.

12. Cases of this kind occur also among the Jews of the Caucasus.

Chapter 16

[For purposes of comparison with the subject of this chapter, cf. Raphael Patai, "The Hebrew Education in the Marrano Community of Meshhed" [in Hebrew], *Edoth* 1, no. 4 (July 1946): 213–26.]

1. Mann, *Texts and Studies*, vol. 1, pp. 480ff., 491ff.

2. Mann speaks of him as "a prominent scholar" (p. 481), probably an exaggeration.

3. Other famous teachers of Amadiya were Ḥ. R. Shim'on (ca. 1640), Ḥ. R. Eliya (ca. 1840), Ḥ. R. Shim'on (ca. 1860). In Zakho, Ḥ. R. Mose Yiṣḥaq Baglugnaya, who died about 1900 at the age of seventy, was a teacher of note. *Sefer Shire Zimra* of Ḥ. Barukh contains several of his poems.

4. In Bashkala, boys are sent to school at the age of six to seven and remain to the age of thirteen to fourteen. Cf. Anglo-Jewish Association, 6th Annual Report, London, 1897, p. 98.

5. Teacher: A. and S. *me'allim* or *mu'allim*; Z. and D. *istaz*, pl. *istazwāsa*; A. (principally women) *istādi*; Arbil *ustal*, pl. *ustala*; S. *kalīfa*.

6. ["The rabbis, busy all day long with slaughtering and dissecting the meat, to remove the nerves and the suet, with going to perform circumcisions in the Muslim homes, with writing amulets, etc., do not have the time to take care of the religious

instruction of the Jewish children" (J. Bassan, *BAIU* 26(1901): 277; trans. from French by R.P.].

7. Cf. a letter of the wife of Ya'aqov Mizraḥi: ["The rabbi, of blessed memory, was occupied with his inspection, and had no time to teach the pupils, so that I taught them in his stead, I was a helpmeet for him" (Mann, *Texts and Studies*, vol. 1, p. 511, lines 68–70 (of the letter); trans. from Heb. by R.P.].

8. On the other hand, ["the Talmud Torah, even in its most primitive and most defective form, does not exist in Seneh. Rare are the Jews who can read the prayers in the books" (J. Bassan, *BAIU* 26(1901): 277; trans. from French by R.P.; Seneh is Sinne]. But perhaps Bassan did not regard the private schools of the *ḥakhamim* as schools.

9. *BAIU* 36 (1911): 74; [trans. from French by R.P.].

10. The groups are called A. *jiwat*; Z. *jewāte*, pl. *jewāteyāsa*; S. *gauqā* or *dasta.*

11. A. *Lūḥā*, S. and A. *dāpā*, S. *takhta.*

12. *Qati'a*, the stick with which the teacher beats the children.

13. Arab. *ḥudh* (Maclean, *Grammar*, p. 94.

14. [They say, "*Sheqer* (lie) has no feet," meaning that the letters *shin*, *qof*, and *resh* have no feet and that a lie cannot remain standing.]

15. Sinne has several variants: *dūsha* (honey), *ḥalwa* (halvah), *zatye* (cakes), *ḥēnē* (henna), and *ṭēnē* (figs).

16. Irene Garbell informs me that these same combinations were formerly used in teaching the Arabic alphabet in the Arab schools. [They are used to this day among the Jews of Iran and many another Middle Eastern country; cf. Patai, "Hebrew Education," pp. 220–21.

17. In Zakho the classes are called *tanyāsa*, *nuqṭa ḥurfe*, and *mehāgōye*, in Sinne, *alef-bēt*, *nuqdē*, and *ḥajūhē.*

18. Sinne; cf. Yosef Y. Rivlin, "Shabtit Dilomkhe," *Zion-Yedi'ot*, 1:4:59.

19. In Sinne the teacher says, *Kha aklēla khūwarta hamēti! kemēti?*, "Bring me a white chicken. Will you ring it?"

20. See also Rivlin, "Shabtit Dilomkhe," p. 59, n. 1.

21. In Bashkala, a string of beads, called *tasbe*, is used in the teaching of arithmetic (Anglo–Jewish Association, 6th Annual Report, 1897, p. 98).

22. In Sinne the father says, *Pisriw ṭālokh garme umishkēw holuwā bākī*, "His flesh is for you, his bones and his skin give back to me."

23. In Sinne the children are beaten every day but without the accompaniment of verses.

24. See also p. 159, however, concerning spittle as a magic remedy.

Chapter 17

1. *EJJ*, p. 303.

2. Z., D., A., and Sulaimani *Knishta*, Arbil *ṣlōla.*

3. [Trans. from Arab. by R.P.]

4. Assaf, "Le-Toldot," *Zion* 6 (1934):111, p. 27.

5. *EJJ*, p. 306–7.

6. [Cf., however, Jacob Z. Lauterbach, "*Tashlik*," *HUCA* 11 (1936): 207–8.]

7. Rough ground plans of the synagogues of Amadiya (Navi Yeḥezqel) and Sundur have been published by Walter Schwarz in *JR*, July 12, 1935. There is also a description of the synagogue at Sundur: ["The synagogue itself. . . serves only in winter as the place of worship. In summer it is the storage place of the community and we find. . . in one of the corners an enormous heap of raisins" (ibid.; trans. from Germ. by R.P.)].

8. *EJJ*, p. 300.

9. According to my informant, this kind of column is found only in Amadiya and only in Jewish buildings.

10. The same is also said of the pillars in the Ezra haSofer synagogue of Amadiya. [This reminds one of talmudic legends, according to which the columns of the Temple of Jerusalem were living trees, deeply rooted in the ground. Cf. Raphael Patai, *Man and Earth* Jerusalem, 1943 vol. 2, pp. 197ff.; idem, *Man and Temple* (Edinburgh, 1947).

11. When, in Sinne, these carpets were once stolen, the governor of the town replaced them.

12. Jaba, *Dictionnaire*, p. 194: *dūshek*, "matelas, lit., banc pour dormir."

13. The old *tīke* of Amadiya were unornamented wooden cases.

14. When on sale, the *rimmonim* are called *'eṣ ḥayyim* in Amadiya. In Sinne they are also called *tāj tora*, "Torah crown."

15. HUBC 38:70. A similar specimen at present in Jerusalem in the synagogue established by immigrants from Barashe, is formed in almost exactly the same way. It dates back to 1783 C.E.

16. Thus, in Amadiya there lived a Ḥakham Reḥamim and a Ḥakham Ḥayyim (about 1890) who were Torah scribes of note.

17. In the *genīza* of the Navi Yeḥezqel synagogue there are said to be more than two hundred unserviceable scrolls.

18. The synagogue of the Jews from Barashe in Jerusalem has five Torah scrolls.

19. HUBC 38:154. It is said to date from the year 1770 C.E.

20. Maclean, *Grammar*, p. 98: *ḥyāṣa*, a girdle. In Sinne the expression *khāsā isirta*, "tied around with the girdle," is used when one does not want to say *sēfer tora* [Torah scroll].

21. [On the bird *simorgh*, see, e.g., Bess Allen Donaldson, *The Wild Rue*, (London, 1938), p. 166; *ERE* 1.514a, 3.448b, 8.294b.]

22. The *genīza* is also briefly mentioned by Brawer, "Mi-Parashot Massa'otay," *Sinai* vol. 1, no. 11 (1938): 438: [In the synagogue there is a *genīza* that has not been emptied for a long time, but I was unable to deal with it. It is possible that scholars will find in it material for the history of the Jews in Kurdistan, of which we know very little" (trans. from Heb. by R.P.]. Concerning the *genīza* of Sundur, see Fischel, "Massa' l'Kurdistan," *Sinai*, vol. 1, no. 3–4 (1938):218–54. p. 10, n. 18.

Chapter 18

1. [Recorded by Brauer in Jerusalem shortly before 1937 from the mouth of a Kurdish Jew from Amadiya, and published in the *Almanach des Schocken Verlags*, Berlin, 1937/38, pp. 164–73, under the title "Der heilsame Granatapfelbaum." To fit the story into the popular style of the Schocken almanac, Brauer presented it in a smooth literary style that must have differed considerably from the original style of his Kurdish informant. In translating the story from Brauer's German into English, I tried to keep as closely to his style as possible. R.P.]

2. The summer shoes are for the smooth mountain paths of Kurdistan. They are made wholly of woven material, and have no leather soles.

3. A raft kept afloat by several inflated goats' skins.

4. Weaving is one of the main handicrafts of Kurdish Jews.

5. The same is true among the Nestorians: "There are said to be Nestorians now in Tiyary who will not kindle a fire upon the Sabbath to cook their food; but their cold winters oblige them to do it for the sake of necessary warmth" (Grant, *The Nestorians, or The Lost Tribes*, p. 215).

6. In Sinne, the Sabbath Kurd is called *ger mala*.

7. Once, on the Sabbath, a spark fell on a woman's dress and began to singe her leg. She screamed dreadfully, but no one ventured to flick away the spark. The *nuraya* was sent for (A.).

8. Not in Zakho or Sinne. In Zakho there are only Muslim barbers. In Yemen the schoolmaster (*mori*) does the shaving; and he, too, does it gratis, as a mitzva. See *EJJ*, p. 308.

9. In Sinne the women bake six small round loaves of bread, *juje shabbat*, two for each of the three meals.

10. Z. *mebōse*, A. and Tchalla *mebīsa*.

11. See *EJJ*, p. 309.

12. In Arbil the Sabbath was formerly announced by blowing the shofar from the citadel.

13. An old *sherā'a shabsa* of iron, whose age is given as two hundred years, is [was] in HUBC (38:101).

14. In Amadiya at present only three loaves are put in the *sīnīya*; formerly, there were twelve.

15. Functions that can be bought are termed *fisle* (A.).

16. The sale of the "third" proceeds in Amadiya somewhat in this manner: A bids 25 rupees for the whole section, B 20 rupees for half, and C 15 rupees for one "foot." C then acquires the "foot" (i.e., a fourth) and B. a half; and the last "foot" is put up to auction again.

17. It is said that in about 1925, when the Jews were compelled to leave Bashkala and Salamas and came to Amadiya, they brought with them the custom of reading the first and last verses of the *hafṭara* in Hebrew and the rest in Targum. The Jews of Amadiya then adopted this custom.

18. Also, the Nestorians pay their calls, instead of going home, after the Sabbath service: "Several of the people then went to the house of the church steward, and partook of a more substantial but plain repast, retiring soon after to their houses or calling upon their more immediate friends"; the Nestorians were no less strict in their observance of the Sabbath rest than the Jews: "Formerly they are said to have regarded the Christian Sabbath with so much sacredness, as to put to death persons for traveling on that holy day" (Grant, *The Nestorians, or the Lost Tribes*, p. 80.

19. In Sinne, for example, he calls out *Re'ūben minḥāya*.

Chapter 19

1. The women call Passover Ēz Parītēlē, Feast That Causes One To Burst, because they are overloaded with work at this time (Z.).

2. This is done also among the Jews of the Caucasus. See Yosef Yehuda Tchorny, *Sefer haMassa'ot*, St. Petersburg, 1884, p. 196. Among the Yemenites, on the other hand, each family celebrates its own Seder. See *EJJ*, p. 341.

3. So defined by an informant from Zakho. The meaning is uncertain, however.

4. The same custom obtains also among the Jews of the Caucasus: ["It is the custom among them even to the present day for the poor women to go to glean spikes in the fields of the gentiles and the princes;. . . and every evening they beat out that which they have gathered and sell it for mitzvot, and the price they get for this *shemura* is quite high" (Zvi Kasdai, *Mamlekhet Ararat* Odessa, 1912, p. 33; trans. from Heb. by R.P.)].

5. [Cf., e.g. Wilhelm Mannhardt, *Wald- und Feldkulte* (Berlin, 1875–77), index, s.v. "Erntestrauss."]

6. [The Jews of Meshhed, Iran, however, also eat rice during the Passover.]

7. E.g., the *pizmon Lō lānū, lō lānū, hinkhem lō lānū—Min Miṣrayim g'alānū, et Toratēnū niḥalānū* (not listed in Davidson's *Thesaurus*).

8. [On salt in Jewish folk custom of Raphael Patai, *On Jewish Folklore*, Detroit, 1983, pp. 388–90.]

9. Wheat is not sold. On the other hand, *gurgur* (burgul) and flour are sold, usually to nomadic Kurds who pay for it after Pesach with cheese (Z.). Sometimes merchants sell their *hames* before Pesach at half price (A.).

10. In Zakho the *maṣṣa shemūra* is baked at midnight.

11. Kurd. *chichine*, from *chichik*, "mamelles de femme" (Jaba, *Dictionnaire*, p. 137); S., Ushnu, and Sulaimani *mama*. A Matzo with a *chichine* from Zakho was in HUBC (39:30).

12. R. David d'Bet Hillel, *Travels*. See also the Hebrew translation by Fischel, "Massa' l'Kurdistan," p. 20.

13. Grant, *The Nestorians, or the Lost Tribes*, p. 383.

14. Fischel, "Massa' l'Kurdistan," p. 23.

15. [Among Ashkenazi Jews the *marōr*, bitter herb, is usually horseradish.] Among the Kurdish Jews *marōr* is the general name for the plant called *taḥlishke* by the Kurds. [According to Ḥakham Avidani, the *marōr* used in Amadiya grows wild and is the same as the *'arqavlin* or *'arqavnin*, mentioned in the Mishna ('Erurin 2:6) and Talmud (B. Pesaḥim 39a), which is taken to refer to prickly creepers on palm trees, palm ivy.]

16. Also, Tchorny, *Sefer haMassa'ot*, p. 108, speaks of the great quantities of *ḥaroset* prepared by the Caucasian Jews.

17. Compare what the missionary Sternschuss wrote from Kirkuk: "The Jews here consider, that the celebration of this feast, as well as of many others, consists in an unusually great indulgence at the table. They especially drink wine, more than they ought, and much more than they can bear, and persons in such a state can scarcely be expected to listen to anything that is holy or spiritual" (Sternschuss, in *JI*, 1848:297.

18. An amulet is worn in the same way in Persia, i.e., on the upper arm.

19. [Similar customs prevail in many an Oriental Jewish community.]

20. A. *maṣṣa meshumeret*.

21. *Jauwāher berēsh de amanita* [pearl in the head of the pledge].

22. See pp. 290–92. Among the Caucasian Jews the custom is practiced in the same fashion; see Kasdai, *Mamlekhet Ararat*, p. 34.

23. [Concerning "ritual" silence, see *ERE*, index, s.v. "Silence."]

24. A. *ṭlōkhe mebīse gō tanūra*, "lentils Sabbath dish in the oven."

25. No explanation of this word could be given. The custom is practiced in Amadiya, Betanura, Rekan, Nirwa, and Dehok. I found it in Ushnu also. The custom is said to be 600 to 800 years old.

26. As he dons his *abāye*, the people sing, *Serī, serī mērāna, benī bene jenāna*, "His head, his head, a man, his abdomen a woman" (A. and Kurd.).

27. HUBC 39:18.

28. [Davidson, *Thesaurus*, vol. 1, p. 227, no. 4939.]

29. The name of the family is Bēt Sīman Ṭov. The play is performed in the courtyard of the Eliyahu Hanavi synagogue and takes place in the intermediate days between the beginning and the end of Passover.

30. My informant from Amadiya told me of such a case from Tchalla. At the home of Ḥ. Yedidya, the *afikoman* was once stolen and could not be located. An inquiry was sent to Ḥ. Raḥamim in Tchalla, who gave the decision that in a case of this kind one must start once more at the beginning of the Haggadah.

Chapter 20

1. [Also, the Jews of Baghdad call Shavu'ot 'Id el-Ziyāra (Feast of the Pilgrimage).]

2. The basis for the reading is the Baghdad edition of the *Seder Kri'a Mo'ed*.

3. In olden times, this *'aliya* was bestowed on the *gevir* in Amadiya also.

4. [Told me by Ḥakham Alwan Avidani of Amadiya, who had heard the story from the old men of his hometown.]

5. One of my informants spoke of twenty thousand participants.

6. This ascent is described by Benjamin II: "At break of day morning prayer is recited: after which the men, bearing the Pentateuch before them, go, armed with guns, pistols and daggers, to a mountain in the vicinity, when, in remembrance of the Law, which on this day was announced to them from Mount Sinai, they read in the Torah" (*Eight Years*, p. 99.).

7. Without waiting for the necessary interval of two hours to elapse between indulgence in milk and in meat dishes.

Chapter 21

1. [The custom is not confined to Zakho. Also, in the Syrian Jewish communities (Aleppo and Damascus) and among the Syrian Jews in Jerusalem, the children used to sew together the clothes of the people absorbed in reciting the Kinnoth on the eve of 9th Av. Making use of the darkness in the synagogue at that service, they also used to pelt the *ḥazan* with peels of water melons.]

2. The mood of the Kurdish youth in Jerusalem is hardly one of true mourning for the destruction of the sanctuary. The boys take advantage of the moment when everyone is lying on the ground to howl in a quite artificial manner. No doubt it is the same in Kurdistan.

3. In the Targum *'Uṣ* is translated as Stambul.

4. HUBC 39:31 from Sinne.

5. In Amadiya the eyes of the *kappara* animal have this significance. An amulet from Amadiya (HUBC 38:99) consists of a cord on which are strung the dried eye, the blue bead with seven holes, and a small blue bead with two holes. Another amulet from Amadiya that I saw consisted of a tin tube that the owner informed me, contained a piece of *neqūsa*, wood pierced by a needle. The dried eye of a *kappara* victim is fastened to the tube.

Chapter 22

1. Called *zewānit ṭum'ā*, "buying of fruits."

2. The Kurds call Rosh Hashana, *'Ida sere Sālē*, Feast of the Beginning of the Year" (A.).

3. [Cf. Davidson, *Thesaurus*, no. 2451.]

4. This practice has been abolished in Amadiya, "because the moths ate up the feather."

5. Benjamin II reports the same thing from Rowanduz: the Kurds forced their way into the Temple, "attacked the women, treated them ill,, and broke the symbolic trumpet and forced the Jews to stop their ceremony" (*Acht Jahre*, 113).

6. The Jews of Barashe eat *khuwarūsa*, because they make their milk products themselves.

7. For pregnant women, the Kurdish Jews do not swing two chickens as prescribed in the *Shulḥan 'Arukh*, but three: two hens and a cock.

8. See also Brawer, "Mi-Parashat Massa'otay," p. 20.

9. The following description of this ceremony pertains to Zakho: "And behold, what did I see? All the Jews were assembled, and in their midst walks the most respected man among them, holding in both hands a large wax candle (the candle for Yom Kippur) and so with dance and beat of drums the crowd moved forward, and the women who were standing on the roofs joined in with loud cries, howling like dogs . . . until they came to the synagogue. There they put the candle in its place" (W. Schur, *Maḥazot haḤayyim*, Vienna, 1884, p. 34).

10. I succeeded in acquiring still another of these rare scourges, a primitively executed implement from Rekan, made of oxhide and ass's skin (HUBC 39:12).

11. It is this scourging that Schur vividly describes: "and at each stroke which the *shammash* gives to the barbarian, the latter cries out loudly in a heart-rending voice. . . . And the unfortunate man's back was covered with wounds. . . . Several Muslim Kurds, who know this preposterous Jewish custom, came to the synagogue, pulled off their shirts and told the *shammash* in jest to give them forty strokes also" (ibid.). My informants denied this last allegation.

12. [This custom prevailed also in Ashkenazi communities among the pious. Of my great-grandmother, who lived in the second half of the nineteenth century in Grossvardein, Transylvania, it is known that she stood in one place during the entire Yom Kippur service and did not speak a word apart from the prescribed prayers.]

Chapter 23

1. [In connection with the custom of representing the soul in the form of a bird see *ERE* 1.525a, 11.729b and 745a (s.v. "Islam"); Sir James George Frazer, *The Golden Bough*, 3rd ed., London, 1922–25, index, s.v. "Soul."]

2. There are some *ḥakhamim* who take the Chair of Elijah out of the synagogue and put it into their *sukka* (Z.).

3. Apparently, there are also social reasons for this: it is not desirable that the rich should have such an advantage over the poor.

4. In Zakho the *lulav* remains at the *gabbai's* house and is not put up to auction until the first day. The price is very high, often £10; and only after the service is it brought to the house of the *merē lulav*. Each day, it is taken from his house and returned to it again after the service.

5. [The dance of the old men may be compared to the dances performed in the Second Temple of Jerusalem by "the pious and the men of good deeds" before the festive crowd in the course of the Sukkot celebrations in the women's courtyard (cf. Patai, *Man and Temple*, p. 28)].

6. [To beat with *five* boughs precisely was prescribed by Kabbalist rabbis; cf. Yeshaya Lurie, "Kavvanot," in Abraham Danzig, *Ḥayye Adam* (Vilna, 1820), sec. 152. Cf. also Isidor Scheftelowitz, *Altpalästinensischer Bauernglaube*, Hannover, 1925, p. 91.]

7. [These are the traditional seven *ushpizin*, guests, whose spiritual presence in the booth is supposed.]

8. [This custom, too, has its historical antecedents in Second Temple days, when on the Sabbath of the Feast of Tabernacles the people used to beat each other with their *lulavs*, (cf. Mishna Sukka 4.1). The beating each other with willow branches is customary in Tripoli, according to Benjamin II: "In Tripolis between each part, Selichot is said, and the Shofar is sounded; much coffee is drunk on the occasion. In the morning they all go to the synagogue, pray, and repeat the Hosheinot. Afterwards everyone takes his Hosheina with him, and they strike each other with the Hosheina over the shoulders. Neither

rank nor station is on this occasion taken into consideration; the women do it also, and each considers the blows with the Hosheina as an honor" (*Eight Years*, p. 331). The custom obtains to this day; cf. N. Slouschz, *Massa'i b'Eretz Luv*, vol. 2, (Tel Aviv, 1943), p. 86. This beating with branches has been explained, by analogy with similar customs of other peoples, as a fertility rite. Cf. Mannhardt, *Wald- und Feldkulte*, vol. 1,pp. 251ff., vol. 3, pp. 115ff.; Edwin Sidney Hartland, *Primitive Paternity* (London, 1909), vol. 1, 100, 108; idem, *The Legend of Perseus* (London, 1894–96), vol. 1, 171; Ovid, *Fasti* 2.425; Sir James George Frazer, *The Fasti of Ovid* (London, 1929), vol. 2, pp. 331ff.; idem, *The Golden Bough*, vol. 2, pp. 97ff.; L. Preller, *Römische Mythologie* (Berlin, 1881–83), vol. 1, p. 389; Angelo di Gubernatis, *Thiere in der indogermanischen Mythologie* (Leipzig, 1874), p. 173–74; Ploss-Bartels, *Das Weib*, vol. 2, p. 315 (cf. vol. 1, p. 764); Patai, *Man and Earth*, vol. 2, pp. 171–72.]

9. In Sinne the main processions often take place on the eve of Simḥat Tora; sometimes, however, not until the day itself at *minha*.

10. In more recent times three honorary posts of *ḥatan* are sold by auction.

11. [So also among the Jews of Achalczik in the Caucasus. Tchorny writes: "After these, every two men took a third one on their hands and carried him after the Torah-scrolls. The end of the matter was: they carried men on their hands, both big and small" (*Sefer haMassa'ot*, p. 154). The other features of the circumambulations (dancing, singing, candles, etc.) are found among most of both Oriental and Ashkenazi Jewish communities. Cf. Patai, *Man and Earth*, vol. 2, pp. 151–52, 169ff., 175ff.]

12. [This custom is observed in many a Jewish community; cf. Patai, *Man and Earth*, vol. 1, p. 215; idem, "Jewish Folk-cures for Barrenness (see chap. 8, n.1), pp. 118–19.]

Chapter 24

1. [In presenting this article here in my English translation, I found it necessary to add a few explanatory notes which I put in square brackets. The unbracketed notes are found in Brauer's original article in *Sefer Magnes*.]

2. [The blood of the sacrificed animals slaughtered upon the graves or near them in the Kurdish Jewish rain-making ceremony reminds us of the role of blood in the rain-making competition between Elijah and the prophets of the Baal on Mount Carmel, described in detail in 1Kings 18:20–40. See R. Patai, "The 'Control of Rain' in Ancient Palestine," *HUCA* 14 (1939): 251–86.]

3. Cf. R. Yosef Ḥayyim, *Rav Po'alim*, part 2 (Jerusalem, 1903), p. 10, paragraph 31. Cf. also Simḥa Assaf, "Le-Toldot ha-Yehudim," *Zion Me'assef* 6 (1934): 85–112.

4. See Mishna Ta'anit 2:1.

5. [In that story, as recorded by Brauer, the name of the father is given as Rabbi Netanel Halevi, and that of his son who fled from Barzan and died in Amadiya as Rabbi Sh'mu'el.]

6. See Mishna Ta'anit 2:1.

7. Also in Yemen they still practice the custom of taking out the Torah scroll from the synagogue when there is a drought. See *EJJ*, p. 367.

8. See Babylonian Talmud Ta'anit 16a, 23b; Sanhedrin 47b; *EJ*, s.v. "Grab." On the visitation of the tombs of saintly men in Salonika, cf. M. Gaster's article in the *ERE*, s.v. "Water," p. 716. Among the Jews of Palestine, cf. Moshe Reischer, *Sefer Sha'are Yerushalayim* (Lemberg, 1870), unpaginated; (reprint, Jerusalem, 1966–67), 33–34.

9. *EJ*, s.v. "Kapparot," p. 914; Bab. Talmud Berakhot 42a.

10. Mannhardt, Wald- und Feldkulte 1:327; W. Wundt, *Völkerpsychologie*, part 4, *Mythus und Religion*, 1:536; Frazer, *Golden Bough*, vol. 1 (*The Magic Art*), 1:272–72.

Cf. also the "Corn-mother," Frazer, *Golden Bough*, vol. 5 (*Spirits of the Corn and of the Wild*), 1:134–36.

11. Frazer, *Golden Bough* 1:274–75.

12. Frazer, *Golden Bough*, 1:275. The pouring of water by a woman is a more original form of the rite, from a magical point-of-view, than the pouring by a man.

13. Frazer, *Golden Bough* 1:275–76, quoting Manuk Abeghian, *Der armenische Volksglaube*, Leipzig, 1899, pp. 93–94.

14. Frazer, *Golden Bough* 1:276, quoting J. Rendel Harris's "manuscript notes of folklore collected in the East."

15. Ibid.

16. My informant emphasized that it makes no difference whether the flock is from Zakho or from another place. This indicates a degeneration of the custom in Zakho.

17. W. Wuttke, *Der deutsche Volksaberglaube der Gegenwart*, 3rd ed. (Berlin, 1900), par. 83; G. Jungbauer, *Deutsche Volksmedizin* (Berlin and Leipzig, 1934).

18. Cf. Jonah 3:7: the people of Niniveh imposed a fast on the animals (as well as on men) so that "they should cry mightily unto God." Cf. also Bab. Talmud, Ta'anit 17a.

19. Gustaf Dalman, *Arbeit und Sitte in Palästina*, Gütersloh,1928,1:1:142.

20. Frazer, *Golden Bough* 1:254, quoting Coulbeaux, "Au pays de Menelik: a travers l'Abyssinie" *Missions Catholiques* 30 (1898):455.

21. [This is one of the very few instances in which Brauer indicates his adherence to the *Kulturkreis* theory of anthropology. Cf. also p. 334.]

22. Pauly-Wissowa, *Real-Enzyklopaedie der klassischen Altertumswissenschaft*, (Stuttgart, 1894–) vol. 15, s.v. "Hermes," p. 776.

23. Pauly-Wissowa, *Real-Enzyklopaedie*, p. 775.

24. Ploughing in water, and ploughing in general, is a means of making rain fall. In the original form of the custom naked girls carried out the plowing. Cf. Abeghian, *Der armenische Volksglaube*, p. 93; Frazer, *Golden Bough* 1:282–83. The custom of ritual ploughing was observed also among the Jews of Amadiya: a few women dressed up as men did the ploughing.

25. Abeghian, *Der armenische Volksglaube*, p. 93.

26. Frazer, *Golden Bough* 1:285, quoting Rendel Harris.

27. Cf. Ezekiel 23:20.

28. See Pauly-Wissowa, *Real-Enzyklopaedie*, s.v. "Esel," p. 670.

29. Ibid., p. 651. In Germany they place the skull of a donkey on the roof as a protection against all evils. Cf. Erich and Beitl, *Wörterbuch*, s.v. "Esel."

30. [The continuation of the rain-making efforts for hours on end was a feature characteristic of such rituals already in biblical times, cf. 1Kings 18:26–29. Cf. also the data on Middle Eastern rain-making rituals collected in R. Patai, "The 'Control of Rain' in Ancient Palestine," *HUCA* 14 (1939):251–86.]

31. Cf. *EJJ*, p. 367; Adela M. Goodrich-Freer, *Arabs in Tent and Town*, (London, 1924), pp. 181–84. Reference to Jewish rain-making ability is found in the *Ḥadīth*, the Muslim traditional writings, cf. S. D. Goitein, *Qovetz 'al Yad* 2 (12):202. [Cf. also R. Patai, *The Seed of Abraham: Jews and Arabs in Contact and Conflict* (Salt Lake City, 1986), p. 172.]

Chapter 25

1. Z., D., Sulaimani, and Ushnu *ḥanuka*; A. *ishra'at ḥanuka*; S. *shrāta ḥanukāye*.

2. A. and Sulaimani *shammash*; Z., A., and Ushnu Kurd. *khedamta*, servant; S. *parwana*.

3. In Rekan, Betanura, and Nirwa those who observe Passover together assemble on the first day at the house of the *merē pisha*, in order to celebrate Hanukka with a great feast (whereas in Amadiya this custom is practiced at Purim, in Zakho, at Simḥat Tora).

4. In the synagogue at Kermanshah there are Hanukka candles that burn for twenty-four hours.

5. The meaning of *qormō bīqā* is not clear. The Kurdish Jews no longer know the meaning of the words, since their present vocabulary no longer contains them. For example, *qormō bīqā* was explained to me as *qor mobīqa*, "very cold." *Qormō* means root, truck, stem; cf. Greek Κορμô (Lidzbarski, p. 558; Maclean, *Grammar*, p. 275). *Bīqā* is said to be an old word for arrack bottle. [Likewise, my informant, Ḥ. Avidani, said that *qormō bīqā* means "firewood and a bottle.]" For this feast, the holiday makers bring along *qormō*, wood for feeding the fire in the stove, and arrack.

6. Note the similarity in sound to *ḥanuka*.

7. In Amadiya this custom was still practiced about 1900.

8. This custom, for which no explanation has survived, is first practiced at Hanukka but is repeated thereafter during the winter months.

Chapter 26

[With this whole chapter cf. Patai, *Man and Earth*, vol. 1, pp. 189–283, which deal with the rich ideological connection between man and the vegetable world as expressed in the customs, beliefs, and legends of Jews and Gentiles.]

1. Jaba, *Dictionnaire*, p. 16: *awis*, "enceinte, grosse."

2. The women also say, *Ilāne shāta māye, smukhlū ilāna*, "The trees drank water, the trees are pregnant" (A.).

3. [Cf. Patai, *Man and Earth*, vol. 1, pp. 213ff., where similar methods practiced by barren Jewish women in other ages and communities are collected. Cf. also Patai, "Jewish Folk-Cures for Barrenness," pp. 117–24.]

4. [This custom, accompanied by similar oral requests, obtains also in other communities. In the Middle Ages, it was customary for barren Jewish women to "dip a paper in the menses' blood, tie it around a fruit bearing tree, and say, "I give thee my illness and my infirmity, give thou me thy power of bearing fruit," Cf. in *ERE*, vol. 2, p. 656b (Gaster). In Raphael Ohana's *Mar'eh haYYeladim* (printed anew in 1908 in Jerusalem and much in use as a handbook of cures and charms at the end of the last and the beginning of the present century among the Jews of Oriental countries) we again find this cure: "Take a long piece of paper and dip it into her menstrual blood and then let her go to a tree full of fruit and insert the paper into a hole or a crack in the tree, and should there be no hole or crack, let her make a hole and put into it the aforementioned paper, and say seven times: 'Tree, tree, I give unto thee my ailment and thou give unto me thy fruits'. And she should not approach that tree again" (p. 35a). This custom had many variants, either accompanied by an oral request or without it. Cf. Patai, "Jewish Folk-Cures for Barrenness," pp. 121ff., including n. 24 for literature as to this custom among other peoples. It thus becomes clear that this custom of barren Kurdish Jewish women is but one local version of a general custom that can be found in many places both among Jews and non-Jews.]

5. [This custom is but one variant of the widespread custom of "tree marriage," which is performed among various peoples in a great variety of forms and for different purposes but always in connection with fertility; cf. Patai, *Man and Earth*, vol. 1, pp. 226ff. and literature there in the notes.]

6. [The comparison of human hair to trees can be found already in *Avoth deRabbi Nathan*, a Tannaitic midrash: "And He created in man everything that He created in His world: He created woods in the world and created woods in man, these are the hair of man" (chap. 31, ed. Solomon Schecther, 2nd ed. (New York, 1945), version A, p. 91). So also in Aggadath 'Olam Qaṭan, ed. Adolph Jellinek, *Beth Hamidrash* (Jerusalem, 1938), vol. 5, pp. 57–59: "The hair of man's head and beard is similar to a forest of trees." This comparison, which is but one of a long series of equations between all parts of the world and all parts of the human body microcosm, obtained also in the Middle Ages. At the end of the book *Orḥoth Ṣaddiqim* we read "And just as He makes herbs to grow from the earth, so man lets grow the hair of the head and the beard." R. Meir Aldabi (fourteenth century) says, "The hair which man lets grow is like a garden which makes it plants grow," (*Sefer Sh'vile Emunah*, "Third path." As to the equation man = world, see Patai, *Man and Earth*, vol. 1, pp. 165–76; idem, *Man and Temple*.]

7. *Wayiqra* refers to the beginning of the third book of the Pentateuch. *Qorqora* was explained as an onomatopoeic word. Cf. Jaba, *Dictionnaire*, p. 208: *qyr-qyr*, "bruit; mot onomatopeique." Cf. Arab. *qarqara*, to coo, to grumble.

8. This refers to the familiar sun-dried sheets of apricot pulp, which must be dissolved in water before using. For a good illustration, see *National Geographic Magazine*, 74:715.

Chapter 27

1. The Christians also practice this custom. Thus, the Christians of Barvilnaye invite their married daughters and sons-in-law to a feast that lasts till evening. Each daughter takes some of the food home with her. If one of the daughters is betrothed, her fiancé and his family are also invited.

2. Jaba, *Dictionnaire*, s.v. *ghaliqandin*, "fermer la porte" (Arab. *ghalaqa*). The custom of "locking the door" obtains also among the Nestorians.

3. In Zakho, the schoolboys with their teacher make a *serāne*, likewise called *ghelāqit tar'ē*.

4. [These words allude to the traditional method of weaving: the woman weaver sits in a pit up to her waist, while the loom rests before her on the ground. (A.)]

5. [The endings of the words *bēlāwa* and *belūka* are arbitrarily changed so as to rhyme with *zāva* and *būka*, respectively.]

6. In this connection, cf. the "begging song" at the *Mereinda* singing during Hanukka, as it is sung among the Sephardi Jews of Turkey. It goes thus:

Damemos azete, el Dio vos empreseinte
Damemos oun ajico, el Dio vos de oun ijico
Damemos ouna seroyika, el Dio vos de ouna ijica.

Give us some oil, so that God may let you live
Give us a piece of garlic, so that God may give you a boy
Give us a little onion, so that God may give you a girl.

Cf. *Revue des Écoles de l'Alliance Israélite Universelle* 4 (1902): 273. [These three lines are but part of the *Mereinda* song. The custom of reciting the *Mereinda* is found also among the Sephardi Jews in Jerusalem.]

7. ["Long before Purim the Tripolitarian Jewish children go from door to door . . . removing mats, brooms . . . and take to their heels, proud of having performed a mitzva.

Since to steal in these circumstances becomes a permitted thing, indeed recommended." *Revue des Ecoles del'Alliance Israélite Universelle*, 6 (1902): 424. Trans. from French by R.P.]

8. In some places the stealing of wood is even regarded as a duty, because wood that is stolen increases the healing power of the fire (Mark Brandenburg). Erich and Beitl, *Wörterbuch d. deutschen Volkskunde* (Leipzig, ca. 1936), s.v. "Ostern," p. 558.

9. A. explained the word as meaning "beauty." Maclean, *Grammar*, 101 *ḥāmutā*, virginity, maidenhood, youth.

10. The Kurds of Sinne call Purim *naurūz* [New Year's Day] because it coincides with the Persian New Year's feast.

11. [Trans. from Heb. by R.P.].

12. [This custom cannot be said to be a general one. The Jews of Meshhed, Iran, e.g., begin reading from the uprolled *Megilla*, which is then slowly unrolled as the reading proceeds.]

13. A., *paqpaqūshke*; Arbil: *toptarake*; S., *taqa*; Ushnu, *bomba*, *bārud*. In S. a stick with percussion caps and fuse is called *fishak*.

14. A. *bambāla*; Z., D., *bumbāla*, *bümbāla*; Ushnu, *dambāla*; Arbil, *batotā*, pl. *batotē*; S., *tīzanq*. This is exploded with powder.

15. Cf. Yosef Y. Rivlin, "Tafsir haMelekh," *Zion-Yedi'oth* 1:43–45.

16. Jaba, *Dictionnaire*, p. 133, *chok*, *jarret*, *genou*.

17. The people say: *lebōke qwīra ābit urza willit smīkha* "Buried (?) *leboke*, you are male but you have become pregnant." *Qwīra* was explained as "buried." Cf. the curse, *sir qwīra*, "May you be buried" (A.).

18. E.g., the song *Hat yarauman, hat yarauman* "Up, let us dance, let us dance."

19. Jaba, *Dictionnaire*, p. 205: *rotl*, pl. *rotlan*, "testicule."

20. See *EJJ*, pp. 333–34.

21. Kurd and Pers. *adabkhāna*, latrine; see Soane, *Kurmanji Grammar*, p. 158.

22. HUBC 39:9.

23. [From Ḥakham Barukh Mizraḥi, *Shīrē Zimrah* Jerusalem, 1930. p. 65. Acrostic: Ani (I), Moshe ben *Yiṣḥaq*. Trans. from Heb. by R.P.].

Chapter 28

1. The word *parug* is the Hebrew translation of the Targum word *fürüch*, chicken.

2. A song by Moshe b. Yiṣḥaq for the Shabbat Shīra is found in Barukh Mizraḥi's *Shīre Zimra* h, Jerusalem, 1930, p. 64.

BIBLIOGRAPHY

Abeghian, Manuk. *Der armenische Volksglaube*. Leipzig, 1899.

Adler, M. N., ed. *The Itinerary of Benjamin of Tudela*. London, 1907. Reprint, London, 1964.

Ainsworth, W. F. "Account of a Visit to the Chaldeans Inhabiting Central Kurdistan." *JRGS* 11 (1841):21–76.

———. *Travels and Researches in Asia Minor, Mesopotamia, Chaldea and Armenia*. London, 1842.

Albala, N. Report in *BAIU*, 1911.

Albrecht, K. *Die im Tahkemoni vorkommenden Angaben über Harizis Leben, Studien und Reisen*. Göttingen, 1890.

Aldabi, Meir. *Shvile Emunah*. Riva di Trento, 1558; Warsaw, 1874.

Allgemeine Zeitung des Judentums. Leipzig and Berlin, 1837–1922.

Alliance Israélite Universelle. *Bulletin de l'Alliance . . .* Paris.

———. *Revue des Ecoles de l'Alliance . . .* Paris, 1901–4.

Anglo-Jewish Association, London. *Sixth Annual Report*. 1897.

Ashbel, Dov. *Annual Report: The Climate of Palestine and Adjacent Countries*. Tel Aviv, 19 (1938/39).

———. *Rainfall Map of the Near East*. Jerusalem, 1940.

Assaf, Simḥa. "Le-Toldot ha-Yehudim be-Kurdistan u-Shkhenoteha." *Zion-Meassef* 6 (1934): 85–112.

———. "Nosafot le-Toldot ha-Yehudim be-Kurdistan." *Qiryat Sefer* 13 (1936–37): 266–71.

Badger, George Percy. *The Nestorians and Their Rituals: With a Narrative of a Mission to Mesopotamia and Coordistan*. 2 vols. London, 1852.

BAIU: reports on Kurdish Jews, 1889:48; 1892:53; 1895:64; 1896:52, 54; 1897:84; 1901:277; 1911.

Barukh, Ḥakham. *See* Mizraḥi, Barukh Sh'mu'el

Banse, E. *Die Türkei*. Braunschweig, 1919.

Bassan, J. Report on Kurdish Jews. *BAIU* 26 (1901):277.

Benisch, A., ed. and trans. *Travels of Rabbi Petachia of Ratisbon*. London, 1856.

Benjamin, Joseph Israel ("Benjamin II"). *Acht Jahre in Asien und Afrika von 1846 bis 1855*. Hannover, 1858.

———. *Cinq années en Orient (1946–1851)*. Paris, 1856.

———. *Drei Jahre in Amerika*. Hannover, 1863.

———. *Eight Years in Asia and Africa from 1846 to 1855*. Hannover, 1859.

———. *Sefer Massa'e Yisrael*. Trans. David Gordon. Lyck, 1859.

Ben-Ya'aqov, Abraham. *Q'hillot Y'hude Kurdistan*. Jerusalem, 1961. Reprint, Jerusalem, 1981.

Ben-Zvi, Yitzḥaq. *Okhlosenu ba-Aretz*. Jerusalem, 1929.

———. *The Exiled and the Redeemed*. Philadelphia, 1961.

Binder, Henry. *Au Kurdistan en Mésopotamie et en Perse*. Paris, 1887.

Borchart, Paul. "Benjamin von Tudela." *EJ*, s. v.

———. "Der Reiseweg des Rabbi Benjamin von Tudela und des Rabbi Petachia aus Regensburg in Mesopotamien und Persien." *Jahrbuch der jüdisch-literarischen Gesellschaft*, Frankfurt a. M., 16 (1924): 139–62.

Brawer, A. J. "Mi-Parashat Massa'otay be-Faras." *Sinai* 1, no. 9–10 (1938): 239–50; no. 11 (1938): 430–38.

Bruhl, J. H. "Journal." *JI*, 1864, pp. 89ff.

Buschan, Georg. *Die Sitten der Völker*. 4 vols. Stuttgart, 1914–22.

———. *Völkerkunde*. Stuttgart-Berlin, n. d.

Clauss, L. F. *Von Seele und Antlitz der Rassen und Völker*. München, 1929.

Cluckhohn, Clyde. "Some Reflections on the Method and Theory of the Kulturkreislehre." *American Anthropologist* 38 (1936): 157–96. Dalman, Gustav. *Arbeit und Sitte in Palästina*. 7 vols. Gütersloh, 1928–42.

David d'Bet Hillel. *Travels of Rabbi David d'Bet Hillel: From Jerusalem Through Arabia, Koordistan, Part of Persia and India to Madras*. Madras, 1832.

Davidson, Israel. *Thesaurus of Medieval Hebrew Poetry*. 4 vols. New York, 1924–33.

Dictionary of National Biography. London, various dates. S. v. "Stern, Henry Aaron," and "Wolff, Joseph."

Diwan, Yehuda ben 'Amram. *Ḥuṭ ha-Meshullash*. Constantinople, 1739.

Donaldson, Bess Allen. *The Wild Rue*. London, 1938.

Dozy, R. P. A. *Dictionnaire detaillé des noms des vêtements chez les Arabes*. Amsterdam, 1845.

Duval, R. *Les dialectes néo-Araméens de Salamas*. Paris, 1883.

EI. S. v. "Kurdistan."

EJ. S. v. "Benjamin, Joseph Israel."

Endres, Franz Carl. *Die Türkei*. Munchen, 1918.

Eppstein, J. M. "Journey to Kurdistan." *JI*, 1893.

———. "Visit to Kerkuk." *Jewish Records*, London, Oct. 1893, pp. 167ff.

Erich, Oswald Adolf, and Richard Beitl. *Wörterbuch der deutschen Volkskunde*. Leipzig, n. d. (ca. 1936).

Field, Henry. *Arabs of Central Iraq*. Chicago, 1935.

Fischel, Walter. "Bei den Juden im kurdischen Bergland." *JR*, Jan. 8, 1937.

———. "Iggerot Kurdistan. *Sinai* 6 (1939).

———. "Kurdistan." *EJ*, vol. 10, 1934, pp. 514–19.

———. "Massa' le-Kurdistan, Paras, u-Bavel," *Sinai* 3:3–4 (1939): 218–54.
Frazer, Sir James George. *The Fasti of Ovid*. 6 vols. London, 1929.
———. *The Golden Bough*. 3rd ed. 12 vols. London, 1922–25. Garbell, Irene. *The Jewish Neo-Aramaic Dialect of Persian Azerbaijan*. The Hague, 1965.
Gerson-Kiwi, Edith. "Kurdistan." In *Encyclopaedia Judiaca*, vol. 10. Jerusalem, 1972, pp. 1299–1300.
———. "The Music of the Kurdistani Jews." In Amnon Shiloaḥ ed., *Yuval* 2 (1972):59–72.
———. *Studia Musicologica* 7 (1965): 61–70.
Goitein, S. D. In *Qovetz 'al Yad* 2 (12): 272.
Goodrich-Freer, Adela M. *Arabs in Tent and Town*. London, 1924.
Gottheil, I. "The Judeo-Aramaic Dialect of Salamas." *JAOS* 15 (1893): 297ff.
Grant, Asahel. *The Nestorians, or The Lost Tribes*. London, 1841.
Gubernatis, Angelo di. *Thiere in der indogermanischen Mythologie*. Leipzig, 1874.
Hamilton, Archibald M. *Road Through Kurdistan*. London, 1937.
Hartland, Edwin Sidney. *The Legend of Perseus*. 2 vols. London, 1894–96.
———. *Primitive Paternity*. 2 vols. London, 1909–10.
Hay, William Rupert. *Two Years in Kurdistan*. London, 1921.
Hovorka, Oskar von, and Adolf Kronfeld. *Vergleichende Volksmedizin*. Stuttgart, 1908–9.
Ibn Verga, Joseph. *Shevet Yehuda*. Hannover, 1855. Reprint, Hannover, 1924.
Idelsohn, Abraham Z. "Aramäisch sprechende Juden." *Die Welt*, Berlin, 30 (1912): 906–7.
———. *Hebräisch-Orientalischer Melodienschatz*. 5 vols. Leipzig, 1912–32.
———. "Sippurim ba-Lashon ha-Aramit ha-Hadasha." *HaShiloaḥ* 29 (1913): 121ff.
Isaacs, A. A. *Biography of H. A. Stern*. London, 1886.
Jaba, A. *Dictionnaire Kurde-Français*. St. Petersburg, 1879.
Jellinek, Adolph, ed. *Beth HaMidrash*. 2nd ed. 6 vols. Jerusalem, 1938.
Jewish Chronicle, London, May 3, 1864. Necrology on J. I. Benjamin.
Jewish Expositor. London.
JI. London.
Jewish Records (Supplement to *JI*, 1861–83).
Jüdisch-Literarische Gesellschaft. *Jahrbuch*. Frankfurt a. M., 1903–32.
Jungbauer, Gustav. *Deutsche Volksmedizin*. Berlin and Leipzig, 1934.
Kasdai, Zvi. *Mamlekhet Ararat*. Odessa, 1912.
ha-Kohen, Joseph. *'Emeq haBakha*. 1558, and numerous editions.
Lagarde, Paul de. *Iudae Harizi Macamae*. Göttingen, 1883.
Laufer, O. "Totenkronen." *ZVV* 26: 16ff.
Lauterbach, Jacob Z. "Tashlik." *HUCA* 11 (1936): 207–8.
Layard, A. H. *Niniveh and Its Remains*. London, 1867.
Lidzbarski, Mark. Geschichten und Lieder aus den neu-Aramischen Handschriften der kön. Bibliothek zu Berlin (Beiträge zur Volks- und Völkerkunde 4). Weimar, 1896.
Löwy, Albert. "Notes on the Jews of Kurdistan." Anglo-Jewish Association, *Sixth Annual Report*. London, 1897, pp. 94–97.

———. "On a Unique Specimen of Lishana shel Imrani." *Transactions of the Society of Biblical Archaeology* 4 (1876): 98–117.

———. "On Kudish Folk Lore in the Kurdo-Jewish Dialect." *Transactions of the Society of Biblical Archaeology* 6 (1878):600–602.

MacLean, A. J. *Grammar of the Dialects of Vernacular Syriac*. Cambridge, 1895; Oxford, 1901.

Mann, Jacob. "Ha-T'nu'ot ha-M'shiḥiyot bime Massa'e ha-Tz'lav ha-Rishonim." *HaTequfa* 24 (1928): 335–58.

———. *Livre d'Hommage a la mémoire du Dr. Samuel Poznanski*. Warsaw, 1927.

———. "Obadia le Proselyte." *REJ* 71 (1920): 89–93. ———. *Texts and Studies in Jewish History and Literature*. 2 vols. Cincinnati, 1931.

Mannhardt, Wilhelm. *Wald- und Feldkulte*. Berlin, 1875–77.

Marçais, Georges. *Le Costume musulman d'Alger*. Paris, 1930.

Minorsky, V. "Kurds." *EI* 4:1132–35.

Mizraḥi, Barukh ben Sh'mu'el. *Shire Zimrah*. Jerusalem, 1930.

Morgan, J. de. *Mission scientifique en Perse*, Paris, 1895.

Mulinen, E. Graf von. "Beiträge zur Kenntnis des Karmels." *ZDPV* 30 (1907): 117–207; 31 (1908): 1–258.

Naumann, H. *Grundzüge der deutschen Volkskunde*. Leipzig, 1922.

Newmark, Ephraim. "Eretz haQedem." *HeAsiph* 1889:39–75.

Nikitine, Basil. "La vie domestique Kurde." *RETP* 3 (1922):334-44.

———. "Rawandiz." *EI* 3:1130–32.

Obermeyer, Jacob. *Die Landschaft Babylonien*. Frankfurt a. M., 1929.

Ohana, Raphael. *Mar'eh ha-Yeladim*. 3rd ed. Jerusalem, 1908.

Orḥot Ṣaddiqim. Quoted in Meir Aldabi, *Shvile Emunah*.

Palmer, H. D. *Joseph Wolff: His Romantic Life and Travels*. London, 1935.

Patai, Raphael. *Israel Between East and West: A Study in Human Relations*. Philadelphia, 1953.

———. "The Hebrew Education in the Marrano Community of Meshhed" (in Hebrew). *Edoth* 1:4 (July 1946): 213–26.

———. Historical Traditions and Mortuary Customs of the Jews of Meshhed. (In Hebrew) Jerusalem, 1945. (In English in) Raphael Patai, *On Jewish Folklore*. Detroit, 1983, pp. 238–50.

———. "Jewish Folk Cures for Barrenness." *Folk-Lore*, London, 55 (Sept. 1944):1170024; 56 (Dec. 1944 and March 1945):208–18.

———. *Jewish Seafaring in Ancient Times* (in Hebrew). Jerusalem, 1938.

———. "Ha-Ledah ba-Minhag ha-'Amami." *Talpioth*, New York, 6 (1953):226–68, 686–705; 9 (1965):238–59.

———. *Man and Earth in Hebrew Custom, Belief and Legend* (in Hebrew). Jerusalem, 1942–43.

———. *Man and Temple in Ancient Jewish Myth and Ritual*. Edinburgh, 1947.

———. "Marriage Among the Marranos of Meshhed." (In Hebrew) *Edoth* 2 (1947):165–92. (In English in) Patai, *On Jewish Folklore*, pp. 203–37.

———. *On Jewish Folklore*. Detroit, 1983.

———. "Problems and Tasks of Jewish Folklore and Ethnology." *Journal of American Folklore* 59:231 (Jan.–March, 1946): 25–39.

———. *The Seed of Abraham: Jews and Arabs in Contact and Conflict*, Salt Lake City, 1986.

Pauly, A. and G. Wissowa, *Realenzyklopädie der klassischen Altertumswissenschaft*. Stuttgart, 1842–61.

Perkins, Justin. *Residence of Eight Years Among the Nestorian Christians With Notices of the Muhammadans*. Andover, 1843.

Pfannenschmidt, H. *Das Weihwasser im heidnischen und christlichen Kultus*. Hannover, 1878.

Ploss, Heinrich, Max Bartels, and Paul Bartels. *Das Weib*. 11th ed. 3 vols. Berlin, 1927

Ploss, Heinrich, and Barbara Renz. *Das Kind in Brauch und Sitte der Völker*. 2 vols. Berlin, 1911–12.

Preller, L. *Römische Mythologie*. Berlin, 1881–83.

Prym, Eugen, and Albert Socin. *Der neu-Aramäische Dialect des Tur-Abdin*. 2 vols. Gottingen, 1881.

Ratzel, Friedrich. *Völkerkunde*. 2nd ed. 2 vols. Leipzig and Vienna, 1894.

Reich, Sigismund. *Etudes sur les villages araméens de l'Anti-Liban*. Damascus, n. d. (ca.1938).

Reischer, Moshe. *Sefer Sha'are Y'rushalayim*. Lemberg, 1870. Reprint Jerusalem, 1966–67.

Rich, C. J. *Narrative of a Residence in Koordistan*. London, 1836. Ritter, Carl. *Die Erdkunde von Asien*. Vol. 9. Berlin, 1840.

Rivlin, Yosef Y. *Shirat Yehude ha-Targum*. Jerusalem, 1959.

———. "Shabtit Dilomkhe." *Zion-Yedi'ot* 1, no. 1 (1930): 9–112, 43–45; no. 4:59–61.

———. "Sippur David we-Goliat bi-Lshon Targum." *Zion-Meassef* 4 (1930): 109–20.

———. "Tafsir ha-Melekh." *Zion-Yedi'ot* 1, no. 1 (1930): 43–45.

Rosenthal, Franz. *Die Aramäistische Forschung seit den Arbeiten Theodor Nöldekes*. Leiden, 1939.

Rubashov, Zalman. "Urmia." *Davar* (Tel Aviv daily), Sept. 6, 1940.

Saad, Lamec. *Sechszehn Jahre als Quarantänarzt in der Türkei*. Berlin, 1913.

Sabar, Yona. *The Folk Literature of the Kurdish Jews*. New Haven, 1982.

Sassoon, David Solomon. *Ohel David*. 2 vols. London, 1932.

Scheftelowitz, Isidor. *Altpalästinensischer Bauernglaube*. Hannover, 1925.

Schmidt. Wilhelm. *Culture Historical Method of Ethnology*. New York, 1939.

Schrader, O. *Die Totenhochzeit*. Jena, 1904.

Schrire, T. *Hebrew Amulets*. London, 1966.

Schur, Zev Wolf. *Maḥazot ha-Ḥayyim*. Vienna, 1884.

Schwarz, Paul, ed. *Der Diwan des 'Umar ibn Abi Rabi'ah*. Leipzig, 1901.

Schwarz, Walter. "Bei den kurdischen Juden." *JR*, July 12, 1935.

Slouschz, Naham. *Massa'i be-Eretz Luv*. 2 vols. Tel Aviv, 1943.

Smith, Eli, and H. G. O. Dwight. *Missionary Researches in Armenia Including a Journey Through Asia Minor to which is Prefixed a Memoir on the Geography and Ancient History of Armenia*. London, 1834.

Soane, E. B. *To Mesopotamia and Kurdistan in Disguise*. London, 1912.

Stafford, Ronald S. H. *The Tragedy of the Assyrians*. London, 1935.

Stern, Henry A. *Dawnings of Light in the East, With Biblical, Historical, and Statistical Notices of Places Visited During a Mission to the Jews in Persia, Coordistan, and Mesopotamia*. London, 1854.

Streck, M. "Irbil." In *EI* 3:521–23.

Tacitus. *Germania*.

Tchorny, Yosef Yehuda. *Sefer ha-Massa'ot*. St. Petersburg, 1884.

Tilke, Max. *Studien zu der Entwicklungsgeschichte des orientalischen Kostüms*. Berlin, 1923.

Vambery, Arminius. *Sittenbilder aus dem Morgenlande*. Berlin, 1876.

Virchow, Hans. "Die armenische Wiege." *Zeitschrift für Ethnologie* (1924):208.

Wigram, W. A., and Edgar T. A. Wigram. *The Cradle of Mankind*. London, 1914.

Wirth, Alfred. *Anhaltische Volkskunde*. Dessau, 1932.

Wolff, Joseph. *Missionary Journal and Memoirs of the Rev. Joseph Wolff*. 3 vols. London, 1827–29.

———. *Researches and Missionary Labours*. London, 1835.

Wundt, Wilhelm. *Vökerpsychologie*. Part 4: *Mythus und Religion*. Leipzig, 1920.

Wuttke, A. *Der deutsche Volksaberglaube der Gagenwart*. 3rd ed. Berlin, 1900.

Ya'ari, Abraham. "Massa'ot R. David." *Sinai* 2:24–33.

———. *Sh'liḥim me-Eretz Yisrael l'Aseret ha-Shevaṭim*. Jerusalem, 1940.

Yosef Ḥayyim. *Rav Po'alim*. Jerusalem, 1903.

Zlotnick, Juda L. *Ma'ase Yerushalmi*. Jerusalem, 1946.

Zobel, M. "Bräuche nach der Geburt eines Kindes." *Almanach des Schocken Verlags*. Berlin, 1938–39, p. 103.

Zohar, The Book of. Many editions.

GLOSSARY

Introductory Note

This glossary contains some 2000 of those words used by the Jews of Kurdistan in their vernacular to which reference is made in the text of this book. No attempt has been made here to indicate the derivation of these words, whose origin can be in any of six languages: Hebrew, old Aramaic, Arabic, Kurdish, Persian, or Turkish. In addition, the vernacular of the Kurdish Jews contains a large number of Hebrew words, especially pertaining to religious matters, which were retained in their original form. These Hebrew words are not included in this glossary. Nor are the Kurdish words used by the Muslim Kurds in reference to Jewish matters, even though many of them are quoted in the book.

Since Targum was a spoken language, not used in writing, its vocabulary did not receive a fixed, written form. Consequently, almost every word was pronounced with marked variations depending on the locality, or even on the individual speaker. These variants, inasmuch as they appear in the book, are listed here, with cross references where necessary.

The local dialects of the Targum language fall into three overall categories:

1. The western dialect (Amadiya, Dehok, Nirwa, Zakho in Iraq; Diar Bekr, Urfa, Mardin, Jezira in Turkey).

2. The northeastern dialect (Salamas, Urmia, Nagada, Ushnu in Persian Azerbaijan; Bashqala in Turkey).

3. The southeastern dialect (Sinne, Sablag, Saqqiz, Bokan, Bana in Persian Kurdistan; Rowanduz, Arbil, Sulaymaniya in Iraq).

In the translation of the words listed in this glossary I confined myself to the meanings in which the words in question appear in this book.

A brief overview of the language of the Kurdish Jews can be found in David Cohen's article "Neo-Aramaic" in the *Encyclopaedia Judaica* (Jerusalem, 1972, 12:948–51). For further study of the language of the Kurdish Jews, see Irene Garbell's *The Jewish Neo-Aramaic Dialect of Persian Azerbaijan* (The Hague, 1965). For the closely related vernacular Syriac, see A. J. Maclean's still most useful *Grammar* (Cambridge, 1895) and *Dictionary* (Oxford, 1901) of that language, and A. J. Oraham's *Dictionary of the Stabilized and Enriched Assyrian Language* (Chicago, 1943).

Pronunciation Guide

In the pronunciation of the words given in transliteration in the text and in this glossary the following should be taken into account:

' stands for glottal stop, e. g., bē'e.

- (macron) over a vowel indicates that it is long and stressed, e. g., āsa, bē'e, īda, adōna, ajūra.

The vowels themselves are pronounced as follows:

a — as in bUt
ā — as in cAr
e — as in tEn
ē — as in Ape
i — as in Is
ī — as in mEEt
o — as in lOt
ō — as in gO
ö — as in French pEU
u — as in lOOk
ū — as in tOOl
ü — as in French rUE

As for the pronunciation of the consonants the following should be noted:

ch — as in CHin
g — as in Go
gh — guttural g (Arabic غ)
ḥ — is a strong, emphatic h (Arabic ح)
kh as in German naCH (Arabic خ)
q — is a deep, emphatic k (Arabic ق)
r — lingual r, as in Italian
ṣ — a somewhat guttural s (Arabic ص)
sh — as in SHe
ṭ — emphatic t (Arabic ط)
th — as in Thin
'ayn — corresponds to the Arabic 'ayin (ع)

The remaining consonants are pronounced more or less as in English.

'aba, 'abāye, abayika, coat
abadkhāna, latrine
abra, raft
ada, weeding
adlēl, tonight
adōde, funeral sermon

adōne, master
afikoman, matzo put aside
aftabha, pitcher, can
aga, aga
'agāla, scalding
āhit, you (*sing.*)
ai, aiya, this
'aīda, feast. *See also* **'ēda, ēza, īda**
ajel, ājil, to go
'ajna, vessel
ajūre, burnt brick
akha, brother
akhel, ākhil, to eat. *See also* **khil**
akhlīla, aklēla, hen, chicken
akhla, akla, aql, aqla, foot
akhtum, you (pl.)
akhura, animal's pen
Ala, Allah, god
'alāfe, grain dealer
'alek, to hurt, hit
alḥad, steps or stone in the grave
alkhalkha, blouse, cloak
alpa, thousand
alūcha, 'alūja, plum
'alwān, sacrifice
ama, woman cook
aman, amāna, vessel
amanita, pledge
amaresa, ignoramus (*from the Heb.* 'am ha'areṣ)
'amra, order
amra, sheep's wool
'amre, life
ana, āna, I
apse, oak apples
aql. *See* **akhla**
aqlasa, section
arakchin, araksin, araqchin, araqṣin, cap, hat
'araqīn, arak
'arāva, willow
arbala, 'arbala, rabala, sieve
arbi, aribi, forty
ardoshavke, flour and grape drink
argaman, byssus
arīsā, betrothal
arkhabke, uncooked flour
ar'ūra, manna, a tree fruit
arzāni, plenty
āsa, myrtle
'asarta, Shavu'ot
āse, ate, athe, ātī, to come, follow
ashadaqāya, ashadagāya, linen cloth, kerchief
ashata, this year. *See* **shata**
ashāye, 'ashāye, evening meal
ashīra, tribe
ashurage, obscene play
'asirta, aṣirta, evening
atīqa, old
auwis, pregnant
avid, awid, 'awid, to do, act
avisla, avisna, wine press
avka barsilqe, beet soup. *See also* **silqe**
awa, strong
awwa, he
azil, āzi, 'āzil, to spin; to go, remove oneself
azīz, 'azīz, *f.* **azīza,** dear, beloved

bāb, bāba, father, daddy
badan, cloak
badūnis, parsley
bahi, price
bahta, baḥta, bakhta, woman, wife
bahūra, behūre, shining
bā'i, bā'e, to desire, want, wish
ba'injāne kōme, egg plant
ba'injāne (balinjāne) smōke, tomato
bambāle, bumbāle, dambāla, bladder
bāmiya, Ochrea bamia
banētha, daughters. *See also* **bata**
bāne, bāni, to count
bāqa, for
baqāla, pedlar

baqlawa, Turkish confection
bar, before
barān, barāne, rain
barata, bata, daughter
barat mishṭākha, low grade grapes
barbūk, old woman
bardāna, liberation
bare, bāri, to create
bārekh, (m)bārikh, to bless
bariqsa, lead bullet
bar sifke, covered porch
barnūt, snuff
bartil, bride-price
bārud, detonating ball
basar, basre, behind, after
bāse, to come
basika, baska, pipe-stem, bone
bata, *pl.* **banātha, banētha, benātha,** daughter. *See also* **barata, bera**
baṭīye, joy
baṭman, measure, = 4 **rotl**
batōta, bladder
bāya, this
bazāzi, textile merchant
bazī, game
bē, without
bē, beta, bīt, house
bedāqa, search, sorting
bedugle, false
be'e, bē'e, eggs
be'elāye, second floor
be genīza, storage room
Be Ḥazāne, "House of the cantors"
behūre. *See* **bahūra**
bejāra, choice grapes
bē khamra, wine room
bekhī, bākhi, to weep
bekhtāya, ground floor
bekhūr, bukhāre, glue made of corn
bēl, house
belāwa, belōke, built up
belinde, tall
benātha, daughters. *See also* **bata**
benīza, corner, foundation
benōke, morning
benōne, sons. *See also* **brōna**
benūda, wrapping, diapers
benunta, shelf
benunim, synagogue officials
berā, daughter. *See also* **bata**
berakha, berakhta, blessing
berē awja, round stone
bereq, carpet
berguza, jacket and trousers
berīkhe, blessed
berīsa, a dance
berōkhe, blessing
beshiyāsa, demons
bē shōde, be shōze, house of joy
besīma, happy
bēta, be'ta, egg. *See also* **be'e**
bēt haḥaime, cemetery
betūna, bottle
bezōke, hole
bichīka, children
bigdāda, mighdāde, together
bīl, willow
bilhāya, shining
bīqa, bottle
bir, loom
birbanke, covered porch
birbiz, (m)berbiz, to scatter. *See also* **rebiz**
birinj, rice
birkar, weaver
birra, come!
birwāna, apron
birye, born, creature
bīsa, dried
biska, a curl, lock of hair
bisle, onions
biyāra, a kind of grapes
bkha, with
bō, with this
bōda, bādi, to begin, to do
bohāre, spring

bōke, buk, buka, bride
bōna. *See* **brōna**
bomba, detonating balls
brikha, blessing, blessed
brōna, bröna, benōne, bōna, son
brünjuk, copper (an amulet)
buchik, sleeve
būk (būke) barāne, rain bride
bukhāre, glue, incense. *See also* **bekhūr**
bumbāla, bümbāla, bladder
buqche, bundle
buqchit kālo, bundle of the bride
buselman, a game

chachiksa, bone
chafta, crooked
chai, tea
chakā, tall fur hat
chakme, leather boots
chāla, shāla, shala, shalo, trousers
chāla chapuksa, trousers and jacket
chape, round about, left side
charchabe, cloth, sheet
charchau, women's coat
charj jolāye, loom
charoke, rectangular cloth
chavīsha, shabīsha, shavīsa, officer, servant
che, what
chehil, forty. *See also* **chilke**
chera, lamp. *See also* **sherā'a**
chichikya, chichīne, nipple
chige, knee joint
chilke, forty. *See also* **chehil**
chochik, chokhik, vest, jacket. *See also* **chukhta**
chūche, chuchiktha, sparrow
chukha, none
chukhta, chukta, vest, jacket. *See also* **chochik**
chūla, shūla, thing, act, deed
chürikchüye, middleman

da, dai, de, mother
dādōka, wetnurse
da'ekh, da'ikh, to extinguish
daftar, ledger, copybook
da'ir, dā'ir, to return, turn back, repent
dāka, dake, court, platform, terrace
dakanitha, shelf
dake, bottles
dakh, like, as
dalke, rope
dambāla. *See* **bambāle**
dan, dāna, time
dān aṣirta, evening time
dān benōke, morning time
danguchka, mallet, hammer
dāpa, board, plank
daipirka, dapilka, dāpirka, midwife
dār, dara, dar'a, wood
darāja, step (in a stair)
dārash, dārūsh, drāsha, sermon, explanation
darbaste, bier
dardāna, release
dāre, der, gate, door
darfe, sheepskin
darga, dargēla, plank, door
darmāne gūre, body hair
darpe, baggy trousers
darze, needle
das gurke, daz gorka, gloves
dasho, dastasho, bowl
dasmal, veil
dasta, group
dastar, oats
dastgul, "hand to the flower,"
davate, dawate, guests
dauwarta, stage in preparing bread
da'wa, wedding
dāya, this
dazga, pillow
dē, to you
debāḥa, sacrifice. *See also* **zabāha**

debancha, pistol. *See also* **tepancha**
debāqa, devhāqa, eclipse
dēbha, wolf
dehena, dehina, tail fat
dēhva, dehwa, gold
delonke, children
demakh, dāmikh, to sleep, die
derā'a, yard, cubit, meter
derāja, stair
deranga, a dance
dermān, poison, medicine, drug
dēta, prison
devēq, to catch
dewāqa, dance
dewaqāne, dwāqa, dancer
dewēt, demand
dewīqa, pickled (meat)
dewōye, ink
dīdī, my own
dijmin, enemy. *See also* **düchmün**
dikāna, shop, store
dikandāre, shopkeeper
dikila, dikla, chicken, cock
dim, quick(ly)
dima, dimma, blood, blood-money
d'ip, d'īpa, folded, bent
diwākh, red cloth
diwambagi, bey of the diwan
dīza, thief
dodīya, cradle
dō'e, buttermilk, sour milk, whey
dō'et kista, "bag cheese," a dish
dōga, dōka, dōqa, baking pan
dōla, dūla, drum
dolma, dolama, rice dish
dorāna, bread roller
doshka, elevated platform
drāsha. *See* **dārash**
duchmin, enemy. *See also* **dijmin**
dugle, lie
dugmi halke, loops and button
duka, dūka, duke, ground, place, shelf
duksa, rug, carpet
duliksa, duluksa, foreskin, long sleeve
dūma, tail
dūma kaske, "green-tail," a bird
dūsha, honey
düshmün, enemy. *See also* **dijmin, duchmin**
dwāka. *See* **dewaqāne**

ēda, ēz, ēza, feast. *See also* **'aida**
ēka where to?
Elāha, Ilāha, God
ēlāka, sleeveless vest. *See also* **hēlāka**
ēlāne, feast time (Sukkot)
ēli, upper
ēlina, cask, jar, vessel
ēlītha, tail fat
ēna, eye, source, spring
ēnit ḥazda, the evil eye
enshē, women
eqla, foot
erūsi, Russian
ērūsin, betrothal
eshkase, policemen
eshlāka, sleeved jacket
'eshq, desire, impulse (sexual)
esiqsa, ring
ēz, ēza. *See* **ēda**

fāke, fēka, fruit
falaq, falaqa, "block" used for beating
fale, sheets of paper
faqīra, poor person
faraji, Torah mantle
faraksēne, round bowl, tray. *See also* **farkhasēni**
farash bāshi, policeman
farek, farekh, pāriq, to save, rescue
farhakīya, snare, noose
farḥīye, farkhīye, gladness, rejoicing, feast
farkhasēni, round bowl, plate. *See also* **faraksēne**

farnīya, a cake
farshe, stone, plank
fasūli, beans
fēḥel, to pardon
fēka, fruit
ferūsh, pārish, to sell, separate
fetāra, fetarta, breakfast
finda, wax taper, candle. *See also* **pinda**
fishak, stick with percussion cap
fisle, fisle, good deeds, synagogue function
fistāna, coat
flān, so-and-so, N. N.
furūch, furūj, chicken, cockerel

gabbai, synagogue head
gabētha, woman-gabbai
gad, as if
gadāra, pedlar
gadle, chains, tassels
gāla, rug, carpet
galē, to reveal
galunka, pipe (for smoking)
gāna, giāna, diāna, soul, person
ganāwa, thief
gāne, this
gara, ritual bath, miqwe
garāga, oar
garāne, livestock
gardana, necklace
gare, roof
garē'eta, knife
gāres, millet
garme, bones
gāsa, lime
gāwe, in it
gawqa, group
gazāra, circumciser, mohel
gazer, to cut, circumcise
gedāni, porch, terrace
gedāya, ghedāya, gadāya, 'edaya, breakfast
gēhenam, gehenna, hell
gelāwesh, planet Mars
gelē, to uncover
gemāla! stop! enough!
genēza, genīza, storeroom
gēra, bread roller, stick, arrow
ger māla, "house Kurd" (Sabbath servant)
gerūsta, handmill
gezāla, covering
gezīrāya, jezīrāya, servant
ghedāya. *See* **gedāya**
ghelaq, ghāliq, to lock, close
ghelāqa, locking, closing
ghezāla, wheat harvest
ghulāma, khulām, servant, slave. *See also* **julāma, khulām**
gifke, fringes
gigla, cord
gilke, onion
gimbashya, similar
gininka, garden, field
ginjower, jinjoger, round, roundish
girgur, burgul. *See also* **gurgur**
girse, grits, groats, ground wheat
girten, capture
gnūna, bridal chamber, ḥuppa
gō, gū, to, until, in, into
goncha, khonche, tray
gōpāla, stick, staff
gōra, man, husband
gōza, walnut tree
grāwa, white linen
grish, grush, a coin
gūba, loom
gubta, cheese
gūda, churn
gūlab, rose water
gulāge, gulangi, sidelocks
gulsa, capital of column
gulul, rice-buttermilk dish
gurgur, gürgur, burgul
gurpāla, rice-chicken dish
gurva, gurwa, stocking
gusa, guṣa, ball of yarn, lump of dough

gusht, meat

ḥababēl, gate-house, courtyard
ḥabirman, pomegranate juice
hādak, so, thus
ḥajūhē, a school class
ḥajūme, wrapped-up (woman)
ḥakem, ḥākim, to rule
ḥakōma, king, government
ḥalal, full, complete
halāṣ, khāleṣ, finished
hāle, hūl, hīl, to bring, give
ḥaliq, ḥiliq, green onions
ḥalva, khalva, khalwa, milk
ḥalwa, halvah
hamē, khamē, kema, to bring
ḥamesta, ḥamusta, khamuṣta, khamüsta, sour food, soup
ḥamil, khāmil, stand
ḥamīra, khamīra, ḥametz, yeast
ḥammin, warm Sabbath food
ḥamüsta. *See* **ḥamesta**
ḥāmuta, virginity, youth
hani, pumpkin
ḥanjar, khanjar, dagger
ḥanukāye, Hanukka
har, already
hāra, quarter
hāret ta'jil, Jewish quarter
ḥaram, ḥarim, forbidden
harīsa, porridge
harzāna, cheap
harzēle, platform
hasīra, ḥaṣīra, straw mat
hashtya, eighth
ḥata, until
haush, courtyard. *See also* **hosh**
have, hawe, to be
ḥavraye, khavraye, comrade, member; the burial society
hawala butzuk (buchuk), "companion of the little one," afterbirth
hawiyātha, living creatures
haya, quick
ḥayāta, woman in childbed
ḥazda, evil
ḥaze, khaze, khāzi, to see
ḥazīne, ḥizīne, mourning
hēkāne, breaking
hēlāka, sleeveless vest. *See also* **ēlāka**
helūla, ḥelūle, khelūle, wedding, wedding feast
ḥēnē, henna. *See also* **ḥinne, ḥuna**
heri bir, weighing of wool
ḥeta, woman in childbed
hevēn, hewil, sour milk
hēy, yes
ḥigga, khigga, dance
hilka, breaking
ḥilyūta, candy, sweets
hināra, pomegranate
ḥinne, henna. *See also* **ḥēnē, ḥuna**
hirga, coat
hitna, khitna, bridegroom
ḥoda, pitcher
ḥor, like, as
hosh, courtyard. *See also* **haush**
hozaban, nuts and candy
ḥozemta, khezemta, nose ring
ḥubra, ink
huchik, huchkiyāta, long sleeves
Hudāi, Hudē, Hulā'i, Huzā'e, Jews
huje, syllable
ḥumus, pea
hüllo, up!
ḥuna, ḥunna, henna. *See also* **ḥēnē, ḥinne**
ḥuppa, bridal chamber, mantle for the Torah scroll
ḥurfa, letter (in the alphabet)
hurka, small
ḥurtumāne, peas
ḥuwāra, khuwāra, white
hyāṣa, girdle

iba, lap, bosom
ibbid, between, in the midst

ich'ah, nine
'ida, feast. *See also* **'aīda, ēda, ēz**
īda, īla, hand
idlēl, this night
ikhāla, meal, repast
il, to, toward
īla, hand. *See also* **ida**
īla, night
Ilāha. *See* **Elāha**
ilāna, tree
ilēl, upper
ilēsa, above
ilattha, upper
iltekh, lower
imnahi, peace
inkan, if
ins, man
inve, inwe, grapes
iqla, stick, staff
iqra, root
irbe, sheep
irkhe, millstones. *See also* **urkhal**
isas, foundation
isehera. *See* **seherā**
ishalla, so God will
ishkāse, testicles
ishra'a. *See* **sherā'a**
isiqsa, *pl.* **isiqyasa**, ring
isirta, sash, belt
isra, ten
istād, istāz, schoolmaster. *See also* **ustal, ustaz**
istatta, woman teacher
Ister, Esther
itli, I have
itrāna, ladle, cooking spoon
iwanta, ewe
ize, goat
izle, he went. *See also* **azil**

jahāzie, bridal outfit
jājik, buttermilk-celery dish
jalab, herd
jalāga, stick with bent top
jamadāni, jemedāni, cloth, headgear
janga, changa, handful
jangoso. *See* **sudra**
jānikh, kind of cheese
janka, juwanka, jwanka, bachelor, young man
jāra, poor man
jarāde, ladder
jashen, baking
jauwāher, pearl
jā zera, Shavu'ot, Pentecost
jeha, Jew. *See also* **ju**
jem'a, jemā'a, community, people
jena, jenān, jenāna, woman
jerban, sheepskin bag
jerde, jiridāne, troop, group
jerīma, punishment
jewātera, assembly
jezāda, cutting
jezīrāya. *See* **gezīrāya**
ji'a, Jew. *See also* **ju**
jidika, midwife
jifke, tassels
jīla, jīle, coat, dress, sack
jille, box
jinjoger. *See* **ginjower**
jins, jinn, demon
jiridāne, equestrian game. *See also* **jerde**
jirik, penny
jiwat, jewāte, group
jīza, jōza, punishment
jizirki, an egg-game
jizna, feast
jōla, weaver
jor, fine, punishment
ju, juhiya, juho, *pl.* **jihiyāna, juhiyāna**, Jew, Jews. *See also* **ji'a**
judda, separate house
juje, loaves
julāma, servant, slave. *See also* **ghulāma, khulām**
jūme, pit

jumma, mother. *See also* **yimma**
jutyāre, raid of plough animals

kabā, mantle for Torah scroll
kabāni, kabaniye, woman cook
kabānit bētha, woman head of the house
kabse, witching woman
kā'de, butter
kāda, kādē, cake
kadkhoda, chief of police
kadya, breast
kaffiye, head cloth
kāhū, horse radish
kāka, tooth
kā'ke, food, a cake
kakla mushān, mice game
kalabdun, cloth with silver threads
kala dīyū, demon's head
kalajāhi, head cloth
kalak, raft. *See also* **kelek**
kalam, Torah pointer
kalāme, kalamīye, white cabbage
kalāshe, slippers
kalba, *f.* **kalibta, kelibta,** dog
kalda, bride
kalīfa, teacher
kalke, low leather shoes
kālo, kalatka, *pl.* **kalawātha,** bride, daughter-in-law
kal sera, red spots
kalunka, clay bowl of pipe
kam, kame, before, in front of
kamar, clasp
kamarband, cloth girdle
kamari, money unit, ca. 2 pence
kame, mushrooms
kameta, first
kamisre, a tree fruit
kangīre, karanga, thorny root
kanina, bottle, goblet
kanun, kanūna, oven
kāpā, bowl
kaprāna, hut in vineyard
kapra shīne, "blue hut" (Sukkot)
kara, sweet butter
karange. *See* **kangire**
karchīne, karsīne, kind of fruit
karkha, small raft
karpīj, burnt brick
karpisa, celery, parsley
kartirja, caravan
kāsa, body, stomach
kāsa, khāsa, good, new
kashke, white cheese
kashkīri, oats
kashkiye, cheese-and-wheat grit dish
kaske, green
kasōye, covering
kasrawan, silk kerchief, scarf
kasut, qasut, messenger, deputy, representative
kate, one
kateb, kātiw, to write
kauwāda, procurer
kāwa, window, niche, chimney
kāwai, ceiling
kawursa, "little fellow", afterbirth
kebā'a, kebā'a, long outer garment
kebista, bewitched woman
kekhil, to apply kohl
kelek. *See* **kalak**
keleyātha, gifts
kema, how much?
kemē, to bring. *See also* **ḥamē**
kenis, kenishta, synagogue
kēpa, stone, rock
kepāsa, kābse, person with evil influence
kepīta, pickled (meat)
keramta, coverlet
kerī, to work
kermit inve, vineyard
kesāne, porridge
kisīla, ksila, felt cap
ketā'eta, qeta'ata, old woman
ketāna, twisted

ketāva, writing, deed
ketāwa, qetāwa, shoulder
ketētha, kethētha, kesēsa, chicken
ketētha, lower
kewāra, kuwāra, *pl.* **kewarāre,** large jar
kezīda, pickled, preserved
khā, one
khabcha, khabṣa, a little, few
khabre, under
khala kōra, midday meal
khalen, to wash
khales, khālis, to rescue, save
khalkāle, khalkhāle, anklets
khalva, khalwa. *See* **ḥalva**
khamē. *See* **hamē**
khamel, (m)kamil, to adorn, make perfect
khāmi, once
khamīra. *See* **ḥamira**
khamra, wine
khamūsa, virginity, beauty
khamuṣta, sour vegetable soup
khanik, khāniq, to strangle
khanjar. *See* **ḥanjar**
khapāra, grave-digger
khāpil, hesitate, neglect, refuse
khāra, dirt
khāre, dirty
kharkhāsa, khāsa, belt; cloth to cover the Torah scroll
khāsa. *See* **kāsa**
khase, horseradish
khashīsha, porridge
khātan, khāton, bridegroom. *See also* **khitna**
khāṭir, to do, give
khatōra, board, for washing or threshing
khātūn, lad, youth
khayāpa, washer
khayāṭ, tailor
khayāṭe, woman tailor
khāye, life
khayip, to wash
khayiṭ, to sew
khaze. *See* **ḥaze**
khazūra, wild boar
khebrāya, khevrāya, community. *See also* **hevrāye**
khedamta, woman servant
khefāka, lap, bosom
khēla, food, meal
khēla bōra, midday meal
khelē'eta, khelēta, grave clothes, shrouds
khelāna, dead
khemāla, woman cook
khenīqa, strangled. *See* **khanik**
khepāqa, body
khepāra, hoeing
khēra, good thing
khēre, benefactors
khesāla, weaning
khetāma, completion
khevar, to anoint
khēy, under, beneath
khezemta. *See* **ḥozemta**
khiaroke, amulet case
khigga, dance. *See also* **ḥigga**
khil, to eat. *See also* **akhel**
khilapta, willow
khilu rashke, dried pears
khilya, sweet
khilyūsa, sweets
khipo, veil
khishte, mud brick
khiṭe, wheat
khitna, bridegroom, son-in-law
khīwa, snake. *See also* **khūwa**
khiyāpa, bath
khlūla, dance, wedding. *See also* **helula**
khlulāye, wedding guests
khōd, khōda, khōde, God
khodāne, lord, master
khokhe, plums
khola, rope

khoshāve, "good water," a fruit drink
khosheba, Sunday
khulām, servant, slave. *See also* **ghulāma, julāma**
khūlawātha, khūrawātha, groups, associations
khule, chule, to wash
khuma, khüma, khima, heat
khumsa, sour
khurāwa, khūrawātha. *See* **khūlawātha**
khurūbi, khurūvi, durra
khusīsa, hat
khūwa, khūwe, snake. *See also* **khīwa**
khuwāna, baking board
khuwāra. *See* **ḥuwāra**
khuwarūsa, milk dishes
khwa, God, Lord
kiapa, bath. *See also* **khiyāpa**
kilōre, doughnut
kilsha, uncut stone
kināra, girdle
kipa, crooked, bent
kirtāka, shirt
kisha, kisha! shoo, shoo!
kisl, with, next to
kisne, corals
kista, stone, pocket, bag, box
kisyāsa, chickens. *See also* **ketētha**
kitan, cotton, shirt
kizākha, pruning
klēcha, nut cake
klīlīlī, women's cry of joy
knis, knishta. *See* **kenis**
kohl, powdered antimony, kohl
kolā, kolāw, felt cap
kolāna, street
kole, kāli, to make, take
kōma, black. *See also* **kume**
korākha, shrouds. *See also* **kurākha**
koru, sons
korunfele, cloves
kotchar, nomads
kozinta, mule
kran, money unit, ca. 1/2 shilling
krās, shirt
kretha, invitation
ksila. *See* **kesīla**
ktēsa, below
kṭoya khā pāra, worth a penny
kuchma, head-kerchief
kud, who
kudakh, as, like
kudkha, each one
kufa, round boat
kufte, dumplings. *See also* **kutēle**
kūla jāh, kulatchā, coat
kulak, ceiling, chimney
kulka, short-haired wool
kulye subeya, goats' wool
kūmik, felt hat
kumlōkhe, night of waking (Seliḥot)
kume, to be black. *See also* **kōma**
kundara, low leather shoe
kuppa, quppa, fund, alms box
kurākha, shrouds. *See also* **korākha**
kurāza, pitcher, jar
kursi, low table, chair
kurta, afterbirth
kurtak, kurtāka, cloak, coat
kushīsa, kusīsa, conical felt hat, skullcap
kutēle, kutilka, dumplings
kutka, jacket
kuwi, wild, vegetables
kwāra, clay container
kwarke, mushrooms
k'wē, salt

lā, no, not
labūsha, lebusha, garb, dress, shrouds
lagan, bowl, plate
laglag, stork
laḥma, lakhma, bread
la'ip, lāyip, (yālip), to learn

lajaga, large head-cloth
lākha, beard
landik, cradle
langeri, round bowl
layla, night. *See also* **lēl**
lebandīya, levandīya, long sleeves
lebōke, Purim masquerade
lebūsha. *See* **labusha**
le'ēfane, long skirt
lēka, what?
lēl, night. *See also* **layla**
lelangāne, Purim gifts
lelange, Purim
lēliye, painting of the bride
lēsha, dough
lewāda, collarless coat
liba, heart
līfe, lifke, sponge, bag for washing the dead
ligbina, liqbina, brick
lil'atha, beet leaves
līsa, cage, chicken soup
līt, there is not
lo! O!
lubia, lubye, a kind of pea or bean
lubna, lubni, mud brick
lūḥa, small board, tablet
lülü, swinging cradle
luqma, a sweet

mā, what
ma'amira, master builder
ma'ārafe, acquaintance
mā'at warde, rose water
ma'az, goat's wool. *See also* **mar'az**
mābes, to warm, dry. *See also* **yāwis**
mabi, to seize
mabikh, to comfort
machrefa, oar
m'adeda, m'adode, m'adode, mourning (wailing) woman
madīra, rice-buttermilk dish
m'adōde, sermon for the dead
magila, copper kettle
maglēla, scythe
mahbūsa, a fast
maḥdar, prepared
makhe, mākhī, to beat
makhfūra, maḥfūra, rug, carpet
makhōra, like this
makhwōya, display
makīna, mortar
makōda, burning
makrūr, the best arrack
maksūd, pickled
mal, māl, house
mala, malla, muezzin
māla, backward
malākhe, angels
malban, rectangular frame
maleq, malek, māliq, to light, kindle
malqut, whip, scourging
malukhve bētha, leader of the house
mama, nipple
maman, mamanji, mamata, midwife
mammi, little brother
mamo, uncle
mampel, to send
mamsata, wetnurse
mana, manna, a tree fruit
mana, he who...
mandurta, roller, press
manikh, to put down
man, mānit, who
mankhēda, Torah pointer
manya, a measure of volume
manzal, manzale, manzar, room, a chamber in the synagogue, storeroom
maqlīle, burning
maqri, to bring near. *See also* **qāriw**
mar'az, wool
marakāb, marakāv, ink
mērāna, man
marāqa, soup

mardasha, once
marigle, tub
marikh, to smell
markan, large kneading bowl
marōr, marūr, bitter herb
marvākha, marwākha, fan
marwada, earring
marzag, marzage, marzaqa, baking plate, cushion
māṣa, matzot
masbaḥ, cap worn by Christians
mashmō'e, mashmō'e, announcement
mashqa, churn
mashqas, clamp
masirka, masirqa, mesraqe, comb
maskir, to make drunk, intoxicate. *See also* **sākir**
maslōqa, fat meat soup
masqe, māsiq, to put forth, raise
mast, masta, leben, curdled milk
mate, matiw, to reach
māya, māye, water
maza, mixed dish of food
māzi, oak apples
mazid, mezid, meziz, mazyid, to increase
(m)bārak, blessed
(m)bāshel, to cook
me'allim, teacher. *See also* **mu'allim**
mebīsa, mebōsa, warm food, sealed oven
mebushle, cooked
mēda, cloth, kerchief
mēdū pisḥa, Seder dish
me'ēkha, mēka, from where?
mefaḥel, (m)fākhil, to forgive
megala, megilla, Purim
mego, grater
mehajōye, school class, syllable
mehmāni, feast
mehīna, meḥīna, mare
mijidi, Turkish money unit
mejo, step (in a stair)
meka, from where?
mekatāna, jacket
mekhūtha, mekhūsa, Torah pointer
maḥala, makhala, quarter (of a city)
menekh, menakh, mānikh, to look
mepiq, mapiq, to go
mepishpishle, (m)pashpish, dashed to pieces
mē pukhta, grape syrup
mem, mother
meqim, māqim, to raise up
mēra, man
merē, owner of, master of. . .
merigla, megīla, big pot
merīji, sparrow
mesāla, scales (for weighing)
mese, to bring
meshāle, like, similar
meshāve, meshāwe, to spread out
mesīna, pitcher, can
mesirka, mesreqe, comb
mete, to send
metutke, wooden mallet. *See also* **mikut**
mewish, raisin
mezaita, ashes
mezīda, skin bag
miangor, shelf in the grave
midrash, school
mighdāde. *See* **bigdāda**
mijāla, hour
mijlis, deputy, representative
mikhwas, mikhwath, like, similar
mikūt, mikutka, wooden mallet, hammer. *See also* **metutke**
mīla khelāna, washers of the dead
milāna, dark blue, green. *See also* **nīla**
milkha, salt
miltāsha, a song
mimlēkha, salted
min, men, I
min, from
minde, mandi, to throw

mindi, a thing
minḥāya, Minḥa prayer
minta, thanks
miol miol, parallel, straight
mīr, mīra, mīre, king, emir, chieftain
mirāni, white grapes
mirōkha, net
mishka, skin
mishka, salted butter
mishmāra, weekly portion of the Torah
mishṭākha, flat ground
misrāja, large wax candle
mista, hair
miṭa, bier
mītha, death
mizākha, grain case
mizdāni, good tidings
m'khizna, trousers
m'nuqsha, embroidered. *See also* **nakish**
mobīka, very much
mokhsim, makhshib, angry
moqdōre, ma'dōre, opening of the Torah schroll
mosē, to bring
mpil, to fall, let fall
m'qodeshta, holy
m'sayōre, excursion, walk
mrozdig, to set (the table)
m'shm'she, apricots
mu'allim, teacher. *See also* **me'allim**
muma, mumta, upright, straight
mukhtar, village head
mümlēkha, salted
mür, mir, death
muṭurbāya, müturbo, musician

na, no, not
na'ala, horseshoe
nābi, prophet
nafshāka, wool of medium length
naftāya, tree trunk
nāḥala, ear
nakesh, naqesh, nāqish, to color, decorate, embroider
nakhīra, nekhīra, nose
nakhpūsa, compensation
nakish, embroidery
nanē, nāne, bread
nānūpaz, bread and mutton
napek, napeq, nepiq, to go out
napel, nāpil, to fall. *See also* **mpil**
naqda, bride-price. *See also* **niqda**
naqdāna, remover of veins
naqsha, clothes
narīke, narīqe, a marriage song
nāsha, nāshe, man
nashāma, nshāme, soul
nasheq, nāshiq, to kiss
naṭer, nātir, to guard, protect, watch
nauruz, New Year
nekhip, nākhip, to respect, to be ashamed
neqish, to dye, tint. *See also* **nakesh**
neqūsa, pierced wood
neshiq, nāshiq, to kiss
newāge, newāqe, grandchildren
nīla, blue dye. *See also* **milāna**
nimōye, lemon
niqda, niqdiya, bride-price. *See also* **naqda**
nishanqa, blemish
nishra, eagle
nīta, intention
nivishk, sweet butter
nūka, hole, point of the needle
nuntha, nunitha, nunya, fish
nuqda, nuqta, point, vowel sign
nuqde, nuqṭa ḥurfe, school class
nūra, fire
nurāya, "fire man"

ōha, this
ōkhō, I

pā'ala, pāla, worker
pā'it, to go, pass. *See also* **pāyit**
pakha, pakhew, dull, bland, lazy
palā, coal
palaw, pilaf, rice-dish. *See also* **pilaw**
palāwe, pelāwe, pilāwe, pelafta, slippers, shoes
palē, sheets
paleṭ, pāliṭ, to go out, take out, discharge
palēṭ nūra, charcoal
palgit yom, midday
panir, panīr, cheese
pāntole, colored trousers
paqa, paq'a, pāqe, to explode, burst
paqin, peqe, to crush
pāqikh, paqkha, to flourish
paqpaqūshke, detonating balls
pāra, penny
parch araqin, distilling apparatus
pardā, perda, cloth, curtain, bridal chamber, ḥuppa, tent
pardāyit mithe, death tent
pāriq. *See* **farak**
pārish. *See* **ferūsh**
parit, to explode, burst
paritēle, bursting
parnasa, sexton
parwana, servant
pāsa, pāse, pāta, face
pasaḥ, to limp
pasen, to praise
pashīva, meal, supper
pashūṭa, final form of letters
pasit, to become
paṣqvi, paṣquvi, deer, stag
pastak, jacket
pāta. *See* **pāsa**
pathpātha, patpāta, kerchief
pātike, wood
patīre, paṭīre, Passover
patōḥe, opening
paw, pi, foot
payis, to survive, remain
pāyit, to go out, pass. *See also* **pā'it**
pāzan, sheep
pechā'i, cloth
pechulka, diapers
pedōma, pemōda, permōda, cover
peke, to rise up
pesarkhe, dinner, meal
peshpish, to break
petākha, petīkha, opening
petekh, to open
petil, pātil, to curl, twist
petīlila, side locks
peze, pāse, to go, walk
pi. *See* **paw**
pil, nāpil, to fall
pilaw, rice dish. *See also* **palaw**
pinda, lamp. *See also* **finda**
piqkha, paqkha, blossom, bud
pīr, old
pirtīqa, small piece
pisḥa, Passover
pisḥāye, Passover guests
pishpishe. *See* **yipraḥ**
pishta, behind
pishta māle, handkerchief
pisle, honoring
pis mīre, son of emir
pisra, meat, flesh
pisra dwīqa, —— kefīta, —— kezīda, ——maksūd, —— qawūrma, corned beef
pisra qadīt, —— vīsa, dried meat
pisrit huwāra, sheep meat, —— **irbe,** mutton, ——**kōme,** black meat, —— **tōra,** beef
plātit kāke, cutting of the teeth
plaṭ, pāliṭ, to rise up, go out
plima, crooked
plit, to cut (the teeth). *See also* **plat**
pōkha, wind
poshīa, poshīye, poshin, head cloth
prāge, millet, unleavened bread
prizla, iron
prūṭa, a small coin

puch, nothing
pukhta. *See* **mē pukhta**
pūma, pīma, mouth
purshāq, open, spread out, elongated
purtakāle, oranges
pūshīn, silken cloth

qabār, gravedigger
qablanta, qablanita, midwife
qachke, a kind of chewing gum
qāda, wood
qadāla, qedāla, neck
qadashta, qadōsha, qadōshe, betrothal
qadit, dried (meat)
qahwa, coffee
qaisa. *See* **qēysa**
qāla, voice
qal'a, citadel, fortress
qalāme, reed pen
qalya, preserved meat
qām, qāme, qamet, before, in front of
qamāya, kamāya, kāme, first
qamjur, tax on the flock
qanāna, horn, antler
qanāra, slaughtering place
qandil, qandela, candelabrum
qantarke, upper chamber, floor
qāp, round case for the Torah scroll
qāpa, satchel, bag
qaprāna, qiprāna, platform, bed.
qāra, borrowed
qara, qar'a, pumpkin, melon
qarachāye, gypsies
qaramta, cover, blanket
qardana, necklace
qāre, flat roof
qar'e, vegetable marrows
qaribāna, qarivāna, groomsman
qāriw, to draw near
qāshā, Nestorian priest
qaṣra, tower
qāsūt. *See* **kasut**
qata, qaṭe, qati'a, to cut off
qatel, to kill
qati'a, qaṭi'a, stick, staff
qāwa sīnī, bowl
qawer, qāwir, to bury
qawirma, qawürma, salted meat
qedāla. *See* **qadāla**
qedāne, veranda, porch
qelim, carpet, rug
qera, qeran, a coin
qēṭa, summer
qeta' to break, tear
qetāwa. *See* **ketāwa**
qeti', broken, cut
qeṭā'a, cutting
qeṭ'ata. *See* **keṭa'eta**
qēysa, wood
qezīra, policeman
qid, yāqid, to burn
qidāna, step
qiprāna. *See* **qaprāna**
qiqwāna, qoqwāna, quqwāna, partridge
qiyāma, qiyamta, rising
qolhītha, qolkhīsa, raisin wine
qōqa, barrel
qōra, grave, earth
qorātha, cemetery
qorban, qorbāni, sacrifice
qormō, firewood
qormüksa, tree roots
qoshmoshīye, a kind of grapes
qu, qum, to arise, get up
qulēra, qolova, durra bread
quppa. *See* **kuppa**
quppat arīkha, "meal fund," welfare fund
qurṭāna, saddle
qutked, mantle, coat
qutnāska, quṭnaska, bead, link
qwīra, burial

raban, fair, beautiful

rabsa, rabta, big one (f.)
rakhamime, mercy
rande, pleasant
rang, dye, color
ranīya, snow-slide
rapthit bētha, the great one of the house
raqam, arithmetic
raqīqa, rug, carpet
rashke, reshīke, reshke, summer shoes made of cloth or felt
rashme'u, long, black grapes
rashraje, rashrashinqa, rattle
raste, right side
ras teri, vineyard
rāyū, bakhad, immunity, forgiveness
rebiz, to scatter. *See also* **birbiz**
refēda, baking plate
rēkha, rīkha, smell, fragrance
rēkhan, wild thyme
reni, butter. *See also* **rom**
rēsa, resh, rēsha, head
reshīke. *See* **rashke**
rēsh shākar, sugar loaf
rēsh shata, New Year
rēsh yarkha, New Moon
reshut, permission
rēspi, *pl.* **respiyana,** "white head," deputy, substitute
rifke, tassels
rimmoniye, Torah crowns
rishtenēsa, dough, noodles
ritla, ritlētwi, testicle
riza, rice; **——kabūli,** rice-and-meat dish; **—— kethēta,** chicken with rice; **—— qoqwāna,** partridge with rice; **rizzit bē kālo,** rice of the bride's house
rizq, lot, share
rizqa, support
roḥēs, washer
rom, melted butter. *See also* **reni, rüni**
roq, to spit
rotl, weight of ca. 2.5 kilograms
roya mazana, "great fast," Yom Kippur
rubār, river, river bank
rüni, melted butter. *See also* **reni, rom**
rūwa, rūya, head chief. *See also* **urwa**

sabatqa, ṣabātqa, chest
sabon, soap
sabūsa, servant
sabūza, shabūda, shabūza, a spit
sa'dani, long white grapes
ṣadāqa, charity
sāj, baking sheet
sāke, seki, seqi, long stocking
sākir, to become drunk
sāko, European jacket
sakū, hole
sakū sede, reading platform (in the synagogue)
sala, sālā, basket
sambūsak, Purim dish of peas and eggs. *See also* **sanbusk**
samikh, samkhan, pregnant
samukh, sixth 'aliya at the Torah reading
sandaq, godfather
sal pisḥa, Seder dish
ṣanaṣēfi, ṣanṣēfi, a fruit
sanbusk, sanbusak, sumbuske, a food, Purim dish. *See also* **sambūsak**
ṣapia, ṣapio, sapya, cloth, linen
sapōya, food
saqāye, water carrier
sar, sere, sire, head, beginning
sar dalinga, sar daringe, lower part, trousers
sardari, close-fitting coat
sardawe, cellar room
ṣarmuksa, foreskin

sarsare, is for . . .
sar sepīye, "white head," old man
sarshüf, long-hair wool
sartāya, upper part of tree
sāwe, se, ṣe, ze, zī, to come, go, depart
se'are, se'āre, barley
ṣeba'ta, ṣeva'ta, ṣubo'eta, dyeing, tinting
seda, side, reading desk in synagogue
sedōde, earthen slab
sedōre, clay mold
sē'era, coarse, black wool
seherā, sihra, moon, month
sehrāne, serāne, excursion
ṣehwin, ṣeḥyon, thirst
sekhōpa, container, vessel
seki, seqi. *See* **sāke**
ṣelōla, ṣlōla, synagogue
selōpi, fine white grapes
ṣelōsa, slōsa, prayer
semakh, sāmikh, to beautify
semākha, semka, smāke, samkisa, pregnancy. *See also* **smīkha**
se'ōda, meal; —— **havrā'a,** recuperation meal
sēpa, sword
sēpe, bough, leaves
sepī, white
serāne. *See* **sehrāne**
sere, sire. *See* **sar**
serē sal, New Year
sēr khelūla, wedding excursion
sershoye, bathing place
sertika, sertun, sertur, cream
ṣēwa, ṣīwa, stick, piece of wood
shabāqa, net
shabāshe, gift, present
shābi, shāwi, is like, equal
shabūda, shabūza. *See* **sabūza**
shahmīza, a drink
shākar, shakra, shakrōke, sugar, candy
shakel, shaqel, shekel, to take, begin
shakhna dusha, honeycomb, band
shāl, shālikh, veil, sash
shāla shapuksa. *See* **chāla chapuksa**
shalōne, shelōna, a skit, a play
shalshalakān, shanshalotka, "like a limping man," a game
shalte, short shirt
shalwar, women's trousers
shām, evening prayer, meal
sham'a, Sabbath
shama, sham'a, candle
shāme, blemish, black spot
shame, shāmī, to hear. *See also* **sme'e**
shamīza. *See* **shahmīza**
shaqlit mithe, bier
sharguma, shargumta, shergumma, shergumta, cucumber, turnip
sharūsa, midday meal
sharwāla, shirwāla, trousers
shasa, shisa, hook and line
shashta, crown
shata, shāta, year
shate, shāti, shete, to drink
shavīsha. *See* **chavīsha**
shebūda, shebūza, spit
shebūqa, stick, rod
she'dē, almonds
shedōra, sending
shekālisit helule, shekalteh khlula, beginning of the wedding
shekel, sheqal. *See* **shakel**
shekāne, eggs
shekh khayāpe, chief of washers
shelāna, shilāna, apricot
shelikh, shālikh, to take off, send, draw (a sword)
shella tirshi, porridge
shelukhta, skin
shemūra, guarded grain
shena, good

shenōye, coming, transfer
shenōyit kālo, escorting the bride
sherā'a, shera', shir'a, shrāta, lamp. *See also* **chera**
sherātha, sitting, serving
sherbāhī, shervāhī, "milk price," bride-price
sherbet, a drink
shesh, six
shetāya, meal
shete. *See* **shate**
she'utha, quarter
shevisa, shevitha, rug, carpet
shewāna, shewāno, shepherd
shewīya, shewitya, pumpkin
shikhta, dust, dirt
shilukhta, shelukhta, skin
shīma, name
shimmē, heaven
shipra, beauty
shir, milk
shirine khorān, "eating of sweets," betrothal
shirwāla, sharwāla, trousers; —— **le'ēfāne,** long shirt; —— **tanāka,** short skirt, trousers
shiṣa, shaṣa, hook
shisha, shishak, silk cloth, cloth to cover the Torah scroll
shishme, sesame. *See also* **shushme**
shiwe, logs, branches
shlikh. *See* **shelikh**
shliq, sāliq, to boil
shō'a, shō'a, seven
shōba, coughing
shoda, shōza, rejoicing
shō'i, seventy
shorba, thin rice porridge
shublāye, gleaners
shublē, ears (of wheat)
shubirsa, shubrāsa, bracelet
shuka, shuqa, marketplace
shūla. *See* **chūla**
shushlātha, ornaments
shushbīn, groomsman
shushme, sesame. *See also* **shishme**
sh'vita, knotted carpet
siābō, celery
siame gurji, cloth shoes
sībak, urine pipe (for baby)
sidanka, earthenware jar, cask
si'era, kind of wool
sikhandōke, sparrow. *See also* **sivandōka**
silqa, beet
sīma, ṣīma, ṣōma, fasting
simalta, ladder
simorg, mythical bird
sinduq, sünduq, chest, box
singür, woodpile
sīnī, sīnīya, bowl, tray
sinja, clay pot
sinjaq, flag
sipsa, edge, end, threshold
sisqe, unmelted fat
sitre, cloth
sivandōka, sparrow. *See also* **sikhandōke**
siwe, wood
ṣlōla. *See* **ṣelōla**
sme'e, to hear. *See also* **shame**
smīkha, pregnant. *See also* **semākha**
smōka, smōqa, red
smōke, smōqe, vegetable with vinegary taste
smōke shanūza, a drink
ṣo'a, dyeing, tinting
sokhwāna, ṣehwīn, thirst
ṣōm. *See* **ṣīma**
somekh, person who points to the text of the Torah, assistant
ṣoṣīya, ṣuṣīsa, ṣuṣīta, ṣiṣīta, braid
spindara, poplar tree, timber
stūna, column
ṣubāyīḥa, dawn, breakfast
ṣubo'eta, finger
sudra, dress, skirt; —— **jangōso,** dress with wide sleeves; ——

mamsanta, wetnurse's shirt; —— qiche, dress of a thousand patches; —— **semāka,** pregnancy dress
sukhma, zakhma, vest
sukhra, compulsory labor
sulāka, Christian Pentecost
sumbuske. *See* **sanbusk**
sünduq. *See* **sinduq**
sūpa, room, hall
sūra, shirt
Sūrai, Sūri, Christian of Kurdistan
susāne, a fruit
ṣuṣīta. *See* **ṣoṣīya**
süswa, siswa, winter
suta, basket, cage
ṣuwa'ta. *See* **ṣeba'ta**

ta, tā, tāl, ṭāl, tar, for, to, so that
ta'alīk, black grapes
ta'ashīr, tithe
tabāqa, basket, sheet, bridal ceremony
tabīla, submersion, bath
tabla, millet
tabūt, bier
tāfiye, mound
tagyāni, for myself
ṭāḥin, ṭākhin, ground sesame
taḥla, millet
taḥlishke, bitter herbs
taḥta, takhta, bed, board, low wooden divan
tāj, crown
tajāra, tijāra, merchant
takhāṭir, for, in order to
tākhir, takhir, to remember
takhlik, a kind of grapes
takhti, lower, beneath, under
takka, money unit, ca. 6 pence
taktakoshkat, "little bombs," a game
tāl, ṭāl. *See* **ta**
talga, snow
tallith z'ora, small tallith
tálma, vessel
talmīda, pupil
ṭalobāya, man accompanying the bridegroom's father negotiating a marriage
talō'e, hanging
taltō'a, hanging
talya, entrails
tambelushka, tambourine
ṭ'an, ṭā'in, to load, carry
tanēsa, tanyāsa, letters, class in school
tanke, type of dwelling
tanūr, tanūra, oven
tapancha, pistol. *See also* **debancha**
tapāya, cemetery
tape, balls
tapiksa, tapiktha, springfall
taptapinka, unleavened bread. *See also* **teftepe**
tāq, tāqe, wall, niche
taqa, exploding ball
taqīya, tekī'a, shofar
tar'a, tar'e, ter'a, door, gate
tarākha, raftsman
ṭarashta, oak tree
targum, the language of the Kurdish Jews
ṭarīs, cured
tarka, branch
tar'oziye, cucumber-like vegetable
tarpa, ṭarpa, twigs, brushwood
tasbe, string of beads
tashi, tashīya, teshi, spindle
tashta, ṭashta, bowl, tray
tata, father, daddy
tavsin, large bowl
tavūt, bier
teftepe, kind of bread. *See also* **taptapinka**
tekī'a. *See* **taqiya**
teliba, ṭeliba, tliba, tlība, bridegroom

telōkhe, lentils
temanīya, eight, eighth
tenāya, test
ṭēne, figs
tepancha, pistol. *See also* **debancha**
tepāya, hill
teqir, was burnt
tēshi. *See* **tāshi**
teva, reading desk in synagogue
ṭevīla, submersion
tever, tāwir, tewir, tvir, to break
tewāra, cutting
tiāma, tyāme, completion
tibn, straw
tijāra. *See* **tajāra**
tīka, patch
tilye, dried meat
tīna, ṭīna, fig, clay
tīq, tīqa, case, box
tita, tīta, band, ribbon
tīzang, tīzanq, bladder
ṭlāba, marriage agreement
tlība, ṭlība. *See* **teliba**
ṭlōbāye, those accompanying the bridegroom
ṭlōkhe, lentils
tluba, *f.* **tlubta,** beloved
ṭluma, ṭlumsa, ṭlumtha, flat, round loaf
tnāshe, hair washing
tō, you
tōka, necklace
tolaqta, divorced woman
tolē, beautiful, good
toman, money unit, ca. 1/4 of a pound
toptarake, detonating ball
toqed kisne, coral necklace
tōra, ox, cattle
torqa lēsa, bag of raisins
ṭrākha, woman who miscarried
tras, gown, dress
trāya, shepherd
trē, two
trinja, etrog
tubarke, sweets
tūka, room
ṭūl, soft stick
tulqa, letter of divorce, get
tūma, garlic
ṭum'ā, fruit
ṭum'e, ṭemā, sweets, tasty things
tūna, straw
ṭura, mountain
tuse, mulberries
tutun, tobacco
tūwa, word of exclamation
tuya, ṭūya, roasted
tvīla, ritual bath
tyāme. *See* **tiāma**

urkha, way, road
urkhel, water mill
urva, urwa, big, great, chief
urza, male
ushpīzin, celestial guests
'ushr, tithe
ustal, ustaz, teach. *See also* **istad**

wa'ada, time
wara, forward, backward
warda, rose
warka, cockerel
waṣla, piece
wazīra, vezir
wēn, yes

yā, O!
yabshāsa, yavshāta, raisins
yahērsiyāt, "Jahrzeit"
yakulta, yagurta, great
yāla, child
yaman, beautiful
yaprakha. *See* **yipraḥ**
yāqid, to burn
yarauman, let us dance. *See* **yārim**
yarīkh, yerīkha, long
yārim, to rise

yarkha, month
yāwa, to give
yāwis, yāwish, to dry up
yek, yeki, one
yēlak, yelāqa, hilka, bodice
yerūqa, green
yeshlak, eshlāka, jacket, vest
yesīra, prisoner
yigdan, chest
yima, jima, mother. *See also* **jumma**
yipraḥ, yiprakh, yaprakh, a dish of rice in wine leaves; —— **pishpishe,** chopped wine leaves with rice
yirke, vegetables
yisāra, binding, bewitching
yōma, day

zā'ata, cake
zabāha, zevāha, dabāha, debāha, sacrifice
zabāsha, watermelon
zabin, zavin, to buy, sell
zada, zade, to fear
zāge, tongue of a bell
zaira, yellow dye
zakhma. *See* **sukhma**
zamṭa, filled, full
zangule. *See* **zingeragi**
zanzōke, swing
za'ora, zara, ze'ora, zora, small, youngest
zaqāra, weaver
zartiāsa, visits
zarvar, to begin
zātit sisqe, fat bread
zatye, zetye, cakes
zāve, zāwa, zawāi, bridegroom
zavin. *See* **zabin**
zawāda, provision
zawe, to bring
zebāre, voluntary labor
zelōbīye, zulubīye, pancakes
zeora. *See* **za'ora**
zerik, best grade of grapes
zēta, zete, zetye, olive
zevaha, debaha. *See* **zavaha**
zevistāna, zistān, zōsan, winter
zewāna, zewāta, bread
zewana, a purchase
ziarta, grave, place of pilgrimage
ziarīya, pilgrim
ziartiātha, ziarye, cemetery
zidāna, zedāna, exceeding, more, in addition
zil. *See* **azil**
zingerogi, zingile, zangule, bells of Torah scroll
zirne, flute, trumpet
zivirta, ziwirta, drinking cup
ziyāna, damage
ziyāra, pilgrimage, Shavu'ot
zōma, summer camp
zōra. *See* **za'ora**
zōzan, pasture land
zūdia, cake
zurta, small, *f.*
zutyātha, cake
zuwā'ata, *pl.* **zudiātha,** cake

www.ingramcontent.com/pod-product-compliance
Lightning Source LLC
LaVergne TN
LVHW010355080826
844660LV00016B/981/J

* 9 7 8 0 8 1 4 3 2 3 9 2 2 *